P9-CDV-477

A
DANGEROUS
WOMAN

ALSO BY MICHAEL AND BARBARA FOSTER

*The Secret Lives of Alexandra David-Neel: A Biography of the
Explorer of Tibet and Its Forbidden Practices*

Forbidden Journey

Three in Love: Ménages à Trois from Ancient to Modern Times

A DANGEROUS WOMAN

The Life, Loves, and Scandals of Adah Isaacs Menken,
1835–1868, America's Original Superstar

Michael Foster
Barbara Foster

LYONS PRESS
Guilford, Connecticut
An imprint of Globe Pequot Press

Adah Menken was the most remarkable mingling of angel and devil.

—Napoleon Sarony, the first celebrity photographer

To buy books in quantity for corporate use
or incentives, call **(800) 962-0973**
or e-mail **premiums@GlobePequot.com.**

Copyright © 2011 by Michael Foster and Barbara Foster

ALL RIGHTS RESERVED. No part of this book may be reproduced or transmitted in any form by any means, electronic or mechanical, including photocopying and recording, or by any information storage and retrieval system, except as may be expressly permitted in writing from the publisher. Requests for permission should be addressed to Globe Pequot Press, Attn: Rights and Permissions Department, P.O. Box 480, Guilford CT 06437.

Lyons Press is an imprint of Globe Pequot Press

Unless otherwise specified, all images are courtesy of the Harvard Theatre Collection, Houghton Library, Harvard University.

Text design by Sheryl P. Kober

Library of Congress Cataloging-in-Publication Data is available on file.

ISBN 978-1-59921-602-7

Printed in the United States of America

10 9 8 7 6 5 4 3 2 1

9001037402

CONTENTS

Introduction: In Search of a Mystery . . . . *xi*
The authors' quest for Adah Menken, superstar, poet, friend and lover to the great.

PART ONE: A COLORED GIRL FROM NEW ORLEANS

Chapter One: Naked *3*
Abandoned by husband John Heenan, bare-knuckle boxing champ, Adah attempts suicide.

Chapter Two: Tales of Adah *9*
Adah's origins—Jewish, Irish, and African-American—and her childhood in New Orleans.

Chapter Three: A Daughter of Texas *20*
Adah's colorful adolescence in frontier Texas. Big men and tall tales. Her love affair with Cuban poet Juan Clemente Zenea.

Chapter Four: Young and Free *33*
She performs in a circus and begins to write poetry. Her brief marriage to a minstrel.

PART TWO: DEFENDER OF HER PEOPLE

Chapter Five: The Jew Menken *41*
Adah marries musician Alexander Isaac Menken. Her theatrical career begins. In Cincinnati she becomes a protégé of Rabbi Isaac Wise, founder of Reform Judaism.

Chapter Six: Entr'acte. *55*
Adah performs in New York, falls in love with Irish-American boxing
champion John Heenan. Her marriage dissolves but she keeps
Menken's name and her Jewish identity.

Chapter Seven: Below the Belt *63*
Boxing in the Gaslight Era. The glamorous Menken/Heenan couple
marry secretly before he sails for London to fight for the world
heavyweight championship.

Chapter Eight: The Year of Meteors *76*
Adah, pregnant, stars in New York. Heenan returns as world champ
and denies he married Adah. Alex Menken denounces Adah as
bigamist. The scandal steals headlines from the election of Abe
Lincoln as president.

Chapter Nine: A Scandal in Bohemia. *91*
Distraught over the death of her infant son, Adah bonds with
America's original Bohemians at Pfaff's Tavern. She writes lurid,
confessional poetry and a brilliant essay defending Walt Whitman.
Adah emerges from the ordeal renewed.

PART THREE: PRINCE MAZEPPA

Chapter Ten: Belle Beauty. *111*
At Albany in 1861 Adah first plays heroic Prince Mazeppa and climbs
a stage mountain strapped to a runaway steed. Adah is dubbed the
Naked Lady.

Chapter Eleven: Pro Patria *121*
Touring the country, Adah becomes a national star. She marries her
fourth husband, editor Robert Newell. She keeps close relationships
with gays and lesbians.

Chapter Twelve: Civil War *135*
Baltimore, winter 1863, Adah entertains the Union wounded. Arrested as a Confederate spy, the Naked Lady is too popular to detain. Suffering from tuberculosis, Adah escapes the New York draft riots and sails for California.

Chapter Thirteen: The Great Menken *146*
Impresario Tom Maguire introduces Adah to San Francisco. She takes the Gold Coast by storm and earns unheard-of sums of money. Courted by reporter Mark Twain.

Chapter Fourteen: Gold Eagle Guy *164*
A drama in which Stella Adler played Adah on Broadway. Adah, in male drag, gambles and wins on the Barbary Coast. Courted by Joaquin Miller, the cowboy poet.

Chapter Fifteen: Sun Mountain *172*
In 1864 Menken performs in boomtown Virginia City, Nevada. Miners shower her with gold and she comes away with a fortune. Her place in the mythos of the Old West.

PART FOUR: A NOTORIOUS WOMAN FROM AMERICA

Chapter Sixteen: The Talk of London *191*
Menken abandons Newell and falls for Paul Barkley, a Confederate agent. In London she does a spectacular Mazeppa and becomes the world's best-known actress.

Chapter Seventeen: Four Aces *205*
Adah's salon attracts Dickens, Tennyson, Swinburne, Pre-Rapahelite painters, former Confederates such as spy Belle Boyd, actors, lords, and psychics. Generous, spendthrift, she flirts with Heenan. Angered, Barkley leaves for New York.

Chapter Eighteen: The Royal Bengal Tiger *221*
Promised a serious drama, Adah is disappointed by friends. Instead, she plays four male parts in the spectacle *Child of the Sun*. She is nearly killed in a fall from the mountain.

Chapter Nineteen: One Last Marriage *231*
Spring 1866, Adah hears Barkley is sick and rushes to New York. She models for Napoleon Sarony, the original photographer of the stars, with striking results. Pregnant, Adah marries Barkley. They quarrel. She collapses and is carried aboard a ship bound for France.

PART FIVE: OUR LADY OF PAIN

Chapter Twenty: City of Light. *249*
Autumn 1866, Adah is the champagne toast of Second Empire Paris. George Sand is godmother to her baby boy. She has risen from despair to the pinnacle of success. Her suitors include a handsome German king.

Chapter Twenty-one: Uncle Tom with Miss Ada *265*
Adah chooses corpy Alexandre Dumas *père* for a lover. The novelist is proud of his part-African heritage. Photos snapped with Adah in Dumas's arms cause an international scandal. Adah's second and last child dies.

Chapter Twenty-two: The Affair Swinburne *277*
Adah returns to London. Sick, disillusioned, she collects her poems for a book, *Infelicia*. Involved with poet Algernon Swinburne in a sadomasochistic relationship. Parties with the kinky Pre-Raphaelite group that includes Dante Gabriel Rossetti and Sir Richard Burton.

Chapter Twenty-three: Know Paris and Die *292*
Summer 1868, Adah returns to Paris to star in another extravaganza. Her health fails and her confidants steal her money. At the end, Adah lies dying in a cheap hotel. Henry Longfellow writes her a farewell poem. Her book, *Infelicia*, will be published posthumously. The funeral is small, with a Jewish service.

Coda: The Sexy Spirit *301*
From the nineteenth to the twentieth centuries, Adah becomes a superstar ghost, her spirit evoked at séances. Her memory has captivated Arthur Conan Doyle, Jerome Kern, Billy Rose, and George Cukor, and she has been played in movies by Sophia Loren, Charlotte Rampling, and almost by Marilyn Monroe. In fiction and film, Adah remains forever young and beautiful.

Acknowledgments *310*
Notes *313*
Bibliography *333*
Index *340*
About the Authors *348*

INTRODUCTION

In Search of a Mystery

At midnight on May 15, 1867, Mark Twain was lounging at the entrance of the New York Hotel shooting the breeze with the desk clerk. The Civil War was over and news was sparse. Twain, a newcomer to the city, was employed as a freelancer by the West Coast newspapers that knew him mainly for his reporting in the gold fields. A tall, gaunt man of military bearing, accompanied by a couple of aides, arrived and checked in. Twain recognized him as Jefferson Davis. No one in the lobby cared that he was the fallen chief of the Confederacy. As Twain reported to the *Alta California*, "the man whose arrival in New York a year or two ago would have set the city wild with excitement had ceased to rank as a sensation, and went to his hotel [room] unheralded and unobserved."

The incident set Twain to wondering what had become of Davis's "limitless celebrity." Next day the local papers barely mentioned Davis, described by Twain as the "head, and heart, and soul of the mightiest rebellion of modern times." Mark Twain had already discarded his birth name of Samuel Clemens, which belonged to a reckless fellow who sought a bonanza in the golden West. Now he was after respectability as a writer—indeed, fame. But what good was renown, even infamy, if Jeff Davis, who had been so widely loved and loathed, could be so quickly forgotten?

Mark Twain's story dispatched to California contained an item of equal length on Adah Isaacs Menken, the glamorous thirty-two-year-old American actress who was the *scandale* of Paris. Twain called her "the poor woman who has got so much money, but not any clothes."

He was joshing about Adah's outsized income and her being dubbed "the Naked Lady" by the press. A mutual friend of theirs, the humorist Charles Henry Webb, had showed Twain a pair of photos sent to him by Adah. These private images of her cozying up to the King of Romance, corpy Alexandre Dumas *père*, had been duplicated and sold by the Parisian photographer. They caused a sensation among *tout le monde*. A tidal wave of gossip swept London and was on its way to New York. Once again the boudoir antics of *La Menken* were front-page news.

Twain described the images for his readers:

> *In one of them Dumas is sitting down, with head thrown back, and great, gross face rippled with smiles, and Adah is leaning on his shoulder . . . beaming on him with the expression of a moon that is no better than it ought to be. In another picture, the eminent mulatto is in his shirtsleeves, and Adah has her head on his breast, and arms clasping his neck, and this time she is beaming up at him in a way which is destructive of all moral principle. On the backs of these photographs is written, in French: "To my dearest love, A. DUMAS." And Menken's note [to Webb] accompanying the pictures betrays that she is extravagantly well pleased with the photographer for publishing and selling thousands and thousands of these pictures to the Parisian public. She knows the value of keeping herself before the world in new and startling situations.*

Twain claimed to be unnerved by Adah's disdain for her reputation. Years earlier, he had overlooked that failing when, as a cub reporter who fancied himself a ladies' man, he had courted the star in booming Virginia City, Nevada, where the audience threw bags of gold dust on stage. When he covered Adah's 1863 opening at the Opera House in San Francisco, the theater packed, crowds outside, Twain wrote: "I went to see her play Mazeppa. She appeared to me to have but one garment on—a thin tight white linen one, of unimportant dimensions. I forget the name of the article, but it is indispensable to infants of tender age." Punning, Twain dubbed Adah "The Great Bare."

While Twain may have been crude in his description of the elder Dumas, who boasted of his African heritage, he keenly noted Adah's ability to scandalize both press and public. From her triumphal parade through the capitals of the world, he learned the importance of publicity and of the photographic image to attract a legion of fans. The Mark Twain that resulted, a fashion plate who we can still appreciate in artfully posed stills, was as thorough an invention as the Naked Lady, the Royal Bengal Tiger, or other tags hung on Adah Menken.

"Before Marilyn Monroe or Liz Taylor commanded first-name intimacy with the public details of their private lives, Menken carefully and cleverly cultivated her reputation," noted *U.S. News & World Report*. Adah's daring photos "foreshadow the *Vanity Fair* cover that propelled a naked, pregnant Demi Moore to new levels of celebrity." But this biracial waif from the wild side of New Orleans became more than a celebrity. Adah's brief life was a shooting star, which went dark slightly more than a year after Mark Twain fretted about her morals.

Adah Menken was the original superstar, both notorious and serious. In the mid-nineteenth century, she revolutionized show business with a modern flair for action, scandal, and unpopular causes, especially that of the Jewish people. It was a time like ours, when revolutionary new technologies such as the telegraph, railroad, and steamboat knit America and the Western world into a cohesive whole. The twopenny dailies captured a mass market, and the photographic album had a place in every middle-class parlor. Adah seized on these developments to become a world-class star.

She could sing, dance, and was a wonderful comic. These talents were brushed aside by the attention given to a sexy, daredevil act that threatened her life. So Adah became the Civil War pinup of fighting men, North and South. For a time, she was *the* ticket on Broadway, the darling of San Francisco, the talk of London, and the toast of Paris. A compact woman, curvy, hair dark and curly, she was fond of gambling the night away dressed in men's evening clothes. She rode horses astride, took and discarded lovers, and wore revealing sheath dresses in an age of hoop skirts. Ultimately, Adah confused fame with notoriety and paid dearly for success.

"Nekkid, Nekkid, Nekkid!" screams a chapter on Menken in *Texas Bad Girls*, a bawdy history of Lone Star women. Clad in a sheer body stocking, Adah was never "nekkid" on stage. But in the melodrama *Mazeppa*, lashed to a runaway steed climbing a mountain, she *looked* naked to rapt audiences. Today, collectors seek her "nekkid" photos, historians write articles on Adah's transgressive behavior, and her confessional poetry is gaining well-deserved respect. Her torrid love life is yet to be fully revealed: "She married repeatedly and made time for a few women as well," claims the gay and lesbian website, Gay Gate. That's putting it mildly!

Reference sources continue to disagree on the origins of this mystery woman. For example, The American Jewish Historical Society holds that "America's first glamour girl" was born in the Jewish faith. Yet the New York Public Library has reproduced Menken's book of poems, *Infelicia*, under the heading "African American Women Writers." Another reconstruction of Adah's childhood describes her as an unalloyed Irish-American beauty! Francophone, conversant with Latin and Hebrew, an actress who in one sketch could play nine different roles, Adah seemed to toy with identity. Beneath her disguises, did there beat the heart of one real woman?

We first met Adah Menken in the window of a rare books dealer near the British Museum. She graced in mezzotint an oversized postcard from London's Theater Museum: young, beautiful, bound to a stallion rearing up at the edge of an abyss. She wore only "a little end of a dimity nothing fastened at the waist," as advertised. This showed off her finely formed thighs and legs that would become famous.

On this evening of a gloomy, drizzly day, Londoners wrapped in mackintoshes hurried home, moving in and out of the light cast by street lamps. Occasionally a face would appear and vanish into the mist like an apparition from a Sherlock Holmes tale. In contrast, the bookstore was inviting, and we could just make out the caption on the postcard: ADAH ISAACS MENKEN IN HER EXTRAORDINARY EQUESTRIAN ACT.

We entered and examined the card. The reverse side informed us that it portrayed a scene from the 1831 melodrama by Henry Milner, *Mazeppa, or the Wild Horse of Tartary*. The historical hero Prince Mazeppa was an eighteenth-century Ukrainian freedom fighter who battled against Russian rule. In the picture, the prince has been stripped bare by his enemies, tied to the back of a fiery, untamed steed, and driven into the wilds to perish. In the text, *he* is pursued by a pack of hungry wolves. The horse, on the rim of a precipice, has nowhere to turn. But in the illustration, its rider—definitely *she*—looks at the audience in a come-hither way.

Mazeppa's legend made its way into the arts. The French Romantics painted it and Tchaikovsky wrote an opera. However, Milner's play, relying on a poem by Lord Byron, turned the warrior into a heroic lover. The bookseller, lowering his voice, explained to us that Byron's version was based on the poet's adulterous affair with an Italian noblewoman and her husband's revenge. "If you're interested in the Naked Lady," he hissed, "I have special pictures in which she poses not only naked, but *in action*."

We had a look. But these Victorian versions of French postcards were faked: Adah's head was pasted onto another woman's flabby body. We bought the original card, thanked the man, and left. Experienced biographers, we briefly resisted the familiar sensation of being drawn into another life. But we were already hooked. We were driven to investigate the life of an American actress who reminded us of Lady Godiva with an attitude.

Milner's *Mazeppa* ran well into the twentieth century. This show had legs! Before Adah took over the prince's role, it was played by a man. To avoid harming him, a dummy was attached to a trained horse. In the climactic scene, horse and dummy trotted up the ramps of a stage mountain built of timbers and painted canvas. The orchestra played bravely but audience response was tepid.

In contrast, Adah made *Mazeppa* into *the* Victorian sensation. After she was stripped down to sheer, pink tights and tied onto a horse, she galloped up the mountain *in the flesh*. *Mazeppa* played to sold-out houses and introduced the practice of advance sales. Meanwhile, the mountain grew in height until it reached four stories. Accompanying thunder and lightning rattled the theater as Adah appeared to leap chasms and climb peaks. At the top, horse and rider exited through the flies—the gallery behind the proscenium arch.

Adah, playing a prince tied to a horse, presented a charged image: male and female, captive and free. Her posture, strapped on the bare back of the steed, legs spread apart, was more suggestive than any actress had previously dared. That she was Jewish made her exotic; that she was rumored to be a woman of color, more alluring.

Part of the electricity generated by the star's performance was the possibility of seeing her destroyed. Several times Adah fell from her horse and was severely injured. We wondered: What was she trying to prove? Courtesy of the British Library, we consulted the standard reference books. We found stale absurdities and so-called facts that contradicted each other. As we graduated to memoirs by Adah's contemporaries and to full-length biographies, we became still less certain. No other significant figure is as poorly served by encyclopedias, histories, and biographies. "Nothing is known about her but lies!" bemoaned her friend Joaquin Miller, cowboy poet and teller of tall tales.

Soon we turned up a second illustrated card, SCANDAL OF THE '60s, which showed a mounted, warlike Adah brandishing a sword. After claiming that she rode the horse completely naked, the text concluded, "Menken went to London, where she conquered the public and became the spoiled darling of genius and royalty." On the side, she burned through five husbands in a dozen years. In reverse order, they were a Rhett Butler–style gambler, a literary editor, a heavyweight boxing champion, a musician, and a minstrel-show performer. In Victorian London she went gunning for bigger game.

At the Westminster Palace Hotel, Adah held a literary salon. Artist and poet Dante Gabriel Rossetti came, and so did "bad boy" Algernon Swinburne and his buddy Sir Richard Burton, the explorer of exotic sexual customs. The poet laureate-to-be Alfred Tennyson made an appearance. Charles Dickens was a periodic guest, as he and Adah planned to go onstage together. The upper crust ate Menken's caviar and drank her champagne, as did down-at-the-heels former Confederates and the notorious spy, Belle Boyd.

We were most intrigued by Adah's personal, untold story. Since she next performed in Paris, we continued our investigations there. In the City of Light her social triumphs equaled those onstage. Friends included top journalists and writers such as George Sand, whose cross-dressing and free love life outraged the reactionary morals of the Second Empire. Adah was escorted by a handsome German king and played to enthusiastic audiences, and, at a gala, before the Emperor Napoleon and Empress Eugénie. Yet her correspondence reveals she was depressed and humiliated by French anti-Semitism, which ridiculed her accomplishments.

In reaction, Adah plunged into an affair with the broken-down musketeer, the elder Alexandre Dumas. The pair was seen together everywhere in Paris, and after they were photographed, their image was seen all over the world. For Adah, this meant asserting her heritage as a woman of color. But the resulting scandal, while it revivified Dumas's career, damaged Adah's. Returning to London, she sought out a liaison with Swinburne, the darling of rebellious youth. Once again the affair boosted her lover, but not Menken. It inspired Swinburne's poem "Dolores," an anthem to sadomasochistic love. Perhaps, that midnight in New York, a rising Mark Twain sensed Adah's downward spiral.

We returned to New York, as Adah did briefly, to triumph on Broadway. The athletic nature of her performance attracted increasing numbers of women, especially at matinees. However, New York was the scene of Adah's past, disastrous marriage to John Heenan, the bare-knuckle champion. The prizefighter had left her pregnant and penniless, leading her to attempt suicide in 1860. This time, despite her stage success, Adah failed to reunite with her last husband, now a Wall Street speculator. Once again she grew melodramatic and had to be placed unconscious on a steamer to Le Havre.

Adah dreamed she would die in Paris. Gravely ill, she held on, waiting for her collected verse to be published. Henry Longfellow, by her sickbed, improvised a poem that concluded: "'Tis Love, fond Love that awakens the strain!" But Adah had gone to sleep. Mazeppa would ride no more. Her book, *Infelicia*—The Unlucky One—arrived one week too late.

Adah Menken's remains lie under a monument in the Jewish section of the cemetery at Montparnasse. The stone reads: THOU KNOWEST.

In order to learn more about this intriguing character, we continued our search into the places and persons that shaped her. In New York, Boston, San Francisco, and Dallas, we were delighted to discover a treasure trove of portraits of Adah by Napoleon Sarony, the Rembrandt of the Camera. This Broadway photographer, who hunted down celebrities to record them on glass plates, caught Adah's varied moods and guises. Whether playing a fine lady in a gown, a *femme fatale* on a tiger skin, or a poker player in men's drag, Adah speaks to us through the portraits taken by the original *paparazzo*.

For thirty-three years Adah lived full out. For an encore, she became a popular ghost at séances, then and now. Novelists have always loved her, but the best fiction is a miniature portrait by Arthur Conan Doyle in his story, "A Scandal in Bohemia." Here she becomes the mysterious Irene Adler, and Sherlock Holmes falls for her. "To Holmes," declares Dr. Watson, "she is always *the* woman. In his eyes, she eclipses and predominates the whole of her sex." Irene—or Adah—is the most intriguing woman in the Holmes canon, and she even outwits the master sleuth.

In the mid-twentieth century, Stella Adler played Adah, "the divine Jewess," for the Group Theater. Jerome Kern collected Menkeniana, and Billy Rose wrote a column about this "lollapalooza who rates with Helen of Troy, Cleopatra, and other standouts in the cuddle-up sweepstakes." Among recent pieces, a prize-winning essay in *The Drama Review* praises "Menken's voluptuous physique and dramatic, charismatic sexuality."

If Adah Menken is not a household name, the fault may be Marilyn Monroe's. In 1953 Marilyn, then unknown, was offered a break playing Adah in Darryl Zanuck's *The Girl in Pink Tights*. At the last moment she backed out. The story, about an actress forced by poverty to become a stripper in a low saloon on the Bowery, resembles Adah's darkest period. Although Marilyn never played Adah, she followed in her footsteps. Their eerily parallel lives epitomize the curse of superstardom: over-the-top success cut short by premature death.

In 1960 the director George Cukor turned a Louis L'Amour novel, based on Adah's triumphant 1863–64 tour of California and Nevada, into *Heller in Pink Tights*, a riproaring Western. The curvaceous beauty Sophia Loren played Menken. Cukor was well acquainted with his subject's life and times. To suit Loren's accent, he called her Angela Rossini. But, says Cukor's biographer, "The flirtatious Rossini was inspired by the real-life actress Adah Menken." The movie has become a cult classic.

Although the great Menken biopic has yet to be made, one can occasionally see her on television. Ruth Roman played the Naked Lady in one of the best *Bonanza* episodes. "A Scandal in Bohemia" is one of the episodes in *The Adventures of Sherlock Holmes*, which runs frequently. In a logical sequel to the Conan Doyle story, the movie *Sherlock Holmes in New York* stars Sir Roger Moore as the master detective and Charlotte Rampling as Irene/Adah. Here, she and Sherlock marry and have a child. In real life Adah had a boy, who, although she cherished him, died in infancy. The most recent incarnation of the Irene/Adah character is in the big screen *Sherlock Holmes*, where her athletic, daring side is brought out by Rachel McAdams.

Adah Menken, naughtiest of Victorians, has come to represent sexual liberation for men and women. In her time, she fought racial, religious, and gender oppression. In our time, women have found freedom in everything from athletics to the current revival of burlesque. Those young, very slightly dressed women vying for the Golden Pasties awards at New York's annual Burlesque Festival are the Naked Lady's godchildren, equally with the French model in a designer tux playing roulette at Monte Carlo, and again, with the crimson-haired punk in torn jeans reading her poetry in a San Francisco coffeehouse. Adah's bright star still glows like a beacon.

PART ONE

A COLORED GIRL FROM NEW ORLEANS

Who were her parents? Where was she born?
What was her name?

—JOHN S. KENDALL

CHAPTER ONE:

NAKED

On the penultimate evening of 1860, twenty-five-year-old Adah Isaacs Menken-Heenan sat alone in her shabby, furnished room in Jersey City. Betrayed by John Carmel Heenan, the prizefighter husband who had ruined her reputation, Adah stared at mementos of a once-promising theatrical career. A playbill on the wall from Wood's Theater in Ohio proclaimed her "The Accomplished Actress and Startling Tragedienne." Tonight she planned to visit friends in Manhattan, and so she wore her best dress, of royal blue satin with lace cuffs, mended here and there. But she had lost hope. She saw no way out of a descending spiral of scandal.

In April in a field outside of London, her handsome Benicia Boy (Heenan's moniker in the ring) had fought the British champ for the world heavyweight crown. Preparations for the illegal match obsessed sporting men from both countries, and at times elbowed Abe Lincoln's presidential campaign off the front page. A large crowd that included the press, members of Parliament, and notables such as Charles Dickens flocked to watch the battle for the championship. After thirty-seven brutal, bare-knuckle rounds, the mob invaded the ring, but the Irish American and the Briton stumbled on to a bloody draw. Each was awarded a championship belt.

Basking in glory, Heenan delayed his return to New York. He refused to answer his wife's letters. Adah, pregnant, was growing desperate. On the advice of Frank Queen, publisher of *The Clipper*, the leading entertainment weekly, she billed herself as Mrs. John C. Heenan on a tour featuring musical and comic pieces, including the appropriate *An Unprotected Female.* Playing before packed houses from Providence to Philadelphia, Adah concluded at New York's Old Bowery Theatre. Here she played her benefit night in a double-entendre farce, *Heenan Has Come!* Taking curtain call after curtain call, Adah felt on top of the world, but she would soon find herself caught in a grim, real-life drama.

Adah awaited the birth of her child and the return of her errant husband. But when the Benicia Boy landed at the Battery in August, he was parading a fashionable English mistress. To the public, America's first world champion could do no wrong. At Jones's Wood, where Adah and John had lovingly picnicked, she was sighted by a sharp-eyed reporter on the fringe of a crowd of 50,000 that cheered on the hometown hero. She could fight her way no closer to the father of her baby boy, who had died a few days earlier.

Adah's troubles grew worse. Heenan's manager, a promoter with a shady past, falsely tipped off the press that the Boy had never married Adah; she was taking advantage of Heenan's famous name. Then Adah's previous husband, Alexander Isaac Menken, scion of a wealthy Jewish family in Cincinnati, denounced her in the press as "an adventuress." Alex claimed she had neglected to divorce him before remarrying and was therefore a bigamist. He had instituted divorce proceedings to rid himself of "this incubus and disgrace."

Newspapers across the country played up the scandal in lurid copy. Because she had left her husband, the presumption of guilt fell on Adah. When she told her side of the story to a curious crowd at Broadway's Hope Chapel, the papers denounced her as immodest for speaking about her private life. Heenan's lawyers struck, claiming in court that she was a common prostitute. In an interview, Heenan delivered the knockout blow, calling Adah "the most dangerous woman in the world."

No legitimate theater would book her by any name. She was forced to perform song-and-dance routines in a saloon damned by the *New York Post* as "a portico to the brothel." Even in this dive the drunken patrons hooted at her. Adah, whose dreams had known no bounds, felt herself a miserable outcast. To earn a meager living she posed in the nude for a Victorian version of French postcards. On the verge of a new year, Adah felt disgraced before the few friends who had stayed loyal.

On the Manhattan side of the Hudson River at Broadway and Bleecker Street, Adah's companions were among the crowd that packed Pfaff's basement restaurant, home to the nightly meetings of Bohemians. This gathering of journalists, poets, and performers had its own long table in the "cave" below the Broadway sidewalk. Proprietor Charlie Pfaff, a Swiss émigré, welcomed one and all. Walt Whitman—vilified by preachers for his "sex poems"—frequented the place. In his prime, wearing a flannel shirt and red bandanna, trousers tucked inside work-man's boots, Walt's glance caught, in his words, "the bright eyes of beautiful young men." Because Charlie welcomed single women, fair-haired Ada Clare, the Queen of Bohemia, held court. Accustomed to captivating the crowd, she was not thinking about Adah.

Amid the haze, the clank of mugs, and smell of tobacco, one of the listeners grew uneasy. He was sensitive to Adah and became concerned about her absence. A slender man who, although a performer, was self-effacing, he took his derby hat and made his way to the door. Outside in the cold, he ignored the holiday sightseers and shook off the ladies of the night. He was headed for the Jersey ferry. He could hardly guess that church bells, tolling in anticipation of the year 1861, were sound-ing the death knell of the American Union—and its first Bohemia. Art-ists and writers, including habitués of Pfaff's, would find their separate ways to Civil War battlefields, some to an early grave.

Adah, shivering in her room, found the courage she needed. She added fuel to the charcoal-burning stove and turned the flue higher. Removing a fringed shawl, she methodically unhooked the back of her dress. Released from the constraint, she went to her desk, strewn with poems in progress and a Hebrew Bible. By the light from an oil lamp, she gazed at her image in a cracked mirror. Perhaps she was beautiful, but disappointment had drawn lines beneath her eyes and hardened her smile to a frown. She was looking at a stranger.

Each winter, many of the poor of New York died from the fumes of cheap, charcoal stoves. Her face glowing with warmth, Adah took up paper, pen, and ink and began to write in an unsteady hand an apology for taking her life. Meanwhile, the gentleman on the ferry, gazing at the fast-flowing Hudson, was, in Whitman's words, one of "hundreds and hundreds that cross, returning home." The ferry plied the river among "the numberless masts of ships and the thick-stemmed pipes of steamboats" that made up the waterborne traffic of the metropolis. As the boat docked in Jersey City, the man hurried toward a rooming house in this riverfront neighborhood. He felt a loving tie to the woman who, slipping off her dress, struggled to write. Her crinoline with all its petticoats made a pile at her feet.

Adah's suicide note is a powerful indictment of John Heenan. In it she accuses him of being a seducer who "drank out *all* my life— absorbed all of good and beauty, and left me alone, desolate, to *die*." Still, she invokes God's blessing on him. And she begs God to "forgive those who *hate* me . . . a poor reckless *loving* woman who cast her *soul* out upon the broad ocean of human love." Since she cannot absolve herself of a deed held by her religion to be unpardonable, she offers the excuse: "Because I am homeless, poor and friendless, and so unloved, I leave this world."

Adah's letter is written on cheap blue paper headlined "12 Mo. 29th D., Jersey City." Observed under a magnifying glass, the paper is marked by what appear to be tear stains. Her handwriting, instead of being bold as usual, is hesitant. Adah had become the butt of jokes in the press and the subject of off-color stories in barrooms. Her life in tatters, she had suffered more than she could bear. She believed death would prove the depth of her love for the Benicia Boy.

Adah undid her corset and slipped off her undergarments. Naked as at birth, she was free of the oppressive clothes designed to constrict her womanhood. Flushed, giddy from the stove's fumes, she might have succumbed from suffocation. But that was too passive for this willful woman. Instead, she chose poison—a lethal, easily available opiate. Adah held the vial in her hand, not quite ready to bid adieu to the face in the mirror.

In 1881 Adah's confidant, the colorful scamp Edwin James, wrote a biographical sketch of his late friend. James, formerly a Member of Parliament, had fled England in 1860 to avoid arrest. Aside from embezzlement, he had been caught making love to a nobleman's wife. Brash New York was to his liking, and he became an influential sports-writer and publicist. Adah grew to think of him as her brother. "But for one solitary friend still living [she] might have followed her child to the grave," wrote James.

Adah lifted the vial of poison to her lips. Her mysterious savior rushed upstairs to the door. He found her naked on the floor, con-scious but with labored breath. He confiscated the vial and threw open the window. In what might have been a scene from a melodrama, he reached Adah's side just in time. Because of the fumes she had inhaled, or because she had swallowed some of the poison, she would be gravely ill for a while. The man put her to bed and stayed to nurse her. James, for whatever reason, would not name him, and biographers have debated his identity ever since.

Adah came within a hair's breadth of self-annihilation. Ironi-cally, her passage through the gates of hell gave her the strength to make her dreams of fame and fortune come true. Royalty would bow before her, generals admire her, celebrated men and women court her. Death, always lurking in the wings, waited until 1868, after Adah had conquered Paris. That year, on hearing the news in distant San Fran-cisco, a lithographer named Billy Low published the *Menken Memorial*, a tribute to her numerous stage roles and actual lovers, which circle her Byronic head in the style of a *thangka*, an oriental painting that celebrates the deeds of a god or goddess. One moment the Menken wields a sword, and the next she reclines scantily clad, or she poses in midair on a rearing steed. Her husbands occupy a corner or two of the portrait. The actress, who could quick-change into nine characters in one sketch, was also a transformation artist in life.

Each Menken persona succeeded and obliterated the last. For a time she lived as a Romantic poet, a female Byron. Briefly, she made a good Jewish wife in the Midwest, before becoming the consort of an Irish boxing champ among the gangs of New York. Down and out, she presently became the rage of San Francisco, throwing over her wimpy fourth husband for a gambler who may have been a Confederate agent. In the capitals of Europe Adah achieved spectacular success and was both worshipped and vilified. The public needs a goddess, if only to sacrifice.

The transition from one of Adah's selves to the next could be violent. Suppose that her friend had arrived too late to prevent her suicide. The Jersey City police would have had to identify a nude body found in a tawdry room, suspecting foul play. The coroner would have demanded the vital statistics—the deceased's name, her date and place of birth. But no one living, including Adah's closest confidant, could have answered the question: Who was she?

Wolf Mankowitz, a colorful 1980s biographer, complained of "a woman whose identity for the first half of her life is, in terms of verifiable facts, virtually unknown." To know Adah, we must listen carefully to her. At times she lied about her origins, burying the truth under a mound of fantasies as though disposing of a telltale corpse. Yet as Mankowitz recognized, those very lies "hit a significant bell-note in [her] extravagant personality." To lay bare the woman's secrets, we need to investigate with the rigor of a detective. We need also to let our imaginations penetrate the artifice of invention created by a superstar who demanded to be both famous and mysterious.

Chapter Two:

TALES OF ADAH

From the Naked Lady's pinnacle of fame in the Victorian era to the present day, biographers, journalists, and scholars have searched for her actual date and place of birth, and especially her lineage. Yet these remain contentious. Three conflicting tales of Adah's origins compete for credibility: the Irish, African-American, and Jewish. In books and articles, proponents of each ethnic identity continue to further their apparently irreconcilable views. And these individuals represent constituencies vital to American cultural life.

Immediately after the actress's death in August, 1868, a pamphlet-sized "life" was rushed out by George Barclay, a comedian from Philadelphia. He dedicated his *Life and Remarkable Career of Adah Isaacs Menken* to her staunch ally Frank Queen, a Philadelphian who became publisher of *The New York Clipper*, the equivalent of today's *Variety*. Barclay stated that Adah was born in Milneburg, Louisiana, on June 15, 1835, "the eldest of three children, there being a boy and another girl." Her father was the Irishman James McCord, "a merchant of eminent standing" who went broke and died seven years later. Significantly, Barclay failed to name or describe Adah's mother.

Barclay's story was seconded by Adah's intimate friend, Edwin James. Originally a London actor, this colorful character became an attorney, charged enormous fees, and was elected to the British Parliament. Unfortunately, James had a habit of helping himself to other men's money, along with their wives. He admitted that he was the model for Charles Dickens's Stryver, the womanizing barrister in *A Tale of Two Cities* who takes credit for the brilliant work done by his clerk, the self-sacrificing Sidney Carton. Dickens describes Stryver in unflattering terms: "Stout, loud, red, bluff, and free from any drawback of delicacy, he had a pushing way of shouldering himself (morally and physically) into companies and conversations, that argued well for his shouldering his way up in life."

On the contrary, by 1860 Ed James was facing charges that could have sent him to prison. He fled from London to New York, where he became associate editor on *The Clipper* and promoted sports events. He was one of New York's first publicists, then a profession without a name. James became friendly with John Heenan, and eventually he turned his attention to Adah, the champion's neglected wife. When she rebuffed his advances, he settled for the role of "brother." Ed grew to be Adah's confidant, the recipient of her most candid letters. Long after she was gone, he treasured her memory.

In 1880, at the age of seventy, James quit journalism to write a series of biographies of sports and theatrical personalities. In his pamphlet on Menken, he confirmed Barclay's vital statistics but stated that Adah was born *Adelaide* McCord. Again, her father had died in 1842, and her mother (still unnamed) remarried a Dr. J. C. Campbell, an army surgeon at the barracks at Baton Rouge. After this gentleman died, Adelaide, aged fourteen, needed to earn the family living. A trained dancer, she and her younger sister Josephine (Annie for short) went onstage at the French Opera House in New Orleans. They were a hit, and engagements in Texas, Cuba, and Mexico followed. When in 1856 Adelaide married Alexander Isaac Menken, she converted to Judaism and changed her name. "Menken was not born a Jewess," James insisted, though he admitted she had the "large lustrous eyes" of one.

Early biographies of Adah tend to rely on her word—either publicity interviews she granted to reporters, or confidences she whispered to well-placed intimates. But Adah, who spent some of her formative years on the Texas frontier, told tall tales with the best of them.

Scrambling up the ladder of success, she talked to her advantage: Settled in the wealthy, Jewish Menken family in Cincinnati, she was a Zionist. Moving to New York, living among an Irish-American sporting crowd, she became Irish. In anti-Semitic, aristocratic France, Adah permitted her infant son to be baptized. We learned to listen to Adah's words, but also to weigh them carefully. More important, we watched the acts she performed over a lifetime.

Attempts at identifying Adah through objective means, such as birth records, have led up a blind alley. Mark Twain once quipped that figures don't lie, but liars do figure. In antebellum America, census takers were unreliable political appointees who set down individuals as white, black, or mulatto according to how they perceived the shade of their skin. These officials could be bought. In New Orleans thousands of persons of color were legally free but lived under crushing social and economic disadvantages. As a result, many free persons of color transfigured themselves into whites in the shadowy phenomenon known as "passing."

In *They Seek a City* (1945), Arna Bontemps and Jack Conroy point out that 10,000 free people of color disappeared from the New Orleans census in the decade prior to the Civil War. That was a decrease in this group's numbers by half. Bontemps and Conroy cite Adah Menken as a famous example of one who was born colored but decided to pass for white. "Obviously," they claimed, "she was at least a quadroon." Although such terms are arbitrary and antiquated, this means one of Adah's grandparents was of African descent. In the South all persons of color were treated legally as black. Among other restrictions, they could not marry whites.

The work of Bontemps and Conroy served as a basis for the statement by James Ivy, editor of the NAACP's monthly *The Crisis*, that Adah was "a colored girl from New Orleans." In a 1961 letter to Dr. Stanley Chyet, editor of *American Jewish Archives*, Ivy playfully recalled these lines from a Creole song about *les gens de couleur libres:*

All you mulatresses there
Are passing for white,
With your white men
You go to the French Opera
But they throw you out.

The Louisiana Creoles, who originated from interracial liaisons under French rule, have perpetuated their "third caste" and francophone culture up until the present. Their complexions range from pale white to tan. The women are famous for their beauty and appeal. In many of her photos, Adah looks Creole, with pale skin, dark, curly hair, violet eyes, a slightly wide nose, and a sensuous mouth. Free people of color had a standing in New Orleans and a proud history of accomplishments, but restrictions on them grew tighter leading up to the Civil War. They responded by passing.

An individual who embarked on this "invisible migration" would do her utmost to destroy her past identity. Scholar Renée Sentilles, who investigated the "high yellow" world, writes that people of color "deliberately misrepresented themselves to sustain a sense of autonomy and anonymity." Put bluntly, at the cathedral on Jackson Square, antebellum birth records had as many deliberately punched holes as player-piano rolls. Early on, Adah learned to lie about her origins and to internalize the lie.

The argument that Adah was of African-American heritage was first made by John S. Kendall in a 1938 article, "The World's Delight." Kendall was a regional historian who had written a history of the New Orleans theater. He understood the society into which Adah, as a woman of color, would have been born, and her motives and conflict in concealing that birth. Kendall discovered the marriage contract dated April 3, 1856, in which a certain Ada Berthe Theodore agreed to marry Alexander Isaac Menken. After taking her husband's name, our subject added an "s" to Isaac, which is often done by French speakers for a more graceful sound.

Kendall also verified that "the Theodore sisters" danced at the French Opera House when Ed James said they did. Kendall proceeded to search the records for a free man of color named Théodore, which he identified as Adah's name at birth. In 1943, Leo Shpall, a writer on Jewish themes, turned up additional evidence to support the Théodore identity. He wrote of an acrostic penned by Adah's admiring brother-in-law Jacob, in which the first letter of each poetic line, if read downward, spells out "Adaberthamenken." By 1980 Wolf Mankowitz had found a Texas certificate from an earlier marriage in 1855, in which "Miss Adda Theodore" entered into matrimony with N. H. Kneass. The signature is unmistakably Adah's. Ada Berthe Theodore is almost certainly our subject's name at birth, the name she used to begin her string of marriages, and her original stage name.

Allen Lesser believed that in his 1947 biography *Enchanting Rebel* he had proved that "Adah Isaacs Menken was born a true daughter of Israel." He insisted that the family name Theodore, accented or not, was Jewish. Adah's poetry, he claimed, "reveals an untamableness of spirit, a messianic zeal, and an unutterable yearning for sublimity that is unmistakenly Hebrew. It is therefore almost inconceivable to suppose that a convert to Judaism . . . could possibly have captured so profoundly . . . the very essence of what would necessarily have been an alien and ancient tradition."

Lesser underestimates the possible zeal of a convert. More to the point is a lengthy interview Adah gave a reporter from *The New York Illustrated News* on March 17, 1860, at a time when she was packing in the crowds at the Old Bowery Theatre. After reading the first installment of the article, she complained about its "light and flippant tone." She denied the reporter's assertion that she had "*embraced* the Jewish religion." Instead, she insisted: "I was born in that faith, and have adhered to it through all my erratic career. Through that pure and simple religion, I have found the greatest comfort and blessing." Then she added, "My first name is spelt 'Adah' and is a Hebrew name."

Lesser gave much of his life to the study of Adah's. He established the basic chronology of her appearances, publications, and husbands. During World War II he served as an intelligence officer in the struggle against Nazism. It is understandable that he would focus on Adah's Jewish identity, her affirmation of it, and her unceasing opposition to prejudice, tyranny, and censorship. He was correct to emphasize her knowledge of Hebrew, her public worship at synagogues, and her refusal to perform on high holidays, though it cost her considerable money.

Unfortunately, Lesser, like other previous biographers, made the mistake of obsessively searching for Adah's father. But in the Hebrew tradition, and in the family reality of New Orleans Creoles, a child's name and identity stemmed from her mother. This serves to emphasize James Ivy's remark that if we assume "Adah was a colored girl of New Orleans, many of the parts of her story which have hitherto been perplexing are inclined to fall into place." Keeping in mind that her family unit was matriarchal, we can ask the question: What was it like to *be* Adah as a child?

Long ago there lived a Jewish clothing merchant who kept a shop in Newcastle Street, London, near the Strand. He employed an assistant named James McCord, a young Irishman who was handsome but poor and who hoped to better himself. In 1837 James sailed for New Orleans, which had a small but growing Irish population. He set up as keeper of a general store in Chartrain, which was in the parish (county) of New Orleans but less costly than the center of town. Later called Milneburg, the village was the terminus of the Chartrain railroad line and a resort on the south shore of Lake Pontchartrain. Once James became established, he looked around for a wife.

The merchant cast his eye on Marie Théodore, a French-speaking widow who had been washed up on this lakeshore when her husband— if the man was her legal husband—had died of consumption (tuberculosis), leaving her with a two-year-old daughter. Adah later described her mother as "beautiful, refined and lovable." Marie was a pious woman of "amiable character and cultivated spirit." Because it is unclear if the name Théodore was her maiden name, or her late husband's, we can't be certain if Marie was born Jewish or converted because of Adah's father.

New Orleans had a number of Théodores resident during the 1830s and '40s. The "City that Care Forgot" may have been officially segregated, but it was multicultural under the sheets. So some Théodores were listed by city directories as white, but others as FMC—free man (or woman) of color. Adah is definite about growing up in a family that was small and close: her mother, one sister, and one brother. In a poetic essay she wrote for *The Israelite*, while living in Cincinnati, she described her New Orleans home as a "cottage . . . almost buried in trees and creeping vines." Here she "first learnt the blessing of a dear mother's love; first knew the sweet influence of an only sister's confidence and affection; first felt the holy spell of a brother's consolation and encouragement." This idealized version of Adah's family is verified by scanty but available information about her brother and sister. We also know something about "Adah's too-numerous stepfathers," as the historian Kendall put it.

However, in Adah's successive tales, her natural father is a dreamlike invention. He grows ever more heroic and high-toned, until, in her posthumously published "Notes of My Life," he becomes Richard Irving Spenser, "a splendid specimen of manhood, strong, healthy, and handsome." Spenser is the scion of a wealthy, slave-owning family that fought for independence in South Carolina during the American Revolution. Adah has created the father she wished for.

This tall tale was presented by Adah in 1862 to her journalist friend Augustin Daly, in the hope he would develop it into a biography. Daly put the material aside. Afterward, when Adah's death was in the news, he forwarded her "Notes" to *The New York Times*, which published them on September 6, 1868. Finally, Adah names her mother: Marie Josephine Rachel de Vere de Laliette, daughter to a French family of royal blood. Daly, already a successful playwright, included a disclaimer that he did not believe Adah's "Notes" in a literal sense. Instead, he thought they were valuable as an honest revelation of her own feelings.

The "Notes," which have a psychological validity, offer intriguing clues. The author depicts herself as "a wonderful and eccentric child," determined to get her way in all things but very affectionate. She describes a girl neglected by her parents but shown too much of the world by a dissolute uncle. "I wanted Love," she proclaims. She may have experienced it too early in a physical sense.

Adah's imagined family seems ill-fated. Her mother Marie is improbably depicted as a blue-eyed blonde twin, whose brunette sister "is drowned at seventeen in Lake Killarney [Ireland]." The family moves to New Orleans where Marie, at death's door, is rescued by "Love, the never-failing messenger of Life," in the person of her husband-to-be, the patrician Spenser. But, with a dose of reality, Adah's father dies of consumption when she is two. Then she and her mother are again rescued, this time by kindly Dr. J. C. Campbell. Her stepfather sees to Adah's education.

Throughout Adah's life, her natural father remained a figure of fantasy, and her relations with men were colored by this image. In contrast, her mother was an actual parent who taught her daughter manners, morals, and French, and without whom she could not have become a beautiful and desirable woman. Robert Roden, who had access to Ed James's collection of Adah's private letters, wrote: "Her mother, who . . . spent most of her life in the 'Faubourg,' New Orleans [the French Quarter], survived at least three husbands, one of whom was a man of low estate named McCord, and another a respectable army surgeon, named Campbell." Adah's love for Marie was deep, but she needed to keep her mother hidden.

Marie was a woman of color—the dark twin her daughter tried to obliterate. In Adah's fantasies there lurks a shadowy side, which is really her other, repressed self. In antebellum New Orleans, with its widespread but concealed racial mixing, the possibility that a white mother would give birth to a black child, thus advertising her relations with a black man, or her own strain of African blood, was an unnerving fear. "In white American society, historically," writes a black historian, "the discovery of black blood meant sudden reversal of fortune, social exclusion, or banishment."

In Adah's "Notes," her dissipated uncle, in whose charge she was left, married his housekeeper—euphemistically termed "a woman of low origin." In time, "a miserable, black-looking baby became his heir." Adah is confessing to a buried African strain in her family. Throughout her life, especially to intimates, she dropped hints of her mixed heritage. According to the biographer Barclay, Adah told her fourth husband, Robert Newell, "I cannot, as the daughter of an octoroon, sympathize with the cause of the Confederacy." Yet, as a woman, she did sympathize with the South, so openly that she would be arrested as a Confederate agent.

The idyllic view that Adah presented of her youth in New Orleans was laced with an inner conflict. As she matured, everyday life painfully reminded her of her position in society. In the French Quarter, she was intrigued by Choctaw squaws at the market, peddling *file* for gumbo. Hefting their babies on their backs, they would casually take them down and give them a breast to suck. She saw French-speaking bankers in cutaway coats stroll into Antoine's for a three-hour lunch, and she watched tobacco-chewing Anglo planters in their slouch hats bidding for human beings, sold like cattle, guarded by overseers with whip and pistol at the ready. She was fascinated by the fancy women of Gallatin Street, the light-skinned Creole beauties. Supposedly free, their slavery was to be kept and traded by rich, uncaring white men. When the young dancer walked along Royal Street on her way to the Opera House, passing by the absinthe houses, sharply dressed men called offers to her *sotto voce*.

But Adah was different. The most intriguing Theodore listed as living in New Orleans during Adah's youth was a certain "Madame Theodore," who resided at the Orleans theater and gave her occupation as a comedienne. The census counted her as white, and she may have been Adah's aunt. If Adah came from a theatrical family, it would explain how at fourteen she and her younger sister appeared as dancers at the French Opera House. Here is a matriarchy at work, of mixed blood but with Jewish values—birthing, raising, and instructing the Theodore sisters. Adah never knew her natural father, and she may not have known his identity.

When the merchant James McCord set up house with the widow Marie Théodore, he did not marry her. Miscegenation was illegal. No matter; they could act as if they were husband and wife, and two-year-old Adah Berthe was their daughter. They had a son, who supposedly died young, and a second daughter. Unfortunately, James McCord was a poor businessman, and by 1840 his general store had failed. Biographers kill him off in 1842, when they also award a new man to the still-attractive Marie. This would be Dr. Campbell, the surgeon, though Lesser nominated a lawyer named Josephs, because Adah's younger sister performed as Annie Josephs.

Clearly, an important influence led Adah toward learning. She spoke English, French, and Spanish. She achieved the fundamentals of a classical education by learning Hebrew, enough Latin to translate Horace and Catullus, and, so she claimed, sufficient Greek to translate Homer's *Iliad* from its native tongue into French. Beginning in her teens in Texas, Adah showed a remarkable ability to hold her own with men of reputation and intellect. This was unusual for a female in the Deep South, even for those from the best families. The schools available to young women were too rudimentary to account for Adah's education. Dr. Campbell must have taken an interest and homeschooled her. Indeed, she called him "a true and loving father in all [things]."

James McCord was a defeated man, but to once again echo Mark Twain, reports of his demise were greatly exaggerated. He simply leaves no trace for a time. However, in 1849, Adah's second stepfather, Dr. Campbell, passed away. Forced by poverty, the Theodore sisters took to the stage. Shortly thereafter the family moved to Texas, where James

McCord was again reported to be the *pater familias*. Adah became a circus performer and earned a good living for the family. Her less than respectable youth was another secret she covered up with tales of an aristocratic pedigree.

From McCord, Adah first learned how to play cards, "the good and bad points about horses [and] the mystery of betting." The well-meaning but debauched uncle into whose hands she falls in her "Notes" is a surrogate for her stepfather, and the exact nature of their relationship remains in the dark. In any case, Adah was an apt pupil. "Fickle, wild, and restless," she wrote of herself in 1862, "she still clings to horses, dogs and her Southern home."

Scarlett O'Hara couldn't have said it better. But there was more to Adah than pretense, not least a destiny that would make her famous across half the world. At New Orleans's Cabildo—the old Spanish courthouse on Jackson Square—there hangs an 1858 painting in which Adah is portrayed as a glowing, starry-eyed Romantic with long tresses. She perfectly personifies a genuine American beauty. But to become this lovely woman, Adah would have to pass through an adventurous adolescence. What a fascinating backdrop for the adventure was frontier Texas, with its traces of Spanish culture, its Rangers, Indians, big men, and dreamers—all of them attracted to our budding star!

CHAPTER THREE:

A DAUGHTER OF TEXAS

Fulton Oursler Sr., best remembered for *The Greatest Story Ever Told*, begins his 1936 novel, *The World's Delight*, on the plains of East Texas. The Draconi circus has finished its matinee just outside of town. A Yankee impresario named Jones from Columbus, Ohio, has caught the act of an eighteen-year-old bareback rider named Dolores McCord, and, like many to follow, he is captivated by her beauty. "Her dark hair was luxuriant and gleaming with life, her black eyes flashed and glistened with an impetuous vitality, and she seemed as high-spirited, mettlesome, and tameless as the young horse she had ridden in the arena." Aside from mistaking the color of her eyes, which are usually described as violet or slate blue, Oursler has artfully portrayed the young woman who is our subject. He has caught that certain something that sets this performer apart from other beauties.

Oursler's Dolores McCord is an adolescent version of the woman who will become the international superstar, Adah Isaacs Menken. Incongruously, the novelist has her engaged to a clown. This fellow Buddy is rude to Jones, and Dolores is too preoccupied with mending the clown's underwear to pay attention to the impresario's offer of an engagement in the bigger, if not big, time. The scenario is unlikely. At no point was the overly serious Adah attracted to clowns. The men who caught her interest were self-important types—"big men," she called them. At seventeen, Adah's own ambitions in legitimate theater were already stirring.

But in 1853 the young woman could find no better opportunity than to join Frenchman Victor Franconi's Imperial Hippodrome, an actual circus that toured Texas during that steamy summer. According to the usually reliable Richard Northcott, a researcher and biographer of the theatrical world, "the ringmaster, Rodney Cullen, instructed her in the business of haute-école." Adah, a quick study who had steady nerves, mastered the art of trick riding, which one day would be the making of her.

Bareback riders are *artistes.* They have to perform their poses with ease on the back of a galloping horse. Nineteenth-century circus man Frank Melville remarked of his training, "As a bareback rider I was required to take all sorts of dancing lessons. I had to walk just so, to hold my hands gracefully." Here is the secret of Adah's carriage and her grace in action.

There is an excellent eyewitness account to an even earlier daredevil act by Dolores/Adah. In 1926 Camilla G. Davis, then ninety-two, recalled that "in the year 1850 I was taken to Galveston, Texas, being then seven years of age. The news came to my cousin's home, where my mother and I were visiting, that Adah Bertha Theodore (her actress name) would give a performance on the tightrope. I was all interest and I and my little cousin demanded that we be taken to see this wonderful show!"

Adah, a precocious fifteen, had some renown. "This was my first performance at a theater and to see Adah Bertha accompanied by her sister, Josephine!" continued Camilla Davis. "Josephine assisted, I think, in a dance. Adah acquitted herself with much glory in pink tights on a wire, balancing her lovely form in mid-air on same. . . . I do not know where they went from Galveston. I heard something said about their being accompanied by their parents, Mr. and Mrs. McCord, into Texas towns."

These are recollections made three-quarters of a century after the fact, but they have the ring of accuracy. Young Camilla, in Texas, was thrilled to attend the theater. It is not surprising she remembered the event her whole life. The most interesting feature of her description is that Adah wore her trademark pink tights. When and where she learned to walk the tightrope remains obscure.

Adah's mother, alive and well, was traveling with her daughters—but what about James McCord? The consensus opinion has McCord killed off when Adah was eight. Here, evidence suggests he was living when she was fifteen, as Camilla had "heard something said" about him. It was unusual for a Victorian father or stepfather to permit his adolescent daughter to earn the family living, especially in a circus. That is, unless the man had failed at his own retail trade and the family had fallen on hard times. Adah's McCord (Irish) identity is verifiable, but remains as shadowy as her Jewish and black heritage.

We know how Adah looked when she was a daring young performer. The copy of an ambrotype has been authenticated as her image. She is beautiful, vibrant, hopeful, with a mop of dark, curly hair. The ambrotype process was invented in the early 1850s and patented in 1854. It was a photograph on glass and occupied a technological niche midway between the daguerreotype and the photo on treated paper. It was really a negative that, when placed against a black background, appeared as a positive. The process grew popular, but it gave way to the familiar photo on paper. In the ambrotype of Adah, taken in her eighteenth year, she retains the look and spirit of innocence.

Yet Adah had already given her heart, and probably her body, to her first lover, the Cuban poet Juan Clemente Zenea. Her journey to Havana in 1852 is substantiated by third-party sources. According to her own "Notes of My Life": "The Montplaisir troupe came [to New Orleans], and Adah joined them and went to the Tacón theater in Havana. There she attracted great attention. . . . On the Grand Plaza, Adah was known as the Queen of the Plaza." The Montplaisir company was popular in both New Orleans and Havana, cities which shared a Latin culture built on the peculiar institution of slavery. However, Adah, just budding, was still in the chorus, and in her recollection she blew up an inconsequential appearance to suit her personal myth. In an instance of poetic justice that took one hundred years to unfold, *Queen of the Plaza* became the title of Adah's most widely read, defamatory, and unreliable biography, by Noel Gerson.

In his day, Gerson, who used several pen names, hastily wrote some two hundred works of pulp fiction and an occasional fictionalized biography. *Queen of the Plaza,* written under the name of Paul Lewis, is based on an intimate diary of Adah's that Gerson claimed to have found at the Harvard Theatre Collection. Actually, he fabricated the diary. For years, Harvard archivists were bedeviled by requests for a document they couldn't locate and feared they had lost. In bad taste, Gerson interpreted "queen" to mean prostitute, and Adah's so-called diary is a record of tricks turned and the prices she got.

Gerson's scenario is that Adah was seduced and abandoned by a roué who brought her to Havana. Turned out of her hotel, she went the rounds of the theaters, looking for work. The managers turned her down, and, walking the streets hungry and broke, she accepted her first customer. "Without a qualm she became a professional prostitute." According to Gerson, Adah enjoyed practicing the world's oldest profession and graduated from finding clients on the streets to fashionable restaurants. Finally, Adah became queen of Havana's whores. We repeat this nonsensical story because Gerson's *Queen,* which is shoddy fiction, has been drawn upon by writers and educators who ought to know better.

Had Adah been abandoned in Havana, or any place on Earth, her bag of circus tricks (witnessed by Camilla Davis) could have provided her a living. She had no need to sell herself as a streetwalker. A little research might have shown Gerson that his fairy tale was impossible. There were no white-skinned streetwalkers in Havana under the colonial regime, which lasted until the Spanish-American War of 1898. In Havana, as in Adah's New Orleans, slavery structured social and sexual mores. A well-dressed, apparently white woman could not walk the streets for any reason.

Cuban historian Miguel Fernandez writes:

Sexual relations between the races and consequent mixed-race offspring were accepted, but only as long as they did not take place between

dark-skinned men and white (especially upper-class) women. Restrictive
codes [were] applied to female behavior based on gender, class and color.
When foreigners visited nineteenth-century Havana, they had to come
to terms with the local customs concerning females on the street. . . . Any
women who tried to break the rules of social conduct would face condem-
nation and even insult. Visitors . . . would almost never meet an upper-
class lady on foot. It was totally against the mores.

Blacks and mulattos, who made up nearly half the population, went about on foot. White gentlemen often rode in carriages—big-wheeled, cumbersome *calesas*—but ladies always did so, when they were not cloistered at home behind barred windows. A white gentleman would marry a white woman for children, but he had *sex* with his black or mulatto mistress. His worst fear was that his neglected wife or closely guarded daughter might take up with a free colored man (who might be his best friend's son). No gentleman could tolerate the example of a white woman prancing about the streets of Havana. Gerson's "queen of the plaza" never existed.

What do we actually know about Adah's visit at seventeen to Havana and her performance at the Tacón? The theater, built in the French style, was the finest in the Western hemisphere and the focus of the city's night life. The auditorium, which could hold an audience of three thousand, was in the shape of a horseshoe and featured a spacious parquet in which sat single men. The walls were adorned by frescos and the whole theater lighted by magnificent glass chandeliers hung from the ceiling. There were five tiers of ornamented boxes, each surrounded by latticework but sufficiently open to display the dresses and pretty feet of young women chaperoned by relatives. Often the young men below ignored the doings onstage and stared longingly at their sweethearts, who responded with fan signals.

Adah, toward the end of her "Notes," offers the reader a description of a peculiar custom at the Tacón: "[T]he loveliest women are to be seen there smoking cigarettes between the acts, which in the dim twilight of the auditorium look like so many fire-flies." She continues with details on this custom of fashionable women smoking in public, which at that time was unique to Havana. Her description of the Tacón reads like a defense of her own smoking habit. Adah began smoking at an early age, and it contributed to her reputation as a femme fatale. She was adept with a fan, and she understood the uses of black lace. Her touch of the Spanish stems from her visit to Cuba at an impressionable age.

Here she began her love life. The historian Fernandez writes: "The culture was obsessed with sex. . . . [G]entlemen considered they had a right (even a duty in terms of macho ideology) to possess any [colored] woman they might desire." The wives of white gentlemen were expected to breed, not to enjoy the sexual act. Adah, who was a romantic, came to distrust the married state. But this early, she fell in love with a young poet and probably hoped to marry him.

In Havana, capital of Spain's last possession in America, the barriers between white and colored, Spaniard and Cuban, fell away when they jointly wagered on bullfights, cockfights, or the lottery. Gambling was a passion for all. A more select class was devoted to plotting independence from Spain. Like Byron, the revolutionary might be a romantic poet. Robert Jameson, a British diplomat, remarked, "Almost everyone versifies here, using gods, goddesses, roses, lilies, gold and diamonds as themes."

The best Cuban poet of the midcentury was Juan Clemente Zenea. Born in Bayamo in 1832, he would marry and become devoted to his wife and daughter, but not until after he knew Adah. In her "Notes," Adah relates a love affair with the patriot, but she turns him into a count, the nephew of the Spanish captain-general. He courted her with "tender words and passionate verses and beautiful jewels." The pair eloped in the midst of an earthquake, and Adah "in honor and reality became the Countess Juan Clemente Zenea."

Hokum, as P. T. Barnum would say. But this is typical of how Adah spins a fabulous yarn around a kernel of truth. In a document meant to be made public, she would hardly admit to sex out of wedlock. As for her desire to wed a nobleman, this was a constant fantasy that nearly came true years after her Havana adventures. However, Adah's actual liaison with Zenea has been confirmed by Cuban sources.

In March 1930 the editor of the influential *Saturday Review of Literature* received a letter from Santiago, Cuba, signed only B.M.A., which, in response to a review of Fulton Oursler's novel, stated:

> *I don't know if you are acquainted with the fact that Adah was the first mistress of one of Cuba's greatest poets, Juan Clemente Zenea, who although he later contracted other ties, was always her faithful admirer and friend.*

The editor responded: "There must have been something about Adah: everyone who knew her seems to have stood up for her so." This *something,* made famous by Clara Bow as *It,* is shared by the line of goddesses from Menken to Monroe. *It* permits them to seem at once sensual and innocent.

In his definitive Spanish-language biography of Zenea, Enrique Piñeyro wrote:

> *In a company which came from New Orleans to play in the Tacón Theater, were two ballerinas, the Theodore Sisters as they were called, and Zenea, who in his capacity as newspaper man went freely behind the scenes, knew one of them and was on terms of great intimacy with her. It was the same one who, under the name of Adah Isaacs Menken, was to achieve great fame in Europe and America.*

Piñeyro adds that Zenea dedicated the poem "Silva" to her, using her initials, "A.M."

It strikes a chord that Adah surrendered initially to a poet, and that afterward she thought of herself as a poet. The impression she made on young Juan was equally strong. His "Silva" describes how he listened raptly to Adah, transfixed by her voice and the gestures of her hands, while she read to him from the arch-Romantic rebel, Byron.

Later, in 1852, the young woman returned to New Orleans. According to the *Diccionario de la Literatura Cubana*, Zenea followed her, and the pair, whom the Cuban poet would compare to Romeo and Juliet, resumed their relationship. Adah improved her lover's French and English, the better to conspire against Spanish domination of his homeland. Zenea and his generation succeeded at poetry, but they would fail at revolution.

While in a dungeon of the military prison of La Cabaña, his fate sealed, the middle-aged poet wrote again of his first love, who had died a few years earlier. In the elegy, titled "Infelicia" (the same title as Menken's famous book of verse), we find this final stanza:

> *I know how from town to town wandering*
> *You whispered, in passing, your grief*
> *While crowns of laurel you trod on*
> *Which multitudes cast at your feet.*

The poem was written shortly before Zenea was executed in 1871, not quite forty. His own laurels would be bestowed only after his martyrdom.

Victor Franconi took his hippodrome to Mexico in 1853. By this time Adah was not satisfied to be a mere circus performer. According to Northcott, "We find her the *première danseuse* at the Opera House in the city of Mexico." She was appearing in Adolphe Adam's ballet *Giselle*, but again, she may have exaggerated her role. By her own account, at the age of twelve she had attracted the attention of "the most prominent teacher of dancing in New Orleans, for she was graceful and beautifully formed." But her lessons before moving to Texas would not have qualified her to become a prima ballerina. Further, the war between the United States and Mexico had ended in 1848, with the grudging transfer of what is now California and the Southwest to the Americans. It is not likely the Mexican public would have tolerated an American starring at their Opera House.

In any case, the most important move Adah made in the mid-1850s was back to the East Texas region, where she had spent much of her adolescence. Several newspaper accounts link teenage Adah with Nacogdoches, an old, thriving settlement in the pine belt across from central Louisiana. The most intriguing stories involve a platonic romance with young Thomas P. Ochiltree, who would grow up to become a Confederate hero, a congressman, lobbyist, and raconteur. Aside from boosting his home state, Tom (as everyone from President Ulysses S. Grant to the jockeys at Saratoga called him) believed in the good life, especially when spending other people's money. "I always suck the orange of pleasure dry wherever I go," he remarked.

Tom, born in 1839, grew up in Nacogdoches as the favored son of a judge on the Texas Supreme Court. With the aid of tutors, Tom received a good education, learning Latin, French, German, and Spanish. According to local historian Francis Abernethy, Adah, still a McCord, "lived with her docile, illiterate, and unenterprising [step] father and her hauntingly beautiful, educated mother in a log cabin" outside of town. The girl inherited her mother's looks as well as brains, and her figure blossomed early. Schoolboys fought over who would carry her books. But Adah had an eye for older men, charming them into stuffing her pockets with coins.

Nearing sixteen, Tom Ochiltree suffered from a crush on slightly older Adah, who found the lad amusing. Tom, against his father's will, joined the Texas Rangers, serving under Captain John Walker. Both Apaches and Comanches were active on the frontier, and Tom saw action against the Indian braves. On Christmas Eve, 1854, the young carrot-top arrived home in Nacogdoches with a company of Rangers. Feeling that he was now a man, Tom blushed with pride as the troopers related his brave exploits to the assembled civilians, including Adah.

The women of Nacogdoches entertained the troopers with a banquet and dance at the fort, which dated from Spanish times. Adah paid little mind to Tom, dancing instead with a handsome lieutenant. Heavy rain caused the guests to spend the night at the fort. Adah urged Tom to hang up his socks for Santa Claus, hinting at a special present. Tom whispered to Captain Walker that he had holes in his socks. The captain suggested he hang up his boots instead. Then everybody bedded down.

Next morning, while the other men examined their presents, Tom discovered that his boots were gone. He and his companions searched high and low without success before blaming the theft on a local Mexican. At breakfast, Adah avoided Tom. He glanced at her feet, jumped up, and shouted, "Now I know what Santa Claus has brought me!" A grinning young Adah wore Tom's boots.

The humor is typical of the frontier, but the anecdote has serious implications. Adah, from a poor family, confronts the well-to-do Tom by putting on his boots—symbol of his newly gained manhood. At nineteen, she is already chafing at the passive role assigned to Victorian women. And what were her feelings when the Rangers casually accused a Mexican of stealing Tom's boots? Shy Tom would grow up to be a ladies' man, as well as the confidant of presidents and kings. His adventures with Adah Menken, who had become a world-famous actress, will be told in due course.

We are faced with a contradiction about Adah: While her education was superior to that of most females of her time and place, she was first noticed as a circus performer, the occupation of an outcast. Part of the answer may be supplied by her mother's cultured background and homeschooling. Nacogdoches itself provides another clue. Founded in 1716 by the Spanish on the ruins of an ancient Indian village, the town occupied a strategic location between Louisiana and East Texas. Americans began to arrive as early as 1819, and the Old Stone Fort served as a base from which to expel both Indians and Mexican authority from East Texas. Nacogdoches University, chartered in 1845, served as an educational center. Adah would claim the ability to read and write in ancient and Romance languages—even German—and the university offered courses in most of these. Adah joined in the intellectual life of this bustling place.

According to Texas historian James V. Polk, who got firsthand information from a distant relative, Adah attended the university and starred in a dramatic club. The members urged the teenager to seek a stage career. Confederate General George F. Alford, in a letter to the Galveston *News,* claimed that as a younger man he had known Adah in Nacogdoches. He lauded her beauty and praised her voice. Adah's singing voice is another bone of contention, some critics complimenting it, others not. In the days before electronic amplification, audiences demanded a clear and mellifluous voice. Adah had a sweet voice—not operatic, but ample for the comic and musical roles she would play.

Reports about Adah's teen years in Texas come from men of standing in a society obsessed with honor and an individual's word. It is unlikely these gentlemen fibbed about events. But Adah herself would weave a Texas-sized yarn about her adventures as a captive of Indians in the southern part of the state. The story was first told by George Barclay and echoed by Northcott, both of whom took it seriously. Subsequent biographers have treated the colorful tale as a dime Western in the style of Ned Buntline.

The gist is that Adah, after returning from her engagement in Mexico, was hunting buffalo in a mixed company of Anglos and Mexicans. They were surprised by a band of (unidentified) Indians, but only Adah and Gus Varney, a coward, were seized. Adah, having fainted, found herself in a wigwam, captive of a self-proclaimed big chief. Eagle Eye also held against her will an Indian maiden, Laulerack, whom he intended to wed—as he did Adah. She asked him (in Spanish) why the chief wanted two wives. "The white beauty in summer, the red beauty in winter!" he replied, as though talking about underwear.

The two young women, left alone, speak: "[A]lthough I have seen you but once I already love you," says Adah, who calls herself "Bertha Theodore." Laulerack, who reciprocates, tells Adah that her father was chief of a tribe defeated by Eagle Eye's band. She watched the massacre of her people and the scalping of her father. Eagle Eye saved her by claiming her as his own. She loathes him but has nowhere else to turn. Adah responds: "If we could escape together you would always be my dear sister and share my home!"

After Eagle Eye makes some insinuating remarks, indicating that the virginal Adah faces a fate worse than death, she and Laulerack flee. The Indians pursue them, but Laulerack scorns the bullets whistling overhead. When the two reach a camp of Rangers, the Texans suppose they are under attack and mistakenly shoot the Indian maid. Laulerack, after bidding adieu to her white sister, passes to the Happy Hunting Ground to join her father and mother.

The Rangers counterattack and capture Eagle Eye, who reveals that it was Varney who gave the alarm when Adah and Laulerack fled. She spares the coward from the Rangers' vengeance and is taken to General Harney's headquarters at Austin. Here she lives for several months in a special apartment in the barracks, rides out with the general on review days, and learns to command a company like an officer. A very tall tale, perhaps, but as Mankowitz points out, "Adah learned her excellent horsemanship, and her style with gun, dagger and pistol from someone military somewhere in Texas." Harney was an actual distinguished general of the time and place, and one of his daughters became an actress. Adah may well have been a guest of the United States Army in the mid-1850s.

Adah's accomplishments along soldierly lines were impressive. Although she couldn't shoot as well as another show-woman, Annie Oakley, her talents were more diverse. She developed a style of command essential to the role of Mazeppa, the warrior prince. But unlike Annie, Adah knew from her New Orleans Creole upbringing that she couldn't get her man with a gun. Charm was a more potent weapon.

The mini love affair between Adah and Laulerack has been cited by the Lesbian History Project as proof that Adah was bisexual. The case is strengthened by a reading of the young woman's first serious poetic effort, "Laulerack." The poem in celebrating its subject abounds with

Victorian sentimentality. Ardent declarations of platonic love between women were not uncommon, but lines such as the following indicate something more physical:

> *[A]s my lips did fondly greet her*
> *I blessed her as love's amulet;*
> *Earth hath no treasure dearer, sweeter.*

"Laulerack" is suffused with regret—"Too late we met!"—and seems to be about a real experience of loss. A few years later Adah would write in an intimate letter to Hattie Tyng, a fellow poet whom she was courting: "I have had my passionate attachments among women, which swept like whirlwinds over me, sometimes, alas! scorching me with a furnace blast." We believe that Menken was bisexual, in a few instances actively so, and that certain of her Sapphic attachments can be identified. However, the Laulerack experience may be about identity of another sort—and its loss.

Adah's amorous relations with women were kept secret. They remain in the shadows, but so do the women in her own family. She seems only sporadically attached to her younger sister Annie (sometimes called Josephine), her mother's favorite. Laulerack, the poem's "lost sister," the "dark-eyed one" for whom Adah grieves, may be her own orphaned inner child. Caring, sacrificial, she takes the part of a filial daughter that Adah cannot accept. The star with worlds to conquer would deny her mother and her family, and thus part of herself.

Adah had done away with Adelaide McCord, circus performer. In order to get on with her next life, as poet and journalist, she needed to eliminate any vestige of the woman of color. In antebellum America dark skin indicated a member of the underclass, slave or free. In contrast, Miss Ada Bertha Theodore was on her way up among the "big men" of Texas. It was time to bid the dusky Laulerack *adieu*.

CHAPTER FOUR:

YOUNG AND FREE

In the early autumn of 1855, Adah, on her own, moved to Liberty, Texas. The town was a shipping point on the Trinity River for locally raised cattle. Founded by a group of French officers after the defeat of Napoleon, Liberty was the site of a French convent that educated young ladies from much of Texas. It was home to the *Liberty Gazette*, one of the state's earliest newspapers, in which the following advertisement appeared on October 8th:

SHAKESPEARIAN READINGS
MISS ADA THEODORE
WILL GIVE FOUR READINGS
FROM SHAKESPEARE IN THIS
PLACE SHORTLY
DUE NOTICES WILL BE GIVEN OF
FIRST READING

During the next two months the *Gazette* published several poems by Miss Ada Theodore. One, *The Bright and Beautiful*, is dedicated to her sister Josephine, the same who appeared on stage as Annie Josephs. Another, dedicated to "R.M.T.," is headlined *New Advertisement!!!* It is a blatant declaration of availability:

I'm young and free, the pride of girls
With hazel eyes and nut brown curls
They say I am not void of beauty

I love my friends, respect my duty
I've had full many a Beau Ideal
Yet never—never—found one real
There must be one I know somewhere
In all this circumambient air
And I should dearly love to see him!
Now what if you should chance to be him?

For Adah's describing her eyes as hazel we have no explanation other than poetic license, in order to match her brown curls. Adah's eyes would fascinate many a Victorian gentleman, but the most vivid description comes from Algernon Swinburne's "Dolores": "Grayest of things gray / And bluest of things blue." At this date Adah continued to wear her hair in many curls, to her waist. Later, after she cut it short in a boyish, Byronesque mode, she sometimes wore a long, curly wig.

Although only twenty, Miss Theodore had been married and separated earlier that year. British novelist and screenwriter Wolf Mankowitz turned up a marriage certificate issued at Galveston, Texas, on February 6, 1855, which shows that "Adda Theodore" married "N. H. Kneass." Previously, the "N" was read as a "W," causing biographers to fail to identify the groom as Nelson Kneass. The *New York Illustrated News* on March 17, 1860, identified him correctly as a musician and composer. Kneass was a well-known member of the New Orleans Serenaders, a minstrel group that included Ole Bull, who later became a celebrated violin virtuoso. Kneass, who wrote "Ben Bolt," a popular tune, would have been considered an excellent match for a mere circus performer.

The marriage failed to last the summer. The newlyweds turned out to be incompatible, but there is no record of a divorce. Adah liked to marry—each wedding promised a fresh start, a new identity. But since divorce meant hard feelings and an end to dreams, she sometimes neglected to obtain one.

Adah was a quick study and learned from Kneass. In minstrel shows a group of white male performers in blackface mimicked the singing and dancing of black slaves. Adah Theodore, who used white lead makeup to lighten her skin, was intent on burying her colored past. But there are borrowings from the minstrel show in her varied song and dance numbers, which, *Mazeppa* aside, became popular in their own right. The minstrel show was the first attempt by white performers to mine the treasure trove of black music. Ultimately, with Adah playing a part, the process would result in such classic American musicals as *Showboat* and *Porgy and Bess*.

The minstrel style was invented in the 1830s by Thomas D. Rice, who under the name of "Jim Crow" performed an act inspired by a black stableman he had watched sing and dance. White entertainers began to search out black music on Southern plantations or riverboats, jamming on the banjo with black musicians. The format of the show was firmly established by the Christy Minstrels, who made famous Stephen Foster's "Camptown Races." The performers, in gaudy, swallowtail coats and striped trousers, paraded onstage and arranged themselves in a semicircle with an interlocutor in the center and point men—Mr. Tambo and Mr. Bones—on the ends. There followed repartee and set jokes, but once the audience started to call out the punch lines, they had to be changed.

Next came the singing of ballads and comic songs, and a series of showstoppers by performers hell-bent on pleasing the crowd. The tone was one of hilarity but with satiric and class-conscious undertones. The minstrels with their exaggerated wigs and clothes made fun of the rich and pretentious, the so-called big men who impressed Adah. Finally, the show ended with a sketch in which the audience participated.

The minstrel craze swept the nation from the Mississippi riverboats to elegant Broadway theaters. The Civil War hardly dented its popularity, and after the war blacks formed their own companies, which finally included women, such as the young Bessie Smith. Adah, who liked pants parts, did play Bones in a regular minstrel show. Later, in her musical numbers performed between acts, she kept the free and easy spirit of the minstrels, especially in the repartee she carried on with the audience. There is no record of Adah performing during the few months she stayed married to Nelson Kneass. In sharp contrast, once she shed her first husband, to whom she never referred, Adah adopted the dual roles of poet and actress.

Pamela Lynn Palmer, a local Texas historian and amateur detective, writes:

> During her stay in Liberty from October 1855 to March 1856, [Adah] contributed poems and essays to The Liberty Gazette, which she sometimes signed "Ada Bertha Theodore." She entertained the town with readings of Shakespeare, as her first ambition was to be a great dramatic actress. Even offstage she retained the tragic mood, rarely smiling and sighing frequently in view of the other guests at the dining table of the City Hotel. Her morose expression attracted comment and people speculated on the cause of her mysterious sadness.

Why was Adah so unhappy? Camilla Davis, who as a child had watched Adah perform on the tightrope, was attending school in Liberty at this time and boarded at the same hotel as she. "I never saw her smile once," she remarked. Adah was often in the company of Henry Shea, who founded the *Gazette*, described as short, well-built, and charming. A young lawyer, Abner Trowel, who became Camilla's first sweetheart, completed an intellectual threesome. Adah's sister Josephine acted as chaperone, and Camilla describes her as plain and inoffensive but necessary.

It is tempting to surmise that twenty-year-old Adah was nursing a broken heart. Certainly, she was not pining over her ex-husband. Adah's outbursts in essays in the *Gazette* show that she was disappointed in her first marriage. "Believe me," she wrote on one occasion, "there are other missions in the world for women, other than that of wife and mother." Yet in "My Home!" she dwelt poetically on her own absent mother and her lost childhood home: "a paradise of innocence and love."

There was a similar contradiction in Adah's scornful attitude toward young women who thought only of catching a husband, employing the feminine arts, and her own advertising for a "beau ideal." Underneath the pretense of a liberated woman beat the heart of a romantic. She was also sensitive to what people said about her, aware that public opinion could be a cruel tyrant.

If we construct a scenario from these divergent emotions, we are looking at a young woman who had been deeply in love with Juan Zenea, but who married another man, Kneass, either on the rebound or for reasons of convenience. Suppose she had become pregnant with the Cuban poet's child? They could not marry, since Zenea was devoted to the revolution. Yet a husband, any husband, would have been essential to retaining her respectability. Once the pregnancy was resolved, either through abortion or a miscarriage, Adah could abandon the loveless marriage. She might have harbored the feelings of bitterness and regret that she expressed at this time.

The above is guesswork, but it may explain a crucial period in Adah's life that has gone unexplained. It denotes a pattern she followed with her husbands to come: Adah was not above using a man, then sloughing him off. At twenty, she bounced back quickly. She was "young and free," with her whole life ahead. Camilla Davis, who saw Adah daily, provides an extraordinary picture: "[S]he was the most charming personality; she was beautiful all over, hand and foot and form . . . Her eyes cannot be described—full of light and love."

Adah had a destiny, which she sensed. "She seemed to be trying to gaze across Time into Futurity," writes Davis. Aware of her talent but lacking focus, she was prey to doubts and loneliness.

Camilla was delighted to learn that Adah, who paid a quiet attention to her, had called her "a lovely child." She recalled that, after a few months, Adah moved from Liberty to Galveston, where "she very soon married the Jew, Menken, and took [his] name. I never saw Menken again."

The woman Camilla knew had passed into memory. Adah's youthful days became a story that, if she remembered it straight, she felt free to manipulate. At twenty-one she was a poet, Jewish, and on her way to becoming a *femme fatale*.

PART TWO

DEFENDER OF HER PEOPLE

The inspired Deborah of her people . . .

—BARON LIONEL DE ROTHSCHILD

Chapter Five:

THE JEW MENKEN

Alexander Isaac Menken was the black sheep of a prosperous German Jewish family settled in Cincinnati, Ohio. He was a musician in a family of merchants. Solomon, his father, born in Prussia, had sailed in 1820 from Holland to arrive at what was then a frontier village. A peddler, his possessions were strapped to his back. Cincinnati grew into the Queen City of the West, its Jewish population increased, and Solomon grew wealthy by selling dry goods. He married outside his faith twice, and Alexander's mother, who died soon after he was born, was descended from a colonial governor of Virginia. Solomon's second wife was a descendant of Napoleon's minister to Spain. When the immigrant merchant died in 1853, he left a considerable estate to his wife and five children, of whom Alexander was the eldest.

Alexander did not receive the inheritance he expected. His name alone was omitted from the family Bible. Allen Lesser describes this eldest son as an individual "of some musical ability but with a particular fondness for chance and change and adventure." Alex, as he was called, was the artistic type, and he clashed with his mundane, social-climbing family. After his father's death, he left Cincinnati to try his luck in the theater.

In March of 1856, this tall, dark, handsome man of thirty was the conductor of the orchestra at Neitsch's Theater in Galveston. A Miss Adah Theodore came looking for work, which she found as a dancer rather than an actress. The pair, thrown together, shared many interests, and they eventually eloped to Livingston, Texas, where they married on April 3, 1856. The newlyweds had prospects but very little

money, and when they moved to New Orleans, they had to stay temporarily with Adah's mother and sister. This was a love match, into which
Adah entered with all her heart.

Adah did see an advantage to the marriage: Alex Menken knew
his way around the theatrical world, and she hoped to get out of the
chorus. Alex became Adah's manager. He decided his wife needed sea-
soning, and she began to act with the New Orleans Crescent Dramatic
Association. No record remains of the roles she played, but by year's
end she drew the attention of James S. Charles, a former actor who
managed a stock company that toured the Red River towns of Louisiana and East Texas.

In March of 1857, "Mrs. A. I. Menken" debuted in her first professional, dramatic role at Charles's theater in Shreveport. She played the
lead in Bulwer-Lytton's *The Lady of Lyons,* a five-act drama set during
the French Revolution. Although the dense, blank verse text was read
rather than staged, Adah got off to a fine start. "The debutante was
self-possessed, graceful, pretty, and capable of reading with correctness
and force," wrote a local reviewer.

Charles's ambitious plans to tour Adah were interrupted by the
stock market crash of that year. Western railroads were the vanguard
of the Victorian New Economy, and the inflated bubble in their stocks
burst. Banks called in their loans and brokers went broke, taking their
clients with them. Businesses and factories closed and many theaters
went dark. The Menkens returned to New Orleans, where, during the
summer and fall, Adah appeared in several brief engagements.

On the last Saturday evening in August, Adah starred in a benefit
for the Crescent Dramatic Association, put on at the Gaiety (aka Variet-
ies) Theater. At a time when wealthier citizens, afraid of fever, had fled
the steaming city for the countryside, Adah chose to make an impression as Bianca in Henry Milman's *Fazio, or The Italian Wife's Revenge.*
Milman was an English clergyman who wrote high-flown drama for a
cultured audience. This was the level of theater to which Mrs. Menken
aspired.

The hard-edged plot of *Fazio* explains why it became a favorite of hers. Bianca is an innocent who wholly trusts her husband Fazio, but he is a calculating philanderer. When his wife's jealousy proves too hot to handle, he murders a rich miser and runs off with a more compliant woman. Bianca, her love turned to hate, informs the police, and she revels in watching her husband's execution. She concludes the play with a stirring speech on the wages of adultery. Years later, Adah could only fantasize about such an outcome to a similar, real-life situation.

In torrid August, the ingenue fanned the interest of New Orleans and filled the house. She was thrilled by the approval of the audience. "The accomplished and talented Menken received constant applause throughout her performance and an enthusiastic call at the termination," proclaimed the *Daily Picayune*.

A few days later Adah starred in a benefit for herself. She showed her versatility by playing in two one-acts: the melodramatic *The Soldier's Daughter*, and the comic *A Lesson for Husbands*. Once again the house was packed and enthusiastic. After the curtain came down, Adah was called out and heaped with bouquets of flowers. The reviewer for the *Picayune* praised her "talent, joined with a good person, a beautiful face, a musical voice, graceful action and perfect self-possession and ease on the stage." In the *Daily Delta* the ingenue was compared favorably to reigning actresses of the day, and by none other than John W. Overall, a critic with a national reputation. He predicted the rising star would let nothing stand in her way.

Overall and Adah Menken would remain friends and stay in touch until the Civil War made correspondence impossible. At his suggestion she produced and staged *The Barbarian*, a romantic drama that has mercifully sunk into oblivion. As producer she was in over her head; the cast mauled or forgot their lines, and only an indulgent audience, won over by the young star, permitted the play to lumber on to its conclusion. In October Adah once again played Bianca, almost living the part of the passionate, vengeful wife, to which the audience responded with curtain calls and thunderous applause.

Despite Adah's success, the wolf was at the door. On November 2 she informed a friend that "circumstances are anything but flattering; I mean privately . . . my means have run out." Alex had been in negotiation with William Crisp, an impresario who controlled several theaters in the upper South. Although Adah's experience on the legitimate stage was shallow, she would accept only the lead in dramatic plays. But the economic depression ground on, and Crisp had to shutter his theater in Memphis.

The Menkens were nervously looking beyond the South. Their gaze was fixed about 750 miles north as the crow flies—on Cincinnati. Alex got in touch with his brothers and sister. Meanwhile, Adah was writing poems and essays on Jewish themes. She published these pieces in *The Israelite,* a Cincinnati-based international weekly presided over by Rabbi Isaac Mayer Wise, the father of Reform Judaism. For most American Jews, Rabbi Wise was the leader and symbolic figure of his generation.

The title of Adah's first essay, published in October 1857, is "Shylock." It protests against stereotypical portraits of Jews in drama. Although the older dramatists were regarded as superior to the modern, she writes, "there can be no question that the Jewish character has received a truer estimate in the present time than in former days." Adah doesn't hesitate to attack Webster, Marlowe, and Shakespeare himself for their willingness to pander to the crowd. Although Jews were banned from England and thus unknown to the Elizabethan dramatists, they are merciless toward their Jewish characters. They depict each as "a combination of the darkest vices and worst passions that could possibly disgrace or degrade a man." Cleverly, Adah points out that in the Italian source of Shakespeare's *The Merchant of Venice,* "Shylock is a Christian and the victim a Jew."

Adah has a few kind words for the Bard. Shylock, as Shakespeare conceived him, is a complex character. But in the play as performed, he is motivated mainly by avarice and revenge. The audience knows Shylock is to be humiliated in the end, and they are not made sympathetic toward him. Yet Adah admires a character that no wrongs can overcome. The essayist looks hopefully toward the future, as did the poet and performer. Later, Adah's companions would include Walt Whitman, far ahead of his time, and theatrical innovators such as Augustin Daly. She herself would instigate sensational changes in American entertainment.

How did Adah, at twenty-two, acquire the sense of Hebrew character and tradition that she demonstrates in her writing? As early as 1857 she began to sound a Messianic note, to identify her personal longings with those of the Jewish people. On November 6 *The Israelite* published her response to the oppression of Jews under the Turkish Empire, which accusation she made the title of her poem. Signing herself "Mrs. Alex Isaac Menken," the poet asserts the historical right of the descendants of Abraham to Jerusalem. Then she demands: "Will *He* never come? Will the Jew / In exile eternally pine?" Her answer would please an ardent Zionist. The Messiah will come, and Jews will be able to live:

> *Where the censer gave od'rous perfume*
> *Where the Holy of Holies had place*
> *Where the Almond of Aaron was laid up in bloom*
> *Where the Ark of the Covenant had resting and room,*
> *Where the Shechinah [God's spirit] gave token of grace!*

Adah has predicted the return of the Jewish people to Israel, which would not become reality till nearly a century later. She has done so with grace and learning. The flowering of her literary spirit occurred simultaneously with the launch of her theatrical career in New Orleans. Allen Lesser writes: "All through her life [both these careers] would complement each other, for the one was the expression of her body, the other of her soul." Actually, as the author/actress observed, she grew more torn as her fame increased. But for the moment, Adah was playing in high drama onstage and, through *The Israelite*, on the world stage.

The Cincinnati weekly featured news items from Jewish communities throughout the world.

Winter 1858 was a fallow period for the actress. She took advantage of this enforced leisure to correspond with Alex's sister Rosina and brother Lewis. She referred to them as *her* "sister" and "brother," and tried to make peace among the fractious family. "How glad I would be to see you all reunited," she wrote Rosina, "and our Alex, and your Adah living in all hearts alike." By now, Alex's family was ready to welcome home the prodigal. But Alex, beyond acting as his wife's manager, couldn't earn a living. Humiliated, he drank heavily.

In spring Adah resumed her stage appearances, first with the Charles company in Shreveport. When Charles leased the Gaiety in New Orleans for the summer season, she returned with the company. On opening night, May 30, she played no less than six characters in *A Day in Paris.* Her ability at quick change of costume, attitude, and gender was a useful talent at a time when protean comedies were popular. The critic Overall insisted that Adah was "an actress of real excellence whose dramatic genius will command the approbation of every lover of superior acting."

The hectic schedule of those years would astound a modern performer. On June 1 Adah played the female lead in *Is He Jealous?* Afterward she performed a number of songs and dances. The next night she played Mrs. Fitzgig in *The Irish Lion* and Mrs. Trictrac in *My Cousin at Richmond.* On June 3 Adah played in *The Lady and the Devil* and as Polly Cripps in *The Unprotected Female,* which became one of her standards. The last night of this run she played the Widow Cheerly in *The Soldier's Daughter,* another of her signature parts. This bevy of roles puts the lie to the allegation, echoed by biographers, that Adah had difficulty learning and remembering her lines!

Adah's connection with New Orleans came to a sudden end. Riots broke out over the municipal elections. In the words of a local historian, "Adah was terrified at the disturbances, and fled unceremoniously to less tumultuous scenes." Here is another piece of evidence that she was born into the class of light-skinned women of color. Rioters, after setting fires and looting, roamed the streets looking for blacks and colored people to lynch. Adah, though in no danger, had broken the law against miscegenation by marrying Alex. She carried with her the unreasoning fear that her secret would be discovered.

On their way to Cincinnati, the Menkens steamed up the Mississippi and Ohio rivers. Walt Whitman, leaving New Orleans, had traveled this route ten years earlier. The fever season and his inability to adapt to slave culture drove the Brooklyn journalist back north. The fever of violence drove Adah, soon to become a disciple of Whitman's, toward the wary embrace of her in-laws. Unlike the muddy Mississippi, the Ohio ran clear blue and steady through high, wooded banks. As Adah looked out from the steamboat's deck, on her right lay Kentucky, a slave state. Where the topography permitted, plantations spread gracefully across the land. To her left lay Ohio, from where she could hear the sounds of ax and hammer—free men clearing their plots and building log homes.

Adah had paved the way for the couple's entrance into Cincinnati's Jewish society. *The Israelite* continued to publish her poems and essays and reviews of her performances. The weekly, which reflected Rabbi Wise's reform and assimilationist views, heartily welcomed Adah as "our favorite and ingenious poetess . . . who comes to us from the south, crowned with the brilliant success genius and talent always meet." The paper proclaimed Adah "a first-class star on the stage all over the southwest."

Adah's in-laws weren't nearly so complacent toward her. In 1877 Celia Logan, whose family was friendly with the Menkens, recalled an evening two decades earlier when, as a child, she had attended a reception at which Alex introduced his wife to the Jewish community. Logan recalled, "There had been trouble about his marrying Adah, the reason of which I was too young to understand, but the old folks had concluded to make the best of it." The "old folks" must have included, beside Alex's stepmother, his three brothers, one sister, and two aunts.

"Never shall I forget the hush which fell upon even the children as the pair paused a moment at the door, as if to ask permission to enter," continued Celia. She reminisced about Adah's "peerless beauty," and called Alex "a remarkably handsome man, with a countenance intelligent as the expression was noble." The couple had a radiant glow and seemed to Celia destined for success and happiness. Considering pater Solomon's two Gentile wives, doubt as to whether Adah was born Jewish could not have troubled the Menkens. It was her career as an actress that frightened the conservative family. However, Adah was already a favorite of Rabbi Wise, the pillar of the community.

Cincinnati in 1858 was the fourth city of the United States, and the largest west of the Allegheny Mountains. It exhibited something of the dynamism later attributed to Carl Sandburg's Chicago, "hog butcher to the world." Fredrika Bremer, a Swedish travel writer, ran into droves of these "respectable four-footed citizens," shipped from nearby farms to the slaughterhouse. "Whole regiments of swine cluttered the streets and stank up the air." Yet this "Queen City" could boast of impressive public buildings, magnificent views from the terraced heights of its hills, a mild climate that encouraged vineyards to grow along the slopes, and, especially, the cultivation of beautiful roses in its many gardens.

Cincinnati loved culture and good beer. It was home to a large, liberal, German-speaking community that had emigrated in force after the failed revolutions of 1848. These folk, often skilled workers, were devoted to politics, music, and their language, and they lived in their own quarter, naming the streets after Old World towns. The Jews, who had joined the general German migration, lived in a tightly knit community within a few square blocks. A majority of them worked in the prosperous men's clothing industry. They encouraged the involvement of women in the arts, and they were partial to religious reform.

Isaac Mayer Wise, born in Bohemia in 1819, the year of a pogrom, first settled in Albany, New York, as the rabbi of a congregation he would find much too conservative to suit him. Largely self-educated and free of dogma, he was a visionary. His view of the Jewish future was to live in a secular country of equals and to adapt Jewish institutions and rituals to the modern world. He believed his vision could come true in America. From his base in Cincinnati, where he had arrived in 1850, he tirelessly fought against discrimination and worked to bring American Jews together into a national union.

The young Adah Menken seemed to fit into Rabbi Wise's plans. The success of Reform Judaism hinged on the increased participation of women. Wise, rather than segregating them, introduced mixed and equal seating in his temple. He encouraged women to sing in the choir. He fraternized with his congregation, and Adah soon became the leading light of a group that frequented *The Israelite* office. She thrived in this intimate atmosphere, and during her year in Ohio, living in a domestic yet stimulating environment, she published twenty-two poems and three essays. According to Leo, Rabbi Wise's son, several of Adah's poems were included in the hymn book of the Reformed ritual.

At this time Adah's poetic style remained conventional, the lines short and rhyming. The message ranged from an outraged cry for social justice to flights of mysticism. Adah's belief that the Jews would return to the land of Israel may have given Wise pause. He believed that America was the Promised Land, the long-sought-after home for the wandering tribes. Adah was far more Zionist than the rabbi, who hoped for secular assimilation. Wise, in a move to enforce separation of church and state, joined with local Catholics in a lawsuit to eliminate the reading of the Protestant Bible in public schools.

Adah's role as defender of her people was sharpened when Baron Lionel de Rothschild was elected from London to the British Parliament. The editor of the influential *Churchman* objected because Rothschild was a Jew, and he dared to proclaim that Queen Victoria, unless she intervened, would be sent to Hell. Adah wrote a spirited defense of Rothschild's right to be seated, taking a fraternal view: "We have joined ourselves to the battle of Israel's right," she declared. The incident stirred up controversy on both sides of the Atlantic. Rothschild is said to have read Adah's piece in *The Israelite* and to have called her "the inspired Deborah of her people."

In the Bible Deborah is the Hebrew Joan of Arc, a prophet. The classical historian Josephus tells us she inspired an Israelite army to fight against the superior numbers and armor of the Canaanites. Although filled with patriotic zeal, Deborah worked through Barak, a general, to rouse her forces. With a little help from the Lord, who sent a hailstorm into the faces of the enemy, then drowned them in a flood, the Hebrew army triumphed.

Deborah, though a judge in Israel, remained womanly. She composed the Ode of Deborah, which praises the Lord for saving His chosen people, and promotes piety and virtue. Perhaps, living comfortably in German Jewish Cincinnati, Adah viewed herself in such a light. In fact, her relationship to that community, as well as her inner conflicts, were too unresolved to result in the sort of peace that followed Deborah's victory.

In 1858 the child Edgar Mortara became a lightning rod for Jewish feelings, rather like the sentiment Elián González would raise much later among Cuban Americans. Edgar, born to well-off Jewish parents in Bologna, Italy, fell ill and seemed to be dying. His Catholic nurse secretly called in a priest to baptize the infant. Edgar recovered, but from the Church's point of view he was now a Christian. Italian law forbade a Christian child to live in a Jewish home. When the facts became known, Archbishop Prèla ordered the six-year-old seized and sent to a convent orphanage. Edgar's father demanded the return of his son, who had begun to train as a monk. Jewish and Protestant newspapers throughout the world seconded the father, while Church authorities supported the archbishop.

In January 1859 *The Israelite* published Adah's militant poem, "To the Sons of Israel," in which she urged young Jewish men to take up arms against their oppressors. She ranted against "the barbarous fiends of priesthood," and demanded of her Jewish brethren, "To struggle or to die!" This alienated the considerable Catholic population of

Cincinnati and disappointed Rabbi Wise. His hard-fought alliance between Jews and Catholics was threatened. To Adah, the Jewish condition of exile was personal, and the Mortara case had struck a nerve. She too felt exiled from a birthright she dared not acknowledge.

To the close-knit Jewish community of Cincinnati, Adah seemed too emphatic a Jew. But there were additional sources of friction between her and the leadership. Leo Wise recalled Adah participating in the give-and-take of younger people at *The Israelite* office. She was the first woman he had ever seen smoke a cigarette. To most Victorians, a woman who smoked in public was a tramp. Adah thought it chic, a reminder of Havana and her first love. After Adah and Alex parted, rumor had it that her smoking was the cause. Actually, the basic incompatibility of the couple was aggravated by Adah's growing popularity.

Soon after the Menkens arrived in Cincinnati in late June, Adah played a week at Wood's Theater. She starred as a coquette in *The Soldier's Daughter* and caused the audience to weep in *The Hunchback*. Parties and dinners were given in her honor. "Flattered, praised and sought after," writes Lesser, Adah "held court with her admirers and suitors as if she were a royal lady." A Dr. Nathan Mayer wrote a poem praising her, and she reciprocated, complimenting him as "the young genius of our ancient race." Alex squirmed and continued to drink heavily.

With his wife receiving such favorable publicity, Alex booked her for a brief run at a nearby Dayton theater. On August 13 Adah had her benefit night, and she played in *Sixteen-String Jack*, her version of the life of highwayman Jack Sheppard. Knowing the reviewer from *The Dayton Empire* would be in the audience, she packed it with seventy-five young male admirers from the local militia, the Light Guards. The high-spirited play featured the athletic Adah in male garb. She had adopted a freedom of movement startling in a woman.

Adah understood that an attractive woman is irresistible in pants. She had learned since adolescence that an audience is a fickle monster, hard to please but quick to fall in love. At Dayton between the acts she sang "Comin' Thro' the Rye," complete with a Scots accent, and then performed a Spanish dance. The reviewer described it as "done with that grace and abandon that ranks her as a finished and fascinating danseuse."

Afterward, the Light Guards marched backstage and invited Adah to dinner as their guest of honor. She was flattered, and under military escort she went along to the local hotel, where an elaborate spread was laid out. Toasts were given and champagne drunk and glasses shattered. Each guardsman was eager to outdo his comrades in proving his devotion to Adah by getting soused. Naturally she had to join in.

The climax of the evening came when the commandant rose and bestowed on Adah the honorary commission of Captain of the Light Guards. Swearing to obey her commands, he drank a toast from her shoe. He passed the shoe down the banqueting table to the officers and men. Each toasted Adah's beauty; it was fortunate she wore a small size, or the Daytonians would have gotten even drunker. No one regretted the absence of Adah's devoted spouse.

Finally, a slightly tipsy Adah was escorted to her room by her fellow officers. Nothing untoward happened. However, word of the festivities was carried back to Cincinnati. It was embellished by the description of a sotted Adah being carried into her room by several military types, who emerged later. Gossip didn't need the assistance of the newly invented telegraph to leap fences and cross neighborhoods. The town was buzzing with Adah's first major scandal. Alex Menken was incensed, believing that his family name had been dishonored. He demanded that Adah give up her acting career. She reacted with shock and hurt, and the pair quarreled.

However, Adah was not yet ready to leave her well-feathered nest, and Alex was not ready to abandon his trophy wife. The couple reconciled. Adah agreed to assume a more domestic role and stick to dramatic readings in nearby towns. She also decided to study sculpture. Cincinnati already had produced one notable sculptor, Hiram Powers, and Adah quickly took to an art that, though immobile, strongly influenced the theater. Actors at a crucial moment had a tendency to pose, at times in imitation of a well-known classic statue. Adah, despite her love of action, would borrow from this technique, relying on her brief but satisfying experience in the sculptor's studio.

On September 3 *The Israelite* published Adah's poem, "Karazah to Karl," a flattering proclamation of her love for Alex and of their reunion. One stanza reveals the passionate woman Alex had married:

> *My burning lips shall set their seal*
> *On our betrothal bond tonight.*
> *While whispering murmurs will reveal*
> *How souls can love in God's own light.*

Typically, Adah lived her private life in public view, going to the extreme in her enthusiasm. In December *The Israelite* published "A Wife's Prayer," in which Adah promised to subjugate her will to her husband's. She prayed to be kept from "all ungentleness and ill-humour," and she swore to be "humble and obedient, useful and observant." Adah meant what she had written. She had a talent for self-delusion that served her well on stage but badly in life. The autumn passed in a haze of high culture that was only dissipated when the incident at Dayton became resurrected in a new light.

The story of Adah's honorary commission in the militia had gone the tavern rounds, but such sexual innuendo was nothing special to the boys at the bar. One evening in New York the popular actor Stuart Robson heard the story, and to a set of reporters, he barked, "By the living jingo, what next? In case of female suffrage, Adah Isaacs Menken will be nominated for President—and be elected too!" Robson's crack made the daily papers countrywide. Suddenly, the name Menken meant something.

Adah understood the power of gratuitous publicity, and since the couple needed money, she prevailed on Alex to resume her bookings. Her first engagement, two weeks in Louisville, Kentucky, was in support of a rising star, Edwin Booth. He was the son of mad tragedian Junius Brutus Booth, the leading "American style" actor, and Walt Whitman's favorite. His younger brother, John Wilkes Booth, was another brilliant performer. But Edwin represented something new in style. Where his father and brother were Romantics, noted for "vigor of voice, and look, and action," Edwin's acting was nuanced and internal. "Pale, thin and intellectual," he had that Montgomery Clift appeal to women.

Adah's meeting with Edwin would be the start of a press agent's dream romance. Rumors about their alleged affair made the gossip-hungry papers. Actually, what developed was a genuine, lasting friendship. Adah's emotional tranquility was destined to be shattered by a very different sort of man.

Next, she made a one-night appearance at the New National Theater in Cincinnati, playing Rebecca in *Ivanhoe*. The performance was held on Christmas night, less a domestic holiday than it is now. It included a surprise that turned Adah's life topsy-turvy.

CHAPTER SIX:

ENTR'ACTE

On Christmas night of 1858, John Carmel Heenan, who claimed to be heavyweight boxing champion of America, gave a one-round exhibition of the manly art of self-defense with a sparring partner at the New National Theater. The actual fights of bare-knuckle boxers were so brutal, they more often fought in exhibition, where they wore gloves. These matches earned easy money and, unlike prizefights, were legal. Because women liked to watch the well-built boxers, legitimate theaters sometimes added an exhibition to the bill.

Heenan, born in Troy, New York, in 1833, was over six feet tall, superbly built, and handsome as a matinee idol. He had thick black hair and eyebrows, rippling muscles, and a potent punch. With an engaging Irish personality, he was the pride of the sporting crowd, and he attracted a higher class of fans than his crude, brawling competitors. In the ring Heenan was quick, strong, and brave. As a man he was a pliant tool of New York's corrupt political machine. When, after the show, the theater manager brought John to Adah's dressing room, she felt she was being introduced to an Adonis.

The electricity crackled. A shock of recognition passed between the two splendid young people: The man who would become America's symbol of courage met the woman destined to become, in Swinburne's phrase, "the world's delight." The perfect power couple instinctively reached toward each other. Unfortunately, those close to them, unwilling to grasp the possibilities, stood in their way.

The brief meeting left Adah excited and uneasy. She couldn't help thinking about Heenan—this magnificent specimen and his gentlemanly bearing and affable manners. Through the winter of 1859 she toured to Indianapolis, then Columbus for three weeks, and in February to Pittsburgh. She played leading roles on the light side, such as the Widow Cheerly in the old comedy of manners, *The Soldier's Daughter*, or the six quick-changes of *A Day in Paris*.

Alex Menken went along, and husband and wife wore on each other. A call boy at the Pittsburgh Theater, who had two weeks to observe them, described Alex as "manager and agent . . . a sort of general utility man to her." Such a figure was helpful to a touring star who played with a different stock company each week. The theater-going public expected a new play each night, and the stars had to bring their wardrobes with them. Adah needed her husband, but their fractious relationship couldn't help her forget John Heenan.

The starlet, hoping to advance her career and to see John, suggested to Alex that he book her into a New York theater. She had complained about how difficult it was to get an opening in a major house. To her surprise, Alex succeeded in booking her at A. N. Purdy's National Theater, where she was engaged for a week beginning March 1. Adah was not greatly saddened when Alex's stepmother died and he returned to Cincinnati. As she chugged along on the Pennsylvania Railroad, bound for America's entertainment capital, she would have plenty of time to make plans for her New York debut—if she could keep her mind from calling up images of the muscular champion.

By the late 1850s the central and eastern United States could boast of a comprehensive railroad grid. This was of enormous importance to the theatrical profession. Clanging and spewing black smoke, trains went everywhere an actor wished to perform. They transported newspaper reviews of his or her latest triumph or failure. The railroad carried trained animals, costumes, and the performers themselves west from New York to Buffalo, Chicago, St. Louis, and places in between. Every city from Richmond to Milwaukee could boast of at least one large, well-equipped theater and a stock company to host traveling stars. For the first time, a performer might gain a national audience.

However, even on a simple journey from Pittsburgh, Adah needed to make three changes of trains before she reached the terminal at Jersey City, where she boarded the ferry to cross the Hudson. Through the years, she would spend an inordinate amount of time bouncing and jolting on the rails, getting covered by soot, and primping in station restrooms. But in late February 1859, Adah greeted the clamor of New York with a smile and an eagerness to succeed.

Purdy's National Theater was located on Chatham Square in lower Manhattan, where the Bowery begins. Today, it would be in the heart of Chinatown. The neighborhood bustled with people on the sidewalks or going in and out of shops and restaurants, while horse-drawn trolleys thundered over the cobbled streets. It was brawny working class. The Irish were a major element, but also the Germans, who frequented beer gardens on the Bowery and had their own theater, the Stadt. Slightly to the south was Five Points, a crime-ridden slum, and a little further on stood City Hall, its moral equivalent.

Nearby on the East River stretched a mile and a half of shipyards that were in constant use, building world-famous clipper ships. As fast as these hit the water they were bought by New York merchants who traded to Europe, California, or the Orient. Three-quarters of the nation's imports passed through New York harbor. The city processed sugar and cotton from the South and made everything from garments to heavy machines. At the tip of Manhattan, Wall Street banks, brokers, and speculators raised the funds to finance all this activity. Forgetting the Panic of 1857, the city's populace, whether native-born or immigrant, followed the lead of its mayor, Fernando Wood: Make money, stay ahead.

New York's theater culture echoed the split in society between the working class (the "roughs," as Walt Whitman called them) and the middle classes. The Bowery, famed for its Bowery B'hoys, a loose-knit bunch of ruffians, was home to one sort of theater district. Here could be seen comedies, musical acts, mime, and "sensation" dramas. Somewhat later, burlesque would arrive with its "leg shows." To the west, Broadway (in the area of present-day Soho) was home to a district that stressed fashionable shopping, classical and moral plays, and ladies' matinees. Often the dramas and the main actors were imported from England. By the late 1850s both districts were thriving.

It is not recorded where in Manhattan Adah stayed during her first visit. She was pleased by the huge three-sheet posters plastered across the National's facade, which billed her as "Captain Adah Isaacs Menken of the Dayton Light Guards." She saw Purdy and he approved the entire week's schedule. For her debut, Adah chose to play the madcap Widow Cheerly in the time-tested comedy, *The Soldier's Daughter.*

Adah could take confidence from the National's record in introducing stars, which included the tragedian Edwin Booth and the great mime, George Fox. She would be supported by Purdy's fine stock company and the experienced J. H. Allen in the role of her suitor, Frank Heartsall, a dashing young banker. On a Tuesday evening, as she peered from behind the curtains, Adah's heart sank at the meager audience that had braved the March winds to see an unknown. She had no idea that Purdy, close to bankruptcy, would resign as manager of the National before the month was out.

The performance on Wednesday became crucial. Adah chose the grim, pseudoclassical drama *Asmodeus,* and, to leaven the evening, the quick-change *A Day in Paris* as a closing farce. Purdy had inveigled William Winter, theater critic of the *Tribune,* to attend the show. When Adah opened Thursday's paper, she found a lukewarm review of the previous evening and the following critique of herself: "Miss Menken has talent, but it is like the gold in quartz veins all in the rough; and so [it] must undergo the refining process of intelligent and critical audiences before she can hope to become an actress." Winter commended Adah's "dashing style," but he warned that "like most western mental products, she wants taming down."

The real issue for the *Tribune's* critic lay elsewhere. In *A Day in Paris,* the actress first appeared as a French dandy, dressed to the nines, then as a bare-legged street urchin hawking papers. She played four more roles and sang and danced. Bare legs, more than ample cleavage, offended

Victorian prudery, and the *Tribune* was hands-on edited by Horace Greeley, reformer and puritan. "When people go to the ballet," huffed Winter, "they expect to see a peculiar and questionable freedom in the toilet [dress]. That style ought never to be outstripped upon the legitimate stage—not even on the eastern side of the city." The censure was especially damaging because of the *Tribune*'s influence and wide circulation.

Winter was on his way to becoming the most important drama critic of the time. That he had an eye for Adah's charms is obvious. It was rumored she rebuffed his advances, causing him to become her enemy. Adah responded to Winter's slap in the face by choosing two more quick-change comedies for her third night, and by showing still more of her legs. Nonetheless, the crowd stayed away. That evening Purdy fired Adah, cutting her out of her benefit night, when she would have received half the gate. Often, the benefit was the only recompense an actor received. But Purdy himself was struggling to survive. As theater historian George Odell says of him, "Purdy did not relax till he gave up entirely."

Adah, rather than give way to despair, complained of her treatment to Frank Queen, publisher of *The New York Clipper*, located at Nassau and Ann streets. The weekly, founded by Queen in 1853, may be thought of as *Backstage*, *Variety*, and *Sports Illustrated* rolled into one. Members of the theatrical world and the sporting fraternity would not miss an issue. For actors, musicians, managers, and circus performers, *The Clipper* ran news articles, employment ads, and personals, and forwarded mail; for admirers of the manly art of self-defense, it reported on and advocated what was then an illegal sport; and for followers of the turf, it listed and reported on horse races. The paper carried news of allied sports, such as baseball, and the activities of volunteer fire departments.

Queen—fat, florid, and sympathetic—couldn't help Adah with Purdy. But from this day on the influential journalist became her friend and champion for as long as she lived, and afterward. Queen agreed to publish her poem, "A L'outrance," *The Clipper*'s first and last venture into verse. More practically, he helped Adah find a booking at a Newark theater, beginning March 7, for two weeks. Less fortunately, he facilitated her liaison with John Heenan, a regular visitor to the offices of the weekly. Queen, like his rival, George Wilkes of *Spirit of the Times*, promoted prizefights and -fighters.

Adah and John probably began their liaison during her March stay in the New York area. Being impulsive, it is unlikely she would have avoided him. There may have been an element of calculation: Adah rarely discarded one man until she had become deeply involved with another. She was still the marrying kind. In a poem written to John, in which she compares herself to a flower, she admits to "a burning unspeakable thirst / to grow all beauty, all grace, all melody to one / and to him alone!"

Adah had grown accustomed to the attentions of men, but she preferred that her lover and husband be the same man. From March 1859 on, the big, strong Benicia Boy was in line for that position, and sensitive, neurotic Alex Menken was on his way out.

Before she began at Newark, Adah took another fateful step. From Henry Chapman, a member of the National's company, Adah heard that an actress named Charlotte Crampton had played the lead in *Mazeppa*. A great admirer of Byron, she was thrilled that the heroic prince might be played by a woman. Chapman had furnished two horses for the production—one for show, and another to carry the dummy, which substituted for Crampton, up the stage mountain.

"You have your horses?" Adah inquired. When Chapman said yes, she asked, "Will you teach me to play Mazeppa?" Chapman took her to James Street, where he boarded the horses and fixed up a run. Adah mounted a well-trained gelding and soon got the hang of it. But since she had no backing, she would have to defer her plans for *Mazeppa*. The incident shows that she took to heart advice given her by James Murdoch, an outstanding tragedian, when she played opposite him in *Macbeth* at Nashville in February 1858.

In his autobiography, Murdoch recounted that Adah had showed up only a few hours before curtain time. She confessed that she did not know Lady Macbeth's lines and was scared to death of the part. "But I must act it," she insisted.

Murdoch coached her. He outlined the play's action, and she swore she could learn the lines in time. When the curtain rose, Adah at first blustered her way through the business. But after reading a letter from her husband, the Scottish lord, she threw her arms wildly in the air. Murdoch was amazed to hear "an apostrophe to guilt, demons, and her own dark purposes" that Shakespeare had never written. To his surprise, the audience loved Adah's improvisation.

Soon she broke down and whispered that she had forgotten everything. "For the rest of the scene I gave the lady the words," wrote Murdoch. He prompted her line by line as she clung to his side. Yet the lady managed to upstage her lord, "receiving vociferous applause, and particularly when she spoke of dashing out the brains of her child." Murdoch helped Adah to wing it through the rest of the play, literally, by referring to a script in the wings between speeches.

The old pro was impressed by this brash ingenue. In what would become an American showbiz tradition, an unknown had stolen the show. Afterward, he tried to dissuade the young actress from attempting Shakespeare again. "Why don't you try something in the sensation line?" he suggested.

Sensation plays, coming into vogue, were the American version of European melodrama. They had lots of action and special effects, such as Mazeppa's perilous dash on the back of a charger up a stage mountain. Now, on the eve of returning to her husband, Adah grasped the brilliance of Murdoch's advice. Before she could act on it, she would have to change the circumstances of her life, to sever her bonds with the respectable.

The engagement at Newark went passably well, but Adah soon returned to Cincinnati. That spring her only appearance was before the Alemannia Society, where she delivered one of her "elegant Poetical readings." Adah and Alex soon found they had nothing left but recriminations. Alex, now head of the Menken family, had become a businessman rather than the aspiring composer she had married. Insecure in this role, he continued to drink, which made matters worse.

In contrast, Adah thought only of success and her new love. By July, with the aid of Rabbi Wise, the couple obtained a rabbinical divorce, which Adah presumed was legally binding. With her marriage ended— at three years, it would be her longest—she packed her wardrobe and boarded the train for New York. Adah carried with her Alexander Isaac Menken's name and left behind a bitter enemy.

Cincinnati's Jewish community never quite got over the shooting star in their midst. In 1864 in *The Israelite*, Rabbi Wise praised Adah's poetry and admitted her Jewish sympathies, but claimed that "as far as the form and birth is concerned, she is no Jewess." Later his son Leo would recall that Adah "requested Dr. Wise to receive her in the fold, going so far at one time as to implore him on her knees to accept her as a convert." Then he added that she was "in faith and ideals an ardent Jewess."

Neither the great man nor his son need be taken at face value. Adah had become the notorious Naked Lady. Wise's Reform community, occupying a middle ground between Orthodox Judaism and the Gentile world, could not afford any scandal. Besides, if Adah was not a Jew by birth or conversion, how could the rabbinical divorce, which Wise had helped obtain, bind her? In the rabbi's defense, Adah was always murky about her antecedents. If she claimed to be a Jew through her mother—in Jewish tradition, the mother is the decisive parent—so also must she be black. The strands of Adah's ethnic and racial heritage were inseparably intertwined.

Other Cincinnatians reminisced with wonder on the phenomenon they had witnessed. "Nature was lavish in her gifts to Adah," recalled family friend Celia Logan. "Every charm of mind, face and form was hers by birthright." Ten years after Menken's meteoric career and sudden death, Celia, now a married woman, pondered: "What led to her incomprehensible recklessness is a mystery which she kept to herself."

CHAPTER SEVEN:

BELOW THE BELT

Walt Whitman completed the third and defining edition of *Leaves of Grass* in 1859, the year Adah Menken came to live in New York. Whitman preferred the name Manhattan or Manhatta, after the chief of the local Indian tribe who had sold the island to the Dutch in 1626. Peter Minuit bought it with trinkets and cloth worth sixty guilders, or a legendary twenty-four dollars. The island was sparsely inhabited, rocky in places and swampy in others. By 1859 Whitman was able to write of "million-footed Manhattan," and indeed, the the most dynamic city in the world was approaching a population of one million, half foreign-born, the largest single element being 200,000 Irish.

Adah had come to marry one of the most famous sons of Erin: John Carmel Heenan, the self-proclaimed heavyweight boxing champion. But her ultimate object of desire was Manhatta itself. In the next several years she played to, courted, and stripped naked for Manhatta, the million-eyed, -eared, and -tongued. In touch with all America by telegraph and the penny press, whose papers were shipped everywhere by rail and steamship, Manhatta was center ring of a circus that today we call showbiz, and its best-known citizen was showman Phineas T. Barnum.

For a moment, envision the ghost of Chief Manhatta, stretched out in the bay waters from head to toe. The Battery Park is his hair; the docks, his headdress; his head is at Wall Street and the mansions along Fifth Avenue are his spine; the robust Bowery is his right arm, fashionable Broadway his left; 59th Street is the chief's belt and Central Park the groin; Third Avenue and the Bloomingdale Road are his legs, feet rooted in the mainland. Manhatta was the lover sought by Adah, the one who would break her heart before finally succumbing to her charms.

In July, after a long, sooty train ride from Cincinnati, Adah debarked from the ferry at Cortlandt Street, just below Washington Market. Perhaps, through the din, her champion called to her. Who was this handsome, genial hunk who claimed first the American, then the world heavyweight title, without winning a single big-time fight? How is it that Nat Fleischer, longtime editor of *The Ring* magazine, could favorably compare Heenan with John L. Sullivan, adding, "As a gladiator, he had earned a reputation for strength, skill, courage and iron endurance second to none in the arena."

Even if Heenan was a natural nobleman, as Adah supposed, he was also a functionary in a dirty racket. Fleischer puts it succinctly:

> *Boxing in the gaslight era of New York flourished in a decidedly malodorous atmosphere of crime and political corruption. Pugilists commonly participated in the gang wars then rampant around Manhattan, wars in which knife, pistol and club worked overtime, and human lives were snuffed out with callous indifference . . .*
>
> *Political factions fought viciously to get and retain control of the pugilistic brigade, from whose ranks were recruited bodyguards for the municipal big-shots.*

Fighters paraded the faithful to the polls on Election Day, kept rival gangs from interfering with voting, and intimidated voters for the other side. Heenan, for his services to Tammany Hall, was awarded a sinecure in the Customs Department, which paid the rent between matches.

Heenan, twenty-five at the time he met Adah, was born at the Watervliet Arsenal in West Troy, where his father, from Tipperary, was head foreman. Young John was a scrapper who led his companions against a rival gang headed by slightly older John Morrissey, who would become heavyweight champion and Heenan's rival in the ring. It is said their fathers, both named Timothy, had fought one another in the Old Country.

John, after some schooling, was taught the machinist trade by his father. There was friction between the two, and at the age of seventeen John sailed for San Francisco. Rather than join the gold rush, he took a job in the workshops at Benicia belonging to the Pacific Mail Steamship Company. In the next two years, dark-haired John developed into a tall, well-formed, muscular specimen of humanity who barely realized the great strength he possessed. To be exact, he was six-foot-two and weighed 180 pounds, with a chest forty-four inches around, sixteen-inch biceps, thighs of twenty-four inches, and seventeen-inch calves.

John's rugged good looks aside, a particular incident reveals the qualities that would win Adah's heart. A bully was used to throwing his weight around Benicia, picking on those who were smaller and weaker. He boasted he could lick any man in California. That was too much for John, who fought him "American style" on the dock. That meant no holds barred, including biting and eye gouging. Our hero trounced the bully, and from then on he was admiringly called "Benicia Boy."

John attracted the attention of political operators, the sort who fought out elections in New York. Ed James, who knew him well, remarked that he was "good on the muscle." The young man fell under the influence of Jim Cusick, a former prizefighter who had sparred with Tom Sayers, the British champ. Cusick arranged sparring matches for the Boy, who with coaching became a proficient boxer and hard hitter, famous all over the Pacific Slope. Yet there continued to be something of Sir Galahad about John.

One day in San Francisco he protected a shop girl from the advances of a well-dressed but obnoxious masher. The men fought and John whipped his opponent, who was confined to bed for a month. A wealthy and prominent man, he decided to take revenge in secret. He hired a gang of hoodlums to waylay John, which they attempted one evening. The fighter ignored their knives and guns, knocked down three, and caused the others to take to their heels. John's reputation soared.

By the autumn of 1857 San Francisco had enough of the operators who brought to California voter intimidation, ballot stuffing, and other niceties of New York politics. A group of the most respected merchants formed a vigilance committee. They rounded up the worst offenders and deported or hanged them. Jim Cusick was on their list, but he and Heenan managed to board a ship for New York before they were apprehended. Cusick was already thinking about issuing a challenge from Heenan to Morrissey, the current champion, to fight for the heavyweight title.

Once in New York, Cusick introduced his fighter at National Hall, Canal Street, in a sparring match with Joe Coburn, who would later befriend Adah. Morrissey, nicknamed Old Smoke, attended the fight and seemed agreeable to a championship match. First the challenger had to raise $5,000, a substantial sum, and to publish a "card" in the sporting papers. Echoing the code of the duel, the card was a formal challenge addressed to the reigning champ, which he had to answer or be publicly shamed. The card was also an advertisement intended to whip up interest in the match.

The fight finally took place on October 20, 1858, at Long Point, Canada, across Lake Erie from Buffalo. Saloonkeepers in all the major cities sold excursion tickets, and by mid-October sporting men from as far away as New Orleans were pouring into Buffalo, centered on a saloon run by Izzy Lazarus, an ex-pug. The newspapers, those like the *Police Gazette* that favored boxing, and those whose editorial pages disapproved of it, sent special correspondents to cover the Mardi Gras–like affair. A reporter from the prudish *Tribune* stigmatized the fight fans as "the most vicious congregation of roughs that was ever witnessed in a Christian city." True, there had been days of drinking, poker, and a few scuffles, after which the spectators were ferried across the lake under cover of darkness. They debarked in the morning to watch the fight on a barren peninsula, where a twenty-four-foot ring had been hastily assembled.

At some point during the summer of 1859, John must have told Adah about the humiliating defeat he had suffered at the hands of his rival, Morrissey. John was not given to excuses, but others provided them for him. While training he was hounded by the authorities so that he frequently had to break camp. Morrissey, who ran a gambling den, was not bothered by the police. Further, a serious abscess on John's leg left him weakened on the day of the fight. He staked everything on a knockout in the early rounds.

Heenan's opponent was just under six feet tall and weighed slightly less than he. Heavily bearded, given to dressing well and spending freely, Old Smoke had an extensive Irish following. Heenan, personable and less associated with machine politics, was embraced by the Native American faction, meaning those born in the United States who were anti-immigrant. Morrissey understood psychological warfare, and just before the fight he offered to bet Heenan $5,000 of his own money on the outcome. The Benicia Boy confessed that he had no money. The two fighters were dressed in tights and boots, bare from the waist up. Their hands were hardened by soaking in brine or walnut juice. They fought under the rules of the London prize ring, which meant that a round ended when a man went down, and the fight was to the finish.

In the first round Morrissey took the initiative, but Heenan's counter punching drew "first blood"—a cry that went up from the crowd. Heenan took charge, pressing Morrissey toward the ropes as he repeatedly hit him with his left. One blow went wild and struck a ring post, which had no padding. This was bare-knuckle boxing, and Heenan badly damaged two knuckles. His quick left was of little use from then on.

Yet in the first few rounds, Heenan landed sledgehammer blows on Morrissey's nose and eye. Old Smoke countered with body blows. To end a round, each fighter would try to grasp and throw the other down and fall on top of him. Choke holds were legal, and so was bending an opponent over the ropes and breaking his back. Bare-knuckle fighters were called "gladiators" for good reason.

By the seventh round Heenan was visibly weakening. Morrissey continued to pound his torso and ended the round by throwing him and falling heavily on top. By the eleventh round the fight was reduced to a question of endurance. Heenan, weakened by body blows, swung wildly in the air. The champ, like a bulldog, bore in relentlessly till he had downed Heenan, who, reported the *Police Gazette*, was "carried insensible to his corner, beaten and terribly battered."

A certain gallantry prevailed among these warriors of the ring. Heenan, revived, was seated next to Morrissey in a carriage, and the two heroes, side by side, were paraded around the grounds. The party steamed back to Buffalo, firing rockets as a large crowd cheered at the dock. In New York and other cities, the taverns and newspaper and telegraph offices were packed with fans, waiting for the news. The police were called out to keep the peace. From this moment on Heenan hoped for a rematch, but Morrissey prudently retired. He would move to Saratoga Springs, open a casino, take part in founding the famous racetrack, and become a respected United States congressman.

Leo Tolstoy, referring to Kitty in *Anna Karenina*—a woman who loves her husband, and, unlike the adulterous Anna, has found content-ment—remarked on how difficult it was for a novelist to write about happiness. It is just as difficult for a biographer. Happiness leaves few traces, while misery tends to be outspoken. During the summer of 1859 Adah was happy. Within a year's time, John Heenan had made her miserable, and therefore we know when they first made love. She wrote the touching poem "One Year Ago" in July 1860, on the anniversary of the date:

> *You took my hand—one year ago,*
> *Beneath the azure dome above,*
> *And gazing on the stars you told*
> *The trembling story of your love.*
>
> *I gave to you—one year ago*
> *the only jewel that was mine;*

My heart took off her lonely crown;
And all her riches gave to thine.

Adah might feel seduced and abandoned one year later, but when she believed in Heenan's love, she entered wholeheartedly into his sporting world. With this "awkward and vulgar crowd of fighters, promoters, gamblers and their women friends," writes Fulton Oursler, Adah shared "a sense of embittered *camaraderie*." Free of the bourgeois fetters of the Menken clan, she let drop the serious side of her nature and gave vent to the playful. She remembered the vices her ne'er-do-well stepfather had taught her.

To the Victorian upholders of strict morality, boxing and gambling were the devil's work. Horace Greeley's *Tribune* described a prizefight as a bloody "festival of fiends," promoted by "gamblers, brothel-masters and keepers of flash groggeries." However, like the other papers, it covered important fights. More and more of its readers were attending sparring matches and demanding blow-by-blow accounts of championship fights.

By the time of Heenan's ascendancy, boxing had transcended its plebeian origins and was becoming fashionable. Professor Mann, the sparring master, had more pupils than he could manage, many of them gentlemen. The attractive personality of the Benicia Boy added to the luster of the ring. Attired in a tall silk hat, frock coat, and striped trousers, Heenan could be seen parading on Broadway with a diminutive figure on his arm, a fashionable woman of striking beauty, but unknown to this side of town, who beamed proudly as the Boy's admirers greeted him.

That summer Adah became familiar with the hangouts of the pugilistic fraternity, taverns such as the Old Crib or the Sporting Museum, which had a ring in the back room. She listened attentively to the opinions of old-timers and young sprouts on horse racing; cock, dog, and rat fights; and boxing. She became friends with a number of the fighters, took boxing lessons, and sparred in the ring. In fine weather she and John picnicked at Jones's Wood on the East River, or rowed a boat on the Hudson, rented at Hoboken. Adah adored John's strength and kindness and attention to her. Despite her two previous marriages, both failures, she was eager to try again.

Adah didn't understand that by divorcing Alex Menken (or so she thought), she had abandoned respectability. In England it took an act of Parliament to grant a divorce, and this was strictly for men. The Free Love movement began as a campaign to emancipate women from the lifelong slavery of abusive marriages, which they were expected to bear. The movement's leading American spokesman, Stephen Pearl Andrews, claimed that most wives were no better off than prostitutes. True, in the United States, divorce was facilitated by states—Indiana granted it for reasons such as desertion or adultery. But divorce continued to turn a respectable woman into a social pariah.

Victorian moralists reacted to the fledgling movement for women's rights by a propaganda campaign in favor of an imagined ideal, "the real woman" (in the United States), or "the genuine lady" (in Britain). Books, articles, and sermons on morals, manners, and health ceaselessly promoted the virtue of this female paragon, and denigrated any deviation from the standard. According to the *Alexandra Magazine* of 1864, a lady was "everywhere recognized, under all circumstances. She is known and judged of according to her works . . . words, dress and manner are but accessories, and merely come into account as the accompaniment of sterling, moral worthiness."

Morals meant sex, and the first qualification of a lady was that she have sex only with her husband and for the purpose of procreation. "A modest woman seldom desires any sexual gratification for herself," Dr. William Acton, considered an authority, assured his readers. "The married woman has no wish to be treated on the footing of a mistress." Essentially what made a woman bad was enjoying the carnal act.

Taking her cue from books such as *The Ladies' Parlour Companion*, a lady exhibited unfailing respect for her husband, loved her children and domesticity, and dressed modestly. Ladies were never seen at taverns, meeting halls, or street parades, and were never unchaperoned at libraries, museums, or promenades, although a married lady might attend the theater in the evening with her husband. The term "public woman" meant prostitute. However, by mid-century, ladies' matinees, often combined with a shopping excursion to the new department stores, were indulged in by pairs or groups of respectable women. The consumer was beginning to nudge aside the puritan.

Actresses occupied a gray area in the social stratum. Laura Keene, who earned her living by managing her own acting company, was admired for her wit. The Shakespearean actress Charlotte Cushman, a lesbian, was applauded by the severest critics, even when she played pants parts such as Romeo. Both were cultivated women whose talent and force of character made them acceptable, if not entirely respectable. Since Adah still harbored the ambition to play dramatic roles, she couldn't offend public opinion. She needed to legitimize her love life.

According to Ed James, Adah "induced" the Benecia Boy to marry her, "the ceremony taking place at a New York roadhouse known as Rock Cottage, kept by a well-known sporting character named Jim Hughes, by the Rev. J. S. Baldwin, on April 3, 1859." Rock Cottage, on the Bloomingdale road (now Broadway) in upper Manhattan, made a convenient locale for a quiet marriage and brief honeymoon. James, who had befriended Heenan from the start, didn't attend because he was in England. He heard the news afterward from Jack Herman, a minstrel who was a witness.

Secrecy was agreed to on both sides. There was the problem of Adah's recent divorce, and a prizefighter was ranked among the lower classes—unless he was champion of the world. Jim Cusick was in negotiations with the handlers of the British champ, Tom Sayers, for a world-title fight, and he believed that a wife might be troublesome. She would soften Heenan's image, and the Boy had little else to make him a contender. In any case, the secrecy surrounding her marriage was going to cost Adah dearly.

In the age before telling all became fashionable, we are left to guess how good a lover the champion made on his wedding night. John would have to overcome obstacles a modern husband can scarcely imagine. The Victorian woman's sexuality was guarded by layers of weighty garments, including a cage made of impermeable material.

One of Adah's sobriquets was "Cleopatra in a Crinoline." A crinoline was a hoop skirt made of whalebone stays on which was draped a decorative fabric, padded with horsehair and supported by fabric petticoats. Through the years the hoops kept getting bigger, which called for ever more petticoats beneath. Finally, in the 1850s, the sprung-steel crinoline became popular, and while it reduced the number of petticoats, it increased the possibility of ballooning. Soon women could scarcely get through doorways or sit on chairs. Later, fashion would become more reasonable with the use of a smaller crinolette or bustle, both made with steel ribs. "It was a most persistent fashion," writes Sarah Levitt in *Victorians Unbuttoned.* "Women were to carry cages around with them for the next thirty years."

Assuming John, panting with love, penetrated Adah's outer layer of defense, he would encounter another impediment: perhaps a tight-fitting chemise, which covered the area from above the breasts to below the knees. More likely, our gladiator came up against a corset, a contraption of whalebone ribs, fabric, and tight stitching. The corset shaped the lady into the Victorian ideal: high, ample bust and an hourglass curve that swooped to a tiny waist and reemerged in rounded hips. Adah already had such a figure, but, like others, she amplified it.

John would waste little time on the hooks, belts, and buckles that strapped on the corset; he was strong enough to rip them away. Now only Adah's drawers remained, like long underwear cut off at the knee. John could dispose of these in an instant, leaving his lady truly naked. Although not an experienced lover, he was a mighty one, and he could also be tender. Their physical love explains Adah's devotion to this handsome, well-endowed numbskull. The upshot of their honeymoon was that, in Wolf Mankowitz's words, "Heenan, showing an attack that hadn't characterized his recent professional bouts, got Adah pregnant in the first round."

Adah, unknowing, felt free to resume her career. She appeared in September at the Gayety Theater in Albany, a city that would figure prominently in her career. In October Adah played for two weeks in Atlanta, her last appearance in the Deep South. Since she had no manager, these engagements were facilitated by Frank Queen. The publisher of *The Clipper* had been born working-class in Philadelphia. Chubby, he was picked on by the tougher boys in the neighborhood. At the *Inquirer,* where he apprenticed himself, a journeyman in the press room taught him to box in the scientific style being practiced in Britain. Frank became a lifelong advocate of the manly art of self-defense. Once he moved to New York, he worked his way up the journalistic ladder. In 1853 he put every dollar he had saved into founding *The Clipper.*

Queen was a shrewd man with a pleasing manner who promoted friends and causes. "A knowledge of the science of boxing is calculated to develop and encourage feelings of manliness, confidence, courage, and love of fair-play," he wrote in his paper. Meanwhile, each edition ran ads for contraceptives, venereal disease cures, and a marriage guide that graphically illustrated how to perform sexual acts. Frank Queen had no truck with pretense or puritans; he loved plain language and he loved every sort of sport.

By early autumn, Adah, realizing she was pregnant, decided to inform friends about the marriage. Typically, she chose to use the newest means of communication: the photograph. Ed James received a photo of the wedded couple: John standing stiffly, Adah in a hooped, pleated dress, smiling with contentment, one hand resting on a pedestal bearing a horse. The picture is signed below: "Compliments to Edwin James from Mr. & Mrs. John C. Heenan." Here is hard evidence, if more was needed, of the marriage.

Adah felt she must keep her pregnancy to herself. The boxing clan in New York and London were feverishly enthusiastic about a Heenan-Sayers match for the world heavyweight championship. Adah would do nothing to impede Heenan, and she urged him to take the match. She was willing to put her own career aside and travel with him to England to be in his corner.

Negotiations for the fight were nearly as complex as those for an international treaty. At first carried out through challenges in the pages of *The Clipper* and responses in *Bell's Life* in London, by November the affair was serious enough for an American emissary to board a ship for London to conclude the arrangements. On November 29 Heenan was the recipient of a benefit night at Hoym's Theater, where he fought one Jack Pyburn. The house, packed to the verge of suffocation, went wild as the Boy demolished his sparring partner. On December 16 Heenan's representative signed articles with Sayers's principal backer and put up 200 pounds to seal the bout for April. The wagering began at once in taverns across the English-speaking world.

On January 5, 1860, at an early hour on the dock in Jersey City, John Heenan, the American champion, with his manager Jim Cusick approached the ship *Asia*, bound for Liverpool. The pair was escorted by fellow pugilists who supplemented their brawn with blackjacks and pistols. Due to the Boy's earlier activities in the prize ring, a warrant had been issued for his arrest by a Buffalo judge, and detectives from that city had been sent to apprehend him. It would have taken a suicidal policeman to attempt it, and such a martyr was nowhere in sight.

However, the champ could not risk a noisy send-off by his fans. Instead, his wife and a few friends bade him good-bye. Echoing Cusick, John had told Adah she couldn't accompany him. A training camp was no place for a woman. He was stating a belief that prevails to this day: a fighter in training must forgo sex. Adah, feeling the child growing inside her, was worried about being left alone, unable to care for herself. Yet she sacrificed her own concern for John's peace of mind. "She therefore permitted him to sail," writes Lesser, "without telling him her secret."

In the taverns working men argued the merits of the two fighters. Toasts were drunk, money bet, and songs sung:

So here's one toast before ye go,
The Yankee land, God bless it,
And for her sake, the Champion's belt
By god, Heenan will possess it!

From this moment on, "The Great Contest for the Championship of the World" was front-page news in every daily and weekly paper. Interest on both sides of the Atlantic built into a frenzy. Headlines about the match were in bold and black, dwarfing news about the impending conflict between North and South. Scarce attention was paid to another fighting man, old John Brown, white-haired and wounded, who was hanged in Virginia for insurrection.

Chapter Eight:

THE YEAR OF METEORS

On January 21, 1860, the *New York Tribune* ran an exclusive that began: "Miss Adah Isaacs Menken, who was recently elected the captain of a military company in Dayton, Ohio, and who is at present playing at the Troy Theater, is the wife of John C. Heenan." The piece continued that she had been anxious to accompany her husband to England, but he had objected for the reason that a training camp was no place for a woman. The news was planted in the daily with the widest circulation, and the other New York papers soon echoed it. Adah's love/hate affair with the press, which went back to her Texas days, was about to kick into high gear.

The notice appeared on the morning of Adah's opening night in Troy, Heenan's hometown, where the *Tribune* was carried by rail. It was the start of a swing through upstate New York. Adah, or her advisors, were making certain she played to packed houses by keeping her in the news. Joseph Daly, in his biography of his brother, Augustin, the critic, playwright, and theatrical manager, wrote that "Miss Menken was a steady correspondent of the dramatic editors, who were all enrolled as 'chums' and 'pals.'" With Heenan gone, Adah saw more of her chums, especially young Gus Daly and the older Ed James, who had become assistant editor of *The Clipper*.

Even with publicity guaranteed by a coterie of newsmen, Adah was having a difficult time. Heenan had left her with no money and the need to earn a living for herself and the child in her womb. She sent for her younger sister Annie, who could live and perform with her. The sisters had barely begun their tour through New York's snow belt when George

Wilkes's *Spirit of the Times* threatened to bring down the curtain. Wilkes, who helped to arrange the Heenan-Sayers match, believed the fighter would have told him if he had married. He printed the *Tribune* story, but, convinced it would harm Heenan's gladiator image, he denied it. When a copy of his weekly reached Adah in Albany, where she was performing at the Gayety, she responded at once in a letter to Wilkes:

> *In your last issue . . . there is an article . . . stating the well-known fact of my being the wife of John C. Heenan. Of this I have nothing to complain . . . I am proud and happy to be known as the wife of the bravest man in the world! But you or your "Itemizer" took the unauthorized liberty of adding: "This is incorrect. Heenan is not married."*
>
> *I have no right to suppose . . . that malice prompted these words, as daggers to stab the reputation of the wife of the man for whom you have repeatedly expressed the warmest and most disinterested friendship. I can only suppose, and hope, it to be a mistake. . . . I beg that you will do me and John C. Heenan the justice to correct this grievous mistake which has caused me the deepest trouble.*

She signed the letter "Adah Isaacs Menken-Heenan."

Adah understood the gravity of her marriage being questioned. In Victorian America, an unwed mother was beyond the pale. She quickly threw a series of counterpunches at Wilkes. She wrote to Heenan's friends in the fight game, alleging that Wilkes really admired Morrissey and not Heenan. She prodded her journalist friends to reiterate that she was indeed married to the Benicia Boy. An interesting addition to her usual partisans was Robert Newell in the *Sunday Mercury.* The weekend papers, such as the *Mercury* or Henry Clapp's *Saturday Press,* like Sunday editions of today's papers, were influential on matters of culture and entertainment. Newell, a humorist and poet, was also a respected editor, and his patronage was an important plus for Adah.

One week later Wilkes published Adah's letter in full, but again he indicated that he didn't believe her. He even stated he had never heard of her, which is unlikely. Rather than the brouhaha dying down, newspapers elsewhere in the country took notice. Finally, the *New York Leader* humorously summed up the "very pretty dispute [that] is going the rounds of the papers as to whether Captain Adah Isaacs Menken is or is not the wife of the Benicia Boy." After stating several points of view, the *Leader* concluded, "Who cares?" The answer would come in Wilkes's weekly on February 18, when he published a mean-spirited letter from Alex Menken, still living in Cincinnati:

> *My dear Sir: I see by the last number of your paper that you have published a letter signed by a woman calling herself Adah Isaacs Men-ken Heenan. In justice to myself and friends, I cannot permit this very delicate effusion to pass unnoticed. Allow me to inform you, my dear sir, that you were perfectly correct when you stated to your correspondent that John C. Heenan was not married, unless it be lawful in your state for a woman to have two husbands at one and the same time. The effrontery and nonchalance with which this woman sentimentalizes in her letter to you, in reference to your damaging her reputation . . . would be very amusing to me were I not so deeply involved in the matter.*

Alex, after indicating when and where he had married Adah, stated unequivocally: "I have never been divorced from her; on the contrary have lived with her up to last July. I go into these particulars merely and solely for the purpose of setting myself right in the social circle in which I have introduced this person as my wife . . . in order that my position in regard to her may not be misconstrued." He added that he had filed for a civil divorce, "which will rid me of this incubus and disgrace." Finally, he dealt her the hardest blow he could think of: a demand that she no longer use the name Menken.

Alex, spiteful and petty, had accused Adah of the crime of bigamy. Still worse, she would be bearing the child of a man not her husband. Wilkes immediately crowed over this justification of his mistrust of the alleged Mrs. Heenan. Following his lead, papers throughout the country piled on her, raking up the old Dayton Light Guards scandal. The *Empire* of that city declared that her poem "Come to Me" (aka, "Karazah to Karl"), a loving offer of reconciliation to Alex, was written "by Adah while enjoying an unnecessarily (so certain parties say!) lengthy rustication in this city about three years ago. . . . Since that time, the poem has been written *expressly* for every paper which would publish it, and 'Come to Me' may now be taken . . . as a general invitation to go in!"

Adah was deemed a prostitute in all but name. Her journalist friends once again jumped into the breach. Frank Queen, editor of *The Clipper*, wrote caustically, "The association of [Adah's] name with that of John C. Heenan has made her the target for almost every newspaper scribbler in the country, who have severally married her to Tom Thumb, James Buchanan, and the King of the Cannibal Islands. . . . We trust that the scribblers have got to the end of their tether, and that they will hereafter assist in her effort to support herself in a legitimate calling." Meanwhile, twenty-two-year-old Gus Daly, drama critic at the *Sunday Courier*, warmly praised Adah and chided other critics for not acting like gentlemen and defending a lady's reputation.

Daly's support is typical of the man. He was tall, handsome, with a crop of dark hair and a mustache to match. His father was an Irish sea captain, but his widowed mother raised him and his brother alone. As a youth he hung about the New York theaters, Niblo's Garden and the Bowery, but especially Wallack's on Broadway and Thirteenth Street. Lester Wallack directed an excellent acting company and put on Shakespeare with scenery and costumes specially prepared for each revival. One day Daly would do the same. From 1860 on he became the drama critic for five New York papers, including the *Times*.

In 1867 Daly would write the quintessential American melodrama, *Under the Gaslight*, which was wildly successful. He went on to become one of the most influential writers and producers in the history of Broadway. Remembering his mother's struggle, Gus was concerned for women living on their own and admired their quiet heroism. *Gaslight* contains the archetypal scene in which a one-legged Civil War veteran is tied by the villain to the railroad tracks and an onrushing train appears to be headed at the audience. The *heroine* rescues the ex-soldier just in time. To this day, variants of this scene have been repeated in countless melodramas, on stage and screen.

Finally, Adah had to mount her own defense. She responded from Buffalo, where she played for two weeks during February. Although she had received three letters from her husband, she was in low spirits. Sister Annie had returned to New Orleans to nurse their mother, dying of tuberculosis. Adah, in her fifth month of pregnancy, wrote to a friend of Heenan (Mr. Robbins of Boston): "I cannot act now, all life and spirits gone." Her listless performance showed in the gate, which, she continued, "proved the worst I ever had the misfortune to experience." The theater managers reneged on her benefit night, leaving her broke.

Still, Adah penned an open letter to the press throughout the country via Wilkes's *Spirit of the Times.* She granted the gravity of Alex Menken's charge of bigamy, but countered that it was Alex who had sought and obtained a rabbinical divorce, which she believed to be legally binding. Adah then turned her guns on Wilkes:

> *The controversy you have sought and are persisting in with me is an unequal one. Your paper has an extensive circulation. It scatters its slanderous insinuations and charges broadcast over the country, while I am comparatively defenceless, dependent on the good opinion of the public, whose mind you seek to poison and embitter against me. . . . Had you been acquainted with my antecedents, and known the trials and adversities through which I have passed to obtain whatever position I now enjoy in my profession, I think you would not have allowed the viper, whose communication you publish, to strike his fangs into my life's current [blood].*

Here, at a moment of truth, Adah dropped any pretense of a privileged background and hinted at her deepest secret—that she was born poor in New Orleans to a woman of color. Through talent, toil, and conniving she had become her own woman, an actress of some reputation, which was now threatened by baseless scandal. Again she took aim at "the viper":

> *Menken may call me "an adventuress." He has been nourished by, and subsisted upon, the fruits of my professional labor, until I would no longer furnish supplies for his bacchanalian career, and such an appellation comes from him with a very bad grace.*

With this parting shot, which revealed to the audience that Alex was an alcoholic, the curtain rang down on the first act of the Menken/Heenan melodrama—but not before America's first media-driven sex scandal had exposed Adah's past and threatened to destroy her marriage. In a letter to Robbins, who she hoped would influence Heenan, she claimed she was ready to give up her career. She planned to return to New York to sell her theatrical wardrobe, without which no actor could succeed. She felt completely disgusted with the theater's toils and trials. At least temporarily, Victorian propriety had defeated Adah Isaacs Menken-Heenan.

In 1857 the telegraph cable under the Atlantic Ocean snapped, and it was not repaired until after the Civil War. For the time being news traveled by ship between the United States and United Kingdom, a crossing that took from ten days to two weeks. Nonetheless, an immense crowd of people gathered at the Liverpool pier where, on January 16, 1860, the steamship *Asia* docked. They had come to see the American champion. John Heenan, warned that the police were about to arrest him, had already debarked with the mail bags and headed by train for London. There his hair was properly trimmed, eyeglasses were stuck on his nose, and he was dressed up like a swell. So effective was his disguise that he could walk the streets without being recognized.

Heenan left the metropolis and went into training in the West Country. Jim Cusick and Jack McDonald, the trainer, turned away numerous reporters and curiosity seekers. But the local authorities ordered the boxers to leave, and the training camp was moved to a village near Bath. Once again the entourage was sent packing and moved to Bedford. Worse, warrants were issued for Heenan and McDonald, and they had to flee. Heenan was arrested and spent a little time in jail. By contrast, his opponent Tom Sayers trained unmolested at Newmarket.

According to the *Police Gazette*, while most Britons wanted to see a fair fight, "there was manifestly an undercurrent of society in London which aimed at the defeat of the American champion by some means or other not in accord with the principles of honest dealing." Sayers, the best fighter Britain had produced in twenty-five years, was not among this set. A London bricklayer by trade, standing at five feet, eight inches tall, he was no heavier than a middleweight. Yet by 1859 he had beaten everyone in sight, winning the heavyweight crown. According to the Brits, Sayers was the odds-on favorite to defeat the American.

The fight was a classic of experience versus youth and strength. It was a case of a good little man versus a good big man. Heenan, five inches taller, thirty pounds heavier, and eight years younger than his opponent, should have been the favorite. But John Morrissey, who came to London to help train Sayers, bet 1,000 pounds on him, which made an impression on the public. Excitement ran wild in England as Parliament debated the morality of the match, while dozens of Lords and MPs made plans to attend. At least 100,000 pounds were bet on the contest, and rumor had it that a disguised Prime Minister Palmerston stood at ringside with orders from Queen Victoria to immediately notify her of the outcome.

In America, as the April 17 date set for the match drew near, business and politics seemed secondary. Nearly all the newspapers, after denouncing prizefighting, sent correspondents to cover the fighters in training and in the ring. Elliot J. Gorn notes in his book, *The Manly Art:* "No matter how much they published on the preliminaries, editors found the public thirst insatiable." Each day, news dealers and their customers would eagerly search for "something new on the great fight." In more recent times, only the two Joe Louis/Max Schmeling bouts were comparable in symbolic importance to the Heenan-Sayers match. Louis represented America—indeed, the entire free world—while Schmeling (unfairly) appeared to be an emissary of Nazi Germany. It was the old tradition of a champion engaging in single combat for his cause.

Since it was understood that Britain would favor the South in the impending Civil War, there was an element of North versus South in this combat, and of Ireland versus England. "All classes of people," observed *The New York Times*, "share this anxiety to hear the results . . . throwing completely into shade all political themes and everything else which can afford to wait." With the cable cut, Americans had to bide their time, swapping rumors at taverns and newspaper offices. Perhaps at one of these sessions, Ed James figured out how to revive the career of an unfortunate actress.

James, in his biography of Adah Menken, remarks in his sly way, "The first really brilliant or sensational move made was fulfilling a successful engagement at the old Bowery Theater—under the name of Mrs. John C. Heenan." The idea to combine a Menken performance with a Heenan rally was either his own or cooked up with Frank Queen. James also arranged for *The Illustrated News* to feature a three-part story about her life, based on a personal interview. The paper had the advantage of being a picture weekly, and though newspapers could not yet reproduce photos, the article featured a flattering sketch of Adah.

"Commonplace people and commonplace events are out of fashion," it began. "Startling sensations are more the order of the day. That a poetess should marry a prize-fighter seems a contradiction of the laws of 'affinity'—but such a fact has occurred." The first installment ran on March 17, just before Adah opened at the Bowery, and the entire piece was reprinted by Robert Newell's *Sunday Mercury* and Horace Greeley's *Tribune*. Although Adah was assured of a good box office, she would still have to please her audiences.

Mrs. Heenan appeared at the Bowery for a week beginning March 19. She appeared in Boston the first week in April, then in Providence, Philadelphia, and Richmond. She regularly packed the houses, first leading a cheering section for the champ, then doing her standard routine of song and dance and quick-change comedy. At the Bowery she impersonated eight different characters in *The Female Brigand*.

Adah's reviews show that she was a fine vaudeville performer. (The term stems from a French town and wasn't yet in general use in America.) *The Clipper* praised Adah as "one of the most beautiful women now upon the boards. [She] has a sweet musical voice, clear and distinct, and a pleasing, fascinating style in all she says and does." Gus Daly outdid himself in the *Courier:* "She is the most charming and versatile *artiste* that has ever appeared in New York." Even George Wilkes's *Spirit* gave Adah a backhanded compliment: "With her personal charms and talents, the perseverance she has exerted to become notorious might have made her celebrated."

In Providence the week before the fight, Adah added a farce specially written for her: *Heenan Has Come!* In fact, he had stopped answering her letters. Wilkes, already in England, had informed the champ of the scandal caused by Alex Menken, and Cusick, jealous of Adah's influence on his boy, continued to badmouth her. As Adah would come to understand, her John was a big child, easily influenced. In the meantime, while she felt heartsick over her husband's neglect, she was growing ever more popular.

In Philadelphia in late April, "Mrs. Benicia Boy" caused a sensation. One paper described her as "a bouncing voluptuous looking Jewess, with a well-developed figure, which she takes delight in exhibiting, a profusion of dark curls, and wicked black eyes." As tales of the Heenan-Sayers match began to reach America, Adah's popularity soared to a new high. Her engagement at the Bowery in early May was a packed-house triumph. Playing in *Satan in Paris,* her appearance onstage was greeted by a wild burst of enthusiasm, concluding with a "three times three" cheer for the Benicia Boy.

During the performance Adah was continually applauded, and when the curtain rang down the audience let loose a yell so wild it sounded like "the battle cry of hell." The pit, boxes, and gallery kept up the shout until the star appeared and thanked them. But she could say no more, she was "too full for utterance." She retired amid a fresh outbreak of cheers for Mr. and Mrs. Heenan. Adah was riding the coattails of the champion who was bravely defending American honor.

The baby was due in little more than a month. How could Adah perform strenuous numbers and exhibit her figure when the pregnancy must have showed? This was at a time when mothers-to-be scarcely left their beds. It is another mystery in a life that always seemed bigger than life.

However, Adah's state of mind remained depressed. Newell's *Sunday Mercury* regularly published her writings, and an essay of May 13, 1860, offers a view into her tortured soul. "Spiritual Affinity" takes up a theme—that the living and the dead are closely intertwined—upon which Adah would elaborate in prose and poetry until it reached a crescendo in her suicide note at year's end. This was a "Year of Meteors," of national foreboding, about which Walt Whitman wrote a poem. During the summer he witnessed "a strange huge meteor-procession dazzling and clear shooting over our heads." Its light blazed through the night to fade at dawn. To add to the anxiety, there was also a "comet that came unannounced out of the north flaring in heaven," which Whitman juxtaposed with the surprising election of Abe Lincoln to the presidency. He concluded by declaring himself "one of your meteors."

To us, Whitman seems more like a galaxy, while Adah is the shooting star, dazzling but liable to flare out. Imminently expecting her first child, she brooded on the attractiveness of death: "These happy dead have rest and peace. . . . They have not vile darts of slander hurled at their defenceless bodies, by cruel vampyres, who live on the innocent blood of wives and mothers." So much for the gentlemen of the press! At this moment she pictured herself as abandoned, sneered at, weeping over her sins. The following lines are prophetic not only about herself, but also the nation:

Why should [love] be so closely linked with death? Why should it hold up to my startled vision the ghastly face, the bandaged chin, the coins sealing the closed eyes, the stiffened limbs, the blood-stained shroud, and the living looking curiously on the corpse[?]

In "Spiritual Affinity" Adah announced that she was a Spiritualist and identified it as the "good cause" and its believers as "my co-laborers." She believed that the living and the dead can communicate, and she asserted that the questions she raised were for the spirits of the dead to answer. This is too heartfelt to be a literary device. Finally, however, her writings of this period are pleas addressed to her husband, John Carmel Heenan, on his way to becoming champion of the world.

When Heenan stepped into the ring on a brisk April morning in a meadow outside Farnborough, Hampshire, he wore belted round his waist the red, white, and blue. His opponent Tom Sayers wore a belt of red and buff surmounted by the British lion. America and Britain were about to settle old grudges toe to toe. In the ring was the English referee, Frank Dowling, who later admitted to betting on his countryman, and in the boxers' respective corners were their trainers and seconds, McDonald and Cusick for the Benicia Boy. Each fighter selected an umpire, who stood outside the ring, and beyond that were ringkeepers, a circle of sturdy men trying to keep back the crowd of thousands, most of whom had come up from London on chartered trains.

Aside from a large contingent of constables, who supposedly had been sent to break up the match, there were in attendance gentlemen of every rank: judges, ministers, physicians, professors, engineers, soldiers and sailors, bartenders, bookmakers, and plain working stiffs who cheered on their man. Visitors came from France and other nearby countries, and according to a contemporary, "The muster of literati included William Thackeray and Charles Dickens." The press was out in force, both British and American. The betting was fierce and the odds changed by the moment, but at the start they hovered around two to one in favor of Sayers. "There never was anything like the excitement," reminisced Ed James twenty years later, "nor will there ever be again, over a fist-fight between two men."

This was the first meeting between the fighters and they shook hands and exchanged pleasantries. They took a liking to each other. But once time was called, they squared away, both men naked from the waist up, wearing tight pants, hose, and boots. The *Police Gazette* lauded the Benicia Boy: "Every muscle on his broad back, his shoulders and arms, was well developed, and gave evidence of enormous power. . . . His skin was exceedingly fair and transparent and shone like that of a thoroughbred." But, continued the *Gazette*, "His mug was hard and looked older than we had expected."

Sayers was in excellent trim—"hard as nails"—and at first, Heenan stayed close to his own corner. His strategy was to draw Sayers in rather than to follow him, which had defeated earlier challengers. James describes Sayers as "very elegant, touching the earth lightly with his feet, and settling himself backward and forward while measuring his man with the ease and grace of a dancing-master." After some sparring, Sayers caught Heenan with a left on the nose and drew first blood. Heenan rushed him, they clenched, and the Boy threw him down, which ended the round.

In the third round Heenan knocked his opponent flat with a straight left. Heenan repeated the knockdown in the fourth round, and the odds shifted to favor him. There was no counting to ten; this fight was to the finish, until one of the fighters was unconscious or disabled. Heenan continued to catch Sayers with his left, but the old pro knew many a move and dodge. So the match continued, with each fighter landing blows and cutting up the other's face. Heenan bloodied Sayers's mouth, and Sayers worked on closing his opponent's right eye. By the seventh round Heenan's eye was "fearfully swollen and projected upward like a cushion," and he was showing signs of weakness.

From the eighth round on Sayers had only limited use of his right hand due to the forearm being fractured from stopping Heenan's blows. Sayers danced and weaved, but Heenan continued to knock down the British champ, who was bleeding from the nose and mouth. By the twentieth round Sayers was looking weak, Heenan chasing him, and the odds had switched to five to one in the American's favor. Heenan threw Sayers about, banging him against the ropes. The twenty-first round was brief because once Sayers came out, Heenan "hit him down clean with a splendid blow and walked away."

Yet each time Sayers was hit, he came up smiling. In round twenty-two Sayers got a second wind, and Heenan's left hand was swollen from smashing his opponent in the jaw. By the end of this round the fight had gone for one hour and eleven minutes. The gladiators fought on with the action more even. Sayers worked steadily on closing Heenan's good eye, and Heenan tried to knock him out with blows to the jaw. The odds still favored the Benicia Boy.

For the next several rounds Sayers dodged, feigned, and kept smacking Heenan in the eye. The British champ drew strength from an unfathomable reservoir, and though shaky on his pins, he kept fighting. Heenan hit better, but if the give-and-take continued, he would soon be blind. By round thirty-four both of his eyes were almost closed and his blows lacked power. Still he pursued Sayers, who fled, turned, and caught him on the face.

By round thirty-six "the Benicia Boy's face was a spectacle to behold, while Tom was very weak." The fight had gone well over two hours when suddenly the constables made their move, struggling to get close to the action. This pushed part of the crowd up against the ring. Heenan rushed Sayers against the ropes, forced his neck across the top strand, and pressed down on his windpipe. He might have broken his neck, but Sayers partisans cut the ropes and stormed into the ring. Some said John Morrissey himself cut the ropes. Dowling, the referee, with money on Sayers, thought it a good time to disappear. In the midst of the confusion, Heenan and Sayers fought on, rolling on the ground and pummeling each other. Since the timekeeper had remained, this went on for another five rounds.

Finally, at the start of round forty-two, after two hours and twenty minutes of combat, Sayers refused to get up from his stool or leave his corner. Heenan charged him but was stopped by the opposing seconds, one of whom pulled a blackjack. He was deterred by a Heenan partisan who drew a revolver. Heenan, though he could hardly see, demanded Sayers's seconds throw in the towel, and when they refused he began to pummel several of them. Cusick and McDonald pulled him off and warned him to run—arrest was the least of what might happen.

So Heenan ran fast as a deer, proving that he was as fit as ever. He evaded the constables, but not himself.

In August, with meteors punctuating the night sky, torchlight parades wound through the cities of the barely United States. The Democratic and Republican candidates, Stephen A. Douglas and Abe Lincoln, were campaigning for the presidency with a swapping of insults not seen since Andy Jackson came out of the West. Barbecues featuring windy speeches, dumb jokes, and mawkish songs pervaded the land. Yet there was no man in America more popular than New York's own hero, John Carmel Heenan, the rightful heavyweight champion of the world. At noon on August 13 the city turned out to celebrate his return home.

At least 50,000 people gathered at Jones's Wood, the picnic ground on the East River in the seventies. Politics were put aside as a chant swelled up from the crowd: "TIGER! TIGER! TIGER!" Heenan was carried aloft on the shoulders of the Ancient Order of Hibernians toward the ring where he would exhibit his glorious form. Flags flew in homage and a brass band blurted a windy satisfaction. In contrast, New Yorkers would shortly greet President-elect Lincoln with an ominous silence.

Four months had passed since the great fight, which was belatedly called a draw. During that time Heenan and Sayers had become friends and toured Britain together, giving sparring exhibitions. The champions amiably shared the title and made more money than ever before in their lives. There would be no rematch because Sayers intended to retire. Now, Heenan had returned home to cash in on the groundswell of adulation.

A sharp-eyed reporter from the *Illustrated News* spotted a veiled woman on the fringe of the crowd. Although she was incognito, the reporter easily recognized Adah Isaacs Menken-Heenan. Next day he would wonder in print: Had the champ deserted Adah? Or had the pair never married? Newspapers across the nation revived the scandal. The *Charleston Mercury,* banishing secession from its front page, asserted: "We will now test the truth of the gossip respecting the marriage of the Benicia Boy. Thus far he has held back and sought no interview with his Adah. . . . Heenan takes the matter as a good joke on a bad subject."

Adah, once recognized, hurried away from Jones's Wood. Her baby boy, born in early June, was ill and running a high fever. He died two days later of what was known as St. Anthony's Fire, a viral infection. Adah's mother was also gravely ill in New Orleans. Meanwhile, Heenan, parading his English mistress and proclaiming himself a bachelor, went on a national tour, giving sparring matches. Adah felt as though she had lost everything. Yet she took comfort in her friends— actors, editors, artists—and she turned to poetry to express her feelings. Over the next few months until the end of this fateful year, she poured out a stream of poems as sensational as the meteor showers that rained down from the heavens.

CHAPTER NINE:

A SCANDAL IN BOHEMIA

If you go strolling on lower Broadway of a Saturday evening, you may notice at number 653, a few doors above Bleecker Street, an unassuming locksmith shop. You are in New York's Noho, which shares with its better-known sister, Soho, just across Houston Street, an upscale, arty beat. Former warehouses and factory lofts have been converted into apartments, boutiques, and galleries. Join in what Walt Whitman called "the vast procession of humanity." You will find yourself in the company of casually but not inexpensively dressed young couples, or perhaps students from the nearby film school, who are heading for a trendy restaurant, club, or movie.

Step back into the year 1860. Again, you find yourself in a busy entertainment district, which extends along Broadway north to Union Square. Some of the decorative four- and five-story buildings are the same, but instead of honking traffic, horse-drawn coaches and buses jam the cobbled avenue. The drivers are as reckless as today's cabbies. Around you are mostly men, some on the town in formal attire. And the women? According to Whitman, once it grows dark the women on Broadway are "tawdry, hateful, foul-tongued, and harsh-voiced harlots."

There are six hundred bordellos in the largest, most dynamic city of a nation on the verge of civil war. No one bothers to count the numerous freelancers on the streets. The police on the beat take their cut and pass it up the line, all the way to Mayor Fernando Wood. Yet Whitman, recently fired from his newspaper job, was too harsh in his editorializing. Often the prostitutes are working women who have grown tired of slaving away for five dollars a week when they can earn fifty dollars by servicing a single customer. Those who hang about fashionable locations such as the St. Nicholas Hotel at Spring Street, or the Academy of Music or Delmonico's Restaurant on Union Square, are pretty and dress nicely, with a touch of color. Prostitution presents a danger to public health but a real temptation to poor women.

Let's assume that, in 1860, you are a gentleman or lady who has convivial pleasures in mind. You are heading toward number 653, the location of Charlie Pfaff's tavern, the informal headquarters of America's first Bohemian crowd. Take the steps down to this cellar *boite*. Once inside, the dim, smoky, confidential atmosphere may bother your eyes, but it's exciting. Ahead, in a large room, men and a sprinkling of women sit at tables, eating, drinking, and puffing on cigars (cigarillos for the women). They have come for the proprietor's renowned German fare and his excellent wine, beer, or coffee. Pfaff, a Swiss, and his waiters serve up everything in the authentic European style.

To your left, extending under the Broadway sidewalk, you see a "cave" that houses a long table; around it are seated several men and one woman—New York's Bohemian elite. Maybe you've heard standup comic Artemus Ward's definition of a Bohemian: "an educated hoss thief." A more polite description is attributed to a British gentleman: "Bohemianism is understood to mean a gay disorderliness of life, cheerful bad manners, and no fixed hours or sexual standards." Pfaff's is one of the few bars in New York that women can enter unescorted; a place where gay men—in the modern sense—can meet one another. To staid Victorians, Bohemia is a land of alarming promiscuity.

The regulars here include Henry Clapp, publisher of the *Saturday Press* and founder of this gathering of jesters and drinkers. The woman, an attractive blonde, is Ada Clare, actress, journalist, and free spirit. The other regulars include the multitalented George Arnold, who is Clare's sometime lover; Fitz-James O'Brien, author of the earliest tales of science fiction; Fitz Hugh Ludlow, a dope fiend and author of *The Hashish Eater*; the nattily dressed *Herald* critic, Ned Wilkins; and the aforementioned Artemus Ward, on the verge of becoming America's most successful comedian. President Lincoln will read one of Ward's humorous pieces to his Cabinet before presenting to them the Emancipation Proclamation.

At a small table to the side sits Walt Whitman. He affects the dress of a local "rough," but his cool gray eyes, scanning the room, tell a different story. His volume of verse, *Leaves of Grass,* is just off the press of a Boston abolitionist publisher. "A foul work filled with libidinousness," scolds the *Christian Examiner,* an opinion seconded by most reviewers. With Whitman is a woman whose notoriety exceeds even his own: Adah Menken, whose private affairs have been publicized in every major newspaper in America. She wears her favorite color: black.

It is not clear who introduced Adah to Pfaff's. Gay Wilson Allen, the Whitman biographer, writes that Adah "had been introduced to the Pfaff circle about the time [February 1860] Whitman went to Boston." Although, until spring, Adah was often away on tour, certain of the bar's habitués would play crucial parts in her life, including Whitman on his return. At first she tried to keep in with the sporting crowd. But once John Heenan denied he had married Adah, she became *persona non grata* to those former friends.

As an actress and writer, Adah retained ties to a number of journalists, including Henry Clapp. Described as short, haggard, and alert, he found her misfortunes a good source of news. His ill-fated weekly, considered on a par with the *Nation,* the *Atlantic,* or *Harper's,* was a focal point for the Bohemian crowd. Clapp didn't hesitate to print Clare's feminist tracts, and he promoted Whitman's poetry, even permitting him to review his own book. His weekly would close its stormy career by introducing Mark Twain's story about a jumping frog to an Eastern audience.

Clapp, a New Englander who once taught Sunday school, was a socialist and believer in Free Love. He returned from his stay in Paris with an idealism championed by La Bohème Galante, a group founded by Théophile Gautier, whose followers drank punch from skulls and knelt before the ideal of Woman. The hard-drinking Clapp was at his most memorable when he was cynical. He quipped about Horace

Greeley of the *Tribune,* "He is a self-made man who worships his creator." In 1860 young William Dean Howells, the future dean of American letters, left Ohio to visit the literary men of the East. When he told Clapp that, in Boston, he had been introduced to Nathaniel Hawthorne but was too shy to say much, and that Hawthorne was also shy, Clapp replied, "Oh, a couple of shysters!"

Adah took to Walt Whitman. Often he sat absorbed, watching the others. He sensed that he was witnessing "the last glorious gasp of antebellum America," a Romantic land where people were garrulous, individualist, and naively trusting. The 1850s bred a host of reform movements, and finally this diffuse energy became focused on the Civil War, the epic struggle between the idyllic Southern past and the industrial Northern future. Whitman, almost by chance, would become the bard of that struggle. Adah, divided within, could not easily choose a side.

Almost alone among her contemporaries, she at once recognized Whitman's importance. In "Swimming against the Current," an essay that appeared in the June 10, 1860, issue of the *Sunday Mercury,* Adah wrote a defense of Whitman when he was most heatedly under attack by moralists. This was not a review of *Leaves of Grass,* though she soon internalized elements of Whitman's style. Rather, Adah praised all who dared to defy social convention and follow their own inner guide. In the midst of the piece, she wrote,

> *Look at Walter Whitman, the American philosopher, who is centuries ahead of his contemporaries, who, in smiling carelessness, analyzes the elements of which society is composed, compares them with the history of past events, and ascertains the results which the same causes always produced, and must produce. . . . He hears the Divine voice calling to him to caution mankind against this or that evil; and [he] wields his pen, exerts his energies, for the cause of liberty and humanity!*

Whitman once remarked that "the girls have been my sturdiest defenders," referring to Clare and Adah. "[H]e swims against the stream and finds no company," continued the essay. The literary Establishment denounced him as "a fanatic, a visionary, a demagogue, a good-natured fool," while Adah predicted that one day in the next century, Whitman and his predecessor Edgar Allan Poe would be justly honored: "marble statues will be erected over the[ir] remains." By now, Adah's "next century" has come and gone, and Walt Whitman has a bridge named after him—connecting Philadelphia with Camden, New Jersey—and a shopping mall on Long Island.

Beyond these two giants of literature, Adah praised the "thousands of philosophers, poets, senators, preachers of God . . . friends of and saviors of liberty, women of inspiration, men of reform [who] have been drowned in the current of life, because they swam against the stream." Some interesting choices made her list, including Jefferson Davis, future president of the Confederacy and historical pariah. Adah is writing not least about herself and her experience of being an outcast.

The essay, if considered, proves several points: first, that Adah knew Whitman personally and was impressed by his air and conversation. Bronson Alcott, Louisa May's father, claimed that Whitman was an egotist, incapable of speaking about anything but himself. Whitman, like Adah, understood that life was a stage and he the principal actor. Second, the literary editor of the highly respectable *Sunday Mercury*, Robert Henry Newell, must have fallen in love with her. He abhorred Whitman and disclaimed responsibility for Adah's praise of "that coarse and uncouth creature." Still, he printed the essay. Newell, however he felt about the denizens of Pfaff's, accompanied Adah like a pet spaniel would his mistress.

Newell, in line to become Adah's fourth husband, was born in 1836 into a wealthy New York family. His father invented an advanced lock for bank vaults. His death, coincident with Robert's graduating from a private school, changed the family's fortunes. Robert and his mother moved to less-expensive Jersey City, and in 1858 he went to work as assistant editor on the *Sunday Mercury*.

Newell first met Adah when she presented him with her memorial essay to Rufus Choate, a United States senator from Massachusetts who had championed the cause of public libraries. Known for his *bon mots,* Choate's remark that "A book is the only immortality" would resonate with Adah till the end of her days. Newell printed the essay in the *Mercury* on September 18, 1859, shortly after its author had secretly married John Heenan. The editor did not see her again until late winter, though he must have been aware of her success onstage and the controversy raging around her.

In March 1860 Newell published Adah's "Fragment of a Heart," the first thing she had written in months. While she complained of her own woes, she continued to identify her fate with that of Israel. Newell headed the column in which the poem appeared "Infelicissimus" (Latin for "unhappiest"), a title and image that Adah would adopt in her work to come. Newell, introducing her to his readers, remarked: "We may state that the lady is a Jewess, and almost insane in her eagerness to behold her people restored once more to their ancient power and glory. Her best poems have been founded on this vigorous sentiment . . . the present prose-poem is strongly tinctured with it."

Throughout the next two years, Newell regularly published Adah's poetry and prose. These poems constitute most of her posthumous collection, *Infelicia.* They are Adah's claim to literary fame and Newell's main achievement as an editor. Reflecting a period of turmoil, charged with despair yet hopeful, the poems break all conventional rules. Resonant with feeling, they turn the Victorian moralist's "real woman" into . . . a real woman. The poems might not have come into existence but for Newell's admiration of Adah's bold and defiant spirit. He was a hesitant champion, but he grasped the worth of her writing.

Newell was in his mid-twenties, a year younger than Adah. Slender, brown-haired, and light-skinned, he sported a flowing mustache that overstated his character. The *Brooklyn Eagle* remarked of him that despite his association with actors, politicians, and Bohemians, "he was absolutely pure in thought, chaste in speech and diffident almost to timidity in manner." The *Eagle* tagged him with its ultimate compliment: "a Christian gentleman." During the war, Newell, writing under the name of Orpheus C. Kerr ("office seeker"), would caricature the rush for appointments under the new Republican administration. He is counted as one of the founders of American humor, and in time he would churn out several volumes of poetry. Only the long poem "Aspasia" (after the Greek courtesan who became the lover of Pericles) shows genius. Newell's finest work is a moving expression of his abiding love for Adah.

As for who introduced Adah to Pfaff's Bohemian den, our nomination goes to her friend, Ada Clare, who was a New Woman and a single mother before either term came into vogue. She was born Jane McElhenney in 1836, in Charleston, to a prosperous, well-connected family. At the age of eleven she was sent to New York, where she grew up under the care of her maternal grandfather. From seventeen on she began to contribute poems and sketches to periodicals, using the pseudonym Ada Clare, after a character in Dickens's *Bleak House.* In the aftermath of a heartbreaking affair with the pianist and composer, Louis Moreau Gottschalk, Clare sailed to Paris, where she gave birth to his son in 1857.

By March 1859 Clare had returned to New York to appear onstage in Shakespeare's *Antony and Cleopatra.* She began to contribute a column on theater and feminist politics to the *Saturday Press.* Like Henry Clapp, she encouraged artists and writers to coalesce into a movement. Unfortunately, drinking and arguing at Pfaff's was as much togetherness as the group could stand. Whitman greatly admired Clare, and he describes her as "slender and elegant," with a "pure white complexion, pale, striking, chiseled features, perfect profile, abundant fair hair, abstracted look, and rather rapid, purposeful step." Her wit and charm earned her the title "Queen of Bohemia."

Clare, who did not lack for material things, held her own salon at home. Whitman mentions meeting theater critic Ned Wilkins there.

Adah, always on the lookout for journalists, surely attended the salon. Both women were committed to writing and acting, but Clare was more political. She was flamboyant about being an unwed mother, and her articles often castigated men for their pretensions of superiority. Adah learned from her in a number of ways, from dressing in black to speaking out in her own defense. Yet in background and temperament, these two Southern women were poles apart. Clare's way of life, as Whitman described it, was "gay, easy, sunny, free, loose." Adah lacked the trust fund and the social assurance that were Clare's by birth.

Adah's "My Heritage," the first instance in which we hear the poet's mature voice, was published in the *Mercury* on June 3, 1860. It is Whitmanesque in its free form but more bitter than anything from that American poet. Without work since early May, Adah writes not only of her own plight but the actor's life in general, applauded one moment, forgotten the next:

> *To think, and speak, and act, not for my pleasure,*
> *But others'. The veriest slave of time*
> *And circumstances. Fortune's toy!*

She knows and fears "Soul-subduing poverty / That lays his iron, cold grasp upon the high Free spirit." She feels she has betrayed her heritage. She has watched passively while her God-given talent went to waste. "Even death shall scorn to give a thing / So low his welcome greeting!"

Adah's forsaken tone has been treated as a convention of Victorian verse, but her desperate situation was very real. Nearing her time to give birth, she was no longer able to perform, and she had to sell off her theatrical wardrobe to live. In her next poetic lament, "Battle of the Stars," Adah sounds bitterly cynical, writing lines worthy of Cole Porter at his best:

> *Souls for sale! who'll buy?*
> *In the pent-up city, through the wild rush and beat of human hearts,*

I hear this unceasing, haunting cry:
Souls for sale! souls for sale! . . .
The hoarse voice of the world echoes up the cold gray sullen river of life.

We are struck by the depth of Adah's sorrow, which she feels for all humankind, and by the precision with which she expresses it. Here is no pretense, no role-playing, no mush. This is the voice of a strong woman, wounded to the quick.

By July Adah had given birth to her son, but he was sickly, and she had received no word from Heenan, his father. Unable to pay the rent due on their room at Westchester House on the Bowery, mother and child were threatened with prompt eviction. In "Drifts that Bar My Door," published on July 29, we find an echo of her actual despair:

O Angels! Will ye never sweep the drifts from my door?
Will ye never wipe the gathering rust from the hinges?
How long must I plead and cry in vain?
Lift back the iron bars and lead me hence.
Is there not a land of peace beyond my door?

The lengthy poem is built on this image of imprisonment and the poet's call for liberation, which can only mean death. Additionally, "Drifts" is colored by macabre, ghastly imagery, without thought toward artistic effect:

See how dark and cold my cell.
The pictures on the wall are covered with mould.
The earth-floor is slimy with my wasting blood.
My wild eyes paint shadows on the walls.
And I hear the poor ghost of my lost love moaning . . .

Extravagance is a hallmark of Adah's writing at its most fevered pitch, and while this results in arresting lines, occasionally she drifts into incoherence. But the woman felt too strongly to care. She wrote these "wild soul poems," as she explained, "in the stillness of midnight, and when waking to the world the next day, they were to me the deepest mystery." Adah herself, startled by the "wild intensity" of her poems, was afraid to publish them. Before the concept had a name, she grasped that her verse stemmed from the unconscious: "[T]he soul that prompted every word and line is somewhere within me, but not to be called at my bidding—only to wait the inspiration of God."

Ironically, the key to the Naked Lady's poetry, in print for a century and a half, is her religious inspiration. In fairness, a few admirers of Adah's verse—such as Pre-Raphaelites Dante Gabriel Rossetti and his anthologizing brother, Michael—understood that the worldly actress was at heart a mystic poet. The force of their literary reputations kept alive Adah's until the postmodern day, when an editor such as Joan Sherman could include Adah's work in *Collected Black Women's Poetry*, calling it, "remarkably dramatic, intensely self-aware and confessional."

Adah, who wrote in haste and anger by a flickering lamp, overlooked the chance Robert Newell had taken by subjecting the *Mercury's* audience to her supercharged emotions. At this time she thought of no man but John Heenan. However, Newell lived in hope that the fair author would forget the boxing champ and look kindly on her editor.

During the second half of 1860 Adah's living situation deteriorated and her mood darkened. Yet she managed to keep hold of herself through the deaths of her baby son in August and her mother in September. A common thread of illness runs through the family. Robert Roden, who had access to Ed James's private collection of letters and photos, claimed that Adah's mother suffered from tuberculosis, which had previously killed her natural father and would one day claim her sister. Despite Adah's sorrow, she appeared on August 20 at Hope Chapel to give an "Evening with Poets." Friends helped her to rent the space and place notices in the newspapers.

Dressed in virginal white, Adah soon dispensed with the poets and launched into a defense of her conduct vis-à-vis her husbands. She accused the newspapers of printing salacious stories that closed every avenue by which she could honestly earn her living, and drove her into a whirlpool of sin. This was the dilemma of any independent Victorian woman, who, if she offended contemporary morals, faced a choice between starvation and prostitution. The press, in the demeaning style of today's tabloids, trumpeted any indiscretion, always adding their hypocritical "tut-tuts."

Adah's diatribe worsened her situation. William Winter in the next day's *Tribune* gratuitously devoted a column to praising Heenan as a distinguished champion and deriding Adah. He described the audience at the chapel as less than human. Even formerly friendly papers berated Adah for hanging out her dirty linen in public. The *Sunday Mercury* scolded her for bad taste, and the *Illustrated News* rhetorically asked what she had expected when she became involved with a prizefighter, whose brutal profession naturally led to desertion. As she wrote to James, "I am so sorry that I appeared at Hope Chapel, and presumed to be anything more than . . . a miserable outcast."

Adah managed to play during the last week in September at her standby, the Gayety Theater in Albany. Back in New York, she found herself embroiled in a nasty lawsuit. Westchester House sued Heenan, who had returned after a successful tour, for Adah's bill. Specifically, the plaintiff asked for "the sum of $196.68, being the balance due for board and lodging furnished to Mrs. Ada I. M. Heenan, as the wife of the defendant, at his and her instance and request, between the months of December 1859, and July 1860." In response, Heenan, prompted by his attorney, declared in the *Herald:* "I was never married to [Adah Isaacs Menken] or to anyone else. . . . I shall not again take any notice of the affair in any manner and it is with great reluctance that I do so now."

In fact, the hotel had Heenan's signature on its register, signed as Adah's husband. His attorney next tried a despicable tactic: He claimed that the marriage was a ruse, and that John had checked in with Adah for a night's dalliance. The attorney accused her of being a prostitute:

> *I will prove that other men, with this same lady, entered her own name at this same house (Westchester) as John Doe and Lady, and that they occupied a room; probably the same as Mr. Heenan is alleged to have occupied. I will prove the character of this frail, fair woman, and that she had her name entered upon the books of this and other houses as the lady of John Doe or Richard Roe, or any who might have money enough to pay for that particular purpose.*

The judge ruled this allegation irrelevant to the case. It was a smear, impossible to prove but effective in frightening Westchester House. Afraid for its reputation, the hotel settled out of court, leaving Adah no opportunity to refute the charge. Worse, the *Herald* printed Heenan's attorney's accusation verbatim. Attempts by Adah to repair the damage proved useless, especially because Heenan referred to her as "the most dangerous woman in the world." *Dangerous woman* was a euphemism for prostitute. Adah's career on the legitimate stage seemed over.

She wrote to a confidant, Stephen Masset, that her reputation as a *femme fatale* caused deserted wives to ransack her lodging, searching for their husbands. On two occasions these women had attacked her and were carted off by the police. "I am confined to my bed today," she complained, "very ill from fright and excitement." Her neck had been nearly broken and her arm badly twisted. Further, she insisted that Heenan was hanging around, spying on her. She feared his bad intentions.

Among those still loyal to Adah, Stephen Masset was the most devoted. Born in Ireland in 1820, he was a performer and songwriter who wrote sentimental ditties such as "My Bud in Heaven." He had set the words of Thomas Moore to music. In the early 1850s he performed in San Francisco, one of the first entertainers to brave the long voyage from New York. Adah refers to him as "Dear Stevey" and "a dear good little fellow" who sent her breakfast when she was ill. Although some who have written about Adah suspect she was having an affair with Masset, it is not likely. Her taste didn't run to "good little fellows," and she was too distraught to be sleeping with anyone. Masset, however, played a critical role in her life at this time.

Adah responded to attacks on her character as best she could. She wrote a letter to the *Herald,* and her essay "Women of the World" was published by Newell in the October 7 *Mercury.* Adah scorned what passed for education for young women: "As girls, they are educated only for display." They were kept from any difficult study and encouraged to be frivolous and vain. Except that in hunting for a husband, young women were taught a strict standard: "Has he money? Can he support me in style?" Those in the marriage market were like baubles, available for purchase. Adah insisted there were higher callings for a woman than that of wife and mother!

This was heresy to Victorian moralists. Then Adah unleashed pent-up anger at the way her own sex had treated her during the Heenan crisis. She excoriated her "sister-women" for "petty jealousy, envy of face and form, love of senseless admiration." If a woman stumbled, she asked rhetorically, would her sisters hold out their hands to help? "Never! If words and sneers could dash a sinking, erring creature to the bottomless pit it would be a woman's work to do it." Adah, by her intemperate language, alienated those women who might have supported her.

Living in a sparse, furnished room on Third Avenue at Fourteenth Street, she had to work. Either Frank Queen or Ed James arranged for an engagement at the Stadt, a respectable theater on the Bowery patronized by German immigrants. On November 11 Adah wrote to Masset that she was certain she couldn't appear the next evening because she lacked music for her dances, proper costumes, and the spirit to perform. "What is the use of trying to do anything?" she moaned. "I am more unhappy than ever."

Masset hurried over and persuaded Adah to go on. She was an excellent mime, and her comic material was so basic it could be performed as a dumb show. After two weeks at the Stadt, another engagement turned up at the Gayety in Albany. Adah played Lucrezia Borgia, the famous poisoner. It was a suggestive role for a woman in a grim mood.

Without benefit nights, Adah's earnings were slim, and the holiday season was dead for theater. It may be at this time that she turned to selling not her body but images of it, seminude. To our knowledge, only three photos of her bare from the waist up survive, though surely more were taken. Stills of the Naked Lady are eminently collectible, and they mostly remain in private hands. But were these three stills faked—Adah's head set on a model's body? From the very beginning of photography, pornography flourished, most obviously in the form of the so-called French postcard. Often, forgeries of celebrities were composed in the darkroom and sold on the street. Later, at the height of Adah's fame, she would be the subject of scandalous, faked porno-graphic photos originating in Paris.

The three seminudes in question are of a piece. They are shot in front of the same drapery and appear to be from a series. We believe that Adah did pose for them, not least because the subject's legs are, from the knees down, firm and muscled. They are the legs of a dancer and circus performer, and few Victorian actresses—the likely class to pose for nudes—could claim such legs. Adah's body, especially around the waist, looks a bit flabby, but that may be the result of carrying a child to term. The facial expression is hers, and so is the body language. She is acting, faking an avid interest.

In later times Marilyn Monroe, unknown and hard up, posed in the nude, and more recently so did Miss America, Vanessa Williams, among other starlets. The resurrection of these nudes, once the women became famous, has caused no end of trouble in our supposedly more enlightened age. That Adah would risk posing seminude is a measure of her desperation. Now we can understand her fear of the whirlpool of sin. Her final engagement for the year, in December at the Canter-bury Concert Hall, snuffed out the light of hope that still flickered.

The Canterbury, a so-called concert saloon, advertised "pretty waiter girls" to lure its male clientele. This, according to Renée Sentilles, "indicated an establishment catering to prurient desires—an equivalent to the twentieth-century clubs advertising topless waitresses." The *New York Post* called the Canterbury a place of "phallus worship" and a "portico to the brothel." In other words, the male clientele came to drink, laugh, and flirt with the waiter girls, and incidentally take in a variety show. If some of the girls, who wore rouged cheeks, jet earrings, and revealing costumes, bedded a customer after work, the management felt it was good for business.

However, the Canterbury was the Waldorf of concert saloons. Located on Broadway between Houston and Prince streets, the spacious theater featured an elevated stage, an orchestra pit, and a mirror-lined parquet floor on which the patrons sat at tables. The orchestra was conducted by Dave Braham. He would compose the music to some four hundred songs written and performed by Harrigan and Hart, America's first great song-and-dance act. The Canterbury might be plebeian, but Robert Newell could explain away Adah's performing there as honest work to earn her living. She herself was dejected by how far she had fallen from her ambition to become a serious actress. Worse, the waiter girls on the floor drew more of the audience's attention than the act on stage. To Adah, being upstaged—or down-, in this case—was the last straw.

The wife of a fellow performer confided to her diary that Adah was hissed nightly. This was Heenan's doing, by sending a claque to jeer and hoot at her. He succeeded in driving Adah from the stage. Helped by Newell, who was secretly pleased, she moved her lodging near his family home in Jersey City. The plan was for the retired actress to write. Newell thought her "the greatest and most original poetess of the day." Sensing her despair, he wanted to keep an eye on her.

Adah's poetry at this time exhibits sorrow curdled to images of revenge. In "Judith" she adopts the role of another Biblical defender of the Jewish people. Unlike Deborah, a prophet who mobilized the tribes to fight their enemies, but who was pious and prudent, the beautiful widow Judith acts directly and with no sense of shame. She enters the tent of the formidable Assyrian general Holofernes, seduces him, and as he sleeps, cuts off his head with a sword. Let Adah tell it:

Ere the last tremble of the conscious death-agony shall have shuddered, I will show it to ye with the long black hair clinging to the glazed eyes, and the great mouth opened in search of voice, and the strong throat all hot and reeking with blood, that will thrill me with wild unspeakable joy as it courses down my bare body and dabbles my feet! My sensuous soul will quake with the burden of so much bliss. Oh, what wild passionate kisses will I draw up from that bleeding mouth! I will strangle this pallid throat of mine on the sweet blood! I am starving for this feast. Oh forget not that I am Judith!

And I know where sleeps Holofernes.

Adah's revenge on John Heenan—Holofernes is his stand-in—would be vicarious for the time being. The poem may have inspired passages in Oscar Wilde's *Salome,* but its rhetoric of sadistic cannibalism goes beyond Wilde's witty iconoclasm. It is a disturbing journey into a land where no other contemporary male or female poet dared venture. As the New Year of 1861 approached, Adah's bubble of retribution burst. Feeling forsaken, she sunk into self-pity. She avoided Pfaff's and saw only a few friends.

An unfortunate aspect of New York Bohemian life was suicide—suddenly, by violent means, or gradually, through using drugs or drink, accompanied by living in squalor. A younger Ada Clare, pregnant and abandoned, had written an essay predicting her own suicide. Instead she gave birth to an illegitimate son and thereafter flaunted him. One young Englishman, a writer of fiction about hunting and fishing, invited his friends over for a feast, after which they watched him blow his brains out before a mirror. Natty Ned Wilkins would die of pneumonia, in his own filth, in a wretched garret. Liquor would finish a washed-up Henry Clapp and the promising George Arnold. Fitz-James O'Brien raised a company of men for the Union Army, in return for which he was shot to death by his own side. These original Bohemians were far from poseurs; they died for their cause.

We return to that stark Jersey City room on the night before New Year's Eve to find Adah, alone and in possession of opiates acquired from the druggist. She felt that all doors were closed to her, as if she had already "died with my fingers grasping the white throat of many a prayer." Yet Adah clung to a thread of hope. Her suicide letter is endearing, almost childlike. She forgives her enemies and apologizes for forgetting "the *God* of my childhood prayers [and] the counsel of my dear old mother." She cannot forgive John Heenan, who "left me alone, desolate to *die*." In effect, she accuses him of murder. Still, she loves him—"one of *God's* grandest handiworks"—which she will prove by dying for the loss of his love. This makes emotional sense if the writer believes in an afterlife, that her soul will have the satisfaction of witnessing Heenan humbled and contrite. Adah believed in the indestructibility of the spirit.

Her body would have proved mortal enough if a visitor had not arrived in the nick of time. Allen Lesser wondered: "Did some gallant Jack Dalton [a stage hero] in the person of Newell, Frank Queen or Stephen Masset come dashing in at the last moment to save the heroine?" Lesser and other biographers have no answer to the question. Each of the above men loved Adah and knew of how she teetered on the edge. But only one, in touch with her every mood, came through the door that evening. He couldn't prevent Adah from taking poison, but he arrived in time to save her life.

Ed James, who grew very close to Adah, purposely did not name the man in his brief biography, but he set the parameters: Adah's "one solitary friend" was still alive in 1881, and she always spoke of him with "the keenest pleasure." The first clue rules out Queen and the second Newell. James had previously ruled out himself. Further, this friend lovingly nursed Adah back to health, a task congenial to Stephen Masset, who was in the habit of bringing her meals and otherwise caring for her. The Irish balladeer played the melodramatic but real-life role of the steadfast friend.

For a time, Adah lay close to death. However, as James comments, "being very courageous, she pulled through." Her stage career, which she had supposed at an end, was only beginning. But upon recovery, Adah was not the same trusting, passionate young woman. Her heart, "a pleasant world / Of sunbeams dewed with April tears" was broken. Neither was she Deborah, defender of her people, nor even vengeful Judith. The phoenix that rose from the ashes of Adah's near suicide was a formidable, unforgiving warrior. Reckless of life, generous to friends, Prince Mazeppa rode and fought for the thrill of it. Woe to any man who crossed swords with this character!

PART THREE

PRINCE MAZEPPA

They always give me a clear stage.

—ADAH ISAACS MENKEN

CHAPTER TEN:

BELLE BEAUTY

John B. Smith, who managed Albany's Green Street Theater, titled himself *Captain*. But he was not the sort to relish a campaign, unless it was in the publicity line. By June 1861 eleven southern states had seceded and formed the Confederacy. While North and South hesitated on the brink of war, fighting began almost by itself on June 12, when Confederate forces fired on the Union garrison at Fort Sumter, South Carolina. Captain Smith, described by Ed James as a "speculative bill-poster," was one of the first to realize this meant good news for his profession.

On a Saturday afternoon in early June he waited impatiently for the arrival of his star actress on the New York Central. She was traveling from the west, where she had been a smash hit in Chicago, Detroit, and Pittsburgh. Jitters caused by the uncertain state of affairs had increased the public's desire for diversion, and currently that was spelled ADAH ISAACS MENKEN, writ bold across a theater poster.

Rehearsal for Smith's new production of *Mazeppa*, to open Monday, proceeded on stage. Knights jousted, damsels cheered, a tightrope walker and clowns performed their numbers. Above the activity a mountain loomed. Constructed out of timbers, canvas, and rope, it was painted with shrubs, trees, torrents, and gorges to simulate a wilderness. A hidden ramp only two feet wide careened up the four levels of the mountain, leaving just enough room for a horse to carry a body to the summit, four stories high.

"I had doubts whether [Menken] could do the piece," Smith reminisced to an Albany reporter in 1879. "In case she failed, I had [prepared]

111

a tournament scene an hour long." Actually, his only assurance that Adah would even show up was a weeks-old telegram from St. Louis. She might still be angry at a dirty trick he had pulled on her. Two months earlier Adah had played at Albany's Gayety, a smaller theater than the Green Street. Founded by a banjo player, backed by a butcher, converted from a carpet store by a dentist, the Gayety was something of an amateur operation. It had been kind to Adah, especially when she performed her comic and quick-change pieces. Capacity audiences of up to six hundred turned out, even during the worst of her marital scandal.

This April, business at the Gayety was mediocre, and Captain Smith hoped to make it worse. He wanted to engage Adah for the Green Street, but as he recalled, "her upstart of an agent would not even answer my letter." The upstart was Thomas Allston Brown, encouraged by Frank Queen to act as Adah's agent after her failed suicide attempt. Brown, dramatic editor at *The Clipper*, was young but knowledgeable. From 1853 to 1857 he had traveled all over the land, compiling his *History of the American Stage*. He knew Smith was running an operation of the sort termed "variety." In rehabilitating their favorite's reputation, the *Clipper* crowd wished to avoid anything lowbrow.

Queen and the others chipped in to buy Adah a new wardrobe, while Stephen Masset nursed her back to health. Ed James recalled that this took some months, and the somber tenor of Adah's poetry, which Newell published in the *Mercury*, shows that she suffered from depression throughout the winter. Work would help her to pay bills and regain her self-esteem. Adah's first engagement was at frigid Portland, Maine, in mid-January, and in February she played briefly in Boston. Brown waited till mid-March to book her for a serious engagement, at Milwaukee's Academy of Music. Local papers were sprinkled with the poetry of Adah Isaacs Menken (no longer a hyphenated Heenan) to coincide with her one week in the German-influenced city. This helped to publicize her performances and to elevate her beyond the actress stereotype.

Adah arrived in Albany on April 9 in a modestly hopeful mood. She had been writing bleak verse, such as "The Ship that Went Down."

Here she compares herself to a foundering craft in a howling storm, which, despite the brave struggle of its crew, "sank down, down, down to the soundless folds of the fathomless ocean." However, by early spring she was composing such poems as "Working and Waiting" and "Wishing and Being." Captain Smith, unaware of Adah's emotional state, got her attention in an underhanded way. On the actress's benefit night, he paid for free beer in all the principal saloons of the city. "Beer pulled stronger than beauty," remembered Smith, "and that night the Gayety was empty." Next morning Smith went to Adah and confessed his deed. She was indignant, but she listened to his proposal.

Smith had used an actor named Miles as the lead in *Mazeppa*, and the drama had been a modest success. Knowing that Adah's beauty was already the talk of the city, he had the revolutionary idea that she could play the prince. Further, in the signature scene, the body lashed to the supposedly wild stallion—actually a mare named Belle Beauty— was a dummy. It had always been so; no actor was crazy enough to attempt the ride up the mountain. If Adah did it in the flesh, wearing as little as possible . . . Smith finished his pitch, letting the actress picture mobs of theatergoers and endless columns in the press.

Adah was noncommittal and left on a tour of the Midwest. At each stop, playing her comic and musical roles, she was enthusiastically received, success building on success. The *Chicago Tribune* admired her "youth, beauty and wonderful flow of spirits, [her] dash and abandon of manner." The *Detroit Free Press* exulted that "the balmy days of theatricals were revived last evening, and for the first time in years the house was crowded from pit to dome. . . . The beautiful Adah carried [the audience] by storm." Before she attempted *Mazeppa*, Adah was a rising star, praised for her versatility. Why, then, did she agree to take on the death-defying role of the captive prince?

The answer may be found at Utica, New York, where Adah played in May. Once again she performed in light, quick-change pieces and the *Utica Herald* praised her acting, charm, and looks. But in a different vein, she starred in *Lola Montez*, which she had written. Lola, born

Marie Dolores Gilbert in Limerick, Ireland, in 1818, was Adah's predecessor on the world stage. She, too, had invented her identity.

Lola's father was an officer in the British army, her mother Irish.
She grew up in British India, where her father was posted, and was
sent to England for schooling. At nineteen she eloped with an officer,
divorced him, and went onstage as "Lola Montez, the Spanish dancer."
Although she conceived of the "spider dance" (using black rubber spi-
ders hung from above), Lola was never a remarkable performer. Rather,
her beauty and wit succeeded where her talent failed. Still a sort of
courtesan, she formed liaisons with prominent men before becoming
mistress to King Ludwig I of Bavaria, who made her Countess of Lans-
feld. Ludwig was overthrown in 1848, but by then Lola Montez had
become a notorious celebrity. She appeared in England, America, and
Australia, playing mostly herself. She gave an interesting series of lectures on "the art of fascination." Men and women paid admission to
see, hear, and speak with this Victorian sex symbol.

In New York in 1858, Lola underwent a religious conversion. She
ended her days as an evangelical Christian and died poor and forgotten
in January 1861, to be buried in Brooklyn's Greenwood cemetery. During the period of Adah's deepest gloom, Lola had been living nearby,
reading the Bible and advising unwed mothers. After her death, Lola's
legend took on new life in fiction, ballet, and film, and Adah's one-act
play was the first of its type. A photo exists of Adah dressed as a Spanish dancer, all we know of the piece. She cared little for Lola's stage
career, but she was fascinated by the social *place* she had attained. Adah
understood that Lola's success stemmed less from the admiration of
the crowd than the love of a powerful few. She intended to beat Lola
at her own game.

In early June, to the relief of Captain Smith of Albany, his star arrived at
the rehearsal of *Mazeppa*. Finding that "[Menken] knew nothing about
the play—business, lines, nor anything else," he dismissed the cast. The

pair decided to rehearse only "the great scene," the one in which she was bound naked to the "wild steed." Miles's trained Belle Beauty was brought out. Smith showed Adah how she would be secured by a kind of bandage fastened to a ring on a leather strap that ran under the horse's belly. The rider held both ends of this bandage, and the tighter she pulled, the closer she was bound to the steed, but if she wished to jump off, she need only let go the ends.

Adah, stripped down to tights and a top, and, according to Smith, "trembling with apprehension," was placed on the mare's back, head against her mane. She requested that instead of starting from the footlights as usual, the horse be led up to the run. Belle Beauty, thrown out of her routine, trotted only halfway up, then, "with a terrific crash, plunged off the planking down into the 'wreck' . . . upon the staging and timbers." Smith thought Adah had been killed and the horse ruined. Stagehands lifted out the dazed woman, blood streaming from a wound in her shoulder. A doctor was sent for. Belle Beauty was hoisted out of the wreck, and Smith was relieved to learn that the mare would be all right.

"Miss Menken's injuries are not serious," announced the doctor, after examining her. "But she cannot appear for some time."

"All the same, the play will be done," replied Smith. "Every dollar I have in the world, and all I can borrow, is in it."

Adah, aroused, said quietly but firmly, "I must go on with the rehearsal."

The doctor argued, but Adah insisted it was now or never. Pale but quiet, she was placed on Belle Beauty and drew the straps around her. She clung to them as the mare bounded up the run, first one, then the next level, finally running onto the "flies," a platform above the top of the proscenium arch. From this height, horse and rider could descend again to the stage. Adah had shown the courage of a Cossack prince. Twenty years later, Smith fondly reminisced, "She is alive now, that mare, and draws an old gentleman to the post office and back to his home, four miles away, without ever letting on that in her time she has borne the loveliest burden ever laid on horseflesh."

For the opening of *Mazeppa,* Captain Smith had done his publicity homework. He informed the New York papers that Adah would star, and he invented a story about a famous trainer preparing a total of thirteen horses for the play. The so-called Menken stud was paraded up and down the streets of Albany. Posters of the scantily clad actress were plastered everywhere. Of course, Smith alerted the local press to Adah's brush with disaster. The story, which would be repeated time and again, might have been headlined NAKED LADY DARES DEATH. The nakedness was an illusion, but the danger was real and inherent in the drama.

The historical Ivan Mazeppa was *hetman,* or chief, of a Cossack band in seventeenth-century Ukraine. Initially an ally of Russian czar Peter the Great, he became a Ukrainian separatist, and at the age of seventy, he threw in his lot with Charles XII of Sweden, Peter's enemy. Their combined army was defeated by the Russians at the Battle of Poltava. Pushkin in poetry and Tchaikovsky in opera treat Mazeppa as a noble but unfortunate traitor; however, to East European intellectuals, he is a freedom fighter. In the West, since Lord Byron's epic poem *Mazeppa,* he has been a symbol of the indomitable lover, who will suffer any torment in order to win his beloved.

In the nineteenth century, Delacroix and Géricault painted Mazeppa bound naked to a wild stallion, and novels celebrated his love affair while a page at the court of the Polish king. In the twentieth century and beyond, movies silent and recent have kept alive the myth. However, only two versions of the story have struck a deep, popular chord: Byron's and Adah Menken's. To Byron, the Cossack courtier, humiliated for an adulterous affair, was a kindred spirit. "Like so many of the heroes of the Romantic age, his heroism is *manqué,*" observes a scholar. Byron's poem focuses on young Ivan's experiences after being bound to the stallion: "A Tartar of the Ukraine breed / Who looked as though the speed of thought / Were in his limbs." The horse becomes a central character, heroic and headstrong like his rider, and the essence of the narrative is the swift and dangerous ride. Despite the use of Oriental trappings, Byron was writing about his own life.

In 1831 Henry Milner, the in-house playwright for Astley's Royal Amphitheatre, Westminster Bridge, dramatized Byron's poem, resulting in his *Mazeppa, or the Wild Horse of Tartary*. Milner was a hack, accustomed to beg, borrow, and steal his material at a time when copyrights were unenforceable. Gone from his version is Byron's language and drive, replaced by sentimental posturing. Milner was good at spectacle, or what we now call special effects. In his *Mazeppa*, thunder roared and lightning crackled as the steed bore its dummy across a mountain range, wolves nipped at horse and rider, buzzards circled overhead, and an orchestra played with all its might.

The drama called for all the audacity and verve Adah Menken possessed. As Northcott observed, "Physically she made an ideal hero. The mere fact of seeing a pretty woman, with her hair clipped short, sustain a part hitherto played by men aroused public curiosity." The actress didn't remind anyone that three years earlier Charlotte Crampton had played Mazeppa, or reveal that she had practiced on the same horse. Adah went much further than Crampton, even to keeping her hair cut short and curly, a la Byron, from this time forward.

On Monday evening, June 7, 1861, the Albany house was crowded from pit to dome. Adah still didn't know her lines, but Smith was prepared to prompt her from the wings, and, by posing as an actor, onstage. Act One is set at the Castle of Laurinski in Poland, presided over by the Castellan, whose lovely daughter Olinska is in love with the page Cassimir, who is really Prince Mazeppa but was found as a boy after a major battle in which the Poles defeated the "Tartars" (the historical Cossacks). It is night and Cassimir and Olinska are having a secret rendezvous on her balcony. Like Romeo and Juliet, they pledge eternal devotion to one another. Unfortunately, the Castellan has determined to marry Olinska to a rich and powerful older man, Count Premislaus, the villain.

Premislas shows up at the castle to hurry the marriage, and Olinska proves too good a daughter to disobey her father. A tournament is held to celebrate the upcoming nuptials. Cassimir is described by Milner as "A

Tartar . . . a sort of wild beast," though attractive to women. The tournament goes forward, followed by hand-to-hand combat. Captain Smith recalled that both scenes were a great success. Adah, as Cassimir, became so excited that she broke two swords on stage—real weapons. Smith had taken the precaution to file them, so they broke easily. Next morning the papers made much of Adah's supposedly superhuman strength.

Cassimir confronts Premislas in his chamber and challenges him to a duel. The count won't fight a social inferior, but Cassimir taunts him: "Aim at my heart; it has no defence but courage and this good sword." They duel, and Cassimir wounds Premislas, who surrenders. The Castellan's attendants burst in, and Premislas falsely claims that Cassimir tried to assassinate him. The Castellan sentences Cassimir to a traitor's death. The page is stripped naked by the soldiers and bound to the fiery untamed steed, which, let loose, is supposed to run like the wind into the wilderness. The Castellan exults that the vile traitor will be tortured by "scorching suns and piercing blasts, devouring hunger and parching thirst," not to mention bruises and wounds, until he is ground up piecemeal.

In Albany the ride was taken along a spiral ramp up a four-story artificial mountain; it looked, and was, scary. To Adah, damp hands clutching the bandages that kept her atop the bumpy mare, her legs straddling its rump and gripping with all her might, it was a brief, claustrophobic nightmare. She closed her eyes, the better to sense the action of the horse. Should Belle Beauty slip, Adah had to instantly let go and leap free. It was bound to happen sooner or later. But a roar of approval from the audience signified she had reached the mountaintop.

The drama's climactic scene ended Act One. If the audience was to sit through the next two acts, Adah's performance had to be first-rate. Act Two opens on a panorama of the Dnieper River winding through wild country. Mazeppa lies exhausted on the back of his dead steed, while wolves—painted heads with jaws manipulated by prop men— nip at horse and rider. Meanwhile the dance of a chorus of fancifully dressed "Tartars" is interrupted by a thunderstorm. Naturally, the folk stumble on Mazeppa, whom they mistake for a demon. However, their king, Abder Khan, is summoned, and he recognizes his long lost son, the Prince of Tartary.

In Act Three, Mazeppa, having proven his valor, leads the Tartar army in an attack on the Polish castle of Laurinski. Ever faithful to his adored Olinska, he arrives in disguise just as the postponed marriage between her and Premislaus is about to take place. Olinska recognizes her lover, and she assuages his jealousy by assuring him that, though she must obey her father's command to marry the count, she holds a dagger ready to kill herself rather than let him violate her. "Ha!" bursts out Prince Mazeppa, "a heroine worthy [of] a sovereign's love!" He then calls in the cavalry.

"A violent battle ensues," writes Allen Lesser, "complete with loud cries, groans and much sword clashing." The Poles are defeated, Premislaus dies fighting, but Olinska successfully pleads with Mazeppa for her father's life. The Castellan resigns his daughter to Mazeppa, which is the pledge of peace. The final curtain rings down on the lovers united, backed by a tableau of subdued Poles and triumphant Tartars on the castle steps. Love, courage, and fair dealing have won out.

Mazeppa is a play with a dramatic story but old-fashioned dialogue, even for its day, and stereotypical characters. Yet it proved immensely popular, gave rise to numerous imitations, and ran well into the twentieth century. Why did this vehicle launch its star into the heavens of fame and fortune? Adah's prince was an instant hit. Captain Smith recalled: "After six weeks fine business here, pretty good for Albany, she played the part in Pittsburgh, Cincinnati, St. Louis, and then in New York, and then in London and Paris, where, as I have been told, she dazzled some of the brightest men in Europe." Adah would get what Lola had wanted.

In the matter of timing, the gods looked favorably on this revival of *Mazeppa*. It is a story of revenge, of defeated Tartars rising to overwhelm the treacherous Poles. *Mazeppa* opened in Albany after Union forces had surrendered Fort Sumter in April and shortly before their humiliating defeat at Bull Run in July. Victories would elude the Union army and its citizens for some time. While watching *Mazeppa*, they could sense the pleasure of eventual victory over the Confederacy and simultaneously gawk at the Naked Lady. Sex and violence, woven together, are the ultimate draw.

During the next two years Adah would play to audiences sprinkled with uniforms in northern cities that had sent thousands of young men to the front, and in border cities where the front was close enough to hear the thud of cannon fire. Mazeppa seemed to be the warrior general for whom President Lincoln searched for years but could not find. The last words spoken by the Tartar prince are ominous: "Let revenge and slaughter be our word of battle!" The curtain falls on a ruined and subdued land, the castle wrecked and the forest burning. Shades of General Sherman's army marching through Georgia!

For the time being, Adah, in her swashbuckling role, could taste a personal triumph over adversity and bad press. She was the darling of Albany, launched on a new career by this staid city of bureaucrats and burghers. Abe Lincoln had stopped here in February 1861, on the way to Washington for his first inaugural. He rode from the railroad station in an open carriage to address the New York legislature. Among the spectators was a handsome young actor, currently playing the role of Iago in *Othello* at the Gayety Theater. He spoke out against the newly elected president but was silenced by those around him. His name was John Wilkes Booth.

CHAPTER ELEVEN:

PRO PATRIA

"In *cartes de visite* for *The French Spy*," writes Maria-Elena Buszek, "Menken was photographed as a glamorous feminine beauty 'passing' in remarkably convincing male drag, posing with a butch swagger that predated Marlene Dietrich's similar vamping in *Morocco* by nearly 80 years." Adah looks great in a sports suit, complete with vest, watch on a chain, and colorful cravat, pants tight, top hat perched at a rakish angle. In a similar photo she sits at a card table, nonchalantly holding a hand at poker. Now that Adah had stepped up the ladder of fame, she smoked cigarillos in public, wore her hair curly and short, and cultivated her flair for the outrageous. Was it a calculated act, or was she expressing a genuinely masculine side of her nature?

Comparing Menken to Dietrich is illuminating. Each performer became a sex goddess not merely through stage or film roles but by doing the real thing. Each had a lesbian side to her love life. Both associated with prominent literary figures. Significantly, each came into her own as an actress in the charged atmosphere of an all-out war. Coming from the enemy side in the conflict, each felt a need to wear her loyalty to the United States on her sleeve. Entertaining the troops was the least both women could do.

Mazeppa, which balanced nudity with combat, was a fine vehicle for Adah to express her patriotism. In a more serious vein she turned to poetry. While touring the frigid Midwest in midwinter 1861, Menken penned "Pro Patria" and sent it off to Robert Newell's *Sunday Mercury.* The poem appeared on March 17, two weeks after Lincoln was inaugurated as president and after seven Southern states had seceded to form the Confederate States of America. "Pro Patria" is a throwback to Menken's didactic, rhymed style. Vague and high-flown, it seems at first glance to be a full-throated defense of the Union:

> *Beware! For the spirit of God's retribution*
> *Will make a red sunrise when Liberty dies;*
> *The traitors shall writhe in the glow of a morning,*
> *And drown in the blood that is filling their eyes.*

On second reading, the "traitors" turn out to be instigators of war between North and South, the disturbers of the peace of an idyllic America. This was the position taken by those who distrusted Lincoln but revered the Union, a respectable crowd that included Horace Greeley of the *Tribune*. "Columbia! My Country! My Mother!" cries Adah. Coming not long after the death of her actual mother, "Pro Patria" is a lament for the dismembered motherland.

Adah made sure the poem was widely distributed. In June 1861, following her resounding success at Albany, she headed west, and that summer and fall she performed before packed houses in Pittsburgh, Milwaukee, St. Louis, and Louisville, ending the year in Cincinnati, of all places. Although Adah played in *Mazeppa* sparingly and continued to rely on her versatility, she insisted that "Pro Patria" be handed out to all her audiences. Few read beyond the first stanza or two, but Adah's reputation as a poet added to the respect with which she was treated in the American heartland.

In Milwaukee, where she spent July, the *Sentinel* heaped praise on her:

> *This distinguished personage . . . whose poetry breathes a high order*
> *of intellect, if not genius . . . this gifted creature, who sings like a lark,*
> *dances like a peri; who rides, fences and talks half a dozen languages,*
> *has come to Milwaukee to delight the habitués of the Academy of Music.*
> *. . . She is beautiful, graceful, self-possessed . . . and she is as original in*
> *her style of acting as she is in the expression of her thoughts.*

Reviews in other cities were equally laudatory. Meanwhile, Adah's manager, Allston Brown, her friends, Frank Queen and Ed James at *The Clipper*, as well as Gus Daly, made certain that local papers never lacked for copy about her, and equally important, images. For the time being they made use of drawings and reproductions, which Adah had disseminated in the weeklies and on circulars wherever she played. She owed much to her publicity team, the first to hype a star through the mass media. These journalists understood the importance of repeated print exposure to ensure name recognition. The emphasis on *image* was Adah's. Still, she was disappointed in early efforts to capture her on film. She had yet to meet *her* photographer.

In Milwaukee Adah wrote a long mash note to another woman poet, Hattie Tyng. Although the letter first surfaced over half a century ago, it has seldom been used by lesbian or bisexual writers to include Menken in their fold. Instead, as evidence of her apparent same-sex eroticism, they cite pants parts, her wearing of men's evening clothes while on the town, and smoking and gambling. These prove mainly that Adah could raise hell, whether in pink tights or men's drag.

Adah's letter to Hattie is far more telling. Dated July 7, 1861, from Racine, Wisconsin, where Adah was resting on the shore of Lake Michigan, it was sent from one stranger to another. Presumably Hattie knew Adah by reputation, and Adah knew of Hattie by reading her book of poems, *Apple Blossoms*. These made such a strong impression on Adah, she felt the author had written them expressly for her. She dreamed of Hattie, who came to her "lovingly and seemed to put [her] arms around me in my most bitter hours of loneliness."

At this time Adah was suing John Heenan for divorce in Illinois. She charged him with nonsupport, abandonment, and adultery with a certain Harriet Martin. In response, Heenan continued his fiction about not having married Adah. Instead of contesting the divorce in court, where he would be liable for perjury, he wrote to the *New York Herald*, insisting he had never spent a dollar of her money. Adah's experience with love had been bitter to the point of nearly destroying her. Yet she wrote to Hattie:

> *Do you believe in the deepest and tenderest love between women? Do you believe that women often love each other with as much fervor and excitement as they do men? I have loved [women] so intensely that the daily and mighty communion I have held with my beloved ones has not sufficed to slake my thirst for them, nor all the lavishness of their love for me been enough to satisfy the demands of my exacting, jealous nature.*
>
> *I have had my passionate attachments among women, which swept like whirlwinds over me, sometimes, alas! Scorching me with a furnace blast, but generally only changing and renewing my capabilities for love.*

Some of this prolix letter may be posturing, but it indicates that Adah had lesbian experience and knew what she wanted. The tone throughout is impassioned. Adah had adopted a cold surface to deal with the press and public, but she promised to reveal her true self to Hattie. She admitted to being demanding, restless, jealous, but blamed her insatiable nature on an excess of vitality. She spoke of an ideal communion between two women that does not look platonic. She has propositioned Hattie, bold as brass.

Adah even assured Hattie that she kept her lesbian affairs secret: "They are unknown to all but the hearts concerned, and are jealously guarded by them from intrusive comment." This affair, however, failed to materialize. Adah's seductive invitation to Hattie was never answered.

In January, Adah again played at Albany. The first half of 1862 resembled the second half of 1861, and she again toured the Midwest, packed theaters, received rave reviews, and kept in touch with friends in New York, including Ed James and Robert Newell. Occasionally she tried on a more serious role. At Wood's Theater, Cincinnati, Adah played Pip in her own dramatization of Charles Dickens's *Great Expectations*. The *Daily Times* called her "the very embodiment of the author's ideal—a pure and innocent character." This pleased her, and she regarded it as a put-down of her ex-husband and the Menken clan.

Mazeppa aside, the light, fast pieces did best at the box office. Adah added impersonations to her repertoire, doing entr'acte send-ups of dramatic actors such as her friend Edwin Booth. In St. Louis she fought a duel of wits over the footlights with a fellow she called "a shrimp of some Volunteer Stay-at-Home Company," who along with his buddies tried to hiss her off the stage. She found out his name and incorporated it, making fun of his manhood, in her song "The Captain with His Whiskers." Adah was intent on becoming truly unequaled on the American stage.

In August 1862, Adah returned to Milwaukee. She wrote to Hattie from her hotel, reminding her of the unanswered letter of one year ago. This letter of August 29 is brief but unapologetic. "Your heart is my heart," Adah insisted, "your life in some time has been my life, your Love my Love."

Again, Adah's attempt to initiate contact failed. Yet her approaching Hattie was surely not unique. Among her female acquaintances we find several who have been identified by lesbian scholars as probable bed partners, including Ada Clare and Lotta Crabtree. However, there is no tangible evidence in these instances. Adah was willing to offer up husbands and lovers on the altar of publicity, but not her female lovers. "[S]ilence and mystery help to guard the sacred spot where we meet alone our best beloved," she assured Hattie. We don't know the extent of her same-sex love life.

<hr/>

In contrast, Adah's supposed affairs with "big men" were pounced on by the press to the point where some were undoubtedly fabricated. In July 1862 in Boston she and Artemus Ward supposedly became an item. They had been friends, but that was all, in the prewar days at Pfaff's. Adah was riding a crest of applause and curtain calls during a five-week engagement at the Howard Atheneum. For the Fourth of July in this bastion of patriotism she went all out by giving a matinee and evening performance of "THE MILITARY DRAMA OF THE FRENCH SPY!," as the broadside screamed in bold. She added a "Grand Broad Sword Combat" with her leading man. Then as now, scenes from an earlier conflict were popular during a time of actual war.

Adah performed a straight week of *Mazeppa* before she switched to other fare. For her benefit night she played nine parts in *Boys and Girls of Modern Times.* She sang, danced, and performed a solo incorporating both, which shows she hadn't forgotten her minstrel days. Menken's and Ward's role in this uncivil war, which killed and maimed more Americans than any other, was to inspire and divert the nervous populace. The front could be almost anywhere.

Artemus Ward, born Charles F. Browne in 1834 on a farm in Maine, had a special part to play in the conflict. He originally made his name writing for the *Cleveland Plain Dealer.* Coming to New York, he wrote humorous pieces for *Vanity Fair* and became the magazine's editor. He resigned once *Artemus Ward, His Book* began to sell prodigiously. The author was about to join the lecture circuit, where serious money was made.

In a letter dated July 18 to Gus Daly, Adah requested that he "contradict all reports of my marriage with Chas. F. Browne ('Artemus Ward')." She had seen the event itemized in the Boston press. "It won't do to be married," she insisted. "Charlie and I 'went it' pretty rapid for a few days here, but—"

The rest was left to Daly's imagination. Ward was a tall, gaunt New Englander, with a craggy nose, drooping mustache, and a mop of curly hair. He dressed simply in black broadcloth but with a gold chain showing. Under his solemn exterior he could be witty and charming. He called his performances a "moral lecture," but he poked fun at people who attended literary societies, where they hoped to become "improved." Ward suspected that secretly the public was sick of being improved. They wanted to laugh at both him and themselves.

Ward invented fanciful titles for his lectures, such as "The Babes in the Wood," and he would later use, or misuse, props, such as an elaborate map when he lectured on the Mormons. He even invented an Old Showman, who was supposed to be giving these moral lectures. Ward's biographer John Pullen describes his typical performance as a "stream-of-consciousness series of jokes and comments that had very little coherence." The comedian's material in print lacks his deadpan expression, the twinkle in his eye, and his perfect timing, yet it is fun to read. He was America's first nationally successful stand-up comic. Young Sam Clemens (not yet Mark Twain) learned a great deal from his drinking buddy, Charlie Browne.

How real was the romance between Adah and Artemus? Pullen believes Ward's heart was broken in Boston in the summer of 1862, when "he loved and lost Adah Isaacs Menken." He is convinced that Adah's letter to Daly "hinted strongly at an affair, a proposal, and a turn-down that may have been not entirely a rejection of Artemus but of the idea of marriage." Pullen feels that Ward was hurt by the out-come of the affair. He loved children, feeling that a bachelor was "a poor critter." Nonetheless, he and Adah would continue as friends for the rest of their lives.

The comical Ward, by deflating the pompous and trite, helped to change the tone of American thought and speech. But his finest hour happened in his absence and without his knowing. On September 17, 1862, the Union commander General McClellan turned back a strike by Robert E. Lee into the North. The Confederate commander had hoped to end the Civil War quickly. The battle of Antietam (Maryland) was the single bloodiest day of the war, and the Union troops fought with grim determination. On September 22 President Lincoln called a meeting of his Cabinet for a closely guarded purpose.

Lincoln began by reading aloud a chapter from *Artemus Ward, His Book*. It was about Ward's Old Showman appearing in "Utiky, a trooly grate sitty" with his usual medicine show of "beests and snaiks" and "wax figgers." How Lincoln delivered Ward's bizarre spelling is not recorded, but the grave gentlemen of the Cabinet grew restless. Secretary of War Stanton thought of walking out of the room. Lincoln wound up the story, which is about a Uticky local mistaking a wax figure of Judas Iscariot for the real thing and bashing in its head. The President remarked, "Gentlemen, with the fearful strain that is upon me night and day, if I did not laugh I should die, and you need this medicine as much as I do."

Lincoln then introduced to his Cabinet the Emancipation Proclamation, which began the process of freeing the slaves. No battle in the course of the long, bloody war would have the impact of this document. The Civil War was no longer being fought over a Constitutional issue, but the principle which underlies the Constitution—human freedom. The part of Artemus Ward in this colossal drama was to keep men and women *feeling* alive by diverting them from the carnage.

At the same time Lincoln was reading the Emancipation Proclamation to a hushed room at the White House, Adah Menken, onstage in New York, was putting her horse through its paces. She had gone through several mares, and she now trained them herself, so they were familiar with her from the start. She was in the midst of her most important engagement to date, at the New Bowery Theater. *Mazeppa* was sold out night after night, attention in the press was constant, and even the swells from Broadway were coming over to see the season's sensation.

The Bowery, with its German beer gardens, Irish pubs, and Jewish shopkeepers, was the central artery of the immigrant's New York. It was a respectable avenue along which families strolled or men sat outside, playing dominoes. It rang with the clatter of horse trolleys and the blare of brass instruments and sometimes a song by a maid off the boat from Tipperary. The New Bowery was its premier theater, and despite the name, was the oldest theater in town.

Here *Mazeppa*, mounted in a full-scale production, came into its own. Among the audience were numerous soldiers in uniform. As patrons took their seats, ushers handed them a card that read:

The Management wishes to announce that attacks on the patriotism of Miss Adah Isaacs Menken are without warrant. Miss Menken makes no secret of her birth in Louisiana, but proclaims no fealty to that misguided state. She is a loyal and trustworthy Citizen of the United States . . . and joins with other patriots in the devout wish that those states which have seceded will return to the fold of the Union.

To drive home the message, on the flip side of the card were stirring verses from "Pro Patria," signed by the author.

Once every last body was wedged in, the curtain rose, the orchestra thundered, a large cast of costumed actors went through their paces, and the special effects went off smoothly. Playing to packed houses, Adah exhibited what a playbill called "sublimely terrific feats of equestrianism" for two weeks in a row. After each act she was called before the curtain and overwhelmed with applause. She began to feel that she *was* the Tartar Prince, or his present incarnation.

Reviewers split into two camps. Typically, Gus Daly praised Adah to the skies, and William Winter at the *Tribune* did his best to ignore her. *The Clipper,* admittedly friendly, made a comment worthy of note:

She identifies herself with the part, and does everything in the most nonchalant manner possible, and with a peculiar fascination that carries the audience with her.

Mazeppa, which hostile critics labeled "Bowery melodrama," demanded of its protagonist a wide range of emotional states—from stealth to wrath to resignation to victory tempered by *noblesse oblige.* Adah, while running this gamut, kept the audience involved. But what really mattered was how she grabbed hold of them in the first place: stripped, bound, riding the wild stallion up a four-story mountain. This was an act harrowing yet erotic, suited to distract from the marching and dying going on outside. Any soldier on leave who could afford fifty cents for a balcony seat could forget the war and empathize with the man/woman Mazeppa.

Adah's androgyny attracted both men and women. When she dressed in a close-fitting man's uniform, such as in *The French Spy*, she appeared all the more a woman. She defied the Victorian code of lady-like behavior and was applauded for it. Adah's freedom of dress was matched by the liberties she took with her lines. As Wolf Mankowitz observed: "It was something new in the theater, very American, passionate, friendly, close to the footlights and directed straight at each individual citizen . . . with a display of sex and temperament which had never before been seen by audiences used to third-rate imitators of the stiff, formal, and painfully dignified European styles of performance."

After Adah's first stint at the New Bowery, she was undeniably a major American star. She made plans to take her act to England and wow the Old World. In a letter to Ed James, she wrote that she planned to make her debut at the Prince of Wales Theatre in Liverpool. However, Adah had not reckoned with the dangers of her manic schedule or her own frailty.

During the spring of 1862 she came down with a severe cold, it seemed. Suddenly she began to bleed from the lungs. Although Adah knew about her family history of consumption, as pulmonary tuberculosis was called, no one else did. Her sister's death in New Orleans on April 28 was an unexpected blow. "I am now indeed alone," she wrote. Attempts on her part to recuperate in the country were cut short by trips back to the city and declarations that she felt fine.

Adah did rest for two weeks before continuing to tour the Midwest. She covered up her symptoms when they appeared and attributed her periodic collapses to exhaustion. An admission that she was consumptive would have ended her career for no purpose. The disease was not understood and the accepted medical treatment wrongheaded. From this moment on, illness threatened Adah's life. Yet she had no intention of surrendering to it, any more than Prince Mazeppa would let himself be defeated.

Despite the fall she took when she first attempted *Mazeppa*, Adah accepted the risk of accidents with a similar *esprit*. In a letter that summer to Gus Daly she described a nasty spill that occurred while playing in Boston. In the second act, after being declared King of Tartary, Adah did a reprise of her run up the stage mountain. The "red fire," a stage effect, was inadvertently lighted under the horse, causing him to shy and tumble from the ramp to the stage, with Adah under his hooves. Pandemonium broke loose and spectators rushed onstage, but before anyone could reach her, Adah was up and seeing to her horse. To the audience's thunderous applause, she mounted and again dashed up the runs.

Adah took her curtain calls, but privately she informed Daly: "The fall was really terrible. Nothing daunts this intrepid and fearless girl." Over the next several years she would suffer various accidents, which led to fractured fingers, a concussion, and a torn ear. The audience watched for horse and rider to fall almost as keenly as they gazed at the lady's nakedness. An injury in Paris, which onlookers scarcely noticed, contributed to her early death.

Body and soul have their limits, and in Boston and New York, Adah exceeded hers. For a time there would be no talk of performing in London. Instead, she dealt herself a fourth hand at that most dangerous of parlor games: courtship and marriage.

Robert Henry Newell, now twenty-six, had conducted a stealthy wooing of Adah. A proper man, he could not speak of marriage until she was freed of her ties to John Heenan in April 1862. Newell has been described as shy, a humorist without coarseness, an affectionate man who loved flowers, little children and animals. While courting Adah that summer in New York he became famous. His book, *The Papers of Orpheus C. Kerr*, which satirized corruption in the nation's war-torn capital, was an overnight success. "The greatest hit of the day," Adah boasted. "It is immense." The diarist George Templeton Strong noted that Newell's satires were "very smart and fresh. These papers are the most brilliant literary product of the war as yet. Their humor is broad and distinctly American."

Today, Newell's satires seem stilted and offensive. With frequent use of an exaggerated brogue, they ridicule the Irish, a point of view shared by high-toned New Yorkers but fueled in Newell's case by his dislike of Heenan. This paragon of virtue had a mean streak. For Adah, he was there when she needed him: the editor who recognized her poetry's worth, the columnist who defended her in the *Sunday Mercury*, the man who stood by her through scandal and attempted suicide. Adah found him cultured, uplifting, one who wouldn't compete with her for center stage. But could she love him?

Newell, with a long, thin nose above a mustache that looked pasted on, was the opposite of John Heenan. This was to his advantage. Adah, in her lifelong seesawing from the aesthete to the hunk, was back on the sensitive side. Marrying the widely acclaimed Newell appeared to create another power combination. Only this time, she believed, she would have the last word. After being spurned by the champ, she enjoyed her new suitor's slavish infatuation. Later he would write: "Adah was a symbol of Desire Awakened to every man who set eyes on her. All who saw her wanted her immediately."

Robert and Adah were married in New York on September 24, 1862, in a quiet Protestant ceremony. They went at once to the Newell home in Jersey City, where he lived with his mother. They had already discussed the possibility of Adah's limiting, even quitting, her stage appearances, in order to focus on writing. Robert rightly felt she had the makings of a great poet. He believed that the theater created a low, coarse environment that detracted from her serious writing. This puritanical attitude toward the theater in America had mellowed by the mid-nineteenth century, but Robert was old-fashioned.

Worse, he was preachy. His poem "The Perfect Husband" shows an unhealthy condescension toward women. The seventh verse describes a husband who treats his wife as a ward rather than an equal:

And ever as a child,
When childish she, he chides her,
And ever as a man,
When she is strong, he guides her:
Through sunshine and through shade,
Through blessing and disaster,
In more than name, her Friend,
In less than name, her Master.

An obituary of Robert Newell, written early in the twentieth century, speculated that he represented to Adah the sort of life she deemed noble and from which she had fallen away. "He believed that he could reclaim and redeem her . . . She believed, but only for a brief while, that he could do so." The brief while lasted four days. On the last evening they quarreled and Adah threatened to leave. Robert locked her in a second-story room. Adah climbed out of the window and down to the street, walked to the ferry, and crossed to New York. A gossip columnist reported that Newell had demanded she give up her Bohemian friends, and she had refused. Adah, a woman of color, made her own emancipation statement.

An obvious but unmentioned problem existed between husband and wife. Robert probably came to the marriage a virgin. After he and Adah had finally separated (this marriage would have a second round), he had no further romantic entanglements over the course of a long life. A widowed sister-in-law kept house for him. From all that we know about Robert, he was unsuccessful as a lover. Perhaps, under Adah's tutelage, he might have made progress, but the pair had too many other issues between them. Robert admitted, "Love never yet blended incompatible natures in marriage."

Robert desired Adah but could not satisfy her. He wrote about her in several poems, his best. In "Leonore" she is the love goddess incarnate:

In the roses of her cheeks
My eager eyes could see

The banners of a regal pride,
That said: come worship me!

Foolishly, Robert insisted on trying to domesticate Adah and keeping her to himself. In the same poem he admits:

There was something in her smile
My heart could not define;
So superficial was its beam,
And yet so near divine.

In verse, he continued to pursue the mystery of the divine yet flawed goddess. Adah went on with her blazing career. She took *Mazeppa* first to Washington, then Baltimore, where war, not love, was made.

Chapter Twelve:

CIVIL WAR

Adah's fourth marriage, to man of letters Robert Newell, had failed more quickly than the others. All her intimate relationships seemed to founder and leave hard feelings in their wake. In her calmer moments, she blamed herself. In an undated letter from Baltimore to Ed James, Adah wrote:

> *With all my longings to find beauty and harmony in others, when found I am most miserable. When I see that some soul has responded to what mine is always seeking, I cannot help shrinking from it far back into the weeds and shadows of myself. Because I find there is nothing in me worthy of answering to beauty and harmony. This failing makes me dumb and cold when I should be all grace and gratitude.*

The letter, like most of her correspondence with James, is candid. This is the woman speaking, not the actress. Ed had assumed the role of her "good brother," all the more because his wife was suing him for divorce and he needed cheering up. She chided him when he apologized for being homely and overweight. Her generosity to those she liked, as well as her powers of introspection, are surprising for a woman who was constantly being admired.

Baltimore, where the star arrived in mid-November 1862, was largely a pro-Southern town. In 1861 while President-elect Abraham Lincoln was on his whistle-stop tour to Washington, railroad detective Allan Pinkerton heard of an assassination plot hatched in Baltimore. Later, Pinkerton would found the Secret Service, which is today charged with protecting the president. He persuaded Lincoln to sneak through the city in the middle of the night.

In April a Massachusetts regiment hurrying to defend the capitol was set on by an angry mob. Responding to flying bricks, some of the troops fired into the crowd. Mayhem ensued, and the soldiers were fortunate to board a train and escape with their lives. Horace Greeley in the *Tribune* demanded that Baltimore be burned to the ground. In May federal troops occupied the city and martial law was declared. Baltimore was governed by a federal provost marshal throughout the war. Adah witnessed soldiers on duty guarding the railroad, telegraph, and government buildings against a hostile citizenry. She could hear the distant sounds of artillery exchanging fire at the front.

The city was tense, and its inhabitants eagerly welcomed the diversion Adah provided at the Front Street Theater. Her comic roles and pants parts drew both men and women. It was Adah's genius that her lovesick sailor William in *Black-Eyed Susan* so affected the ladies that several, she claimed, "were removed from the theater in a fainting state." *Mazeppa*, however, proved the big hit of this engagement. On December 9, after two weeks of the horse drama, Adah informed James that business was still "*immense* . . . we must turn people away. . . . Such a run of a piece was never known in Baltimore."

Adah, playing for a percentage of the gate, was earning outsized sums of money. The amounts she made, the equivalent of a Hollywood star, need a large multiplier to make sense today. Her success helped to improve the way other actors were recompensed. Her popularity was indeed *immense,* and after her benefit performance, a group of leading citizens marched onstage and presented her with a diamond bracelet. "It was the greatest present ever got up in Baltimore," Adah wrote James.

To her friend and publicist, Adah has nonchalantly described an accomplishment that would lay the foundation of the modern theater: long-run engagements, advance sales, and a star who transcends the stage to appeal directly to the public. At a time when plays were changed nightly, *Mazeppa* filled the house for three and four weeks in a row. Because each performance was sold out, theatergoers broke the custom of buying tickets on the same day as the show. Producers could use the advance cash to invest in costumes, scenery, and machinery for special effects. Supporting players, who for ten dollars performed in six shows per week, could *hope* to be paid a living wage. American show *business* really began with *Mazeppa* in the depths of the Civil War.

The fighting ground on. Publicity played no part in Adah's entertaining the wounded in hospitals after the mid-December Battle of Fredericksburg. Hesitant but talented General McClellan had been replaced by mule-headed Burnside as commander of the Army of the Potomac. The general recklessly threw his men against Lee's entrenched Confederates, whose deadly fire brought down 12,000 federal troops on the last day of the battle. Federals, still pinned down after Burnside ordered retreat, piled up corpses as makeshift breastworks. Finally, the many wounded were carried back to Baltimore hospitals by rail.

Adah sang comic songs for the men and danced a sailor's hornpipe. She pulled out her old minstrel tricks. The men laughed and applauded, even those missing an arm or leg, or worse, but Adah was horrified by the carnage among young lives. She quietly donated her diamond bracelet to the cause to furnish the lads in hospital with a few comforts. However, the experience turned her decisively against the war and those who had perpetrated it.

Adah's friend from Pfaff's, Walt Whitman, reacted differently from a similar experience. The poet had remained in New York, writing marching songs and watching others enlist. But once he learned that his younger brother George was wounded at Fredericksburg, he headed south to care for him. On the train, Walt's pocket was picked before he landed, broke, in Washington. He would remain there for the duration of the war, a volunteer nurse at the hospitals. In his upbeat, caring way, he diverted and solaced the wounded men. Whitman became committed to preserving the Union through war. He drew inspiration even from defeat, and he would write the poetry—such as "O Captain! My Captain!"—that makes him our national bard.

In Baltimore Adah was not well. She admitted to suffering from what she called neuralgia, and now one eye had swelled shut. She felt weak, irritable, and depressed. She brought down the curtain on her engagement and holed up in her hotel suite, seeing no one. In New York Allston Brown was negotiating by wire with a California impresario, Thomas Maguire, to bring Adah to the Golden State. Although she warned James that she felt out of sorts, she asked him to inform the California papers about her great success. She added, "My health is not good enough to venture before the pleasant weather comes."

In the meantime, Adah herself negotiated a return engagement at the Front Street Theater. She was to receive a larger portion of the gate than any other American actor of the day. Among the demands she made of the Baltimore manager was that he redecorate her dressing room in Rebel gray. She added a Confederate flag and inserted along the edge of her mirror photos of Jefferson Davis, Robert E. Lee, and other Southern notables. The terrified manager warned that the federal provost marshal's police would arrest them both. But Adah insisted, and he agreed to play dumb, in return for which *Mazeppa* would run for the entire month of February, 1863.

Adah had switched from being a defender of the inviolate United States, who publicly called on "those states which have seceded [to] return to the fold of the Union," to a Rebel sympathizer. Her motive has been ascribed to a keen nose for publicity. Baltimore leaned toward the Confederacy, so why shouldn't she? This ignores the real conflict— a personal civil war—which Adah experienced between her Southern roots and her feelings as a woman of color. She balanced precariously over this inner schism, hiding it behind a show of bravura. Besides, to this transgressor of Victorian mores, the rebellious stance of the Confederates made a romantic appeal. A daughter of the South, she never entirely accustomed herself to the North.

Provost Marshal Fish, a colonel who came from a distinguished New York family, tried to overlook Adah's posturing until one of her regular callers was arrested as a spy. The man, a fellow actor, had been under surveillance for some time. Adah informed Ed James of the result:

> *On Monday I was arrested and brought before the Provost-Marshall for being a Secessionist. Of course I did not deny the charge; but I denied having aided the C.S.A. They wanted to send me to Dixie but would not permit me to take but one hundred pounds of luggage. Of course I could not see that. So after a great deal of talk they concluded if I would take the oath [of allegiance] to let me off. This I refused most decidedly. . . . I tell you, Ed, I gave them "particular fits."*

Adah's arrest presented a dilemma for Colonel Fish. Actors, moving from place to place, had special opportunities to receive and transmit intelligence. It was an actor, John Wilkes Booth, who recruited a ring of Confederate agents in Washington and Maryland in an attempt to kidnap President Lincoln. When that failed, the conspirators assassinated Lincoln. The question arises whether Adah knew Booth, and if the actor who called on her at the Front Street Theater, and aroused the suspicion of Colonel Fish, was part of his network.

Adah was well acquainted with the performing members of the Booth family, who during the winter months kept a house in Baltimore. John Wilkes, a nervously attractive bachelor and a ladies' man, was a successful and prominent actor, especially admired in his hometown. He didn't bother to hide his Confederate sympathies any more than Adah hid hers. That winter, between engagements in Boston and Philadelphia, Booth spent time in Baltimore, and he was surely aware of Adah and where she stood. After Abe Lincoln's 1860 Cooper Union speech in New York, Adah had predicted in the *Sunday Mercury* that, if elected president, he would not live out his term. We believe John Wilkes Booth did call on Adah, whose views were similar to his own. While there is no evidence that she knew of his plans, she may have crossed the hazy line between being a Southern sympathizer and an informant.

A number of women collected intelligence for North or South during the war. Once caught, they were rarely punished beyond a brief imprisonment. Women spies detained by Union authorities could be released on signing an oath of allegiance. Even if they refused, they were held long enough for their information to become irrelevant, then sent over to the enemy lines. No woman other than Mary Surratt, who was implicated in Lincoln's assassination, was hanged by either side. No gentleman—and an officer was expected to be one—cared to play jailer to a lady. In practice, the Victorian code of conduct trumped the War Department's "Rules of Land Warfare."

The derring-do of Adah's friend Belle Boyd is a case in point. When the war began she was eighteen, living in Martinsburg, West Virginia, on the border between North and South. Her intensely Confederate family ran a hotel where Union officers stayed and could be overheard talking. Belle, learning of a scheme to capture General Stonewall Jackson, risked her life to cross a battlefield to reach his staff. Her dress was riddled with bulletholes. She received a note of gratitude from the general himself.

Belle was a slender young woman, graceful if horse-faced. Known as the "Siren of the Shenandoah," she continued her spying ways far from home. Come discovery or capture, Belle could use her feminine charms. When taken prisoner on the high seas, she seduced the naval officer guarding her and made her escape. After the war Belle went onstage to give dramatic readings from her autobiography, *Belle Boyd in Camp and Prison*. In London and Paris she became warmly attached to Adah, who held a salon that welcomed Confederates in exile.

Adah, when arrested by the provost marshal, acted in a highhanded fashion. She realized that Colonel Fish was not likely to carry out his threats. Appearing to persecute a popular actress, one who had entertained the Union wounded, would put him in an unenviable position. Besides, she spoke no more favorably of the Confederate cause than several New York papers did daily. Colonel Fish slipped out of the noose he felt round his neck: Adah would report to him in thirty days. *If* she continued to parade her Confederate sentiments, she could choose between taking the oath and being sent south with minimum baggage.

Adah exited, smiling. She planned to leave town before then. In the meantime, she permitted word of her encounter with the Union authorities to leak out. Her romance with Baltimore burned still brighter. "It has done me a great deal of good," she informed James, "and helped me to knock Mr. and Mrs. Barney Williams 'higher than a kite.'" These were the first of a growing tribe of Adah Menken imitators, some of whom burlesqued *Mazeppa*. But they could not touch the original: "[T]here seems to be more excitement about the piece than ever," she assured Ed.

Adah now owned an impressive wardrobe, expensive jewelry, and the trained horse in her act. She was not yet living so extravagantly that she spent more than she earned. At the peak of her popularity, illness struck. In mid-February she caught what she claimed was a cold, due to stripping down to her sheer body stocking in a drafty theater night after night. Because of her weakened lungs, Adah became bedridden. She bled from the mouth and nose and suffered days of complete prostration. The symptoms are those of pulmonary tuberculosis, the scourge of early industrial society.

The run of *Mazeppa* was canceled. Adah, not yet twenty-eight, fought for her life and pulled through, though she was confined to her sickroom for a month. Then, thin and drawn, she left for the Jersey shore to recuperate. Adah always sensed that her sensational life would be a brief one.

⌐⌐

Josh Billings was a popular stand-up comic who influenced Artemus Ward and Mark Twain. He did a routine about Long Branch, New Jersey. In summer the town was a lively beach resort with a gambling casino and, as Billings put it, a crop of "young widders" hunting for husbands. "The biggest thing they hav got at Long branch," Billings wrote, "iz the pool ov water, in front ov the hotels. This pool iz 3,000 miles in length, and in sum places 5 miles thick. . . . The scenery here iz grand, especially the pool, and the air iz az bracing az a milk puntch." Here Adah took the cure prescribed by Victorian doctors for their tubercular patients—sea air and sea baths. Regularly at ten in the morning, wearing an ungainly wool dress, Adah would wade into the breakers. Very gradually she regained her strength. She remained at Long Branch until mid-June, but she stayed in close touch with the *Clipper* crowd and Gus Daly, who was supposed to be writing a play for her.

Adah returned to New York, staying at the St. Nicholas Hotel on Broadway, the city's finest. The newspapers relayed or invented rumors about her future. Wilkes's *Spirit of the Times* stated as fact that playwright Dion Boucicault, manager of Astley's Theatre Royal in London, had engaged Adah to open the redecorated house. Others gossiped about the state of her health, and, since she advertised her horse for sale, concluded that she had quit the stage. Actually, Allston Brown, with the help of Ed James, was finalizing negotiations with Tom Maguire, California's leading theatrical entrepreneur. He was eager to have Adah but balked at the price.

There is a story that comedian Artemus Ward received a wire from Maguire in San Francisco: "What will you take for forty nights in California?" Artemus wired back: "Brandy and water." Concerning Adah, Maguire finally capitulated. During a run of one hundred nights at his new Opera House, the Naked Lady would receive one-third of the nightly gate (box office receipts), and on Friday evenings and matinees, one-half the gate. Brown, before enlisting in the Union army, had won spectacular terms for his client. No actress, no singer—not even Jenny Lind, promoted by Barnum—had been rewarded so handsomely on the American stage.

Fittings for Adah's new wardrobe, both stage and personal, took up much of the next few weeks. There were affairs to be settled before she sailed. Then came the return of Robert Newell. Profuse with apologies, the offending husband begged to be reunited with his dearest wife. He swore he was a changed man. Could they not give their marriage a second chance? Despite reservations, Adah weighed her decision.

She knew the journey was dangerous, beginning with Confederate privateers off the East Coast. Once the steamer reached Panama, the trip across the Isthmus by narrow-gauge rail was through primitive country. Finally, the Gold Coast of California was man's country, where even a wimpy husband provided some protection against unwanted advances. Adah was impressed that Robert was willing, at the height of his literary success, to resign from the *Mercury* and place himself at her disposal. Beneath her captivating exterior she harbored intense self-doubt. Robert, on the contrary, appeared modest, yet his breeding made him inwardly confident.

Adah agreed early enough for Robert to reserve a stateroom in the name of "R. H. Newell and wife" on one of Commodore Vanderbilt's steamships, the SS *Northern Light*, sailing the afternoon of July 13. This turned out to be the first day of the infamous New York draft riots. The turmoil in the streets would have caused a less determined person to postpone her trip. Adah, however, was set on the glory and gold awaiting her in California. She had eight trunks of clothing and innumerable hatboxes packed and ready. She had hired a maid to accompany her, and never again would she do without servants.

The riots were caused by a series of wartime events. Lincoln's Emancipation Proclamation was followed on March 3, 1863, by the Act of Conscription, which provided for drafting men from eighteen to forty-five years old. By the time it was implemented in New York City, Lee had invaded Pennsylvania, the carnage of the Battle of Gettysburg was being reported in the papers, and Lincoln had called for an additional 300,000 soldiers. To the workingman, the war looked like a conspiracy to subdue the South, to pry loose its slave labor and drive down his wages. Blacks and Irish were already competing bitterly for jobs on the docks and in construction. The last straw was the act's exempting the monied class, who could buy out of the army for three hundred dollars, nearly a year's wages for a laborer.

On Sunday, July 12, the papers published the names of those drafted the day before. There were Confederate provocateurs in the city, who plied their trade among the angry taverngoers over the weekend. On Monday morning the "Black Joke" Fire Engine Company No. 33 headed a mob of thousands that marched on the federal provost marshal's headquarters on Third Avenue. They stormed and burned the building and its draft records. The mob swelled, and the provost marshal in Washington estimated its size at 30,000 strong. Furious men, many of them unemployed Irish laborers, roamed the streets, at times razing entire city blocks, cutting telegraph lines, tearing up railroad tracks, and causing factories and shops to close.

Provost Marshal Colonel James Fry noted in his report that the home regiments had been posted to Gettysburg, and "the military and the police force of the city on duty were overwhelmed and dispersed." The governor of New York, an anti-Lincoln Democrat, was on vacation in New Jersey, and the police chief and sheriff were pro-South almost to the point of treason. While politicians temporized, for three full days and nights drunken mobs terrorized the city, setting fire to entire blocks, looting the mansions of the rich, and beating, shooting, stomping, burning, and lynching any black persons they found. New York was under siege by a mob crazed by race hatred.

We don't know how much of the terror Adah and Newell experienced on the way to board their steamer. However, since Adah's hotel was on lower Broadway at Spring Street, she and Newell needed to travel across town to the docks now known as South Street Seaport. Their cab would not wish to cross the Bowery, where the mob was strongest. Headed straight down Broadway, the cab would need to swing east around tough Five Points, which crawled with rioters armed with pistols and homemade hand grenades. Their mood was as nasty as the bottles of sulfuric acid they carried to throw in policemen's faces.

Whichever route the cab took, the air was acrid with smoke from torched buildings, including the Colored Orphan Asylum (although the orphans were rescued). The *Tribune* building at Printing House Square was under attack because of the pro-Union sentiments of its publisher, Horace Greeley. On Cherry Street the rioters swarmed over Brooks

Brothers, parading its clothes on their backs. Illumined red from nearby blazing warehouses, corpses of black men dangled from lampposts. On each chest was pinned a sign that read WE'LL BE BACK FOR MORE TOMORROW! The only resistance came from a company of invalid soldiers, who fought bravely but were beaten back.

Adah left no record of her fright and anger at these sights, but she could not help feeling the anguish of the victims as she remembered her own past. Her party safely reached the steamship *Northern Light*, guarded by armed sailors. They boarded and the ship loosed its moorings and steamed out of the harbor. Once south of Chesapeake Bay, no lights were permitted in the evening because of privateers. It is assumed by previous biographers that during the uneventful voyage to Aspinwall (now Colón), Panama, Adah and Robert enjoyed an eight-day second honeymoon. Since the couple was not sexually compatible, we doubt that. After taking the railway across the tropical Isthmus to Panama City on the Pacific, the pair boarded the SS *Golden Gate*, bound for California.

Not until they reached San Francisco on August 13 would Adah and Robert hear the details of the draft riot, finally put down by federal troops returning from Gettysburg. In total about 120 persons were killed, many more injured, and property damage ran into the millions of dollars. Irish rioters had shot at and been shot by Irish policemen, the fires were fought by Irish firemen, and the returning New York regiments were filled with Irishmen. There is no accurate number of blacks killed, but it was mercifully low because most had fled or been given shelter by well-meaning citizens, including Catholic priests.

Adah reacted to the news as though one side of her had tried to murder the other. The madness of the events she witnessed mirrored the turmoil of her own soul. She lost some of her desire to succeed in New York, and her focus shifted to other capitals. She would have understood Herman Melville's comment on the riots: "The town is taken by its rats—ship rats and rats of the wharves."

CHAPTER THIRTEEN:

THE GREAT MENKEN

Handsome Tom Maguire was short but well made, with a piercing gaze and a flowing mustache. Usually wearing a top hat at a rakish angle, he was dubbed the "Napoleon of the Stage." The master of theatricals for California and Nevada, he stood on the dock on August 7, 1863, peering through a glass at the *Golden Gate* steaming past its namesake entrance into San Francisco Bay. Behind Tom gathered a committee of notables, the press, and a brass band of volunteer firemen. Farther back on the long pier massed a crowd of a dozen nationalities, eager for a glimpse of the notorious Naked Lady.

Maguire, the incredible impresario, was all decked out for the occasion. His kid boots gleamed to match a diamond stickpin, his diamond-ringed hand gripped a slim cane, and a Cuban cigar jutted from his jaw. Irish, from New York, Tom began life as one of Walt Whitman's "roughs." He drove a hack, ran a saloon, and did dirty work for Tammany Hall. In 1849, moving to San Francisco, he built a theater as an adjunct to a saloon that fronted for a gambling parlor. When each of Maguire's wooden theaters burned down, he built a new one—the Jenny Lind I, II, and III. Finally, the promoter constructed the large, plush Opera House on Washington Street, which also incorporated a saloon and casino, the Diana. In a good year, Diana paid her proprietor over one million dollars in profit, big money in those days.

Maguire demanded the best talent for his theaters. When he opened the Opera House in 1856, he booked the San Francisco Minstrels, who became a local institution. The next year, armed with an inexhaustible purse, he sailed east to New York in search of star performers. Maguire also developed an excellent stock company to play the latest dramas from Europe. He opened a playhouse in Sacramento, close to the gold fields, and another in Virginia City, Nevada, where the real wealth of the Gold Coast was mined from the depths of Sun Mountain. He remodeled the Opera House, adding ventilators and gas lighting and painting the ceiling with cupids and angels. As a local paper wrote, "The interior has been magnificently decorated, the dome and circles in the rich and gorgeous style of the reign of Louis XV."

Maguire was obliged to maintain a constant stream of stars flowing into his theaters. Opera singers, tragic actors, comedians, magicians, and animal acts were lured by the jingle of gold coin. Performers from Britain and the Continent risked weeks at sea to arrive at San Francisco. Their mission was to entertain a surprisingly sophisticated public, drawn from everywhere in America and the cities and palaces of Europe, not to mention the Orient. Maguire, the gambler, spent money the way Napoleon used armies in battle, but to date, his biggest bet had been placed on Adah Isaacs Menken.

The *Golden Gate* steamed past the barren island of Alcatraz, where Confederate agents were held. Sea lions lazed on its rocks. On deck, Adah could make out San Francisco: brick and stone buildings were gleaming new, while wooden shacks scrambled up hillsides with the heartiness of goats (which still roamed the distant hills). The harbor bustled with cargo skiffs scooting out of inlets and between sleek clipper ships and white Pacific steamers at anchor. San Francisco was midway between Europe and the Hawaiian Islands, Australia, and Asia—the focal point of a global economy. Its docks were lined with shipping that flew flags from all over the world. Its women wore the latest Parisian creations and its dirty laundry was shipped to China to be washed. In fifteen years the parvenu city had grown past 100,000 inhabitants, a size it took Boston two hundred years to attain. Adah, who thrived on the expansive, thought she might like it here.

Once the *Golden Gate* docked, the band broke into a march. Citizens fired their revolvers in the air. Adah, wearing a taffeta suit of yellow and black checks and a feathery creation perched on her black curls, descended the ramp with an appropriate sense of the moment. She was thrilled that no woman had caused so much commotion since the arrival a decade earlier of her idol, Lola Montez, the Countess Landsfeldt. Despite arriving with all the paraphernalia of romance, Lola had failed onstage and secluded herself in the gold country before sailing for Australia.

Adah's husband Robert Newell, overseeing a mountain of luggage, struggled after *The* Menken, as Adah had come to be known. He was confident about his reception among the literati of the Bay area. He knew that the leading weekly, the *Golden Era,* had run a notice of the arrival of a famous author and his actress wife, without mentioning her name. He did not guess that the *Era*'s contributors, Mark Twain and Bret Harte, were given to little jokes. Newell was hardly aware of the weekly's ancillary contributors, such as Joaquin Miller, Charles Warren Stoddard, and poet/librarian Ina Coolbrith, who would make their own marks on American literature. The notion that on this far-off shore the literary life of the nation was taking a definite shape would have struck the New York author as absurd.

Tom Maguire took charge. Shepherding Adah and her entourage into a carriage, he escorted them to Russ House, where he had reserved a suite. It was San Francisco's finest hotel and one of the few buildings west of Chicago that could boast of an elevator. On the way Maguire told Adah of how he had assembled the finest dramatic corps ever known in San Francisco. He promised that the special effects for *Mazeppa* would be something new, the scenery startling, the costumes gorgeous. Nor had he spared any expense in advertising The Menken. She was amazed to see a poster of herself in the window of nearly every shop on Montgomery Street. Top-hatted swells from the stock exchange jostled elbows with miners, ranchers, Mexicans, and Chinese to stare at *her* portrait.

Among the gawkers was a young writer named Charles Warren Stoddard. Forty years later, he well remembered Menken's "head of

Byronic mold; a fair, proud throat, quite open to admiration . . . The hair, black, glossy, short and curly, gave to the head, forehead and nape of the neck a half-feminine masculinity suggestive of the Apollo Belvedere." In person, Adah's eyes would transfix Charles. He described them as "not wholly human . . . intoxicated eyes." This is the gaze of the self-absorbed goddess, stage or screen, which only appears to look outward.

Of Menken, her admirer continued:

Garments seemed almost to profane her, as they do a statue. She was statuesque in the noblest sense of the word. . . . The moment she entered upon the scene she inspired it with a poetic atmosphere that appealed to one's love of beauty, and satisfied it. . . . She possessed the lithe sinuosity of body that fascinates us in the panther and the leopard when in motion. Every curve of her limbs was as appealing as a line in a Persian love song. She was . . . a living and breathing poem that set the heart to music and throbbed rhythmically to a passion that was as splendid as it was pure.

Charles Warren Stoddard was born in Rochester, New York, of Puritan stock that included the reverend Jonathan Edwards. The family moved to San Francisco in 1855. Charles was sent east for schooling, under the supervision of his evangelical grandparents, who tormented him with the fear of going to hell. By the time he returned to the Bay area, he was a nervous wreck whose main interest was writing poetry. Signing his verse "Pip Pepperpod," he submitted it to the *Golden Era* and was thrilled when they printed it. He was a clean-shaven, fine-featured, sensitive young man, who would solve his religious quandary by converting to Catholicism. His sexual identity caused more of a problem.

Stoddard is the first identifiably gay American writer. Of course, he was not the first to *be* gay; nor should we overlook Walt Whitman's homoerotic poetry, which came as a revelation to the younger man. But Whitman's verse was often mistaken as heterosexually pornographic by the moralists of his day. In contrast, the sensibility of Stoddard's travel writing, whether about the South Seas or Near East, or his confessional autobiography, stems from a special outlook. Charles was a lover of men who in print remained discreet but unmistakable. Under a thin veneer of conformity, he signaled his gay identity and its emotional cost. In life, he openly adopted a series of young lovers and left no doubt about his sexual preference in the minds of his fellow writers and friends, ranging from Mark Twain to Ambrose Bierce.

In later years, Stoddard calmly remarked to young Jack London, Ina Coolbrith's protégé: "I am what I was when I was born." But as a youth of twenty when The Menken hit San Francisco, Charles was nearly prostrate with doubt. Compared in looks to Shelley, he was attracted to Adah's courage, her ability to fall upon, but surmount, the thorns of life. From Walt Whitman on, Adah formed friendships with talented gay men. Stoddard cherished knowing her, and they would continue to correspond after she left California. Her example prompted him to travel and write, and in the process he became a defender of the so-called savage (colored) peoples, a collector of curios who employed a French cook, and an outstanding American character.

In a little over two weeks before opening night, Adah had to train a full-blooded California mustang and rehearse with a diverse supporting cast. Yet shrewd Maguire encouraged her to see the town, especially on horseback. Adah in the flesh was his best possible advertisement. A biographer of Maguire remarks, "Men lined the streets to catch sight of her, and women were irked with curiosity and disdain as the male sex emulated the Menken's spit curls!" The promoter floated the rumor she would abandon her pink tights and appear on stage in "the little end of a dimity nothing fastened at the waist." This turned popular enthusiasm into mass hysteria. Maguire was able to make a nice advance sale, charging an additional fifty cents to reserve a seat.

Adah explored the mother of boomtowns. Each year fifty million dollars' worth of gold from the California and Nevada mines flowed into San Francisco's assay offices. The specie soon found its way into the pockets of saloonkeepers, gamblers, and stock speculators. But there was plenty left to ship east to support the Union forces, and the local economy knew no bounds. The city boasted of numerous four- and five-story buildings, with more going up by the week. At its core was the grid of streets downtown—between today's Market and Battery—lined with fashionable shops and elegant buildings but still poorly paved. In the gullies beyond lived squatters, while millionaires' mansions strutted across the hilltops. Newly rich wives sprinkled gold flakes in their hair as casually as they applied face powder.

The Barbary Coast, centered on Pacific (called "Terrific") Street, was a raucous district of saloons, gambling dens, and whorehouses. In a town that counted five men to each woman, the houses did a brisk business. So did the theaters located around Portsmouth Square, today's Chinatown. Melodeons, which featured waiter girls and burlesque shows, were popular, but only the Metropolitan and American theaters offered competition to the Opera House, and Maguire owned an interest in both. The liberated atmosphere of San Francisco made it fertile territory for entertainers, charlatans, Bohemians, and a lively press. Newcomers with a shadowy past were considered intriguing rather than dangerous. Westerners had little use for enforced standards of behavior.

Adah instinctively responded to the city's "go for broke" spirit. At the Opera House, however, she met determined resistence. Maguire had assembled too professional a company. The seasoned actors, led by Junius Brutus Booth, looked on *Mazeppa* as a circus play. June Booth, as he was known, was the eldest of three acting brothers, Edwin and John Wilkes being the younger two. He was a fixture on the West Coast stage, who became chagrined at the attention and salary Adah was getting. Assigned to play the villain, Booth felt that *Mazeppa* was too old a chestnut. Day after day he predicted failure and disgrace.

Watching from the wings as Adah struggled with her mustang and a mean set of actors stood tall, blond, long-haired Joaquin Miller, the original Cowboy Poet. Born Cincinnatus Hinus Miller in Indiana in 1839, his family had settled in Oregon in 1852. The lad ran away from home, cooked for the miners, lived with the Modoc Indians, fought alongside their braves, and, in a native ceremony, married one of their women. Miller adopted the Modoc custom of stealing horses from the whites, got caught, broke jail, studied law, became a Pony Express rider, and then edited a newspaper in Eugene that supported the Confederacy. Along the way he adopted Joaquin as a given name, in honor of the bandit Joaquin Murieta, the Robin Hood of California. After Minnie Dyer wrote to him praising his poetry, they married, and he called her Minnie Myrtle. Joaquin's politics were so unpopular that to avoid being lynched, he and Minnie left for San Francisco, where he proposed to support them by his writing. Let him continue:

> *I had a friend, Pres Dean, who was then bringing out Lotta [Crabtree] at a little place called Gilbert's Melodeon, on Portsmouth Square, and as I was with him much and doing some small newspaper work only, I was enabled to be behind the scenes at most theaters. . . .*
>
> *On one occasion [during a rehearsal of* Mazeppa*] the man who was hacking swords with Booth let his iron slip from his hand, and it went whirling past Booth's head. Then Booth threw down his big broad knife, and rushing up and down the stage, simply roared. He disappeared then, vowing he would never, never return, and Menken after him; and I holding the horse which some fool "super," in the excitement, had turned loose to roam about and browse or burn his nose on the footlights.*

Adah returned with a more docile Booth and noticed handsome Joaquin, who had performed a similar miracle with her horse. She and this rough-and-ready character bonded at once. The next two weeks were tense. While the cast slowly thawed toward Adah, she was the object of all eyes in public. Newell, who found San Francisco vulgar, especially hated the crowds that gathered at the hotel and theater entrances, hoping for a glimpse of his wife. There was a saying that New York dressed better than Paris, and San Francisco better than New York. But no other woman dressed like Adah, who had tailored for her a Chinese-inspired sheath. Thirty years later Joaquin vividly recalled that "all her talk, dress, action, was vivid with color. Who of those days does not remember that graceful, yellow figure on the streets of San Francisco—[in] a single garment of yellow silk?"

Yellow was Adah's color in California. To ten-year-old David Belasco, the future author of *The Girl of the Golden West* (the play that became a Puccini opera and a Jeanette MacDonald movie), Adah seemed a vision in gold. Belasco was destined to become the top producer on Broadway, reigning for decades, but as a lad he ran errands for Tom Maguire. He could see that Adah, like the others, developed jitters as opening night came near. Only Tom Maguire remained unruffled. Once, a man with a grudge shot him in public, but Maguire simply turned and walked away.

Adah, in a dramatic shift of mood, took Joaquin on a ride to Seal Rocks shortly before the opening of *Mazeppa*, scheduled for August 24. "The road [present day Geary Boulevard] was all sand then," recalled Joaquin. They approached a little mountain of sand in the road: "Our horses plunged in and wallowed belly deep, and she shouted with wild delight: 'I was born in that yellow sand once, sometime and somewhere, in the deserts of Africa.'"

Again Adah had dropped a strong hint of her measure of African blood. She also sounded a Spiritualist note about the indestructibility of the soul. Here in California, she grew more sure of her spiritual nature. Freed of puritanical constraints, she was able to let loose both her worldy and otherworldly sides. As Joaquin remarked, Adah played at being the bad woman, but "with her soul and her soul's friends she was very much another woman."

Adah continued to talk rapidly as they rode on, about the "lion-color, the old-gold color . . . the light, the life in the moving moun-tains of sand about us." Joaquin was astonished: "It was my first lesson in color." The man who would become godfather to today's thriving genre of cowboy poetry claimed that he originally owed his ability as a colorist to Adah. His best known poem is "California's Cup of Gold," a tribute to the golden poppy.

The riders passed under Cliff House (still standing today). To Joaquin, Adah seemed happy until they got down to the Great Beach, opposite the rocks. Then she threw herself from her horse, "fell with her face almost in the ocean and sobbed and cried as if her heart were broken." Gaining control, she got to her feet, smiled through the tears, and told him: "I had to do it. They are killing me at that old playhouse, and I had to come out here and cry or die."

Adah was not speaking metaphorically. Long hours at rehearsals and the pressure of being a star, both on- and offstage, were undermining her fragile health. She turned to Joaquin and told him of a vision that haunted her. She was lying alone in a shabby room, and "my dog slips off my bed and slinks away. Dogs smell death." Adah saw Death beckoning in the wings and knew she was rushing into his arms. But she was driven to accomplish what frightened others, and she seldom complained. After she had tossed her handkerchief to the ocean and bid good-bye to the "grey old grandfather," the pair rode back to town.

For a time, Joaquin and Minnie Myrtle lived in a garret, making do on scraps. Once Joaquin learned that the *Golden Era* could not pay its contributors (other than Mark Twain and Bret Harte, who received ten dollars per article), the couple decided to return to Oregon. But not before Joaquin had attended to Adah's horse on opening night. By the early evening of August 24, Washington Street and the surrounding blocks were thronged with theatergoers pushing their way into the Opera House, eager to get a seat or a place to stand. Women—ladies—were plentiful in attendance. The *Daily Alta* declared this to be the largest audience ever gathered in San Francisco. Speculation on what Adah would wear, or perhaps not wear, had turned into widespread wagering.

Notables in richly gilded boxes included General John C. Frémont and his politically connected wife, Jessie; banker William C. Ralston; and Democratic senator William Gwin, who fronted for the Copperhead crowd. An orchestral flourish announced the curtain's rise, and the audience whispered furiously. Menken—the disguised Prince Mazeppa—came on clothed as a humble page. Her Cassimir courted beautiful Olinska on her balcony, as Romeo had Juliet. Then a military procession arrived, sent by villainous Count Premislaus to claim the fair one as his bride. The tourney was fought in the grand arena, after which Mazeppa defeated Premislaus in hand-to-hand combat. The Prince, surrounded by Polish soldiers, was stripped—and, it was hinted, violated—and the fiery, untamed steed was led onstage. As beacon fires flared across the panorama of mountains, the audience held its collective breath.

Adah's body appeared so nearly nude that the crowd gasped. They murmured as cords were knotted around her loins and she was bound to the steed's back. To a roll of drums the horse reared, then galloped up the mountain trail past jagged rocks, across a perilous bridge over a roaring stream, and finally lost in the shadowy heights behind the proscenium, four stories above the stage. It happened so quickly there was no agreement on what Adah wore. Some called her brief costume a Greek chiton (tunic), others a chemise, and Mark Twain would obliquely refer to it as a diaper. Those in the boxes swore Adah's pink tights had been left in the dressing room.

Regardless, the audience was on its feet, clapping, stamping, cheering, here and there a woman weeping. The star appeared in front of the curtain to receive a standing ovation. She received a similar reception after the second act, which concluded with Adah, mounted on the steed she had tamed, leading a Cossack army sworn to rescue Olinska from the clutches of Premislaus. Between the acts women socialized and men drank and gambled at Maguire's saloon. This evening all the talk was of Adah's beauty and grace. At the drama's conclusion, after Mazeppa and Olinska headed a grand and imposing tableau, the star was called out again and again. Bouquets of flowers and gold watches were tossed onstage.

Over the next few days the reviewers, those who didn't wax moralistic, echoed the judgment of the audience.

The *Daily Alta* claimed to be pleasantly surprised:

She showed herself more of an accomplished actress than we had been led to believe from the sensational notices which have beset her career. Aside from her personal attractions, which are great, she is quite an actress—calm, considerate, careful and judicious—of the modern natural school: one whom we judge would shine as a dashing comedienne more than a tragedian. She reads well, has a fine voice, is fully self-possessed. . . . She is all grace—a model for the sculptor and painter, every action being the "poetry of motion."

The *Golden Era* was equally positive, dwelling on "Menken's superlative athleticism and equestrian skill," subjects that Eastern papers had neglected. To a modern reader the most interesting review is one by a young, smart-aleck correspondent sent by the Virginia City, Nevada, *Territorial Enterprise:*

The Menken—Written Especially for Gentlemen

When I arrived in San Francisco, I found there was no one in town—at least there was no body in town but "the Menken"—or rather, no one was being talked about except that manly young female. I went to see her play "Mazeppa" of course. . . . She appeared to me to have but one garment on—a thin tight white linen one, of unimportant dimensions; I forget the name of the article, but it is indispensable to infants of a tender age. . . . With the exception of this superfluous rag, the Menken dresses like the Greek Slave [a nude statue]; but some of her postures are not so modest as the suggestive attitude of the latter.

Here every tongue sings the praises of her matchless grace, her supple gestures, her charming attitudes. Well, possibly those tongues are right. In the first act, she rushed on the stage, and goes cavorting around after Olinska; she bends herself back like a bow; she pitches head foremost at the atmosphere like a battering ram; she works her arms, and her legs, and her whole body like a dancing jack; her every movement is quick as thought; in a word . . . she carries on like a lunatic from the beginning of the act to the end of it.

Although the piece is signed "Mark Twain"—an early use of the pen name—it resonates as the voice of Sam Clemens, novice reporter for the Nevada paper. Mark Twain would become a great writer, but Sam stayed wet behind the ears. His job was not so much to report facts or opinions but to amuse the hard-bitten readers of the *Enterprise*. San Francisco was maturing, and its entertainments ranged from the Italian opera at Maguire's to the strip joints of the Barbary Coast. Virginia City, or Washoe, as the locals called the region, remained a raw, lawless, mining town. Sam succeeded on the *Enterprise* because he could pull off a hoax or ridicule a target. However, notes one of his many biographers, "He could not stand to be on the receiving end of a practical joke." When Sam's insulting tone toward the volunteer women of the Sanitary Commission (the Civil War's Red Cross) caused him to be involved in a duel with a rival editor, he skipped town, much as he had skedaddled from the Confederate militia in Missouri.

Sam had begun to regularly sign his work "Mark Twain," after a measure of soundings taken by Mississippi River boatmen. Born six months after Adah Isaacs Menken in 1835, the year of Halley's Comet, he came of age in Hannibal, Missouri. Although he lacked formal education, Sam's stint as a pilot on the Mississippi River taught him something about life. He arrived by overland stage in Nevada Territory in August 1861, a hard-drinking carouser given to taking the long shot. Like most, he hoped to strike it rich by finding gold. Sam was imbued with the prejudices typical of the frontier: He looked down on blacks, mistrusted Jews, and loathed American Indians. Mark Twain would become not only a better writer than Sam Clemens dreamed of, but a finer human being, a dedicated fighter against injustice, colonialism, and racism. He would so improve his mind that he became a significant social philosopher.

In regard to sex, Sam seems never to have reached a sophisticated maturity. Even his uncensored writings as an older man are scatological—toilet humor. In reviewing Adah's *Mazeppa*, he stressed her androgynous appearance and actions; for example, he compared her to an obviously phallic battering ram. Sam, a good-looking fellow with a fine head of curly, red hair, lived in an environment where men were intimate but that contained few women. He received and felt homoerotic attractions. Andrew Hoffman, in his recent *Inventing Mark Twain*, writes, "Though most western men appear to have visited female prostitutes, they also typically lived in male pairs, sharing resources and beds . . . [which] were often understood as metaphorical marriages." Sam roomed with another man on two occasions and both times caused barroom snickers about the nature of their relationship.

Witnessing a woman who projected a cross-gender sexuality—who blatantly exhibited "the bare Menkenian thigh"—disturbed Sam. Her muscular calves made him nervous. In Virginia City, when he finally got close to Adah, she would frighten him. His review for the *Enterprise* is headed "especially for gentlemen," a backhanded slap at the large number of women who attended the show. To Sam, women were either angels or devils, and after meeting Adah he redoubled his search to find an angel to marry. Once he did find her, the couple slept in a bed with wooden angels adorning the posts.

The cub reporter, who valued success, soon modified his views on Menken's act. "*Mazeppa* proved a great card for Maguire here," he informed his Nevada readers. "He put it on the boards in first-class style, and crowded houses went crazy over it every night it was played." Maguire estimated that in the first two and a half weeks *Mazeppa* drew thirty thousand spectators, over one-quarter of the population of San Francisco. Before Menken left for the East in 1864, at least one of her roles would be seen by nearly every town dweller, farmer, and miner in the Northern California/Nevada region.

Tongue in cheek, a journalist quipped, "Livery stable horses could no longer be persuaded to carry ordinary burdens and refused to be mounted by any person wearing clothes." The Naked Lady caused what has been described as "the frenzy of 'Frisco." This went beyond the wildest dreams of other performers. Menken's success—and it was hers personally—points toward a new era in show business. It was on the Gold Coast of California, crowded by wealth seekers from all over the world, that this Jewish woman of color became the first superstar. The warrior prince, careening "naked" up the mountain in *Mazeppa*, arrived at the apex of the entertainment world.

Ironically, the punster in Sam Clemens captured Adah's astral phenomenon. For a San Francisco weekly, he penned a piece entitled, "A Full and Reliable Account of the Extraordinary Meteoric Shower of Last Saturday Night":

> *About this time a magnificent spectacle dazzled my vision—the whole constellation of the Great Menken came flaming out of the heavens like a vast spray of gas-jets, and shed a glory abroad over the universe as it fell! I have used the term "Great Menken" because I regard it as a more modest expression than the Great Bare, and consequently better suited to the columns of The Californian, which goes among families.*

Punning was another bad habit that Sam, in becoming Mark Twain, largely abandoned.

Sam caught *Mazeppa* at the end of the drama's run. Although Adah had opened at Maguire's for an engagement of sixty nights, the bill was changed after only sixteen performances. The horse opera proved too strenuous for its star to perform without a respite. For the next sixteen nights Adah played in *The French Spy* and *Black-Eyed Susan*. The main character in the former piece was an Arab boy, and in the latter, William, a lovesick sailor. Charles Stoddard considered William "a wonder; of course there never was anything like it on ship or shore. . . . A sailor boy so dainty and delightful as this sweet William would have been devoured by the sweethearts in any port, or even petted to death by the crustacea on a desert island."

Adah's cross-sexual appeal delighted both men and women, straight and gay. Reviewers, in discussing the propriety of the shows, noted that many respectable women attended. A modern-day scholar might ask: "Did they mean to hint at homoerotic curiosity on the part of the female viewers?" Certainly the audience, which watched a swashbuckling actress in male drag make love to a passive woman, got its kicks. The Opera House continued to sell out each night. The exception was Yom Kippur, the Jewish Day of Atonement, when the house went dark and Adah attended services at the community's synagogue. This brief rest was hardly enough. By late September Maguire's star was again felled by so-called neuralgia, and he posted closing notices. Adah would be unable to perform for nearly two months.

That she concealed the true nature of her illness from the public is not surprising. The younger Dumas's fictional Camille did the same, and so does Satine the courtesan, played by Nicole Kidman in the film *Moulin Rouge*. A woman who lives by inciting desire cannot afford to appear incurably ill. Pulmonary tuberculosis, from which Adah suffered, was the nineteenth-century equivalent of AIDS, especially in the denial with which it was treated. Adah, still young and strong, recuperated, and the illness went into remission. With time to spare, she wrote some of the best verse of her life, a sufficient achievement to rank her among the serious American poets.

Adah's poems were published in the *Golden Era*, along with reprints of earlier verse, from September 1863 through January 1864. "Aspiration" is rhymed and regular in rhythm. It comments ironically on a soul that "fixes its high hopes / In the dim distance, on a throne of clouds." The poem concludes that such ambition is illusory: "a spark *thou* art, and dost but see / Thine own reflection in Eternity." Here Adah has transcended the Victorian view of the human soul as being rock-solid, like one of their houses, to view the totality of her life as an electrical moment in universal time. This is no mere echo of Whitman but an instance of her own spiritual belief.

"Resurgam," which is prose-like on the order of Whitman, harks back to an earlier phase in New York. The verse is angry, accusatory, and harps on the theme that John Heenan, by betraying their love, has killed her. Menken insists that she is *already* dead; her strange, strangled imagery was written by a woman struggling to breathe. The poem contains striking moments, as when the poet claims she:

> *Died this uncoffined and unburied Death*
> *Died alone in the young May night*
> *Died with my fingers grasping the white throat of many a prayer.*

A third poem, "Infelix," the Unlucky One, could be Adah's theme song. Regular in cadence and rhyme, when read aloud it can move a modern audience. Again she sounds the theme of failure and renunciation. She declares her life "vain / A desert devoid of peace." The lament concludes:

> *I stand a wreck on Error's shore*
> *A spectre not within the door*
> *A houseless shadow evermore*
> *An exile lingering here.*

It is incongruous that the *Era* published this dirge on January 3, 1864. Adah had recovered her health and resumed a schedule no modern actor would undertake. She had traveled by riverboat to Sacramento, played at Maguire's Metropolitan Theater, and returned to open another horse drama at the Opera House. In Sacramento she was a hit, packing the house for fifteen nights. "Prudery is obsolete," declared the *Sacramento Union* in honor of the Naked Lady. Menken was "an exhibition," wrote its reviewer, "a voluptuous experiment on American taste for amusement. And it pays." However, although Adah had become the highest paid performer in the land, money meant nothing to her. She gave it away or spent it. At times she agreed with her husband Robert, who sulked in the shadows, that the theater was a crass environment, ruining the talent of a serious poet.

In 1863 San Francisco contained 41 churches, 105 schools, 12 daily papers, and 231 saloons. Among these means to enlightenment it is the weekly *Golden Era* that still matters to us. Its attendant literary set called themselves Bohemians, after the crowd at Pfaff's in New York, but they hung out at the plushest offices west of the Mississippi. The *Era*, run by "Colonel" Joe Lawrence, a genial gentleman from Long Island, was a strange potpourri of agricultural and mining intelligence, baked bean recipes, and literary content that ranged from theater reviews to gossip, stories, and poetry. Despite paying its contributors next to nothing, the *Era* attracted such writers as Mark Twain, Bret Harte, Stoddard, Miller, and Charles Henry Webb, who would found the rival *Californian*. Webb was a worse punster than the young Twain, calling Adah "a thing of beauty and a boy forever."

The *Era* was located in the Occidental Hotel on Montgomery Street. Rustic Joaquin Miller called the weekly's offices "the most gaudily carpeted and most gorgeously furnished that I had then seen." However, it was at the hotel bar, where cocktails such as the Blue Blazer and Tom and Jerry were invented, that Lawrence entertained literary visitors to town. Here he painlessly inveigled contributions from the likes of landscape painter Albert Bierstadt, Sir Richard Burton, Artemus Ward, Adah Menken, and Ada Clare. *San Francisco's Literary Frontier* is an aptly named study that claims the *Golden Era* of the 1860s combined "European intellectualism and Pacific Coast empiricism . . . to create one of history's most exciting intellectual atmospheres." The *Era* continued to "penetrate the wilderness as persistently as canned oysters."

Adah bonded with the *Era* set as easily as she had with their brethren at Pfaff's. A notable exception to those who adored her was Bret Harte. An Easterner of twenty-seven, Harte was married and a father, the recipient of a sinecure at the United States Mint. His book learning, combined with his serious attitude and great care in dressing, permitted him to act as elder statesman to the likes of Stoddard, Clemens, and the rest of the crowd. He was apparently immune to Adah's fascinations, physical and literary.

Harte took his cues from the New York scene, and he was eager to publish in Robert Newell's *Sunday Mercury*. Yet even he could not coax the man out of his shell. Newell was both appalled and fascinated by the praise showered on his wife. He realized that his love for Adah could not compete with the adulation she received from sycophants and moochers. He fought against what he saw as Adah's degradation into Queen of the Night. He reasoned with her, scolded, forbade, but all to no avail.

Harte and Newell both wrote about this phase in Adah's life. Harte, the shrewd professional, would feature her in one of his least successful novels. Newell, a man of limited talent, would write a stunning poem about losing his wife, his best literary effort. Meanwhile, Adah carried on entertaining a hard working, drinking, and gambling town. By Christmas Eve she was back at Maguire's Opera House, and on New Year's Eve she introduced a new horse opera, *Rookwood*, that she had adapted to her needs. Although less demanding than *Mazeppa*, it featured a strip scene and a run on horseback up a stage mountain.

This time Adah's California mustang slipped and fell to the stage. She was not badly hurt, but the horse had to be taken out and shot. Adah limped through the rest of the show, to the great appreciation of the audience. Again Maguire staged Adah's quick-change pieces while she trained a new horse, Sweepstake. "It has taken most of my time," she informed Ed James by letter. "But now I am happy to say that he is brilliant and talented. My health is excellent. I am now playing *Mazeppa* to crowded houses. My *Rookwood* ran 12 nights."

Adah entirely commanded the attention of a civilization as glamorous as her own life. Showered with gifts and praise, she blazed like a comet across the night sky of the Gold Coast. But, only human, she was headed for a different sort of tumble: "from the high altar of Passion."

Chapter Fourteen:

GOLD EAGLE GUY

Much of downtown San Francisco is built on fill. The practice began during the Gold Rush, when sailors jumped ship to go prospecting. Absent a crew, owners sunk the hulls to add to the growing shoreline. Other deserted ships were beached and converted into hotels, saloons, and dance halls to help alleviate the building shortage. In November 1934 New York's Group Theater performed a commissioned play: *Gold Eagle Guy*, set in just such a ship converted to a saloon. The central character is Adah Isaacs Menken, or at least a conception of Menken by the author, Melvin Levy. She was played by none other than Stella Adler, whose school of acting thrives today.

Despite an excellent cast that introduced young John Garfield, *Gold Eagle Guy* flopped. But guided by directors such as Elia Kazan and Lee Strasberg, and with an emphasis on psychological posturing, the Group's influence on American theater and films has been profound. What does the title *Gold Eagle Guy* mean, especially in relation to Adah? During the flush times, those who had struck it rich scorned paper money or small coins. They paid bills or gambled with gold eagles, a coin worth ten dollars (today's value is far more). A sport in evening dress, who liked to jingle the coins in his pockets, was called a "gold eagle guy." Why the tag stuck to Menken will become obvious.

> *Pearls are asleep in the waves of her hair,*
> *Gems on her bosom are dreaming;*
> *And from the smouldering worlds of her eyes*
> *Glories of ruin are gleaming—*

Glories that glow from the ashes of hearts,
With a smile over them beaming!

Thus Robert Newell described his wife in a poem for which he deserves to be remembered, "Aspasia." The classical beauty he references was a *hetaira* (courtesan) of the Golden Age of Athens who became devoted to Pericles, the great statesman. Aspasia was brilliant, well educated, and the center of a salon attended by the notables of Athens, including Socrates. Pericles divorced his wife to live with her, which was a major sex scandal at the time and caused him much trouble in the Senate. Newell's comparison of Adah to Aspasia is highly flattering, though he presents her as a *hetaira* manqué:

This is her Court in the Kingdom of Night,
Princes are bending before her;
Nobles and warriors wall her around,
Ready to serve and adore her;
Even the sage breathes the incense of love
Cast by her majesty o'er her.

Newell sees himself as the sage, blinded like other men by the light of this shining star. He can't help loving her, though it will lead to his ruin. His picture of his wife as a *femme fatale* seems exaggerated until we recall that it corresponds with Alex Menken's view. These two were the sensitive type, men Adah married *entr'acte*—in between her more-masculine lovers. If she did not entirely ruin them both, she inflicted considerable damage.

From the moment they docked at San Francisco, relations between Adah and Robert steadily deteriorated. He continued to regard himself as her teacher—indeed, her savior. In its 1901 obituary of Newell, the *Brooklyn Daily Eagle* wrote of Adah: "Hers was an experience of unregulated friendships and attachments, which contained in them excitement, variety, stimulation, tragedy. . . . [U]nderneath all of it, was a nature essentially spiritual but perverted, an imagination fine, subtle and fragrant, but trained neither by high associations nor by uplifting studies." Even at the beginning of the twentieth century, a woman who exercised her sexual freedom needed reforming.

Newell, and the *Eagle*, supposed he was the man for the job. "He represented to her much that she brokenly or intermittently wished she had realized. He believed that he could reclaim and redeem her and vindicate his love and confidence in her. She believed, but for only a brief while, that he could do so." In fact, Adah's overwhelming success in the West made a mockery of Newell's pretensions and extinguished her own doubts. In "Aspasia," the jilted husband saw clearly the folly of his hopes:

> *What is the sternness and strength of a man,*
> *Barbarous, monkish, or knightly,*
> *When the Imperial Passion commands,*
> *Ruleth it ever so lightly?*

Newell was confronted by the reality that "Passion" was synonymous with a four-letter word, and, in the words of Wolf Mankowitz, "[he] was unable to deliver." Adah never entirely bought into The Menken, the superstar construct she and her promoters invented. But she understood that her fame and its demands excluded her present, conventional husband. However, until the couple parted, Newell would either sulk or lecture her to make her feel guilty. Adah, fearing a fourth divorce and another scandal, couldn't easily escape out a window this time.

In a letter to Ed James, she expressed her resentment:

> *You know not what a dark, heavy cloud casts its shadows over my life. With all my professional success there is not a day of my life that I do not pass the fiery ordeal of tears and prayers. It is now only eight o'clock in the morning. I am in tears. I have not been to bed all night. I cannot, in this letter, tell you all the cause, but suffice it to say that I married a*

"gentleman"! Perhaps you do not know what that word means as I do. It means a far superior being to either of us, and who occasionally condescends to tell us what low, wicked and lost creatures we are.

This raises the question of where Adah had been all night. In reaction to Newell's nagging, she took to cruising the Barbary Coast in male drag with June Booth and other companions from the supporting cast. Top-hatted, in evening dress and smoking a cigar, Adah won a bet with Booth that she could get away with gambling at the toughest dives. Fortune's favorite, she won at the tables, whether playing poker or faro. The time is immortalized by a photograph of her suavely attired, seated, holding a winning hand. Kate Davis writes of "her winnings at faro, up to $25,000 a night. Often she ended with a roll of bills from which she would peel off the top one for the first beggar, careless of the denomination." Perhaps Adah was recognized and occasionally *permitted* to win, but that would have taken a saloon operator as clever as Blackie Norton (played by Clark Gable) in *San Francisco*.

Adah's propensity to unwind from her performances by carousing along the Barbary Coast was aggravated by the arrival of Artemus Ward, who showed up with his manager Hingston in December. He made a hit, lecturing in his nonsensical way, and then he went on to Virginia City. Adah threw a going away party for him, which Newell attended, glowering. He needn't have worried, because Adah was much too purposeful to engage in Ward's aimless dissipation.

In Nevada Artemus bonded with Sam Clemens and the boys from the *Territorial Enterprise*. Joe Goodman, the paper's editor, remembered him as "bright and handsome as a young Apollo, but exhausting himself by foolish excess and feverish activity." At the end of one night's debauch, Artemus inveigled Sam to clamber along the roofs of the town, at the risk of being shot by street patrolmen who fired on sight. Ward and Hingston returned to the East via the overland stage, traversing the mountains and plains in the midst of winter and an Indian uprising.

Midwinter 1864 saw the arrival of Ada Clare, New York's Queen of Bohemia. In San Francisco she would find herself a mere lady in waiting. The positions of Clare and Menken had been reversed since the old days at Pfaff's. Then Adah was desperately poor while Clare, dressed in her finest gowns, lorded it over her own literary salon. Now Clare's Charleston family fortune had gone with the wind. Needing to work, she had an agreement with the *Golden Era* to write a weekly column. The peripatetic pianist and composer Louis Gottschalk, the father of her boy born out of wedlock, was playing the Gold Coast at about this time, but he refused to recognize their son. Clare writes of him as "one sweet face that I loved without tumult and kissed without passion, which I have now lost sight of forever."

Clare had a reputation not only as a scandalous woman but also a witty columnist, a combination the *Era* was counting on. The paper, advertising her column, called her "beautiful, accomplished, talented, and brilliant." Adah Menken and Ada Clare got on well and influenced one another. Ironically, each wanted to do what the other was best at. Clare thought of herself as an actress and asked Adah to intercede with Tom Maguire to present her in a play. Adah wanted to write a novel, and Clare was already at work on her confessional *Only a Woman's Heart*. Her column at the *Era* instantly caught on, though her views were feminist and her style often acerbic. Clare's most controversial remark was made in a March column, and it remains insightful today. Observing a variety of Californians, she wrote:

> *They seem to be people without any remembered Past. . . . Though I cannot exactly specify why, there surely is a certain something in their general expression of countenance, tone of converse, movements and aims, which suggests to me . . . the novelty of sentient creatures whose entities are all in the present hour, and inseparable from the present place.*

From the Gold Rush to Silicon Valley's New Paradigm, California has radiated optimism; its culture has denied the weight of the past and, at times, convinced the rest of the world that the New Age is dawning. Clare caught on to this phenomenon before anyone else. Her remarks on Victorian gender relations were equally trenchant. She wrote an amusing satire called "The Man's Sphere of Influence," which turned the tables on the sort of moralist who wanted women kept at home. "There is something effeminate in the literary or artist[ic] man that our sex repudiates," she claimed, tongue in cheek. "We do not want man to be too highly educated; we want him sweet, gentle, and incontestably stupid."

Adah was preparing to leave for Virginia City, and Clare would come along. Their friendship throws into doubt Newell's assertion that his wife ruled in a "womanless court." He insisted in "Aspasia" that "to her altar and unto her throne / Cometh no form of a woman." In fact, Adah had several close women friends, but they were as far removed from the Victorian standard as she. In San Francisco Adah's act was reviewed on occasion by women. Tess Ardenne, writing for the *Golden Era*, described her William the sailor in *Black-Eyed Susan* as "handsome enough to turn the heads of all the girls in any port her ship may enter."

Ardenne raved over Menken's body language: "You never saw hands speak like hers . . . I did not know they could use so perfectly the language of affection." Victorian women gave a variety of excuses for being excited by Adah in pants, and current commentators dwell on social or psychological explanations. Simply put, a pretty woman in drag is a turn-on for all, *provided* she looks handsome and has the style to pull it off. Garbo and Dietrich did, and they effortlessly appealed across the gender line. Often there is an androgyny about the superstar: look at Madonna or Michael Jackson. Adah had that quality of universal (or undifferentiated) sexuality that appeals to the widest audience.

Adah's closest pal in San Francisco appears to have had no sexuality at all. Seventeen-year-old Lotta Crabtree, then unknown outside the state, was spoken of as "the most talented juvenile actress California has yet produced." Beginning at the age of six, Lotta had been tied onto a saddle and lugged around the mining camps by her mother. Mrs. Crabtree, married to a ne'er-do-well, determined that Lotta would make their fortune. She subjected her daughter to every manner of hardship to make her a musical entertainer. Maguire, leery of the Crabtrees (it was Lotta's father who shot him), was finally obliged to feature the teenager in his productions. Mrs. Crabtree never let Lotta out of her sight, pocketed the monies owed to her, oversaw her wardrobe and act, and otherwise tyrannized over Lotta until she died when her daughter was sixty.

Lotta was permitted few friends and no love life. Consequently, she could play only one of two roles: the tomboy or the pert little girl, and these she kept up to popular acclaim until she retired from the stage at forty-five. Shrewd Mrs. Crabtree did permit her daughter an occasional intimacy—first, with Lola Montez when she played the mining camps, and then with Adah Menken when she became the rage of San Francisco. That the pretty young woman was emotionally stunted was not yet evident. That she was never permitted to develop an interest in men is clear, but whether she had any lesbian relationships is unknown. After Lotta's death, when a woman claimed to be her daughter and heir to a large estate, medical evidence was produced to prove that Lotta had died a virgin.

Lotta and Adah were seen together frequently, driving through the streets of San Francisco: "an odd pair, Lotta in the plainer elegances of the day, hoops and capes and bizarre little hats, Menken in her free-flowing barbarous yellow." Adah, while playing the part of mentor, courted her young friend. She took her horseback riding to the Cliff House, where they could admire sea lions on the rocks, and beyond them, the great bay. Or they went to the races at a track outside the city, where Adah bet and won for them both.

Adah's final hit show before leaving for Nevada was *Three Fast Women*. She adapted a tired English burletta by impersonating or telling jokes on well-known San Francisco figures, who were often in the audience. She sang, danced, and quick-changed between six very different roles, three men and three women. According to the *Alta California* of January 20, she showed "a wonderful versatility, and passes from character to character with almost lightning-like rapidity." Quick-change involves a total switch: *everything* must change, including appearance, voice, and attitude. It is the ultimate test of a comic actor, and in modern times has been attempted by only the best, such as Peter Sellers or Eddie Murphy.

This should put the lie to the remark made by Walter Leman in his *Memories of an Old Actor* and mindlessly repeated by others: "Miss Menken played nothing else but *Mazeppa* and faro, which she played with skill and success." Had she never seized on *Mazeppa* as a vehicle, Adah still would have been a star. As to her talent at the gaming tables, perhaps she owed that to the Irish in her.

The boys in the back room at Washoe, including Sam Clemens, were about to fall victim to the Menken charm. Tom Maguire had built a new Opera House in Virginia City, and there, after alerting the *Enterprise,* he sent his superstar at the end of February. Deep down in Sun Mountain the gold eagles were first hatched, but above ground—in dozens of saloons, bordellos, and Maguire's theater—they were more easily caught.

CHAPTER FIFTEEN:

SUN MOUNTAIN

Oh, Washoe
That's the land for me
I'm going to Sun Mountain
With my washtub on my knee.

—FOLK SONG

South of present-day Reno, Nevada, lay the rugged mining district of Washoe, capped by the town of Virginia (no one bothered with "City"), perched along the flank of 8,000-foot-high Sun Mountain. To the east lay the River of Death and the Forty-Mile Desert, which to the miners seemed "haunted by hunger and thirst, pestilence and Piutes, death and dust." From the west, the 150-mile journey from San Francisco crossed the High Sierras and skirted Lake Tahoe, passing mining camps abandoned and lively. It took thirty hours by stagecoach, unless there was a blizzard or mud slide, when the route became all but impassable. Washoe's supplies came up from the coast, and the gold and silver bars needed by the Union to fund the Civil War were trucked to the mint at San Francisco. So important was this traffic that, weather permitting, Wells Fargo ran three stages per day.

On February 27, 1864, Adah Menken and her entourage arrived at Virginia. Already a semi-mythical figure, she looked up to see the Naked Lady, bound to a charger, in a gigantic poster high on the face of the mountain. Impresario Tom Maguire had flooded the town with 1,000 *carte de visite* photos of Adah, dressed and undressed, and these had become collector's items among the "boys" of Washoe. Regal, she descended from the coach into the arms of welcoming admirers. Ada Clare followed, along with her pack of pet dogs, and then several members of the supporting cast.

A reporter noted that Robert Newell rode atop the baggage in the hind boot, an uncomfortable and precarious roost. He was "dressed in a black mustache, a plug hat, and a gray blanket, and looked like a Georgia major just returned from the war." Adah's humiliation of her husband was seconded by the local press. The Nevada *Gazette,* for example, called him "an unutterable fop."

The actress had entered on a stage well suited to her irreverent mood. Virginia, crowning the fabulous Comstock Lode of gold and silver, echoed San Francisco of ten years past, before the vigilantes drove out the bad men. The desperados had moved on to Nevada: card sharps, stock swindlers, horse thieves, murderers, and lawyers. So rich were the deposits of metals lodged in Sun Mountain that they revolutionized world finance and produced a crop of instant millionaires, mud from the mines on their boots.

Mark Twain recalled in his memoir, *Roughing It,* "There were nabobs in those days, in the 'flush times,'" whose main complaint was their inability to spend money as quickly as they made it. The Comstock riches seemed so endless that fantasy replaced truth: "A gold mine," quipped Twain, "is a hole in the ground with a liar standing next to it."

Joe Goodman, in his mid-twenties, was editor of the *Territorial Enterprise,* the most influential newspaper between San Francisco and Denver. The man who hired an unlucky, dead-broke prospector named Sam Clemens, and gave him his first literary job, later described Virginia:

Wildcats [dubious mines] flourished without number. Mills clattered. Furnaces roared. The heavens were smutted with smoke. The earth rocked with subterranean detonations. Streets rocked with traffic. Throngs rocked with tumult. Stacks of bullion poured out of mills and were rushed over the old immigrant road to California coffers. San Francisco had nothing

worth boasting about but what she owed to Sun Mountain. . . . Economy
in the presence of fabulous fortune became a senseless sham. . . . Life
became a spree of spending.

By the time Wells Fargo had delivered Adah, sending on separately
her horse Sweepstake and a spare untamed stallion, Virginia had grown
from a mining camp into an oddly shaped habitation of 40,000 people,
mostly vigorous young males. From top to bottom, Streets A, B, C, and D
curved along the steep mountainside, and an occasional side street clawed
its way up the slope. A, the shortest, was occupied by the mansions of
those who had struck it rich, and B, by the houses of those who were up-
and-coming, as well as the courthouse and Maguire's Opera House. C,
the widest, was a bustling thoroughfare of commerce: coaches, wagons,
horses, and pedestrians jostled amid the typically Western buildings of
hotels, assay offices, stores, saloons, and the *Territorial Enterprise*—at which
Sam Clemens had begun to sign his contributions "Mark Twain." D
Street was the red-light district, which meant bordellos plain and deluxe,
gambling dens, and more saloons. Below that was Chinatown, where
Chinese folk cooked, cleaned, washed, and mended for all of Virginia.

The San Francisco *Bulletin* remarked dryly that Washoe was a
"receptacle for the vagrant, the vicious and the unfortunate, who has-
ten to find in the excitement and social license incident to frontier life a
condition congenial to their perturbed spirits and blasted hopes." From
today's view, the scene looks far more romantic. Virginia was the wildest West, beyond any Hollywood fantasy. In *Mark Twain's America*, Bernard DeVoto wrote:

In Washoe, a code of the duello existed: two of Sam's colleagues on
the Enterprise *had stood up at the proper distance, offering themselves*
to formal gunfire . . . Manslaughter in a fair fight carried with it no
social stigma whatever, and in the city streets, unmolested by the law and
unavoided by the citizens, walked hundreds of men who had settled argu-
ments by the one invincible syllogism.

Mining itself was fraught with danger. Prospectors in the small camps that abounded among the hills were subject to claim jumpers, Indian attack, searing heat and freezing cold, scurvy, influenza, and plain boredom. They named their mines whimsically: "Wake-up-Jake," "Gouge-Eye," "Let 'er Rip," and "Root Hog or Die." These were the lucky ones who, to make a stake, had survived digging for the big mines, working shifts twelve stories down in the Hades of Sun Mountain, where the temperature was 138 degrees Fahrenheit, day or night. Times of day were meaningless in Virginia, since the mines and smelting and stamping mills worked 'round the clock and the air rang with their clamor and the earth shook with detonations at all hours.

The miners dreamed of a rich strike, but also of womankind, and this sustained them in their perilous and grinding routine. Women were either saints or the other kind. The pioneer mother was worshipped, but few could be found. When the territorial legislature met at Carson City, its session was inaugurated by playing the national anthem. In the midst of "The Star-Spangled Banner," an infant started to cry. The band was silenced and the legislature stood in awe of that wail. When a nun appeared on C Street, hardened characters bent down and kissed the hem of her habit.

The other kind of woman was to hand, and the pricier ladies gained respect. "They civilized the Comstock," admitted the most American of historians, Bernard DeVoto. To their bawdy houses the boys came to play, and they minded their manners or they were hustled out the door. Julia Bulette's Palace was the most elaborate bordello the West has ever seen. Run by a handsome woman of color from New Orleans, the rococo mansion exhibited all the mahogany furniture, stained glass, Persian rugs, and satin wall hangings any *nouveau riche* could desire. Julia served fine wines to complement French cuisine, dressed herself and her girls in the latest Parisian style, and decked her palace with fresh-cut flowers rushed by Wells Fargo express from San Francisco. She was one of *Life* magazine's Fabulous Women of the Frontier: "To the lonely, rugged miners she brought touches of long-forgotten grace and gentility."

Julia, a compassionate fund-raiser for the Sanitary Commission, the Civil War's Red Cross, was a madam with a heart of gold. She was the premier belle of the hard-drinking, rough-and-ready boys, until Adah arrived with the force of a Washoe zephyr—a wind so strong it could overturn a stagecoach. Menken's challenge to Virginia's sweetheart would not go unopposed by her steady clients. Although the newcomer had softened up Joe Goodman by contributing poems to the *Enterprise,* Joe and Sam Clemens and his roommate, Dan De Quille (a pen name for William Wright), conspired to ruin her time in Nevada. The boys had driven other performers off the stage, and their reviews were reprinted all over the West. Dan, a mining expert, had a dry, benign wit. Sam was the instigator of this prank, which, like many of his articles for the *Enterprise,* was cunningly mischievous and aimed at a particular person.

On the evening of March 7, 1864, Virginia's Opera House was packed to the doors for the opening of *Mazeppa.* Tom Maguire's new theater seated around 1,600 persons, with a spacious stage lit by gas lamps in sconces. An Italian artist had painted the curtain, which showed a view of Lake Tahoe from the Sierras. Boxes on either side were furnished with gilt chairs and velvet railings. Glittering chandeliers hung from the ceiling. The adjoining bar was all mahogany and mirrors. Everybody from mining barons to the politicians at Carson City milled about on the thick carpeting, dressed in their formal best. Instead of onyx studs in their shirtfronts, the millionaires sported diamonds. Julia Bulette was seated in a stage box with half-drawn curtains, wearing rubies and a low-cut white satin gown. The drapery was management's nod to Nevada's growing sense of propriety.

In the pew reserved for the *Enterprise* sat the unholy three newsmen. The bell rang for the curtain to rise, the hubbub quieted to a whisper, and gas flares dimmed. Sam got ready to vivisect this mere circus rider. Now the trio faced the courtyard of the Castle of Laurinski with lofty mountain scenery in the background, and Adah as Cassimir the page moved stealthily in the moonlight to woo his beloved Olinska, the betrothed of a powerful count. The boys stared at the lithe, graceful figure in cloak and tights. That proud, dark, curly head—did it not bring to mind Lord Byron, who also defied society to love whom he would?

The boys fell silent and listened to Cassimir speak. As George Lyman, historian of the Comstock, writes, they sat "open-eyed, open-eared, open-mouthed, drinking in the beauty of that matchless voice." It "overwhelmed them with its melody." Stirred to the tips of their toes, the boys were caught up in the action of a melodrama that "consummated the lust of an era and a locality born of melodrama." What is the history of the West, in song and story, but a melodrama of good guy fighting bad guy for the love of a good woman—and a bad one on the side? The audience on the Comstock saw in *Mazeppa* their own life stories immortalized by Byron, the poet/hero. They too would pass into legend.

Mazeppa was hardly more dramatic than Adah's life. She brought to its core story of a romantic triangle, which she understood too well, a fresh, athletic skill. She moved with the decision of a man and the grace of a woman. The boys watched the tournament in awe, amazed at Adah's realism in the dueling scenes. They belonged to a gymnasium for fencing and boxing, and Sam prided himself on being expert with foils. According to his buddy Dan, "in attack he was fiery and dangerous." Adah's ringing blows with a blade were echoed by applause from the amateur swordsmen.

Came the climactic strip scene and the audience grew hushed, the tension running like an electric current through the aisles. The stage mountain, which poked its head above the proscenium arch, reminded them of their own Sun Mountain. A narrow trail zigzagged from the stage level upward to the flies, obscured at times by a cardboard gorge or tree. The height was real, and as menacing as the soldiers who ganged up around Cassimir, doing to him/her something unspeakable. Now the snorting stallion was led out and the abused page—stripped to reveal the woman—was bound to it, legs spread wide.

"Her body was beautiful and to the Comstock it signified infinite desire," observed DeVoto, just warming up. As the orchestra increased its tempo, Adah was carried "white, violable, and orgasmic" up along the narrow path. Thunder crashed and lightning illumined the Naked Lady on high. She and the horse disappeared into the flies behind the proscenium arch. The curtain fell on a stunned house, which exploded in applause, demanding Adah take call after call. The boys were swept along like chips in a flood. Adah seemed to them "a goddess . . . eternally virgin!" Her dangerous ride up the mountain brought home the heroism of men on the battlefields of a distant war.

The boys rushed back to the *Enterprise* office. They wrote seated at one long table, scribbling, chatting, and consuming bowls of noodles fixed by a Chinese cook. Their articles often represented a kind of consensus. Next day the review of *Mazeppa* "exalted Menken to the skies, piled ecstasy on ecstasy. Never had there been anyone like her; she was 'divine, remote, inaccessible, holding the world in contempt.'" According to Albert Bigelow Paine, Mark Twain's chosen biographer, Sam Clemens joined in the rapture: "Like all other men who ever met her, he became briefly fascinated by the charms of Adah Isaacs Menken." He would not buck his pals' enthusiasm or Adah's spectacular success.

At the Opera House the applause went on. Cheering miners tossed bags of gold dust on the stage, and merchants their gold watches. These were only the first of the many presents heaped on Adah. A newly found ore ledge was christened The Mazeppa Mounting Ledge, and an entire underground section was named The Menken. Mixing the ribald and serious, The Menken Shaft and Tunnel Company was formed and issued stock certificates bearing the picture of a naked lady. The promoters gifted the original with fifty shares worth $100 each, which she soon sold for a handsome profit.

Silver bars were ceremoniously presented to Adah, including one worth $3,000. It was so heavy that Wells Fargo had to brace a coach to carry it down to the railroad at Reno. As the scholar Kate Davis remarked, "In their way, these crude men of a fabulous era tendered their honest tribute to Adah Menken." She was also honored in less tangible ways. Tom Peasley, proprietor of the Sazerac, the largest, most ornate saloon in Virginia, nominated himself her chief protector and escort. A man of personal courage, Tom took her dancing at the Melodeon and assembled a band of chums beneath her hotel window to serenade her. Menken played faro at Peasley's saloon, open twenty-four hours a day. Because Tom ran a square game, she generally won.

Attending bear- and bullfights and boiling an egg in the scalding underground waters of the rich and deep Ophir mine were additional pastimes of this goddess. Rather than patronize the boys, she became one of them. One day at his saloon, Tom, who was chief of American Engine Company 2, announced that Adah had been elected an honorary member of the fire brigade. He presented her with an engraved, silver-buckled morocco belt to prove it. The only other woman so honored had been Julia Bulette. Since Adah was fond of dressing in drag and touring the town into the wee hours, including visits to bordellos, we wonder if she met Julia, and if so, what the two queens of the night talked about.

Another open question is whether Adah took her admirer Tom Peasley as a lover. "She delighted in his soft, panther-like step," writes Lyman. Tom was handsome, politically powerful, an older, more savvy version of ex-husband John Heenan. Adah had again ricocheted from the sensitive pest, Robert Newell, to the macho guy. If Tom lacked the poetic element, he was kind and considerate. Adah could have done worse, but she was holding out for someone more suitable.

Adah's state of mind was divided. "There was something in her that denied happiness," observes Lyman, "that could not be appeased with applause [or] bought with bullion." Adah throbbed with the pulse of her surroundings, yet she felt no real satisfaction. She claimed that she loved raucous Virginia City, whose miners dug day and night and then rose to the surface to raise hell. But within, she cried for her lost art. Her being was an aesthetic one, and its inner voice would not be still. Adah wrote no poetry while in Washoe.

Newell's verse portrait of his wife, "Aspasia," cuts through the clatter:

Think of her, lonely, with hundreds around . . .
Think of her, truthful and pure in herself,
Lost by the falsehood of others!

Certainly the *Enterprise* heaped outlandish praise on Adah. Joe Goodman declared that she was a "great actress . . . [an] eloquent delineator of human passions." Rival papers became irritated at Joe and Sam and Dan's applauding the star's every move. The nearby *Humboldt Register,* under the heading of "Menkenized," wrote that "the local [editor] of the *Enterprise* is awfully spooney in his comments on Menken's performance." A California paper remarked: "[T]he editors of the *Enterprise* have gone crazy—but they didn't have far to go." The suggested remedy was a laxative and a good night's sleep.

While Ada Clare envied her friend's triumph, Adah decided she wanted to write a confessional novel. She would avoid sentimentality and tell the truth. With an uncanny eye for literary talent, Adah reached out to the one man who could help: Sam Clemens, who was morphing into Mark Twain. She was *not* romantically attracted to this unkempt young man with a shambling gait, bad temper, and worse-smelling pipe. Sam, in Virginia City, had a reputation so unenviable that the father of his future wife, Olivia Langdon, when he learned of it, initially rejected him as his daughter's suitor. He responded to Adah's feelers in his own mischievous way.

In a letter to his sister Pamela, Sam wrote that he had received a rather formal note from "Miss Menken, the actress—Orpheus C. Kerr's wife," attached to a sketch she wished to publish in the *Enterprise.* He responded at length—"3 pages of 'legal cap'"—in a manner "extravagantly sociable and familiar." Then he added:

She has a beautiful white hand—but her handwriting is infamous; she
writes very fast, and her chirography is of the doorplate order—her letters

are immense. I gave her a conundrum—thus: "My Dear Madam—Why ought your hand to retain its present grace & beauty always? Because you fool away devilish little of it on your manuscript."

I think I can safely say that woman was furious for a few days. But finally she got over it. . . . She is friendly now.

In response, Adah decided to give a dinner party for Sam, Dan De Quille, Clare, and herself, at which she would discuss her literary ambitions. From Sam she wanted the sort of advice on her novel that she would later receive from Algernon Swinburne on her poetry. The other two guests were more or less chaperones. Dan reminisced about the shindig thirty years later:

The dinner was given in The Menken's rooms at the International Hotel, and was the best that could be obtained in the city. It was given on a Sunday afternoon . . . and to do anything like justice to the many courses required over three hours. Menken kept a whole procession of waiters moving to and fro between the kitchen and her rooms, many courses being no more than tasted before they were removed.

It seemed a little rough on Orpheus [Newell], glimpses of whom we caught as he patrolled the hall in front of the rooms . . . that he should have only a smell of the good things as they were carried past him by the waiters. For some reason he was just then in bad odor with his more energetic half.

Adah's torturing of her fourth husband, with whom she was otherwise finished, seems a step down the moral ladder. While her cruelty accomplished nothing for her, it incited Newell to do his best work.

This was not a well-chosen group for an intimate dinner. Blonde, blue-eyed Clare tried her best to intrigue the boys, and Adah was lively and complimentary. But Dan, in his mid-thirties, though beloved in Washoe, was hardly a man of the world. He was married and supported a family in Ohio, which he rarely visited. Sam, single, though a frequenter of houses of ill repute, had little experience with sophisticated women. Later, Dan claimed his roommate didn't like Menken, but Sam's actual feelings were ambivalent. She attracted him, and he hoped to use her influence in New York; at the same time he was frightened by her sexual independence. He knew if she were a "good" woman, he wouldn't be sitting uncomfortably close to her while her husband fumed in the hallway.

Dan continued:

The object of the dinner appeared to be, on Menken's part, a sort of literary consultation. For the time being she was full of her proposed novel. Aside from this talk, and some talk of getting up a new play for Clare, the dinner was rather dull. It was thought to enliven the occasion with some short flights of song.

Sam's rendition of a ditty about a horse named Methusalem put an end to that idea.

Dan counted nineteen small dogs in the room, most of them Clare's. The women had been feeding them cubes of sugar soaked in brandy, and the dogs were drunk. One of them nipped Sam's leg. He aimed a kick at it under the table, but miscalculating the distance, Sam gave Adah a tremendous kick in the shins. She bounded from the table to a sofa, rolling around in agony.

The boys apologized but took the opportunity to beat a hasty retreat. Saluting Newell in the hall, they got a dirty look in return. So Adah's novel died on the vine, and we may never learn the revelations about friends and lovers it would have contained. Due partly to Sam Clemens's skittishness, we have lost a choice item of historic telling-it-all.

Adah received another blow from an unexpected quarter, which sped her departure from Virginia. Tom Peasley had commissioned an artist to paint a portrait of her to hang behind the bar at his saloon. These Western bars of mahogany with inlays of rare woods and gleaming brass rails were themselves works of art. Progress was kept secret until the night scheduled for the portrait's unveiling. Adah, accompanied by Dan, attended after her performance. Three cheers and a "tiger"—a loud *Hooray!*—greeted their arrival at the crowded Sazerac. After a number of speeches, the cloth was removed from the painting—or, rather, paintings. To the left of the Naked Lady, who occupied the place of honor, hung a portrait of Lola Montez, and to the right, one of the Benicia Boy in sparring tights. John Heenan remained a great favorite among the miners.

Allen Lesser relates that a furious Adah was lifted atop the bar, from where she put down both of her associates. Lola, she said, may have begun with a king (of Bavaria), but she had ended with a miner (in California). "I began with a prizefighter," she boasted, "but I'll end with a prince." Once the cheers had died down, she reminded the boys that Heenan had taught her a thing or two, and she offered to box anyone in the room. Dan, who boxed daily at the gym, went a couple of rounds with her. She treated him roughly and ended by throwing him down and out. "Her left," Dan would recall, "was a thing with which to conjure."

In the midst of the mayhem, Adah, without a word to Tom, disappeared into the night. Fighting back tears, she went directly to the Wells Fargo office. Although it was midnight, doctor Allen Hamilton had hired a stage to take him to San Francisco. When the company agent asked if he would accept a lady in distress, he agreed. A gentleman, he left the inside of the coach to her. He would ride up top with the driver.

At Placerville, where they changed horses, Dr. Hamilton caught a glimpse of the mysterious lady and realized it was Menken. "In the early morning, [she] looked anything but attractive in all her frowsiness and overnight change in facial decoration." Adah had spent the night crying. The old, deep wounds caused by Heenan would not heal. She would have to go far away, where no one had ever heard of the Benicia Boy.

Ada Clare crossed the Sierras some days later. She arrived at Russ House, along with Adah's maid and baggage, to find her friend translating *Mazeppa* into French. Newell was off in Sacramento. Adah was set on new horizons. She had conquered California and accumulated a war chest sufficient to attack those fortresses of culture, the capitals of Europe. The pianist Louis Moreau Gottschalk, who was received tepidly in California, remarked that "the circus flourishes, and Miss Adah Isaacs Menken, after having driven all the people crazy, has carried away with her fifty thousand dollars." Ed James thought she sailed past the Golden Gate worth twice that. To get a present equivalent, we must think in the multimillions. But during these last weeks in San Francisco, money was not on Adah's mind.

The francophone had previously half-jested that her soul would ascend to heaven through the gates of Paris. She had dreamed she would die in the City of Light. More seriously, in a recurring nightmare she imagined she was ill, struggling for breath, alone in a shabby room except for her dog, who suddenly fled from her bed. Clare offered to take her to Emma Hardinge, a Spiritualist medium and clairvoyant.

Spiritualism was the mid-nineteenth-century version of radical feminism. It was the only religion in which women were preeminent and could preach from the pulpit or platform. Often, women acted as trance mediums, whether in a séance or a more public gathering. Today's channeled writings are directly descended from the Spiritualists, and, rather like New Age gurus, certain of their medium authors achieved great popularity. Converts numbered in the millions, among them (it was rumored) Abraham Lincoln. Emma Hardinge was one of Spiritualism's most charismatic figures.

An Englishwoman with a pleasant, intelligent face, Hardinge was a lady by birth. Commanded by her spirit guides, she traveled by herself across the United States to California. Between trance-guided meetings, she stumped for the reelection of Lincoln. Outdoors, she attracted thousands of spellbound listeners, and the *Golden Era* praised her brilliant speaking ability. Spiritualists were outspoken on all aspects of women's rights, but they particularly disliked marriage as they knew it. The wife was expected to surrender her name, property, and body. A few mediums were advocates of Free Love. According to Charles Stoddard, a certain "priestess among the modern pagans" had tried but failed to seduce him.

Adah, Clare, and the medium met privately. Hardinge explained that California was a wonderful place to experience spiritual phenomena. This was due to the heavy charges of mineral magnetism from the gold deposits, as well as the animal magnetism emanating from seekers who came there from all over the world. Adah asked to contact the spirit of her mother, which Hardinge facilitated to her satisfaction. She also comforted Adah about her nightmare. The wealthy star responded with a generous contribution and rededicated a poem to the medium, "Dreams of Beauty," that she had originally written for Stephen Masset.

In April Adah performed for a week at Maguire's Opera House. No matter the show, the theater was packed and tickets scalped for high prices. As usual Adah had her detractors. The Stockton *Independent* dismissed her acting as "decidedly of the Bowery style," while the Nevada *Gazette* called her "a brazen harlot." The papers that were most preachy still printed every hint of news they could find about her. They had to admit Menken's shows "were patronized by young men and curious women . . . of the first families of California." One last night of *Mazeppa* on April 17 left the audience and reviewers rapturous.

The *Golden Era,* after putting down the prudes as hopelessly naive, editorialized: "The star that flashed across our Western Hemisphere from an eastern glow of triumph, lighting up the old time dullness of our theaters with a meteoric grace and brilliancy, is about to disappear from our gaze—we hope not forever." Adah steamed out of the bay on the *Moses Taylor* on April 23, bound for Panama. Robert Newell went along for show, a favor she granted him to save face. She felt no regret at their parting, probably at the Isthmus, where they could board different ships for New York. Men of the world would find the marriage of the prudish intellectual to the brazen Naked Lady a good subject for barroom jokes. To Newell, the loss of his one and only love was a tragedy. He continued to write poetry and novels, but would live as a man without a heart.

Adah would not return to California, and her leaving signaled a shift in its cultural climate. With the Civil War nearing its end, the best performers sailed for the Eastern states or shunned the long voyage to San Francisco. June Booth and his daughter were aboard the *Moses Taylor,* and Lotta Crabtree and her mother followed within a week. Tom Maguire kept up his business for a time, but his passion for importing Italian opera stars would nearly ruin him. In 1867 he sold his Virginia City Opera House to a saloonkeeper named Piper. *His* theater still stands as a tourist attraction in a town that clings to olden times.

The San Francisco Bohemian scene would also fracture. Eventually New York and Europe drew the best of the writers. Joe Lawrence abandoned the *Golden Era* when, in 1865, it became outclassed by the *Californian,* then the *Overland Monthly,* both edited by Bret Harte. The latter left in 1871, having already written his colorful stories of Western life. These are the hard-luck tales of miners, gamblers, and prostitutes that give the name to today's "Bret Harte Country" in central California. In Europe, the author would try to repeat his early success, while living on borrowed money and evading his family for the rest of his life.

In 1887 Harte published the novella *Crusade of the Excelsior,* which features a *femme fatale,* Belle, who destroys her sensitive, intellectual husband. Harte admitted in a letter to his wife that the character was "a study from some of my recollections of Adah Isaacs Menken, in the old California days." Although he presented Belle as "shameless with a desire for notoriety," he admitted he hadn't done justice to Menken. *Crusade* was another rung down on Harte's descent into banality.

Joaquin Miller, with the generosity of a cowboy, gave Menken her due and then some. He claimed he owed his writing style to her. He divorced Minnie Myrtle, and in 1870 he went to London, where he laid a myrtle wreath from the Sierras on Byron's tomb. He published *Song of the Sierras* and followed it with a realistic account of his life among the Modoc Indians. Miller was lionized by the literary world, and he dressed California style, including sombrero and moccasins, in the most fashionable drawing rooms. Lillie Langtry remarked on his "yellow hair so long that it lay in curls about his shoulders . . . and a dreamy expression in his light eyes." Later, after traveling through Europe, Joaquin returned to California and lived on the Oakland heights overlooking the Golden Gate. He became an apostle of free love. He liked to hint to visitors that, in his younger days, he had slept with the goddess, Adah.

Tom Peasley, who had a better claim to being Adah's lover, died with his boots on after she left Washoe. Gunned down without warning, he propped himself up on his elbow and blew away the varmint, then breathed his last. Still more romantic, after Adah sailed from San Francisco, Ada Clare ran off to Hawaii with gay Charles Stoddard! They were friends, acting as cover for one other. What they did with the bronzed native lads is hinted at in Stoddard's *South-Sea Idylls*. Clare was back by December 1864 to play Camille at Maguire's Opera House. She was a flop, and afterward she and her pups sailed for New York to inflict her acting upon what she hoped would be a more appreciative audience.

Stoddard spent additional sojourns in Hawaii and wrote several books, including *The Lepers of Molokai*. He corresponded with Adah in Paris. Although her life was packed, she took time to reply with warmth and consideration. No wonder, at the turn of the century, that Stoddard continued to think of her with a feeling that mingled pity and love. She had introduced the isolated, nervous youth to Walt Whitman's work, and via a mutual correspondence Whitman became his pole star. Menken's influence on Stoddard and Miller—indeed, on the creation of an American style—is important but subtle. The prose of both writers, especially the reportage, is far better than their reputations, and their defense of the despised and downtrodden is entirely relevant in our global age.

Finally, what can be said of the collision between those two children of Halley's Comet, Adah Bertha Theodore and Samuel Langhorne Clemens? Clearly, they traveled on opposed paths. Sam, though a dissolute young man, craved fame *and* respectability, which meant he would have to tame his language and demeanor. Adah lived her time full out. Each created a public persona that was different from, and even at odds with, his or her private self. Sam lived in Mark Twain's skin for much of the seventy-two years between appearances of Halley's Comet. Adah burnt through the night sky like a shooting star.

Andrew Hoffman in *Inventing Mark Twain* claims that Clemens learned from Menken the necessity of presenting a public persona that was *not* notorious: "Don't *live* outrageously if you want to *perform* outrageously." Hoffman perceives that the up-and-coming author dared not befriend the Naked Lady. Through connections Sam made in Nevada and San Francisco, the name "Mark Twain" became known to readers of Eastern weeklies, and he eventually followed the migration of talent to New York. But though the boy left the country, he brought along his provincial prejudices. In 1867 he objected to the popular burlesque *The Black Crook,* a "leg show" for which Menken's theatrical nudity had opened the way. Twain thundered that such license onstage, along with pornographic literature, was "corrupting America's youth and would stock thousands and tens of thousands of houses of ill fame." While traveling in Europe, this innocent abroad objected to Titian's painting of the nude Venus!

Adah Menken's influence on the West, as experienced firsthand by its pioneers, and vicariously by us, cannot be diminished by the moral judgments of even the great. *Life* magazine understood that to the miner, cowboy, gambler, or storekeeper, "Adah was the premier sight of the West. . . . Many an old-timer had as his proudest boast not the fact that he had looked the fierce Comanche in the eye or had a drink with old Jim Bridger, but that he had seen Adah on that horse."

PART FOUR

———⚬⚬⚬———

A NOTORIOUS WOMAN FROM AMERICA

We are menaced with an invasion of impurity.

—H. B. FARNIE

CHAPTER SIXTEEN:

THE TALK OF LONDON

On July 23, 1864, Adah Menken sat at a desk in her newly occupied suite at London's Westminster Palace Hotel to write to Ed James, her "dear brother." First she apologized for being tardy:

> *You know very well what a whirl it is to live in London. And I have had to see a great many people and go to lots of places. And then during the day wrangling with managers about my terms, pieces, etc. And so the time has flown. But all is settled now and I am your devoted sister to write you letters and to send you photographs.*

Adah had accomplished a major coup, but she put off the glad tidings until letter's end. She might well have reflected on the problems she'd had since sailing away from her triumphs in California. Nothing seemed to go according to plan. Landing at New York on an overcast spring day, she was last year's news. No brass band, no crowd greeted the arrival of The Menken. The scandal over her marriages had gone stale. John Heenan had sailed for England, where he fought Tom King for the championship and was badly beaten. Walt Whitman was nursing the wounded in Washington, writing the poetry of "Drum-Taps," snapshots of men at war that evoke Mathew Brady's grim photos. The Bohemian crowd at Pfaff's had scattered to the winds. The war and the coming presidential election were all anyone talked about. In a choice bit of political skullduggery, Lincoln would win a second term because of the electoral votes of California and Nevada, two new states admitted to the Union for that purpose.

Adah made the rounds of Manhattan. She saw her journalist friends Frank Queen and Gus Daly, and she consulted a new admirer, Joe Brice, president of the Board of Aldermen (the City Council), about divorcing her fourth husband, Newell, who was acting sticky. She was shocked to hear that Ed James had failed to book her act in London. Too many American performers, hoping to escape the war, had fled to England. Not one had succeeded in winning over the press or public. James hesitantly reported that Edward Tyrell Smith, manager of Astley's Theatre Royal, did make Adah an offer, but at a lowball figure. It made her angry and more determined.

In June Adah, her maid, and a retinue of trunks took passage on a transatlantic steamship. For reasons of propriety and health, she also traveled with a woman companion, the well-bred Nelly Stewart. On the voyage she was accompanied by a still more interesting companion, the mysterious Captain James Paul Barkley, C.S.A. He has been described by Menken biographers as a gallant Confederate officer, wounded and retired, who made his money on the San Francisco stock exchange. Wolf Mankowitz depicts Barkley as akin to "Bret Harte's gambling gentleman . . . a typical Western hero-figure, with an approach both strong and tender, cool and passionate, a natural wooer, but always with the threat of a derringer in his coat-tail." We like to think of him as a real-life Rhett Butler.

There is a lack of hard evidence concerning this man. Supposedly he came from Memphis, Tennessee, and Adah would claim she had known him since adolescence. Barkley may have been a trader on the Cotton Exchange, the training ground for a number of big-time speculators. That his name does not show up in Memphis birth records is not surprising for a man who preferred the shadows. We know that he dealt in mining stocks, and after the Civil War he would become a broker in New York. However, the story about the captain being wounded and relieved of duty is an invention; he showed no sign of serious injury. Further, from what we can learn of his character, he was not a man to desert his cause.

Because it solves the mystery of Captain Barkley's shadowy presence in San Francisco, then London, we believe he was a Confederate agent. During the war the Confederacy tried desperately to win over California and Nevada, and, failing to accomplish that, to get their gold into Southern hands. A speculator on the stock exchange was well positioned to learn where mining was richest, and when and how bullion would be transported. Once California became staunchly Union, the Confederacy concentrated its best agents in England, where a loan might be floated to sustain the cause. What makes Barkley a likely operative is that despite being Menken's consort at a time when she was constantly in the public eye, and often photographed, he leaves no trace. Barkley surfaces in Menken's confidential letters and nowhere else. This very lack of evidence points to a man who has the skill to avoid being noticed.

The affair between Adah and Barkley began in California, and they sailed jointly, if not together, to Southampton. Mankowitz believes the attraction was what the French call a "*coup de foudre* style of love-affair, the stroke of lightning which ignites an instant flame of passion." Menken was given to such sudden, all-consuming infatuations, especially in her younger days. Allen Lesser concocts a romantic tale of a chance meeting on board ship, a star-filled night at sea when Adah succumbed to Barkley's charms in spite of herself:

> *She felt herself drawn to him, held so tightly she could hardly breathe while his ardent words wove a spell of enchantment about her. . . . Slowly her lips yielded to his kiss, and then as she gripped him in a frenzy of passion she knew.*

After so many months with the limp Robert Newell, we can imagine what Adah learned about Barkley that night. However, she chose her next lover in a more calculated fashion. Yes, she was attracted to this dashing figure, but she had known him earlier, indeed, "intimately for *fourteen years*," she insisted to Ed James. Adah sensed that Barkley was right for the campaign she planned in London. Newell had been dismissed, and it wouldn't do for The Menken to be flitting from one man to another. A strong, silent figure in the background was ideal. At her hotel, Barkley unobtrusively took rooms adjoining hers.

Finally, almost casually, Adah's letter to Brother Ed informed him that manager E. T. Smith had agreed to present her at Astley's to inaugurate the new theatrical season. *Mazeppa* "is to be produced in the most magnificent style," she concluded. "Everything [possible] is to be done for my success." Moreover, Smith had met her terms in an agreement so generous that he later disowned it as "wicked and preposterous." Adah, the waif from New Orleans, was about to become the highest-paid actress in the world. How had she successfully struck a deal in London, after the savvy James failed?

The capital of the British Empire, a sprawling city of nearly four million inhabitants, was a world away from decadent New Orleans, or pushing and striving New York, or gold-struck San Francisco. London had righteous Queen Victoria, a widow in perpetual mourning for her deceased consort, Albert. Its glorious palaces, parks, and mansions, with their displays of pomp and circumstance, put out of mind the disease-ridden warrens where the poor eked out a living. Rows of bordellos lined shady streets, including those in St. John's Wood that specialized in the so-called English vice (sadomasochistic sex), and children of both sexes openly solicited at Picadilly Circus. Hard to fathom were the apparently complacent middle classes, who would decide the box-office fate of The Menken.

Adah first chose a small hotel near the Theatre Royal Drury Lane, where she hoped to make her debut. Stage manager Edward Stirling patiently explained that Drury Lane put on Shakespeare and that Astley's in the Westminster Bridge Road would be more appropriate for her sort of show. Since the reign of George III, Astley's had been known for equestrian dramas, and *Mazeppa* originally played there. The house was built around an amphitheater, and to it came large, plebeian crowds to cheer and hoot at action melodramas such as *The Battle of Waterloo*. An attempt by Irish-American playwright Dion Boucicault to elevate the level of production—the amphitheater was replaced by stalls and potted plants—failed at the box office. Management fell into the hands of Smith, who Stirling offered to contact. Smith replied: "Thanks. Menken can go to Drury Lane or to the Devil. She won't do for me. She was kicked out of America."

Smith got this notion from John Heenan, who continued to bad-mouth his ex-wife. The former champ had turned to making book at the racetrack and remained a respected figure in sporting circles. Smith sincerely admired his battle against Sayers. The latest lessee of Astley's, the outstanding theater on London's south bank, began his career as a policeman, then became a wine merchant, a real estate dealer, man-ager of a circus, and proprietor of the *Sunday Times*. He once operated the infamous Cremorne Gardens, where randy pleasures were for sale. Smith was a plunger, but he was careful to conclude his shows early enough so that suburbanites could make train connections home. He understood the uses of publicity better than any man in England. Since he had been poisoned against Menken, she spent her time seeing other theater managers. Each time she was rebuffed.

One day, dressed in her finest, Adah barged into Smith's office. She was likely wearing a favorite royal blue dress to match her eyes, with a jaunty cap over long, curly hair (a wig), pendant gold earrings, and a gold and garnet necklace—an outfit in which Napoleon Sarony would photograph her. She was closeted with Smith for some time, and when she emerged she held a contract that guaranteed her half the nightly receipts for the run of *Mazeppa*, a professional company to support a first-class production, and a stage box and dolled-up dressing room to receive visitors and the press. Rumor had it that Adah got what *she* wanted by pulling a Lola.

The most famous scene in the life of Lola Montez, Adah's role model, was played offstage. In 1846 she insinuated herself into the pri-vate chamber of King Louis I of Bavaria, danced for him in the alto-gether, spent the night, and became the Countess Landsfeldt. Adah merely showed her prospective employer the merchandise, because under her proper Victorian guise she wore her pink body stocking. To persuade Smith to put on *Mazeppa*, Adah stripped for him. He must have liked what he saw. While Lola gained an aristocratic title, Adah was thrilled to have the best deal an actress could desire.

Impresario Smith wasted no time in moving Adah to the fashionable Westminster Palace, from where she was convenient to Astley's (across the Thames) and to Hyde Park, and in sending out press releases. Vacationers returning to town were greeted by such "puffs" as the following:

> *Miss Adah Isaacs Menken, the popular young American actress, is now in London. Every fine afternoon she appears among the aristocracy in Hyde Park, either mounted or on her famous black mare and escorted by a groom in full livery, or else airing herself in an open carriage with a liveried coachman and footman complete. Her equipage is much admired by the fashionables.*

Adah joined the parade of those who rode to be seen: gentlemen, ladies, and impostors; officers from the botched Crimean War, hoping for promotion; hunters of fortune or love; the self-satisfied, self-made men and their wives and mistresses. Each morning she trotted down The Mall past St. James's Park, swept around Buckingham Palace to Hyde Park's Rotten Row, impassive, glancing neither left nor right. The public, who came on foot to watch the display, ignored the noble and famous to stare at La Belle Menken, as Smith dubbed her. She was indeed the observed of all observers.

Adah began with the great advantage of being a superb horsewoman whose image was wedded to that four-footed status symbol. She came from the American West, where horses were a common means of transportation. But in Britain and on the Continent, the horse divided the gentleman from the commoner and the lady from her maid. Those who didn't bother to keep a horse, though otherwise respectable, took a hansom cab—a light, fast, two-wheeled vehicle for a single occupant.

The driver sat behind, a reference to the uniformed footman. Adah, because of her part in the equestrian drama, was able to wedge herself into this tightly knit society where everybody knew his or her place and how to signal it.

Adah played the *lady* of Naked Lady as though to the manor born. Smith proceeded to plaster London with oversized, lithograph posters of Mazeppa bound to the untamed steed. This prince was a study in androgyny, entirely naked except for the "diaper" at his/her crotch. From the waist up he looked like a young man with a mustache; yet his smooth thighs and legs were womanly. The poster read MISS ADAH ISAACS MENKEN AS MAZEPPA! Smith cleverly figured he could get away with showing a man nearly naked while meaning a woman. Rumors flew that on opening night Menken would appear in the buff. The promoter stirred up the press, but he was caught by surprise by one critic who claimed to be outraged.

The *London Orchestra*, a leading entertainment weekly, launched an attack on the morals of American art: "There is a depth of degradation in the drama which England has not yet reached, and which she, hopefully, never will; however common may be that degradation beyond the seas. . . . We [are] menaced with an invasion of impurity against which we cannot but protest." The editorial, written by H. B. Farnie, went on to damn Menken and all American "corruptions in language, in religion, in art." It ended on a racist note by lumping "a Yankee audience" with "a Sepoy [Indian] community."

Farnie was a dandy and London insider who had a reputation as a womanizer. He had no personal scruples but supposed that Menken, as an American Jew, was vulnerable to the insidious charge of "impurity." Farnie's motive was increased circulation, and possibly he wished to play giant killer. Adah, coached by Smith, responded by letter, knowing Farnie would print it:

To begin with the play is Lord Byron's Mazeppa *and I impersonate the hero, but my costume, or rather want of costume, as might be inferred, is not in the least indelicate. . . .*

I have long been a student of sculpture, and my attitudes, selected from the works of Canova, present a classicality which has been invariably recognized by the foremost of American critics. I may add that my performance of Mazeppa *had a most prosperous career in America, and, as is usual in such cases, my success created a host of imitators, and some of these ladies, I hear, have adopted a style of drapery inconsistent with delicacy, or good taste.*

Menken then compared her outfit with that of a ballerina, or a dancer in the "burlesques" popular at several legitimate theaters, claiming it was no skimpier. Finally, she invited Farnie to come to Astley's and see for himself. So in one brief riposte she had defended her morals, implied she would wear very little, knocked her competitors, and put in a plug for the show. Farnie got the message, and in the next issue of the *London Orchestra* he was more conciliatory. He was on the way to becoming (so he would later claim) a Menken intimate.

Smith, who had invested a large sum, walked the narrow line between arousing the public's interest in *Mazeppa* and having the production banned by the Lord Chamberlain. Whenever possible he invoked the name of Byron, a pariah while alive but afterward a pillar of English literature. Adah played her part, receiving callers at her hotel and attending the theater on the arm of John Oxenford of *The Times*. Discretion was the lubricant of Victorian society. Men of privilege often kept a mistress, while their wives were expected to be faithful. Then, as now, the crime was in getting caught. Yet society admired the virility of the transgressor. Prime Minister Palmerston, an octogenarian, was accused in court of having relations with a married nursery maid but was acquitted. His rival Disraeli quipped it was a good thing, for if the public believed he kept a mistress at his age, they would make him dictator!

In Albany, Adah had played *Mazeppa* after two days' preparation. Smith insisted on two *months* of rehearsal, so that his star would mesh perfectly with an excellent cast, headed by the clever actress Lucy Rushton as Olinska. In addition, the movements of the advertised "Grand Stud of Forty Horses, Two Hundred Soldiers, and a Superb Ballet" had to be plotted and integrated. Finally, this Victorian Cecil B. DeMille declared the spectacular ready to open. Secretly, Smith felt as much trepidation as had the earlier Smith, manager of Albany's Green Street Theater.

An eager crowd pressed into Astley's on the evening of October 3, overflowing the pit, boxes, mezzanine, and two balconies. They stirred impatiently while a curtain-raiser called *The Double-Bedded Room* was being played. Adah, from the wings, was delighted to see the boxes occupied by gentlemen and ladies in formal attire. In the stalls were "real swells from the West-End," as Charles Roydant, all of thirteen, phrased it. There were journalists, too, personally invited. Adah was troubled by a rumor that Heenan would bring a claque to force her off the stage. But as Ed James remarked, "this served to excite the cockneys, usually rather phlegmatic."

Finally the great chandelier dimmed, the orchestra struck up, and the curtain rose to reveal the page Cassimir, in Turkish pantaloons, approaching the balcony of the Castellan's daughter to declare his love. The subdued lighting kept in shadow the looming mountain. From the start Adah had this crowd in her pocket. She accompanied her declaimed speeches by striking a classical pose—"as if with a view of satisfying an audience of photographers," noted a reviewer. Her style was similar to that of a silent screen actress, such as Clara Bow. Poses were exaggerated and held to create an impression on the viewers. Menken, like Bow, communicated to her breathless fans by sign.

In contrast, where Cassimir duels Olinska's suitor Count Premislas, Adah fought with vigor and spirit, charging the entire cast with her energy. However, London's *bon ton* had not traveled to the south bank to see *that* sort of action. At last came the strip scene. With the soldiers ganged up on Cassimir, he/she being violated was left to the audience's imagination. Suddenly the Naked Lady appeared, bound to the wild steed, which charged up the illuminated stage mountain. The scenery looked real, and from the cataracts flowed real water. Mechanical wolves nipped at the horse's heels, vultures flew overhead, and the illusion of breakneck speed was aided by artificial thunder and lightning and the orchestra's crescendo. The lady's nudity was illusive, since she wore a body stocking and a white dimity "nothing."

The curtain rang down on the first act to a roar of approval. Smith led Menken forward to accept the ovation. John Heenan got to his feet and applauded louder than the rest. Acts Two and Three of *Mazeppa* went well, keeping an enthusiastic audience on the edge of their seats. Whenever Menken vanquished a foe, the audience cheered, and she waved an acknowledgment from the saddle. At the final curtain, Smith approached to lead her out to the adoring crowd. The star waved him aside. "For heaven's sake, man, stop fussing," she said.

Adah Isaacs Menken took her bows and bouquets alone.

Reviewers, while more modulated, reflected the approval of the first-nighters. The journalists complimented Menken's athletic figure but remarked mainly on the propriety of her costume, or lack thereof. John Oxenford noted that Adah "goes through perils that were never contemplated by her male predecessors." He too praised her "magnificent figure," then wrote: "The lady's costume . . . is not a whit more objectionable than those of the female Highland boys and mythological beauties who are now accepted as matters of course." He would remain a staunch supporter.

The *Daily Telegraph* began with a comment that since America was "the country where woman's rights have been so strenuously claimed," it was no surprise to find an American star playing a man's role. Nonetheless she had "an excellent figure associated with a pretty face," although that figure was "somewhat lavishly displayed." Still, "no eyes need be shocked by the appearance Miss Menken presents when divested of her sumptuous apparel."

Adah's performance received many more yeas than nays. The *Morning Advertiser* found that she "vividly and gracefully portrayed" her part. The reviewer noted that "the female portion of the audience were as enthusiastic in their applause as the masculine." *The Age* raved about

Menken's "beauty of person," to which was added "a genius which burns and glows in every movement and gesture." The reviewer concluded: "She stands peerless in *Mazeppa.*"

However, *The Queen,* an ultrarespectable lady's weekly, claimed to be offended by a woman who "emulated the muscular power of a man." *Punch* attacked viciously, calling Adah, "a bare-backed jade on [a] bare-backed steed." The editor Mark Lemon referred to her as a "vulgar Jewess." *Punch,* and the conservative males who read it, would remain opposed to Menken. Farnie's *Orchestra* again sounded a moral note, blaming the public for attending the show. "The attraction which draws full houses to Astley's lies undoubtedly in its impurity," opined the hypocrite. But here was the money line of which publicists dream.

Smith printed a booklet of reviews and placarded London with more posters, screaming of the Naked Lady's unprecedented success. He sent puffs to all the press but especially to those who had disapproved of the show. He arranged an interview with the respected *Illustrated London News,* which ran a mostly fictitious biography that stressed Adah's French background, her youthful mastery of the classics, music, and painting, her marriage to Heenan (but not the others), her great popularity in America, and Smith's cleverness in engaging this nonpareil. The promoter knew his public, for the *Court Journal* summed up the result of his efforts:

> *MENKEN is the fashion of the metropolis. She is the most talked-of actress in London; and in society, at the clubs, in the streets, and on [the Stock Ex] 'Change, the name of MENKEN remains paramount. The lady Mazeppa will make a fortune for both herself and her manager.*

Money, except to spend it, held little interest for the lady. Fame was her addiction. She instructed ticket sellers and ushers to warn her if anyone special was in the house and to direct them to her box. According to a list provided by Smith to the press, the Duke of Cambridge, the Duke of Hamilton, the Earl of Chesterfield, the Earl of Uxbridge, Lord Chelsea, and Lord and Lady Lincoln were among the titled who attended

Astley's during the first month of *Mazeppa*. Generally they visited Menken in her dressing room after the show, and those she favored would be invited to her soirees at the Westminster Palace. In Ed James's words, Menken had begun to host "breakfasts, dinners, and reunions there that would break a Belmont's heart or purse . . . if continued long."

James, who visited Adah in London that autumn, begged her to put aside something for the proverbial rainy day. She laughed, saying, "Ed, when I get so that I have to *borrow* money, I want to die." He did not like the tone of her voice. James, portrayed by Dickens as pushy, couldn't help being impressed by the attendees who gathered at Adah's for good food, wine, and conversation:

> *At the Westminster we frequently met such men as Charles Dickens, Charles Reade, [playwright] Watts Phillips, the Duke of Edinburgh, [tragedian] Charles Fechter, the Duke of Wellington, John Oxenford, Algernon Swinburne, Prince Baerto . . . Lieutenant Wylde Hardynge and his wife, Belle Boyd (the Confederate spy), together with Mad[ame] George Sand, Jenny Lind, and many others of note.*

Among the others were a gaggle of reporters and playwrights—the young, rising men Adah had learned to cultivate. They wrote drama reviews, did interviews, and could be employed as moral defenders in case of need. Another group was patronized by Adah out of conviction alone: theater people. She had seen hard times and knew how it felt to be down at the heels. "Her generosity was unparalleled," wrote a nineteenth century biographer. "She squandered money recklessly, but seldom upon herself." Adah gave liberally to those who even hinted at being needy, whether they were stagehands, out-of-work actors, or beggars on the street. Her friends knew that "with all her faults, she was a noble creature."

Adah retained her loyalty to the losing Confederate cause. Belle Boyd was always welcome, and Belle's making off with and marrying one of her jailers, Lieutenant Hardynge, was a story to warm Adah's heart. Perhaps Paul Barkley's influence was felt, for he introduced

General John Breckinridge, C.S.A., a former vice president of the United States, into their circle. Adah's salon was the most desired ticket in town, and the Prince of Wales was any day expected to attend.

More from a distance, Adah won the favor of those all-important middle classes, so memorably drawn in Dickens's novels, who packed the pit and galleries of Astley's night after night. The *Orchestra* wrote of "applauding shouts that go up from an over-crowded house at every bold movement of the semi-nude actress." The audience, demanding curtain calls, declined to drop orange peels or whelk shells from the balconies. Because there was never a vacant seat, Smith did a lively trade in advance bookings at a premium price. This staple of the modern theatrical business was made possible by the popularity of Menken's *Mazeppa,* which ran uninterrupted until the Christmas pantomime season, an unbreakable tradition in London. Indeed, during the annual cattle show, Smith put on special matinees for the farmers who had come to town eager to see the saucy wench in tights.

Menken was able to use her reserved box to good effect. She was delighted when Charles Reade wrote asking for seats. Reade, in his middle years, was the leading playwright of the realistic school, a prolific writer who focused on social reform. Involved with the actress Laura Seymour, Reade would become Adah's friend and advisor. Meanwhile, she knew that to be regarded as more than a sensation actress, and to have her poetry taken seriously, she needed the patronage of a truly great man. In England of the 1860s, this meant Charles Dickens. Since Adah's luck was running, the novelist, known for his night rambles about town, walked into the lady's arms.

According to John Forster, Dickens's friend and biographer, the novelist, then in his fifties, walked to Waterloo Bridge to cool a boiling head. There he saw a poster of Mazeppa being carried away by her untamed steed. It brought to mind earlier, pleasant memories of the horse dramas he had seen at Astley's. Dickens went to the theater and asked the man at the box office for a ticket in the stalls. To Forster, he described the following exchange:

"None left, sir."

"For a box-ticket."

"Only standing-room, sir."

Then the man (busy in counting great heaps of veritable checks) recognizes me and says: "Mr. Smith will be very much concerned when he hears that you went away, sir."

"Never mind; I'll come again."

"You never go behind [backstage], I think, sir, or—?"

"No, thank you, I never go behind."

"Mr. Smith's box, sir—"

"No, thank you, I'll come again."

Now, who do you think the lady is? If you don't already know, ask that question of the highest Irish mountains that look eternal, and they'll never tell you—Mrs. Heenan!

Dickens did come again. But his attitude summed up Adah's problem in a name: Despite the fame she had acquired, to some she was still Mrs. Heenan. In fact, John Heenan was back in her life! He had arrived, derby in hand, repentant, falling to his knees to beg forgiveness and declare his eternal love. She sent him away, but not without encouragement. Adah had something in store for the older-looking, handsome ex-champ, who needed her far more than she needed him.

Barkley, a man of intelligence, got wind of Heenan hanging around and that Adah had flirted with him. He threatened to return to New York. From that metropolis, licking its wounds from the war, Adah heard that Robert Newell was bent on causing her trouble. She hoped to avoid scandal, and she feared that her cast-off husband might do her reputation great harm. She wrote to Ed James, imploring him to have Newell watched. Adah, the most successful American ever to play in London, who was fast becoming the spoiled pet of genius and royalty, felt as if life was a lovely dream, from which she might awaken to harsh reality.

C.H. FOSTER
WITH SPIRIT OF ADA ISAACS MENKEN
SPIRIT PHOTO BY MUMLER.

Adah Menken passed on in 1868, but her ghost was often called up in séances. She has become immort

Suffering from tuberculosis and injuries from her daredevil act, Adah—at thirty-three, and at the height of her fame—was doomed.

Sitting by Adah's sickbed in Paris, Henry Wadsworth Longfellow composed a beautiful love poem.

*Adah and her friend,
novelist George Sand.*

*Adah with Algernon Swinburne,
who boasted of being her lover;
their affair was a strange one.*

*The "infamous" photograph of Menken and Swinburne. It shows a declin
Menken.*

...dah is posed intimately with her lover, novelist Alexandre Dumas, who boasted of his African heritage. These photos caused a global scandal.

CH. REUTLINGER PHOT.

Adah with her son, who died while she performed in Vienna in 1867.

MISS DADA MENKEN
(THÉÂTRE DE LA GAITÉ)

A caricature from Paris, where Adah packed the Théâtre de la Gaîté with Les Pirates de la Savane. *The racist attitude is obvious, as is the pun on her name ("Dada" was slang for "hobby horse").*

Belle Boyd, notorious Confederate spy, attended Adah's London salons along with celebrities ranging from Jenny Lind to Charles Dickens.

Adah, married to her fifth husband, Captain James Barkley, is pregnant.

ADAH ISAAC MENKEN.

Joaquin Miller, the original cowboy poet; Adah's good friend, she hinted to him about her racial background.

Sam Clemens, cub reporter, at the time he became Mark Twain; in 1863–64, he covered Adah for Nevada's Territorial Enterprise, and was both attracted to and frightened by her.

Adah was photographed by Napoleon Sarony in a costume from Child of the Sun. She had become the toast of London and successfully toured England.

Adah with a winning hand in San Francisco during the California Gold Rush; she was the talk of the town, had bags of gold dust tossed onstage, and won still more gambling.

Robert Newell, journalist and critic, was Adah's fourth husband.

H.W.Smith. N.Y.

Walt Whitman, Adah's friend and mentor; his groundbreaking poetry collection, Leaves of Grass, *was described as obscene for its overt sexuality.*

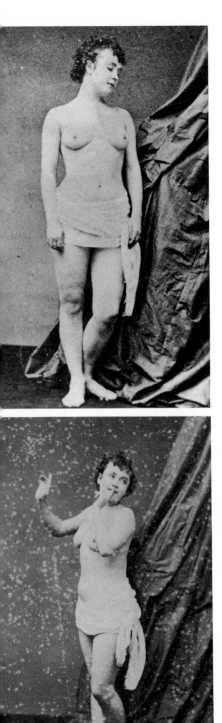

Did Adah pose for these seminude photos, or did the photographer paste her head on another woman's body? Either way, they sold briskly under the counter.

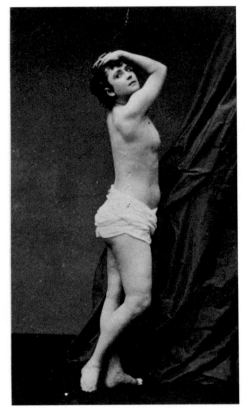

MAZEPPA WALTZES.

Adah, as Mazeppa, tied to the untamed steed; a popular composer made use of Adah's even greater celebrity.

Adah in her body stocking, which was actually flesh-colored.

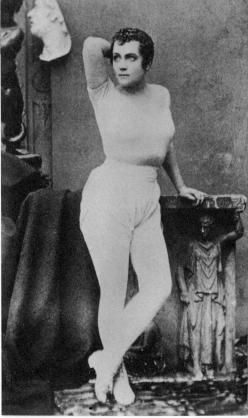

Edwin James, Adah's "brother" and publicist, served as Dickens's model for the barrister Stryver in A Tale of Two Cities.

Prizefighting champion John Carmel Heenan, Adah's third husband and great love.

Chapter Seventeen:

FOUR ACES

She lands in London, takes a gorgeous suite
In London's grandest hostelry, entertains
Charles Dickens, Prince Baerto, and Charles Reade,
The Duke of Wellington, and Swinburne, Sand
And Jenny Lind; and has a liveried coachman;
And for a crest a horse's head surmounting
Four aces, if you please. And plays Mazeppa,
And piles the money up.

So Edgar Lee Masters, the homegrown Chicago poet, imagined Menken's London triumph. Masters had it right, except for the stanza's last line, because his subject went through money faster than she earned it. Throughout the autumn of 1864 Adah's glad-hand entertaining began nightly in her spacious dressing room and continued at her hotel suite into the small hours. After the show, guests were as plentiful as the banks of flowers that lined the mirrors, and witticisms from the *bon ton* flowed as freely as the host's champagne.

Ed James wanted to share in the good fortune of his "sister." In August he was lobbying Frank Queen of *The Clipper* to send him to Dublin to cover the fight between Briton Jem Mace and American Joe Coburn. Then Joe, Adah's friend from the Heenan days, showed up in London and amiably barged into her hotel room. He found her at breakfast with Paul Barkley. The moment was embarrassing because a man and woman who breakfasted together were assumed to have spent the night together. Adah knew Joe would report back to Ed, and she was afraid her "brother" would disapprove of the liaison.

She wrote him a letter denying the obvious:

> *I am very much afraid that Joseph misunderstood me in speaking of a certain gentleman that he met at my rooms. I have since believed that J. C. thought there to be an undue intimacy existing. I only joked J. C. about the gentleman but . . . I think he made the mistake I allude to. He may even have said something in his letters to you of it. But I assure you it was all a mistake on Joseph's part.*

This heavy-handed fibbing failed to satisfy James. When Adah did not receive a reply for two weeks, she chided him: "Have you a new love? 'Be off with the old love before you are on with the new' is an adage to be remembered by you. Besides I am not to be thrown off at all." Here she tweaked her "brother" about his philandering, which had gotten him into trouble in both the old country and the new. Adah and Ed had deep feelings for one another, but these were not sexual on her part. Ed was older, and he lacked the dash, or the literary standing, that attracted her. Whatever his initial wishes, over the years a platonic intimacy took root between the pair, a devotion that proved more lasting than Adah's infatuations or marriages.

Finally, Ed informed his "sister" that he was coming to London and longed to see and kiss her. She shot back: "I shall see you [soon], and then if you are tired of kissing the picture you shall kiss me. . . . But you need not give up the picture, for you can kiss that as often as you like, and you can only kiss me once." This flirting with a leash on it served Adah well with Brother Ed, whose straying had caused his wife to divorce him. It did not discourage but rather bound him closer to Menken, the star.

When Ed arrived in October, he was amazed at how quickly society had taken up Adah, who lived like a princess. He recalled that "she had her team, with liveried coachman and footman, and a horse's head surmounting four aces for a crest." At E. T. Smith's suggestion, she had the brougham (a four-wheeled carriage) built to order, and when ready it was the fanciest coach in town. Silver bells jingled from the yellow harness, the wheels were studded with silver-plated nails, a rampant horse leaped from each corner of the roof, and gold foliage bordered the doors, in the center of which Menken's crest was emblazoned. It bore the motto IMMENSABILIS. When she rode out everyone stared at the mysterious figure behind the fringed curtains.

The coach would come to a tawdry end. It was so expensive that Smith had laid out the money and Adah signed notes payable over a period of four years. She never did pay them, and the carriage ended up in New York, where in 1866 she sold it for the cost of its materials. But in London that autumn Adah was in top form, tossing bags of coins at street beggars, never thinking of money. A complicated love life was her great vexation.

The prizefight in Dublin was called off. Some said that the handsome Joe Coburn, a boxer, did not want to risk his looks in the ring with slugger Jem Mace. While Ed James was in Ireland, he met John Heenan. Hurrying to London, James warned Adah against Heenan. Strangely, she was more concerned about Robert Newell, and wished to be divorced as soon as possible. Meanwhile, James and Barkley were thrown together. Although the captain behaved in the manner of a Southern gentleman, Brother Ed distrusted his intentions toward Adah. After the opening of *Mazeppa,* James boarded ship for New York. It was dangerous for him to linger in England, where he had avoided prison by going into exile. *The English Churchman* dropped a broad hint, referring to him as "the same person who recently 'left his country for his country's good.'"

Heenan began to pay court to his ex-wife. With honest Jem Mace as chaperone, the former Benicia Boy hung about Menken's dressing room and wheedled his way into her salons. John was a better man than the cocky youth who had fought Tom Sayers for the heavyweight championship. Tom King had knocked the stuffing as well as the false pride out of him.

Adah did not discourage the fawning of "Lord Carmel," as she dubbed him. This angered Barkley, and in November he returned to New York. With the Confederacy on its last legs, he would turn up as an outside broker on the stock exchange. Traditionally the American Exchange was called "the curb," because it took place on the sidewalk outside the New York Stock Exchange building. Here a lively trade was practiced by those who lacked an inside seat. Barkley made a risky living, and it was this poker-player aspect of his personality that James distrusted. The gambler might be flush at the moment, but how long would it be before he was asking Ed's "sister" for handouts?

By letter, Adah reassured James about Heenan: "I will throw him off whenever I want. I do not care for him, but that does not prevent him caring for me." Meanwhile, she continued to fret over Newell, and she urged James to befriend her new love, Barkley:

> *Pray keep me posted about him [Newell]. He means mischief. If he finds [Barkley] is in N.Y. he will take his life. Say nothing of this, but be my guardian angel in this matter as far as you can. I have no other friend to confide in but you. The "Prince" [Barkley, given a title] is my heart's blood. If you love me, as I believe you do, write me everything and keep your eyes open for my sake.*

Newell, living with his mother, was writing forgettable fiction and holding down an editor's position at the *Daily Graphic*. He had begun to suffer from the so-called writer's cramp and word blindness that would cut short his career. He would die alone and forgotten in Manhattan during a heat wave in July 1901, his body undiscovered for several days. An unfinished novel about his former wife, who became a lifelong obsession, lay nearby. Adah's fear of this shy, introverted man probably stemmed from guilt, a feeling she had wronged him. At some level she grasped that Robert Newell had seen what was finest in her, though he lacked the strength to bring it out.

Toward Heenan, a less worthy character, Adah felt a mixture of sorrow and contempt. She wanted revenge and took it. In a remarkable letter to Ed James, she revealed the state of her soul:

There is only one love to one life. Carmel [Heenan] would die for me tomorrow. But it is too late. He has been the ruin of what might have been a splendid life. It was he who taught me to disbelieve in man; it was he who made me callous and unfeeling. I can never be what I once was to him, truthful, pure and good. He destroyed a beautiful and bountiful nature. He seeks to revive that which is dead. Now, Ed, it is my turn to inflict suffering.

Adah led on the ex-champ, and she was pleased when he sent his mistress, Sarah Stevens, packing to California. She smiled inwardly when he swore he had always loved her. When, on his knees, the big man proposed all over again, she had won her victory. To Ed she wrote:

I do not mean to hurt the only man I ever really loved, but I cannot help it. It is too late. I do not tell him all of myself, for when he is with me the old dead power comes up, and I am silent and let him talk of his love and the reward he thinks he can bring me in his devotion and conscious faith. I know he is now true, but—too late. I can not believe again. He killed me—I died. There is no resurgam. I cannot tear the bandage from my dead eyes even to say: "You crucified me." He knows it, but he hopes. Alas!

For her penitent knight, Adah deliberately exhibited her newfound wealth, fame, and fancy friends. She let the washed-up fighter, broke as ex-champs often are, salivate at the feast. For a time she dangled hope before him, keeping him on as a suitor at her court. After all, he was ornamental at her salons.

The Menken was more talked and argued about than any other actress of the time. All of London was either mad about or at her.

Photos of her poses were for sale at every news dealer, porcelain figurines were cast to resemble the Naked Lady, and Michael Balfe composed the "Mazeppa Waltzes," to be played by the Guards' Band at that Victorian institution, the Crystal Palace. Playwrights wrote broad burlesques, actresses imitated Adah's act, and sidewalk buskers sang Menken-inspired doggerel. The *London Review*, on the other hand, called her "a notorious woman from America" who had nothing more to offer than "pink legs [and] bare arms."

The outcast from New Orleans, stemming from poor and obscure origins, had proved she was the brightest star in the firmament. Alex Menken, who had called her an adventuress; Heenan, who had labeled her a prostitute; and Newell, who had mocked her desire for fame—they would have to eat their words. Yet Adah's emotional life was a shambles. She feared her ex-husbands, was estranged from her current lover, and she could fully trust only Ed James, former rogue. Adah's solution was to reach out toward the most famous man of all.

Ever since she arrived in London, Adah had been dying to meet Charles Dickens. Then in his mid-fifties, the novelist, editor, and social reformer had become a national institution. He was a man of some vanity, not only about his accomplishments, but also his dress and looks. Everyone was struck by the brilliance of his eyes and his smart, even dandyish, appearance. Yet, while attempting to keep up his breakneck pace, Dickens had aged badly. A sketch of him toward the end of his life—face lined by care, hair turned gray—looks like a man much older than the sixty years he would never see. Dickens and Menken both lived full out.

Immediately after the incident at Astley's box office, when the great man was turned away because there were no seats, Adah wrote an apology and offered him the use of her own box on any evening he wished. Dickens, an amateur but devoted thespian, attended with his friend, the handsome Charles Fechter, who was London's leading actor. To Menken's delight, they visited her dressing room between the acts. This was the beginning of a warm friendship between Adah and both Charleses, though that with Fechter would be longer lasting. Initially, Dickens became involved in her plans to visit Paris once *Mazeppa* closed. On December 12, shortly before the Christmas pantomimes began, she wrote to James:

> *My good friend, the great Fechter, is to be present at the reading of my new piece, and is to make the suggestions suited to my talent. I cannot tell you how kind F. has been to me. He has conducted all my Paris engagement, and made me out a great creature to the French Press.*

She added that Dickens had also encouraged her performing in Paris. Menken referred to negotiations with the Porte Saint-Martin theater for a joint appearance with the famous author. She would do scenes from *Mazeppa* while he would read from his novels. Dickens, the best dramatic reader of his day, had performed earlier in Paris, and the proposed theatrical bill was not as incongruous as it seems. Dickens always needed money to support his country home at Gad's Hill, Kent and a London establishment for his daughters' social life. He provided six hundred pounds annually to his estranged wife, Catherine, and there were continual outlays for the rest of his brood of nine children. Besides, Paris meant to Dickens, as to many other Englishmen, a place to kick up his heels and do the unusual. That the negotiations fell through was probably best for all concerned. Onstage, Dickens was no match for the female Mazeppa!

Looking ahead, Adah demanded that Ed James immediately collect her poetry that had appeared in the *Sunday Mercury* since 1860. "I have the advice and patronage of the greatest literary man of England who will revise my poems for me," she boasted. "Such a blessing may never occur again." But she had permitted wish to become fact. Dickens, who edited a weekly magazine and wrote his novels serially against deadlines, was pressed for time. Moreover, the separation from his wife left him in a precarious social position. Adah did not seem to understand that the author of *A Christmas Carol*, who was spokesman for a charitable Christmas philosophy, could not risk a close association with the Naked Lady.

Fortunately, James was delayed in accomplishing the task set him. Dickens didn't care for Menken's poetry. He felt she was talented but lacked discipline. He agreed with the remark of playwright and novelist Charles Reade, a friend of his and of Menken's, that her poetry "was as bad as other people's—would have been worse if it could." However, Dickens's taste in poetry was, as the *Britannica* puts it, "imperceptive." The Menken oeuvre, *Infelicia*, would not be published in England until after her death in 1868. The book was dedicated to Dickens with his permission, but it was actually published with the help of that *enfant terrible*, Algernon Swinburne.

Dickens spent Christmas 1864 at Gad's Hill. Here, as was his custom, he handsomely entertained company: Charles Fechter and John Forster (the author's future biographer) and their wives. Georgina Hogarth, his wife's younger sister, acted as mistress of the house. Since May 1858 Dickens had lived apart from Catherine, the mother of his nine children. Forster claims that "the satisfactions which home should have supplied, and which indeed were essential requirements of his nature, he had failed to find in his home." A rumor, fanned by his mother-in-law, flared into a national scandal: Dickens was sleeping with Georgina. Since she was his sister-in-law, this meant, in biblical terms, incest. If true, it would have ruined him.

The great man had come up the hard way from a lower-middle-class family that spent time in debtors' prison. Now he fought back with a front-page airing of his marital woes in his weekly, *All the Year Round*. Playing a Victorian trump card, he claimed that Catherine had never been a caring mother to their children. Along with motherhood, there was an opposite female state equally revered, and Dickens played this card also. A medical doctor was brought in to examine Georgina, and he gave a written opinion that she was a virgin. Dickens, by exposing others, kept his reputation.

What his readers didn't know, and neither did Adah, was that the great extoller of domestic bliss was secretly keeping a mistress, a much younger woman. In 1857 Dickens hired a Mrs. Ternan, a professional actress, and her two daughters to play in an amateur version of Wilkie Collins's *The Frozen Deep,* in which he himself starred. Dickens was forty-five and the younger Ternan sister, Ellen, eighteen. She is described as having "a pretty face and well-developed figure," and Dickens instantly fell in love. He persuaded her (or, more probably, her mother) that, to keep her virtue, she must quit the stage. He installed her in a house at Slough (Kent), convenient to a railway junction. There he could secretly visit her on his way to and from London, and, on occasion, take her on a trip to France, where their relationship would be unremarkable.

Dickens's daughter Katie said that Ellen "came like a breath of spring into the hard-working life of Charles Dickens and enslaved him. . . . Who could blame her? . . . He had the world at his feet. She was elated and proud to be noticed by him." Their liaison on the sly—wealthy older man keeps young, impoverished lover—was typical for its Victorian time. Even in Paris Victor Hugo's lifelong liaison with an actress and Émile Zola's with a serving girl were cloaked in secrecy. In nineteenth century Europe divorce was too difficult a proceeding for a woman, and scandal too risky for a man, for either to act honestly. This meant a lonely life for Ellen and a fractured emotional life for Charles. However, by the 1860s Catherine was out of the way, and Ellen could visit the Dickens home at Gad's Hill. His family and inti-mates kept his trust. Ellen was present at his deathbed, and in his will Charles left her the Scrooge-like sum of 1,000 pounds for her twelve years of devotion.

This was the system of sexual hypocrisy that Adah Menken confronted. Not only was there a double standard, but prostitution, though cloaked, was better understood than passion. Sexual free-dom for women was simply denied. As an American actress who had stripped onstage and divorced several husbands, Adah could not hope for respectability in Victoria's England. Yet she did gain the respect of the literati and the adulation of the public. In truth, the middle classes, stifled by their dreary, ultrarespectable lives, were desperate for entertainment. The Menken promised thrills, and she delivered. She described December 17 at Astley's, the last night of *Mazeppa*, as "a great event. I received many presents, and was crowned by one of the audience with the *Laurel*."

The symbol of the victorious warrior was appropriate. Adah had given her all, for as she informed James, "I was very near 'used-up.'" Yet Smith was urging on her a new play by John Brougham, a mediocre American actor and writer, called *The Child of the Sun*. She would go into rehearsal immediately after the New Year. "I shall wait a little longer if I can," she wrote wistfully. "I should like to run off to Paris—two weeks for a 'lark.' I'll try it."

In Paris Adah had introductions from Fechter, among them to his friend Théophile Gautier. The poet, novelist, and art and ballet critic had been for decades a central figure on the Parisian literary scene, and he knew everyone. Gautier is associated with the doctrine of art for art's sake, which was a revolutionary fanfare opposed to the moralistic drone of the mid-nineteenth century. He believed the artist must leave off preaching and pursue perfection of form. A forerunner of Baudelaire, he was a married man who kept two mistresses, and he became an immediate admirer of The Menken.

They had a nice chat, and Gautier recommended she cultivate a pair of younger English poets, Dante Gabriel Rossetti and Algernon Swinburne. He thought he could provide the star with an appropriate vehicle, a classical drama, since they both admired Greek art. There was talk that he had drafted a synopsis, which she approved. However, Adah returned to London and no play was forthcoming from Gautier. This was only one of the attempts she would make in the following years to secure a first-class drama in which to show off her acting ability.

In London, Smith had soured on Brougham's *Child*. Why bother with the expense of a new production when the tried-and-true *Mazeppa* could be sent on the road? Fechter agreed, and he found Adah a manager, a shrewd Scot named John McKenna, to shepherd her on a tour of the British provinces. The cities were prosperous, crass, sharply divided between owners and workers, and as straitlaced as the cities of the American Midwest in which the actress had done so well. McKenna was worried about her reception among the supposedly dour Scots, but Menken promptly visited the *Glasgow Herald* and chatted up the newspaper lads. Good reviews packed the theater for two weeks straight.

Liverpool was still more receptive. The amphitheater was crammed every evening, and Adah was heaped with presents and love notes. She drove through the city streets, visited the Exchange, where the worldwide price of cotton was set, and called on the mayor and council. The reviewer for the *Daily Post*, the organ of business, took careful inventory of her assets—figure, limbs, bust, face—and declared himself pleased. He also assured the ladies there was nothing improper in her performance. Meanwhile, the sons of the city's first families escorted Adah home after each performance.

There were some attacks on her in the press, but these were ill-natured jeremiads against her country and the freedom it fostered. America, one journal ranted, had given the world "Spiritualism, Mormonism, and Barnumism . . . but *La Menken* surpasses and transcends all in utter worthlessness." Adah brushed it off and informed James that "the excitement here has exceeded London. Twenty policemen have to nightly guard my carriage the crowd is so immense." To her joy, Paul Barkley joined her for three weeks. After each performance her prince tossed her bouquets, then waited in her dressing room while she changed before they went out for supper. Adah had taken to wearing black velvet, not in mourning but to create a daring, minimalist look that she mixed with long gypsy earrings, barbaric bracelets, and glittering diamond rings. Declining to rouge her cheeks, she looked pale and mysterious, and the men were entranced.

News of Lee's surrender at Appomattox sent the former Captain Barkley back to New York. His past allegiance no longer mattered, but Barkley had to attend to business. Adah, looking ahead to engagements at Birmingham and Leeds, was too preoccupied to mourn the defeat of the South. Fan mail overflowed her writing table. In London Brougham was still working on the play Smith hoped to mount in the fall. From Paris the manager of the Théâtre du Châtelet offered to star Adah in a French version of *Mazeppa*. From New York she heard via Colonel Allston Brown that producer James Nixon hoped she would do a play on Broadway. Adah hurriedly wrote to Gus Daly, known as an adapter of European plays, pleading with him to find something new and challenging for her.

The star put off her personal correspondence, apologizing to Brother Ed:

I'll tell you how it is, old fellow: sometimes, I am afraid, I neglect you, and for that my conscience will not let me sleep the "sleep of the just." I mean to do everything that is right, pleasant and proper. But you know what hell is said to be paved with. I believe that I am a very large shareholder in the pavement. I would like to sell out, but so many wretches have invested largely in the same stock that I fear it will be rather difficult to find a victim.

The language is that of a hustling broker, Barkley. It seems odd that Adah would console Ed in the tone of a man he didn't care for, but she continues on about Barkley: "He was my child-ideal. He is now the light of my life."

The first part of the admission has been treated as another of Adah's fibs, but taken literally, it indicates that a portion of her formative years were spent in Memphis, Tennessee (Barkley's hometown), as well as New Orleans and Texas. While this adds little toward identifying Adah's biological father, it places Barkley as the ideal father figure she sought in her lovers. Because of her heightened expectations, this declaration of love foreshadows an unhappy ending.

Adah makes a second, startling revelation in this letter: "You know, dear Ed, I have had no real opportunity of telling you my story, although I sincerely wished to do so in London. I could tell you things you little dream of." So not even Brother Ed had been told the truth of the early struggles from which emerged Adah Menken, superstar. As for tales she spun to eager reporters from the metropolitan dailies . . . she could put on a life story with the ease of lipstick.

Back in London in June after a wildly successful tour, Adah agreed to a limited season of *Mazeppa*. She was receiving a fifty/fifty split on the gate, which made her by far the highest paid actress in the world. She could afford to be amused by the crop of imitators that sprang up in the provincial cities, in America, and even in London. At a theater in Cardiff, Wales, there appeared "the most beautiful Mazeppa seen anywhere"; at Hull, "the unforgettable Mazeppa"; at the City of London theater, "the Beautiful Menken, together with her celebrated steed, Ada." Their acts consisted mainly of a prolonged striptease, especially interesting in the case of drag queen Adah Inez Montclain, "a regular New York guy," according to Ed James.

As word of Adah's success got back to the States, the ranks of her imitators swelled. She joked with Ed, who had been slow in writing, "I presume some of the army of 'Mazeppas' have captured you. Let them beware! If they are worthy of my steel, let them remember that I wear a sword, and can use it too!" But it was no jest when the beautiful Leo Hudson's mount missed his footing on the runway, tumbled off the stage mountain, and fatally crushed his rider beneath him.

The danger of Menken's act, and her spirit and eloquence in performing it, once again packed Astley's. John Oxenford in the *Times* wrote that her reception resembled a Roman populace applauding the return of a victorious general. Enthusiasm ran higher than ever, and during July, when the other London theaters closed, Menken drew capacity audiences. Nor did it matter that, wearied by the demands of *Mazeppa*, she switched to her old sailor-boy standby, *Black-Eyed Susan*. The crowds came, Oxenford applauded Adah's "genuine pathos," and

Smith begged her to stay through the summer, after which he would arrange a triumphal tour of the European capitals.

She missed Paul Barkley, she smoked too much, and her temper was growing short. When a noted critic took his son backstage to meet the star, the lad was shocked to see a woman smoking a cigarette. "While she was acting," continued the critic, "a page boy stood in the wings with cigarettes on a silver tray in readiness for her." On occasion Adah preferred a Havana cigar, a taste she shared with George Sand.

On August 12, 1865, Adah sailed for New York. She needed to see her man and rid herself of the clingy ghost of Robert Newell. She traveled with "Lady" Nell Stuart as companion, and she debarked without fuss in a city chaotic but confident. The war had ended, and New York was back to making money and millionaires. With all her success abroad, Adah hadn't allowed herself to be forgotten here. She had sent Brother Ed a stream of news for *The Clipper*, including an imagined puff about Queen Victoria attending a performance of *Mazeppa*. The American press multiplied her husbands to seven, which kept her on the front page but complicated her relations with Barkley.

The latest rumor—that Adah had secretly wed one of the Davenport brothers, Spiritualist mediums much in vogue in England—surfaced after she established herself in a suite at the St. Nicholas Hotel on lower Broadway. Here she received her friends: Ed James, Gus Daly, Artemus Ward, and Ada Clare, who had returned from Hawaii. She embraced Stephen Masset, who she hadn't seen since the dark days of her despair. Adah promptly called in the press and denied the Davenport story, which she attributed to malicious sources. She had in fact attended the brothers' open meetings, and perhaps séances, but she rarely advertised her Spiritualist allegiance. Of course, she saw Barkley and explained all to him. Their romance flourished, but fear of scandal and the fluctuations of the stock market limited their time together.

Menken and Clare had much to talk about. Clare's Southern family had been bankrupted by the war, and she was writing for the newspapers to earn a living. She and every other woman who visited raved over Adah's sable coat, which cost thousands. Except for the impression created, it was useless in the dog days of August. Adah did the town with Gus Daly. They were good friends, and it did the young playwright's reputation no harm to be seen with an international star. They went to hear Artemus Ward at Irving Hall. He was at the peak of his fame, rambling on about Mormons or the "Children in the Wood," his sly mischief convulsing the audience with laughter.

A few days later Adah and Gus went to Artemus's hotel rooms, only to find him doubled up with intestinal pain. He had come down with dysentery, but he was lively enough to question Adah about London, where he was booked for a later date. He had offered to write a farce for her but turned the task over to Daly. Artemus knew he was suffering from pulmonary tuberculosis, against which his joking made a weak shield. Adah never again saw him in an intimate situation. The man who had made Lincoln laugh during the darkest hours of the Civil War died at Southampton in 1867, aged thirty-three. In Britain he was long regarded as the father of American humor.

Adah, in her own words, was "run to death in New York." Her stay was for only twelve days. During that time she set in motion the divorce from Newell, which was granted in Allen County, Indiana, in October. She prodded James to hunt for a complete file of her poetry. She harangued both Clare and Daly to write her a play. She talked business with Allston Brown, warning him that the producer Nixon must quickly meet her terms if he wished to star her in a Broadway production. E. T. Smith was counting on her to do Brougham's melodrama in the fall, after which he would ask her to sign for Paris and Madrid. Because of Barkley, she preferred New York, but Nixon hesitated to meet her minimum of five hundred dollars a performance (today, about twenty thousand dollars).

On the day before Adah was to sail for England, she went to her French hairstylist, a *monsieur* Gentil. The young dramatic actress Rose Etyinge, appearing at the Winter Garden, came in afterward and saw "a swathed and betowelled form occupying the operating chair." Rose was about to leave, when the figure turned to her, and she saw "one of the loveliest faces I ever beheld and [heard] a voice that begged me to remain. Never, either before or since, have I heard anything so perfect in sound as that voice. It transfixed me; it was like the softest, sweetest sound of an aeolian harp."

Later, on inquiry, Gentil explained to Rose that she had met Adah Isaacs Menken. Rose treasured the cameo of that memory, and a half-century later, she relived the moment in a memoir of her life in the theater.

Chapter Eighteen:

THE ROYAL BENGAL TIGER

E. T. Smith was not the man to wait for time or tide. While Adah's ship lay at anchor off Cobh, Ireland, in September 1865, he put *The Child of the Sun* into rehearsal at Astley's. Smith, looking over the playwright's shoulder, urged Brougham to concoct a spectacle: a series of scenes resembling Menken's greatest hits. The drama was set in Mexico, then much in the news because of the rebellion against the monarchs imposed by France, Maximilian and Carlotta. Adah would again ride a live horse up a stage mountain, then switch to a dummy mount across real-looking rapids. She would play not one but four male roles, including a wealthy *caballero*, a Comanche chief, a mute slave, and the hero, Leon. The slave wore next to nothing, which permitted Adah to amply display her charms.

The cast of brigands, peasants, Moorish servants, *caballeros*, and *señoritas* was grand. Furnished with songs by Irving Berlin and choreography by Busby Berkeley, *Child of the Sun* might have made a Hollywood spectacular. There were native dances, there was action, including a battle against the Indians, and there was The Menken, talking and mute, riding, dueling, and loving. Charles Fechter volunteered to fit the pieces together to make an actual drama.

Fechter, usually referred to as French, was born in London in 1824 of a German Jewish father and an English mother. He was educated in France and blessed with matinee idol good looks. He began his illustrious stage career in Paris, and he became well known in the major cities of Europe. In 1861 in London he caused a commotion playing Hamlet. Discarding the old tradition of bombast and gloom, he played the Dane as a natural man, active and emotional, with a slight French accent. His interpretation was acclaimed, and *Hamlet* became his signature piece. Dickens greatly relied on Fechter as an acting coach and a friend. He even tolerated his notorious borrowing of money that was never repaid.

Fechter and Adah hit it off at once. They shared an active, physical style of performance, and they even liked the same earthy dishes, such as sheep's head. On a deeper level, Adah was attracted by the tragedian's art, and he by her audacity and potential. Fechter saw in Menken the germ of a superb tragic actress. Soon the era of Sarah Bernhardt, Henry Irving, and Ellen Terry would arrive, but presently there were few serious plays being written or performed. So Fechter interested himself in management and the mechanics of presentation. He invented a method of sinking part of the stage to the theater basement where a scene could be set and then raised to view. Fechter helped with the theatrics of *Child of the Sun,* and his best efforts were sorely needed to enliven the turgid melodrama.

Rehearsals left Adah free in the evening. Although she complained that potential escorts were too old for her, she made certain to be out and written up in the press. Critic John Oxenford of *The Times* was her escort to the theater, and they appeared together at a number of first-nights. This caused the *London Review* to renew its scurrilous attacks on her:

> *The Menken has been airing herself at various places of amusement during the past week. On Monday she was at the New Royalty, and her peculiar conduct there attracted much attention. The gentlemen applauded her; the ladies hissed her.*
>
> *On Tuesday Miss Mazeppa occupied a stall at the Christy Minstrels. She rattled a metal fan through the first part of the programme, and let the world know that she was there. During the interval she left her place and her masculine escort tore her dress. She cursed him roundly in bad "French." We have had enough of Miss Menken, and wish the public had.*

Menken replied in a cutting style that should have caused the *Review* to take cover. "[A]t the New Royalty," she began, "the ladies did not hiss. *Ladies never do.*" The rest of her rejoinder was equally sarcastic but failed to silence the *Review's* tirades. Their object was to increase circulation, and a letter from Menken guaranteed robust sales of the rag. But she, too, had learned there was no such thing as bad publicity. She sent the *Review* one of her worst poems and the editors printed it.

On October 4 Oxenford took Adah to the opening of Charles Reade's *It Is Never Too Late to Mend,* an indictment of prison conditions. Then, Reade was nearly as popular as Dickens, but the timeliness of his plays and novels have caused them to be forgotten. He openly lived with an actress, Mrs. Seymour, and was an incessant crusader for political and social reform. He was friendly to Adah, and she sat in his private box. To his diary, Reade confided his thoughts on the star:

> *A clever woman with beautiful eyes—very dark blue. A bad actress, but made a hit playing Mazeppa in tights. She played one scene in* Black-Eyed Susan *with true feeling. A trigamist, or quadrigamist, her last husband was John Heenan, the prizefighter. I saw him fight Tom King.*
>
> *Menken talked well and was very intelligent in private. She spoilt her looks off the stage with white lead, or whatever it is these idiots of women wear. She did not rouge, but played some deviltry with her glorious eyes, which altogether made her spectral.*

This was a style she adopted in later years, a forerunner of Soho chic, which included dressing all in black. Menken had a way of inventing trends that would reappear at a much later date.

Child of the Sun never got off the ground. Early in the play the action drew round after round of applause. Leon, mounted on a white charger, dashed to the rescue of fair Juanita, threatened by a seething panther. The hero's dash, and frequent change of costume to play different roles, partially compensated for the leaden dialogue. The spectacle of horses, Indians, scalpings, and rescues was vast even for Astley's. In the next day's *Times*, Oxenford wrote, "Miss Menken never appeared personally to better advantage." However, the piece was "a chaotic mass, awaiting some master spirit who could reduce it to order." The action dragged, and the intermissions were interminable. When the curtain finally rang down, boos were mixed with applause. Adah hadn't heard the like since playing New York dives.

Failure never entered the star's mind. The show was cut and speeded up and the Menken mystique still drew crowds. As she reminded Ed James, she was the idol of the town. "They have given me a new name at the clubs. Instead of the 'Royal Menken,' I am now the 'Royal Bengal Tiger.' Is it not an engaging title?" In a follow-up letter she confided:

> *My carriages and horses are the finest in even gay London, where everything is beautiful. I have bought a charming villa in Brompton Road [South Kensington], furnished in a princely manner. I call it "The Lair."* . . . *"Beware how you rouse the Tiger in the Lair" is an old stage speech. It is said every evening in* The Child of the Sun. *Lord Carmel revels in the new title. I have everything I could wish for, but I am very miserable. Always remember that in the little coterie in the old* Clipper *office lives the remains of Dolores Adios Los Fuertes, known as Adah Isaacs Menken.*

Again, Adah thought of herself as dead, or at least alienated from an imagined true self. Writing to Brother Ed, she would reveal her innermost feelings:

> *I cannot truly love anyone since I suffered. Even you can never be compensated for your devotion to me. Yet I know that for you I would do all that love requires. Nothing can ever change me. If you were a murderer, a thief, imprisoned, I could die for you.* . . .
>
> *If there is any of the old fresh good soul of me left, you, Ed, have it entire.* . . . *God will bless and reward your great heart for its untiring*

faith. I can never imagine why you are so fond of poor me. I cannot imagine why anyone should be fond of me. . . . I am too cold and passionless since my crucifixion.

So the steadfast love of this woman known as the Naked Lady—the object of desire for males around the world—was a paunchy, middle-aged reprobate, a man she never slept with. And the one man who had really excited her desire she now kept like a pet on a leash, toying with him. She no longer wanted Heenan but couldn't let him go.

On the fourth night of performance Adah had a bizarre accident. She was riding the dummy horse, which was pulled across papier-maché rapids. A trap door had been left open and she and the horse disappeared through it. Adah's fall was broken by a stagehand who happened by, and though stunned, neither he nor Adah was badly hurt. To much applause the star went on with the show.

A few weeks later, Adah, careening up the stage mountain on a live horse, was again injured. It happened out of view of the audience, and the manager called for a doctor. A surgeon from Guy's Hospital responded, and with him was a young intern. Here is his description:

The manager led us to the green room. There, upon the floor, lay the beautiful Menken, with her silk fleshings stained with blood. "I don't think I am much hurt, doctor," she said. "I am only frightened." In turning a corner the horse had gone too near one of the flats and had grazed her limbs, tearing the flesh all down. Expedition being required, the room was cleared and we set to work. The wound, which was not dangerous but must have been very painful, was soon dressed, and the fair sufferer taken to her home at Brompton. It was my duty to visit her there, day after day. The injury healed, but the shock remained.

The intern's remarks show that The Menken was made of flesh and blood. The psychological effects of the injury lingered. There would be further accidents, and they would take a toll on her health.

Till Adah recovered from this one, an understudy, made up to resemble her, played her four roles for several nights running.

When Adah returned to *Child of the Sun* she found herself playing to houses only half-full. Smith tried his publicity tricks, but they did not work. The Menken, no longer London's focus of attention, grew irritable. She missed her lover in New York, and she smoked too much and slept badly. She put on weight, but Victorian men liked their women on the plump side. Those with thin legs often padded them to look curvier. In Menken's case, this led to a wager.

At one of the clubs a young lord loudly insisted that Adah padded her legs. A sculptor, with a keen eye, declared that the lady's calves were her own. A bet of ten pounds was agreed on. Side bets were placed and the clubmen bribed an actor in the cast, James Fernandez, to prove the point. In one scene he helped Menken to mount her horse. At a given performance he grabbed hold of her calf and squeezed. Menken leaned down and smacked him across the face. Fernandez had earned his money, and the lord paid up.

At another performance, according to humorist Sir Francis Burnand, the star made a memorable show of her hot temper. He attended Astley's with a friend, a stage manager who had gotten on the wrong side of Menken. During an intermission Burnand went to speak with E. T. Smith. Returning to the box, he found his friend cowering behind a chair, with Adah holding a raised dagger:

> She ignored me, except to acknowledge me with a nod as a witness, and addressed herself to him. Her eyes flashed more brilliantly than her dagger, and in other, and far different circumstances, they would have had quite a killing effect.
>
> Then she resumed the vituperation, which my entrance had temporarily interrupted. Menken was a fine, natural tragedienne, and never had I seen her do anything on the stage half as powerful as her performance at this moment in private life, and in a private box. . . .

Finally E. T. Smith burst into the box, and rushed the raging Men-ken back into her dressing-room, whence, a second later, she emerged on the stage, kissing both hands apologetically to the impatient audience, who now generously and enthusiastically testified their forgiveness of her on the spot.

On November 18 Smith closed *Child of the Sun*. Instead, he ran *Mazeppa* for the rest of the fall season, and again Astley's was packed nightly by cheering crowds. The question of why *Child* failed while *Mazeppa* continued to succeed cuts to the quick of the appeal of melo-drama. The genre presents "a dream world," writes Michael Booth in *English Melodrama*, "inhabited by dream people and dream justice, offer-ing audiences the fulfillment and satisfaction found only in dreams." This is a world of clear and simple good versus clear and simple evil, where the outcome is certain: "good triumphs over and punishes evil." Moreover, virtue is rewarded in a tangible way: marriage, a promotion, an inheritance.

However, *Mazeppa*, unlike *Child*, was based on a historical hero and dealt with serious issues of loyalty and betrayal. The Cossack prince Mazeppa's allegiance had been as changeable as Menken's mood or stage gender. His fate onstage was known, but each evening the woman who portrayed him might fall or be killed. Thus, a note of chance mocked the predictability of the standard melodrama. *Mazeppa* echoed Menken's life, which was the real, compelling drama her audiences had read and gossiped about, and had come to see. To them, Adah *was* Mazeppa.

This identification answers the question posed by W. S. Gilbert, a young dramatic critic not yet teamed up with the composer Sullivan: "Why doesn't somebody provide The Menken with a sensible play in which to display her talents?" Writers of renown would promise and try, but it was for the larger-than-life Mazeppa, rather than Adah her-self, that they failed to create a role. At that moment, in December 1865, Adah was writing to Gus Daly, "I am angry, disappointed, restless and annoyed." First she boasted of her riding habit, made by Poole of Savile Row, then berated Daly for not sending her a script to read. Of course, the flip side of Menken's annoyance was that she owned both the part and the myth. *Mazeppa* imitators have come and gone, but since Victorian times, the image of the Naked Lady has become fused with the heroic Cossack prince.

Adah Menken is seldom associated with the English Pre-Raphaelites, but her poetry is easier to place in connection with this iconoclastic, pictorial, pro-American movement. She was on easy terms with perhaps the most talented figure in the loose-knit, Bohemian group. Toward year's end, Adah was able to spend leisure time with the painter-poet Dante Gabriel Rossetti. He lived in a large old house at Cheyne Walk in Chelsea (from which he had recently evicted Algernon Swinburne). In true Romantic fashion, he shared his home with a menagerie that included peacocks, monkeys, and a wombat fond of cigars. Adah allowed Rossetti the use of her private box at Astley's, and he in turn encouraged her to seek a publisher for her poetry. The pair frequented oyster shops near Leicester Square, sampling old port wines. Sometimes Adah, incognito, went along while Rossetti and an American friend, James Whistler, hunted for the blue-and-white porcelain the artists collected and used as background in their paintings.

Rossetti and Adah were never lovers. Short, a bit thick, with a goatee and bright, popping eyes, the artist made an unlikely but busy ladies' man. He employed a series of attractive models at more than painting, and he would have a famous affair with Jane, wife of his best friend, William Morris. Rossetti's portraits of the long-necked Jane are among the most prized of Pre-Raphaelite paintings. However, he is best remembered for the bizarre gesture of burying his unpublished poetry along with his young wife, Lizzie Siddal, who died of an overdose of opium. It was an act of contrition that Rossetti would undo years later by disinterring the corpse to retrieve the moldy manuscript. His *Poems,* published in 1870, contain some of the finest verse of the Victorian period, and it is significant that he championed Adah's poetry, especially in its more mystical aspect. Unfortunately, in later years, Rossetti would descend into paranoia and finally succumb to drug addiction.

Menken, as a working actress, had less time for self-indulgence. During the winter of 1866 she again rode the rails to tour British cities, beginning with Liverpool. At Birmingham she met the photographer who would mean so much to her fame, Napoleon Sarony, a French Canadian residing in England. The theater manager was able to provide every lady seated in a box with an autographed *carte de visite* photo. Adah had to skip Edinburgh, where the city fathers were too prudish to permit her act, while at the busy spa town of Cheltenham a theatergoer complained to the local paper that Mazeppa was too *modestly* dressed. In Menken's posters she looked nearly naked, and the customer felt swindled!

Adah slipped away to Paris, where the managers of the Théâtre de la Gaîté were eager to have her perform. Théophile Gautier called on her at the Hotel du Louvre, bringing with him Anicet Bourgeois and Ferdinand Dugué, successful writers of melodrama. He felt their talents were better suited to Menken's style than his own, and, in fact, a play already existed, *Les Pirates de la Savane*. Once the pair had adapted it to Menken's specifications, she would appear at the Gaîté, home of spectaculars. With everything arranged, Adah's dream of starring in Paris seemed about to come true.

In March Adah resumed her English tour. Then she heard that Paul Barkley was ill in New York, and she canceled her bookings and rushed to London. She put her house and horses on the market. Preparing to sail, she dismissed John Heenan for good. It is suggested that she paid him off. At any rate, he sailed from Liverpool with a traveling circus, and over the next several years he sparred in exhibitions throughout America. Boxing fans remembered the fighter he had been and came to see him in fair numbers. In 1873 the Benicia Boy, on his way to California to join his former mistress, Sarah Stevens, died at

Green River Station, Wyoming, of a sudden, massive heart attack. The one-time world champion was thirty-eight years old.

Once she had fired him, Adah gave the great love of her life no further thought. She was not callous, but bent on flying to Paul, now her "heart's blood." Should he perish before she reached him, she would never forgive herself. This was a fine, stirring melodrama, the life of Adah Isaacs Menken, née Théodore, McCord, Heenan, Newell, and a forgotten name or two. What's more, her life was about to be captured in a series of star photos—an American first.

CHAPTER NINETEEN:

ONE LAST MARRIAGE

On March 23, 1866, several gentlemen in the bustling City of New York headed for the dock on the Hudson (then the North) River at which Adah's steamship of the Cunard Line would terminate its transatlantic journey. If not their precise thoughts, their feelings and fears about the woman who had become the most famous actress in the world are known.

Take Gus Daly, stuck in Broadway traffic in a cab. Formerly he had been Adah's escort in "charming flights of vagabondism," of which she reminded him in flirty letters. These, however, often chided him for not writing the drama he had promised her. The young playwright was becoming successful by adapting works from French and German. His *Leah* was a major hit in London. It made him uncomfortable that the drama was based on the biblical story of Deborah, a Jewish heroine whose mantle Adah had worn. Another actress, Kate Bateman, had achieved the respect Menken still sought. Daly felt even worse because he had not been paid for his efforts! To make a living he wrote criticism for the *Sunday Courier* and a half-dozen other papers. Overworked, he put aside the piece he was supposed to write for his friend.

Ed James, proceeding on foot from the *Clipper* office, looked forward to embracing his "sister." He couldn't help feeling neglected. He had done so much to make Menken famous, and now he was left out of her plans. Her letters to him were profuse with declarations of love, but lately they had been laced with snobbery. She was putting on airs, chumming with aristocrats, a world he had been forced to abandon. Nor was James pleased by Adah's romantic escapade with the gambler

Barkley. He was sure that, like Heenan, Barkley would use up her money and leave her.

Hanging from straps on streetcars, lesser members of the press headed for the debarkation of The Menken. They knew that printer's ink was the life's blood of a theatrical reputation, and that Menken's love life made the best copy. Each hoped for an exclusive, a tidbit not fed to the others. Their hopes would be dashed by a man they had never heard of—the mysterious Captain Barkley. Using money from a booming stock market, Paul had paid the shipping agent to learn exactly when the big steamer would dock. He was driving his own carriage, and he had a big surprise for the woman every man wanted.

Adah was accompanied on this voyage by an Englishwoman, Mrs. Susette Ellington. She occupied an intimate place in Adah's life, one reserved for a woman. Susette was secretary, confidante, and, on occasion, nurse. Paul arrived just as the steamship's whistle sounded across the pier. On board, Adah thought he looked amazingly well for a sick man. She was less pleased when he insisted she come with him at once. New York theater producers were balking at her price, and she needed her friends the reporters to make front-page news. But Adah gave in to the manly man. Paul arranged to transport her entourage and baggage and swept them past the clamoring crowd to his carriage. Away they went up Seventh Avenue to 39th Street to see his surprise: a newly built, four-story brownstone.

Inside, the mahogany furniture, wallpaper, plush carpets, and crystal chandeliers were the finest money could buy. The house alone had cost Paul thirty thousand dollars, and he presented it as a gift to Adah. She understood that his intentions were honorable, but she did not want to get married. Being a wife was one thing she had failed at, and she hoped she and Paul could remain lovers. Yet she moved in. She hadn't the heart to refuse Paul, and so she stalled. She named her new home Bleak House, after her favorite novel by Charles Dickens.

Adah realized that the ornate, crested coach she had shipped would make the wrong impression on postwar New York. The city was run ruthlessly by Boss Tweed, the Grand Sachem of Tammany Hall. This corrupt organization treated New York like a private fiefdom whose reason for being was to line the pockets of the clubhouse gang. Before Tweed and his boys went to prison, they stole municipal millions and facilitated the larceny of far more millions by robber barons such as Jay Gould, Jim Fisk, and Commodore Vanderbilt. The ill-gotten gains of these operators stemmed from bogus railroad stock and bonds. They were crude, tightfisted men, while Tweed was a glad-hand buyer of votes, charitable to the poor.

In Ed James's words, New York in victory was "dirty and democratic." Mounds of garbage and carcasses of dead animals littered the streets a few blocks from Fifth Avenue's mansions. Boatloads of immigrants from southern and eastern Europe were filling up the neighborhoods of Hell's Kitchen and the Lower East Side. The migration would raise the city's population from one to three and a half million people by century's end. The poor comprised the so-called *other half,* whose level of income, sanitation, and health were what we would term Third World. Smallpox, typhus, and infant cholera ravaged the slums, and tuberculosis was common but unnamed. Yet even among the lower classes, men prospered and spent their wealth where it made a splash.

George Templeton Strong, of the old rich, complained, "Not a few ladies in most sumptuous turn-outs [carriages], with liveried servants, looked as if they might have been cooks or chambermaids a few years ago." He may have referred to the wives of newly prosperous saloon-keepers or proprietors of gambling dens, or to the madams of posh brothels on West 23rd Street. Adah, who didn't wish to be confused with such parvenus, sold her precious coach.

She needed to be seen and talked about, and, weather permitting, she strolled with Susette along Broadway's Ladies' Mile. During the afternoon, it was *the* rendezvous spot for ladies of leisure. Here were found the fashionable department stores of Messrs. Altman, Macy, Stern, and Lord and Taylor. Here were the legitimate theaters that showed matinees: Laura Keene's, the Broadway, Wallack's, Niblo's

Garden, and a dozen others. James opined in *The Clipper:* "It's worth a walk to look in at one of our matinees, if only to gaze at the gay plumage of the female birds." After the show the ladies adjourned to a nearby restaurant for "ice punch and cream cakes." Respectable women had become a crucial audience for the theater, and Adah had always succeeded with women.

She began to give lavish parties at Bleak House. No expense was spared on food, wine, and musicians. Wall Street was well represented, as were the leading newspapers and theater companies. Politicians came often, especially John Price, president of the Board of Aldermen (now the City Council). Prudes stayed away, and so did New York's "four hundred," the old-rich families found in Edith Wharton's novels. Menken cared nothing for these relics anyway. But hosting at Bleak House failed to satisfy her in the way her old-world salons had. James supposed that Adah "longed for aristocratic London and gay Paris." There, business was never discussed at soirees, and titled persons mingled with artists of every sort.

In New York, Adah missed her Bohemian friends. Ada Clare was back in town, and the two of them went to Pfaff's to talk over old times. Charlie Pfaff was the same, but the place had changed. It was larger, fixed up, and serving a more prosperous clientele. There wasn't a Bohemian in sight. Henry Clapp had been carried off to the lunatic asylum; Walt Whitman was working as a government clerk in Washington; and other spouters of poetry and prose were silent among the rows of war dead. Clare, though she talked about an acting tour of the South, seemed to have lost her *joie de vivre.* She was tired of being regarded as a curiosity. She was writing a tell-all novel, *Only a Woman's Heart,* in which, as she put it, "for the first time she opened the book of her own heart and turned over its crimson leaves."

Clare was reliving in print her youthful affair with composer Louis Gottschalk. Understandably, she would give the story a sentimental ending, for their son had died. Clare admitted she had tried to live "a life of pleasure," in which she would "skim over all the flowers of existence, tasting only the sweets." Clare now understood that this was impossible, but she was trying to make art out of the pain of reality. Clare would never provide the play she had promised to write for Adah, loosely based on the ups and downs of The Menken's life.

The old friends were too preoccupied to see much of each other while both were in town. After Adah left, Clare published her novel. The reviews were dreadful, and the style is sentimental in the stock Victorian manner. But *Heart* is a landmark of frankness in women's literature, and others would build on it. Clare continued to act in journeyman fashion. In 1874, while returning by train from an engagement, she cuddled another passenger's lapdog, and it bit her in the face. She died in Manhattan of rabies. Walt Whitman jotted down a brief obituary: "I have been inexpressibly shocked by the horrible and sudden close of her gay, easy, sunny, free, loose, but *not ungood* life." Indeed, it is for her liberated life that Ada Clare is remembered.

To theatrical producers, Adah may have appeared nonchalant, but she was nearly broke and fearful of becoming dependent on Barkley. She stuck to her asking price, which was half the gate with a minimum of twelve thousand dollars for twenty-four performances, and in the end, she got it. George Wood, of the theater owning Cincinnati family, recently had become manager of New York's Broadway Theater. He reasoned that Menken in *Mazeppa* would surely make money—and his reputation. Wood signed her and set the opening date for the end of April.

Within a month's time the theater was refitted for the horse drama, and a cast and orchestra were assembled. Rehearsals got under way, and promotion was launched. Menken, backed by James and *The Clipper*, were masters of the latter art. The first step was to float a rumor that Adah would appear on stage minus her trademark pink tights—actually naked. The city, though wide open and corrupt, flew into an uproar. Naked dancers were appreciated, but only behind the curtains of bawdy houses on East 14th Street. *Would she or wouldn't she?* became the question on everybody's lips. The answer George Wood wanted came in unprecedented advance sales at the box office. Well before opening night the theater was sold out, and to The Menken we can likely attribute the origin of another Broadway custom: the ticket scalper.

Adah gave considerable thought to advertisement, and she had begun to rely on the wide distribution of *carte de visite* photos for the purpose. She was prescient about the importance of the camera to enhance a star's image, and she had used stills for publicity since 1859. Yet she had still not achieved the effect she wanted. So in Birmingham in 1865, when the French Canadian photographer Napoleon Sarony pestered her to pose, she refused. "All attempts to photograph me as Mazeppa have been failures," she told him. Finally, she agreed to a trial run of eight poses, which she herself would choose. Sarony, an elfin man with a bushy beard and mustache, knew the result would turn out poorly. He agreed, but on condition he could pose her in eight different attitudes. Then they went to work. According to Sarony's later recollection:

> *When the photographs were ready, I hunted her up in her dressing room at the theater. I gave her those of her own posing first. Her exclamation was: "They are perfectly horrible. I shall never have another photograph taken of myself as long as I live." Then I presented the photographs of my own posing. She threw her arms around me and exclaimed: "Oh, you dear, delightful, little man. I am going to kiss you for that," and she did.*

Menken's *cartes de visite*–sized photos (about four inches by two and a half inches), when printed and vigorously sold by Sarony, proved a great success in Britain. He was earning a good living in Birmingham, but the man was driven, a dynamic blend of artist and entrepreneur. Earlier in New York, he had abandoned a lucrative trade as a lithographer on the order of Currier and Ives. Sarony had the knack of spotting and drawing popular subjects, but in 1858 he sold out to his partners. For six years he traveled in Europe, studying painting. While Mathew Brady recorded life and death on the battlefields of the American Civil

War, Sarony haunted the art galleries of Berlin, Paris, and London. He became interested in portrait photography, which he was determined to make into an art form. Once the war had ended, he returned to New York, on the verge of its first golden age of theater. Sarony set up a studio at 630 Broadway, south of Pfaff's, in what is now Soho. He was beginning a glamorous career that would make him the master of celebrity portraiture, the "Rembrandt of the Camera."

The woman who visited Sarony's Broadway studio one day in April, for her second shoot with him, was at the height of her fame and beauty. Thirty-one, she had little more than two years left to live. Perhaps she had an inkling of this, but in any case, she was eager to leave a pictorial record of her accomplishments. In a black sable wrap over a dress of royal blue, she barely managed to navigate her hooped dress up the narrow stairway. Sarony had his studio on the fourth (or top) floor in order to take full advantage of the sunlight, his only source of light. Behind Adah Menken struggled a stagehand, carrying a trunk laden with her costumes.

Sarony's weird reception room was filled floor to ceiling with props: Russian icons, classical heads, mummies, stuffed crocodiles, life-size dummies. Wearing a long, white tunic stained by chemicals, Sarony showed Adah into a spacious loft whose ceiling consisted of skylights through which streamed the morning light. The hustle of the street fell away, and she felt herself close to the sky and a few drifting clouds. Glancing around, her attention was caught by iron braces for the neck and back that looked like torture devices. Stacked about were screens, draperies, and a few basic pieces of furniture, including columns. Adah was already familiar with the large, bellows-like object on legs: the camera, whose two bulging lenses reminded her of the eyes of an insect.

Sarony and The Menken went to work. Notes Marianne Fulton, chief curator at George Eastman House, here is the first instance of "the confluence of celebrated artistry and the popular photographer" that combined to make a superstar. The artist's point of view includes the intelligence and beauty of his subject. The hope is to create a transcendent image—"a magic place for us to live, if only for a little while."

Sarony, aided by two assistants, created a miniature set in which he positioned Adah. She was seated, a red drapery thrown across her lap, a bright Astrakhan cap placed at a rakish angle on her head, the braces hidden, the sunlight adjusted by means of venetian blinds. Sarony, seeing her unease, explained that each glass plate that he inserted into the camera was coated with a light-sensitive, silver compound and could capture eight images. He reminded her to hold the pose until he gave the signal, which took twenty seconds or longer, depending on the light or if a cloud passed by.

For Sarony, each so-called position told a story. Each picture conveyed an aspect of character, a moment of joy, sorrow, or longing. This fidgety artist, like a movie director, hated the stiff, lifeless poses that most photographers of his day reproduced. Yet the lack of an adjustable lens (aperture) in the camera doomed his subjects to immobility. Therefore, his positions must be carefully chosen to *suggest* movement. To his past admirers and present-day collectors, Sarony's stills seem "all life and expression, only with far more abandon and intensity of action."

The protean Menken was the artist's ideal subject. To Adah fell the interpretation of the photographer's positions, the mood, the aura. At first, in elaborate dress boasting a flowing hairpiece, jeweled earrings, and necklace, she acts demure, her eyes turned down in a self-reflective gaze. Adah calls up the Victorian lady, beautiful, expensive, with her bustline acceptably revealed. Such a convention would not satisfy the hyperactive Sarony for long.

Adah had brought a variety of costumes to illustrate her roles. After ducking behind a screen, she poses as Leon from *Child of the Sun:* a serape around her shoulders, sombrero on her head, dagger at the waist of her tight, fancy pants. With hands on her hips, staring straight at the viewer, she is one tough *hombre*. In another shot Adah holds a sword with a jeweled hilt; she wears a decorated Mazeppa-like costume but with a skirt rather than pants. Her hair is short and curly. A miniature of a man is pinned to her blouse, next to her heart, but we cannot make him out.

In another mood, Adah, wearing a semi-sheer body stocking and her "little dimity nothing," assumes a variety of poses designed to show off her curves. The positions have become classic to the pinup: an arm behind the head to emphasize the breasts (a la Lana Turner, the sweater girl), or a leg casually crossed to show the thighs from both side and front. Or Adah stretches out on a divan with a look that both attracts and distances. Postfeminist women have caught on to the power of the pinup, using pinups of themselves to enhance awareness. In *The Drama Review,* Maria-Elena Buszek writes approvingly: "[T]he photograph's focus was upon Menken's voluptuous physique and dramatic, charismatic sexuality."

The drama depends first on the props chosen by the photographer. Adah, semi-reclining on a tiger skin, wearing an abbreviated outfit dressed up by bangles, Oriental hangings in the background, suggests Cleopatra of Egypt. She reminds the viewer of her trials with Heenan the gladiator. Here, in Sphinx-like profile, the queen of women has conquered the queen of beasts. It would be a long time before so much action was packed into a celebrity still. Although very different, we think of George Hurrell's 1930s portrait of Jane Russell in *The Outlaw,* where she reclines in the hay, arm back to show her ample bust; one knee up, she toys with the outlaw's pistol, pointed at her groin!

One of the most striking examples of the collaboration of Menken and Sarony to predict the libidinous future are two portraits of her in a man's white dress suit and black top hat. In one, standing, she portrays the sport from *The French Spy,* complete with cravat, vest, and watch fob. Writes Buszek: "Adah Isaacs Menken poses with a butch swagger that predates Marlene Dietrich's similar vamping by nearly 80 years." Actually, Adah plays more winsome than Marlene, and there is something of the "teenager in his father's clothes" about this shot. In the second photo, Adah sits at a card table, pleased to hold a winning hand. This calls up her exploits as a gambler on the Gold Coast. It reminds us that, like Marlene in World War II, she played a vital part in the life of her times.

Perhaps the sky clouded up on the first day of the shoot. The electric light, let alone the flashbulb, had not been invented, and so Sarony would have to quit. But he and Menken shot on a second day, until he had over 100 negatives of her in various positions. These his assistants would turn into many thousands of positives, which would be pasted onto cardboard backing, then sold in a variety of stores and hawked by newsboys on the street and outside theaters. Ordinary folk bought them as souvenirs or to spice up a family photo album. They were as ubiquitous as today's baseball cards. Olive Logan, an actress critical of Menken's style, acknowledged: "The sale of these photographs is immense. People buy *cartes de visite* of well-known persons for as many reasons as other people resort to the convivial tumbler."

Menken and Sarony's work, over a brief period in the springtime of photography, established the guideposts of sexual glamour then and now. Of similar importance a century later in New York, Marilyn Monroe posed for Richard Avedon in a shoot for *Life* magazine. She impersonated five "fabled enchantresses" of earlier days. These included opulent Lillian Russell, silent-screen vamp Theda Bara, "It" girl Clara Bow, platinum-blonde Jean Harlow, and sultry Marlene Dietrich. *Life*'s article, which appeared in the Christmas issue of 1958, has fallen victim to its own popularity. If you locate a copy of the magazine, you will probably find the Marilyn story torn out.

Marilyn's husband, Arthur Miller, present at the shoot, wrote a sidebar that looks back at the progress of desire from the Gay Nineties until the sexual revolution of the mid-twentieth century. Avedon's direction points the way to Marilyn's interpretation of the superstars of past generations. Together they evoke the spirit of beauty, which underlies these disparate, and sometimes desperate, lives. "Marilyn is their heiress," wrote Miller. Another fifty years later, in 2008, actress/ singer Lindsay Lohan, a favorite of the tabloids, recreated Marilyn's last photo shoot for *New York* magazine, with an emphasis on seminude shots, as well as the tragedy of her early death. Lindsay felt honored, a spritual granddaughter to the greatest of sex symbols. Yes, and Adah Menken is godmother to the lot of these beauties, so often unfortunate in their personal lives.

The Marilyn Monroe/Richard Avedon shoot fulfilled the promise of Sarony's painting of Menken's moods with natural light, his only tool. Adah had foreshadowed Lillian Russell's favorite sailor-girl garb, and, as the lovesick William, she clung to a phallic mast. Marilyn portrays Russell as all hat, bust, and thigh. She plays Theda Bara, the vamp (short for vampire) as the sister to the skinned tiger whose head she holds. Clara Bow is manic jazz, surrounded by cigarettes and booze, while Harlow is serene against a sofa, white on white, quick to soil. Marilyn's Marlene, in top hat, sheer, gartered stockings, and spiked heels, is pure *femme fatale*. Avedon brilliantly captured the past, but it was Sarony who predicted the future. Indeed, the recipe for superstardom runs true from Menken to Madonna: sex, danger, drama.

Avedon remarked about Marilyn: "She gave more to the still camera than any woman I've ever photographed, infinitely more patient, more demanding of herself and more comfortable in front of the camera than away from it." In contrast, Sarony had to coax Menken to pose. One senses a latent reserve in Adah's photos. *There are depths to me*, she implies, *that I will not show you.* One of Sarony's most striking portraits of Menken was later echoed by Edward Steichen in 1928, when he photographed Greta Garbo, another reticent beauty. Adah is wrapped in Victorian black lace, which serves to isolate her face, an oval whose serious mood is contrasted with a red rose in her hair. Standing out from her amorphous dress is a bar and lock below her waist, like a chastity belt. Equally unwelcoming is Steichen's Garbo, another pyramid of black that isolates Garbo's face with a straight-ahead look. The feel is Art Deco, the mood severe and neurotic. Both artists have captured the self-imposed loneliness of the superstar.

Yet Menken had a resource the other goddesses lacked. The most famous portrait of Marilyn is that of a young girl stretched out nude on a throw of velvet. The shot is entirely physical. As Billy Wilder observed, her flesh photographed as flesh. Even more typical is a little known shot of a gowned Marilyn in front of four mirrors, each of which reflects her smiling image. She is a female Narcissus who adores herself first and last.

Menken, in contrast, grew increasingly self-critical toward the end of her life. Sarony saw the side of her that caused scandals and filled theaters, but he also saw her nobler aspirations. He remarked: "Adah Isaacs Menken was the most remarkable mingling of angel and devil that ever wore petticoats." In one pose he remembered that she was a poet. Adah is garbed in a satin gown with white lace cuffs, seated but leaning forward with her crossed hands resting on an upright book. She wears a wedding ring and looks at us hopefully, asking for our under-standing, our prayers.

⸎

Mazeppa starring Menken as the heroic prince opened at the Broadway Theater on April 30, 1866. Every seat was sold out and people stood three rows deep. The packed house presented a serious fire hazard: The aisles were cluttered, and men stood on the windowsills. The best seats were occupied by distinguished army and naval officers and celeb-rities from the worlds of politics, art, and commerce, along with their wives. Menken's initial reception was tumultuous, her riding and duel-ing wildly applauded, and when the curtain rang down, the audience rose as one and cheered. The show was a smash hit. Gus Daly's *Courier* put it succinctly: "The female 'Mazeppa' is the sensation of New York. It should continue to draw for months to come."

Most of the important papers agreed. The main quibble, often stated indirectly, seemed to be that Menken was overdressed, even in the so-called nude scenes. The reviewer in the *Herald*, published by Gordon Bennett, one of the reigning press lords, found Menken's voice weak, but she may have been drowned out by the enthusiasm of the audience. Wilkes's *Spirit*, Menken's old enemy, didn't dare openly attack, so the reviewer satirically praised Black Bess, the untamed steed, and hardly mentioned her rider. He concluded that "the person called in the bills 'Mazeppa' . . . is best *on* the mare, and the worst *off* that I have ever seen or expect to see."

William Winter, writing in Horace Greeley's *Tribune*, remembered his old grudge against Menken. He first attacked her morals, complaining that "a woman would exhibit herself, in public, in a condition closely bordering upon nudity." Winter, because he collected his articles in books, and simply because he lived so long, has become the critical standard referred to by later writers. But he was ever the puritan, and his views, if applied to the modern theater, would be laughable. He was shocked that Menken invited attention "not to her emotional capabilities, her intellectual gifts, or her culture as an artist, but solely to her physical proportions." Although he grudgingly admired her courage and daring, he claimed she had no idea how to act.

In classical terms, that's true enough. But Winter was enamored of the rhetorical past, and the physical acting he excoriated would not come into its own until our own action-packed time. Winter's prejudice is shown by his description of the first-night audience, which he called:

> *the coarsest and most brutal assembly that we have ever chanced to see at a theater on Broadway. Every variety of dissolute life was represented in it. The purple nose, the scorbutic countenance, the glassy eye, the bull head, the heavy lower jaw, the aspect of mingled lewdness and ferocity—all was there. Youths, whose attire exhibited an eruptive tendency towards cheap jewelry, lolled in their seats, champing tobacco and audibly uttering their filthy minds. Old sports were abundant. The atmosphere fairly reeked with vulgarity.*

Winter concluded by warning the respectable to stay away from the show. That way, they could not see his fabrication for themselves.

Menken was wounded by the tone of the article. She wrote to Gus Daly that she did not mind criticism, but that Winter's was too low to answer. It had "the eloquence of Billingsgate or of Fishmonger's Hall." Since she knew Winter from nights at Pfaff's, and had rejected his advances, she believed his review was poisoned by "petty personal spite." Still, Adah felt discouraged, despite *Mazeppa* outdrawing all other attractions, including the San Francisco Minstrels' burlesque, *Mazeppa a la Menken.* Demand was so great that Wood added matinees to the schedule of performances. He attempted to prosecute scalpers who sold tickets in front of the theater, but in a landmark case, the judge ruled their activities legal.

Mazeppa might have run into the summer had not Adah, after the curtain rang down on her benefit performance, collapsed on stage. She was rushed to Bleak House, where she lay unconscious for two days. Several doctors were called in, and beyond pronouncing the patient to be exhausted, they could do little. Pulmonary tuberculosis, though epidemic in Adah's time, had no name or means of diagnosis until the close of the nineteenth century. The tubercle bacillus lingered in her lungs, the disease not sufficiently advanced to overcome the woman's strong constitution and stronger will.

Adah revived, and, in a typical show of generosity, two weeks later she gave a benefit performance for the stage manager. Offers for engagements poured in from around the country, and Susette outlined an extensive tour that would carry *Mazeppa* from Boston to Washington, then into the Midwest and South. A return to Europe could be postponed. Barkley argued against the American tour. Adah, indulging in nostalgia, recalled the youthful adventure of appearing in strange theaters and winning over fresh audiences. Forgotten was the torture of nights on jolting trains and the difficulty of breathing air fouled by coal smoke.

In the end, Adah's health wouldn't permit such strain. The tour was pared down to Cincinnati, Nashville, and Louisville, places where the Wood family owned theaters and Menken had a large following. Despite Barkley's protests, she decided to play a week in July in each city. Why did she bother? Allen Lesser writes of an "inner force" that impelled her to return to "the scenes of her early successes." Perhaps it was the memory of a young, idealistic self that drew Adah to the locales of her ambition to be a serious dramatic actress, a poet, and the voice of her people.

Adah found Cincinnati bigger and pushier than she had known. Gone were her favorite haunts and gone were the Menkens. The brothers had moved their business to Memphis, and there Alex would reside, nursing wounds real or imagined. The Cincinnati Jewish community, although fascinated by Adah's singularly romantic career, dared not openly welcome her. But they did pay to see her perform, and on July 2, *Mazeppa* opened to a packed house. Hundreds were left in the street because there were no places for them. The audience cheered whenever the hero appeared, and finally threw her bouquets. Adah was by now a favorite daughter, and the reviews were kind. The *Daily Gazette* enthused: "She wore a magnificent costume, and appeared young, plump, and fresh, evincing no signs of either illness or dissipation." This was the sort of praise that warmed the lady's heart.

By Nashville, Adah realized she had a more involving problem than exhaustion. However, the local excitement was such that she had to fulfill her engagement at the Old Theater. Reviews in the local papers were raves, and again they dwelt on her person rather than the play:

By universal acclaim Miss Menken is the acknowledged Queen of beauty and drama. Her admirers of other days were astonished to find her looking so young. . . . Time has dealt leniently with her, and instead of marring the good looks, for which she was long ago distinguished, has but retouched them with a richer and lovelier glow.

In Louisville the next week, Adah reminisced with Susette about having played opposite Edwin Booth. She still hoped to be taken seriously as a dramatic actress. But she could no longer deny, to herself or Susette, that she had morning sickness: She was pregnant. In a few days the pair returned to New York, and Adah told Paul Barkley that she accepted his long-standing proposal of marriage. He was even more pleased to hear he would be a father. Involved in preparing for the wedding, he felt certain she had forgotten Paris.

The couple married on Sunday, August 19, 1866. The ceremony was performed by alderman John Brice, a Tammany stalwart, and was followed by one of the most star-studded dinners the city had ever seen. This, Adah's fifth marriage, lasted for all of three days. She and her Prince quarreled bitterly. He wanted her to be a conventional wife and mother, while she insisted her career had greater heights to scale. Adah loved Paul, but she loved her dream more.

She was accustomed to supporting her husbands, which usually gave her the whip hand. But Paul had money and could not be intimidated. Although Adah made use of her acting experience to cajole, cry, implore, and demand, Paul was adamant: She must choose between touring Europe and staying home as Mrs. Barkley. Faced with a decision she could not make, Adah copped out by attempting suicide.

Adah's second try at poisoning herself was serious, but failed. Pregnant, she may not have intended death. Susette's part is unclear, but she did contact Ed James, who arranged immediate passage for the two women to England. Paul chose not to interfere. That we don't have his side of the story is to be expected from a man given to secrecy. Ed James is our sole authority for what happened. He writes of a "misunderstanding" between the couple, and then:

> *She was so ill from an overdose of poison, whether taken to soothe her nerves or for self-destruction was never perfectly ascertained, we had to carry her from the tender to her stateroom on board the Cunard steamer* Java, *on August 22, 1866, and the last we saw of this strange genius was when she could recognize nobody.*

Thus, The Menken's greatest triumph to date ended in ignominy. Barkley, accepting his loss, sold Bleak House and returned to California. Unconscious, Adah sailed away to her star-bright destiny. As she had dreamed, it would climax in Paris.

PART FIVE

OUR LADY OF PAIN

A life deeply sensible of loss . . .

—WILLIAM ROSSETTI

CHAPTER TWENTY:

CITY OF LIGHT

Adah's conquest of Paris began in London in late 1865. Days of cloying fog had lifted, and while driving through the streets, she showed off her carriage and its comely passenger. Ever unconventional, Adah was seated next to the driver, the better to be seen. The Prince of Wales was out riding in Rotten Row, and she hoped to catch his eye. Instead, the carriage brushed a man trying to cross Regent Street and knocked him down. The driver, reining in his team, went to the rescue. Fortunately, the man was unharmed, and on his feet, he began to vent his anger in French. Glancing up, he was surprised to see "a beautiful creature, whose black eyes rested on me with interest."

Adah, holding the reins in her left hand, reached down to shake the man's hand as a gesture of peace. The poor, confused fellow introduced himself as Adrien Marx, a Paris journalist who wrote for *Le Figaro*. Adah replied, also in French, "I am so glad that the carriage of Menken has not erased you." She invited M. Marx to visit her at Astley's, and to come backstage between the acts. At the time, her agent was negotiating with manager Louis Dumaine for an engagement at the Théâtre de la Gaîté. When Marx visited her dressing room, Adah gave him the full treatment. Stripping to her famous pink tights, she nonchalantly changed costumes in front of the young man, all the while keeping up a one-sided conversation about Hebrew philosophy, music, and the immortality of the soul.

Marx took notes as best he could. Later he recalled that this modern Venus had shown him "the marvelous beauty of her body." Victorians, conditioned by neoclassical paintings, expected a goddess to be blonde and antiseptic. But Adah's curves were sexy, her skin tanned by the sun, and her nostrils flared as she spoke passionately. Finally, it was her eyes that captivated the young man, quickly changing in expression from loving to ferocious.

Adah, in response to questions about her youth, launched into a Texas tall tale about her noble birth, her capture by Indians, miraculous escape, and service to the Confederacy disguised as a male soldier. To illustrate the captivity narrative, she let Marx feel the groove in her scalp left by a tomahawk thrown at her while she fled. She then hoisted her skirt above the thigh to show him "the trace of the balls she had received in war." Finally, about her much discussed love life, she had to confess she was the blind slave of passion.

The journalist may have realized the actress was pulling his leg, but he knew good copy when he heard it. Once the interview had appeared in *Le Figaro*, Menken's place in French romantic lore was assured. Her delay in appearing on the stage in Paris only whetted the appetite of a capital that lived for show and pleasure. When the expectant mother arrived in September 1866, accompanied by Susette Ellington, she encamped at the Hotel de Suez in the Boulevard Strasbourg, a short walk from the Gaîté. The hotel was favored by Americans of modest means. Without Barkley, Adah was having trouble making ends meet. She reached a formal agreement with Dumaine to open at the theater early next year, which she supposed would put an end to her money troubles.

Adah saw only a few friends, among them George Sand. She had admired the author, thirty years her senior, since reading her novels as a youth. Sand took the part of women who had "fallen" in the conventional sense, but who, through suffering, rose in moral stature. In her works of fiction, Sand upheld what was then known as Free Love. Her heroes and heroines spurned arranged marriages, fell in love with persons of the working class, and even married them! "It is always the same fight," she insisted, "against the same enemies, prejudice and narrow-mindedness."

Sand the woman (her actual name was Aurore Lucie Dudevant, the surname being that of a husband she had left long ago) loved as she wrote—deeply and tenderly. Both Sand and Menken were Romantics, great women who ran afoul of a society whose rules were increasingly suited to the *petit-bourgeois* mentality. The women's serial love affairs, and the notoriety bestowed on their liaisons by the press, horrified nineteenth century prudes. Indeed, today's *Encyclopedia Britannica* still assures the reader that "it would be a mistake to accept the popular impression of [Sand] as a nymphomaniac." It would be equally boorish to think of Menken as promiscuous, despite her collection of husbands.

Both Sand and Menken adopted what were considered to be men's dress and habits. They wore pants in public, and in their domestic relations, they also tended to wear the pants. They smoked cigarettes and sometimes cigars. They chose their careers, earned lots of money, and played a significant part in the events of the day. This may have become commonplace, but in Victorian America or Britain, and still more in Louis Napoleon's reactionary Second Empire, Sand and Menken shocked the establishment. In France it was against the law for a woman to dress in men's clothes. Sand got away with it because of the loyalty of her family to the first Napoleon, and because of her friendship with Prince Jerome, cousin to the Emperor. Menken got away with almost anything because she was an actress, a beauty, and a charmer.

Slight evidence remains of the friendship between Menken and Sand, which was warm, personal, but relatively brief. Biographers have insisted that their extensive correspondence was lost. In fact, the letters never existed. Menken herself, replying to Charles Stoddard, who was hunting autographs, remarked: "Geo. Sand came to me. We have seen too much of each other to leave many writings. And have greatly abounded in telegrams." Not surprisingly, the telegrams were discarded.

Sand, in a letter to her son Maurice, mentions seeing the actress perform in January 1867, and how she found Adah very attractive and friendly. The lesbian relationship promoted by an American biographer of Sand, Noel Gerson (alias Samuel Edwards) is clumsy fiction.

Gerson is the same hack who faked Menken's licentious Havana diary. At the time the two women met, Sand, sixty-two, had retired to her family estate, Nohant, in the province of Berry. She came to Paris on occasion, usually to gratify her love of the theater.

Sand, her beauty faded, looked like an older woman. The diarist Edmond de Goncourt described her face as "mummified." Matthew Arnold wondered whether it was worthwhile "to go so far to meet such a fat old muse." She had lost the last of her significant lovers, an engraver named Alexandre Manceau. A friend of Maurice, he was much younger than Sand. In a replay of her famous romance with Chopin, Manceau suffered from tuberculosis, and he died in her arms after a long, painful struggle. Months of nursing him day and night, changing his bloodstained bedclothes, left the woman exhausted yet spiritually uplifted.

Sand claimed she had reached "the age of impersonality . . . free from egotism." A respected figure in French letters, it is unlikely she would subject herself to the caprices of a notorious foreigner half her age. Instead, she was given to "motherly and grandmotherly affection, devotion to her family, and enthusiasm for all that is beautiful and noble." Because Menken reminded Sand of her own younger, wilder days, she felt all the more protective of her.

There is extant one photo of Adah and George. Read with care, it depicts the sum of their relationship. George, standing, has her right arm around the seated Adah's shoulders in a motherly way. Both women wear billowing hooped skirts and embroidered jackets over white blouses, a Victorian uniform. George's hair, usually worn pulled back, is curled like Adah's. No doubt the tribute is to Byron, whose hairstyle Menken imitated. The women are regarding an object that, on close examination, turns out to be a bird's nest. This would be singularly appropriate since Adah was expecting her child shortly. Either the photo was taken at Nohant, or George brought the nest from the country to her friend. Adah appears almost childlike, while George looks like the woman Dumas *fils* spoke of as "*la mère Sand*." She has adopted

Adah as a member of her talented entourage, which regularly paid obeisance to her at Nohant.

It is not surprising that, after Adah gave birth in November to a premature yet healthy boy, Sand stood as godmother to the lad and bestowed on him her married name. Susette Ellington wrote to Ed James that the baptism ceremony took place "at the grand cathedral, with a prince for a godfather, and his godmother one of the first authoresses of Paris. The name given to this royal stranger is Louis Dudevant Victor Emmanuel Barkley!" The prince, whose name she did not reveal, was surely an Italian, since Victor Emmanuel was the first monarch of newly united Italy. However, that the steadfastly Jewish Menken would agree to have her child baptized is strange, and biographers have seized on the episode to assert that she had reneged on her faith. But Menken made no greater sacrifice of principle than did Sand, who was hostile to the Church and preferred Protestant ceremonies for her own family.

The Catholic nature of the baptism was likely insisted on by the unnamed prince. Menken was swept away by the glamour of the occasion. Italy was the focus of Europe's attention, the great cause that Greece had been for Byron. King Victor Emmanuel, placed on the throne by the military victories of Garibaldi, was enormously popular. Menken was impressed by the benefits of such a connection. Already she had begun to feel the heat of anti-Semitism, a monster that would show its fangs later in the Dreyfus case. Recalling the pain and degradation of her youth, she acted to shield her infant son from racial hatred. The two photos we have of Adah with the boy, three months old, his tiny face resembling hers, show a tender and sheltering mother. Adah would not permit her background to tarnish the prospects of *her* prince.

❧

Menken wasted little time in returning to the stage, playing a brief engagement in *The French Spy* in Liverpool. Then, in December, she turned to the Gaîté, looking forward to the meaty role she had been promised in a reworking of the hackneyed melodrama, *Les Pirates de la*

Savane. All along Dumaine, who both acted and managed, had assured her that writers Dugué and Bourgeois were devising a vehicle especially suited to her talents. Although *Mazeppa,* devoid of Byron's language, lost too much in translation, the new drama would feature its action sequences and Adah's death-defying ride up the mountain. Her part would be the best one in the play, promised Dumaine.

The cast had already begun rehearsals when Adah first attended on December 12. To her surprise, she learned that her role would be performed entirely in mime. Dumaine was afraid that her Creole French would sound humorous to the Parisian ear. Adah, feeling betrayed, let loose the tiger that was her temper. The pudgy manager bore the brunt until he and his forebears had been thoroughly trashed. Yet his judgment on the matter was sounder than Adah's, and presently he was able to calm down his star.

Dumaine produced a copy of a pamphlet, done in fancy type, that was supposed to be a history of Menken's life. In the main it was a translation of an interview she had given to the *London Illustrated News,* which stressed the allegedly high tone of her antecedents. However, it was stated that her parents were Franco-American "Israelites," and that Adah herself was "a scrupulous observant of their ancient Faith." So clearly she continued to identify herself as Jewish. Her stepfather, now a Scot, was promoted to "Sir Campbell." The pamphlet had gone out to the press and would be sold at the theater for thirty centimes. Like everything else about Adah's time in Paris, it proved very successful.

Next evening *La Menken* attended the Gaîté's current production. According to Susette Ellington, "She was the loveliest and handsomest dressed woman in the theater." Seated in the Imperial box, dripping with jewelry, Menken drew more attention than the play. Even the actors dropped their lines in staring at her. A pair of magnificent diamond earrings was most admired, especially by those who knew the story behind the sparkle.

Supposedly a British lord, Albert Avon, had sent the earrings, along with a proposal that Menken become his mistress. She refused the offer but kept the diamonds. Her reply to m'lord, made available to the press that day, declared:

I shall wear the diamond ear-rings, not for the donor's sake, but in hopes that their magnificence may create an impression upon the audience of the Théâtre de la Gaîté. As for my accepting your Palace as a home, I can only say that my hotel is preferable. Go to your friends and tell them that Adah Isaacs Menken is an American woman, and there is no French in her blood, and that all further attempts at intrigue are useless.

This was a signal shot fired in the publicity campaign leading up to the opening of *Les Pirates de la Savane.* Since there is no Lord Avon in the peerage, he was another of Menken's inventions. Her assertion of a strictly American identity, which contradicted management's tales of French descent, was aimed at the manager, Dumaine, and stemmed from anger at his duplicity. She warns him that she will not tolerate further tricks. Certainly the diamond earrings did cause a stir at the theater and beyond. But if the fictional lord did not give them to her, who did? Even Adah could not afford them. Perhaps the answer is that she was in the process of becoming the supposed mistress of a king.

Parisians were fascinated by this American sex siren to a degree that would not be repeated until, in the 1920s, Josephine Baker performed her famed banana dance and strutted about with a jaguar on a leash. Adrien Marx had written up Adah in *Le Figaro,* one of a half-dozen papers controlled by Jean de Villemessant, who was "a great believer in scandal and indiscretion of every kind." De Villemessant employed a staff of clever young writers, such as Émile Zola. The escapades of Menken were made to order for them as a means of expressing their political and social dissatisfaction. Additional journals were predisposed toward a woman who broke the rules but got away with it. *Le Mousquetaire,* which the aging lion Alexandre Dumas *père* wrote and edited single-handedly, devoted a column in praise of Adah's beauty and wit. The puffs handed out daily by Adah's manager, M. Karel, whetted the appetite of the press, and stage-door johnnies were lined up in hopes of making her acquaintance.

Opening night of *Les Pirates* was set for December 30, on the edge of that fabulous year, 1867, the apogee of the Second Empire. Louis Napoleon, the ill-favored nephew of Napoleon Bonaparte, a constant schemer, had been elected president of France in 1848, after a liberal revolution overthrew the monarchy. It was said the peasants thought they were voting for the *first* Napoleon. In 1851 Louis presided over a coup d'état, and shortly thereafter, backed by what Karl Marx termed a collection of "vagabonds, disbanded soldiers, discharged prisoners, fugitives from the galleys, sharpers, jugglers, professional beggars, pickpockets, conjurers, gamesters, pimps, and brothel-keepers," Louis declared himself Emperor Napoleon III.

Karl Marx's description of the emperor's followers characterizes the moral tone of the Second Empire and its comic opera court. From a distance of a century and a half, Louis Napoleon looks either ridiculous—"*le petit Napoleon*," Victor Hugo called him—or sinister, the first fascist dictator. Certainly the Bonapartist coup was brutal, protesters were shot down in the streets, and thirty thousand citizens were imprisoned, transported to Algeria, or otherwise disposed of. Louis is described by a historian of the period as "a gauche little man with a large nose and a lusterless expression about the eyes." Théophile Gautier said he looked like "a ringmaster who has been sacked for getting drunk." Louis's defining trait was a sexual avarice that demanded he possess any attractive woman he met for at least one night. At a time when syphilis was common, he may have contracted the disease, and he suffered from severe problems of the urinary tract.

In her sphere, the Empress Eugénie was at least as important as her husband. A beautiful Spanish socialite of twenty-six when she married Louis, she brought to the court at the restored Tuileries Palace a cosmopolitan air, an eye for fashion, and a hauteur that counterbalanced Louis's nightcrawls. For twenty years Eugénie would set the style in clothing for women the world over. She began the crinoline craze and, by patronizing the Englishman Charles Worth, helped to establish the first great house of *haute couture*. Eugénie and her pal Princess Pauline Metternich, wife of the Austrian ambassador, presided over the innumerable masked balls, imperial dinners, and pageants held at the Tuileries and other palaces. While Pauline paraded the streets pretending to be a prostitute, Eugénie concerned herself with family and position. She thought of herself as the Marie Antoinette of the Second Empire, and her place in history is nearly as unfavorable.

Otto von Bismarck, Germany's Iron Chancellor, famously remarked of the Second Empire: "From a distance it's stunning. When you get up close, however, there's nothing there at all." Louis Napoleon, determined to echo his uncle, revived titles and protocol from the First Empire and made a great show of France's military prowess. Gorgeously accoutred soldiers—mounted lancers, hussars, and cuirassiers—were paraded along the new *grands boulevards*, then dispatched to fight in Italy, Algeria, Indochina, the Crimea, and finally Mexico, with considerable loss of life and few lasting victories. Mexico was such a fiasco that in 1867, the year of the Great Exposition (or World's Fair), Louis announced a so-called liberal empire and eased political and censorship restrictions. Uniforms gave way to formal attire and ball gowns, and march music was replaced by the waltz and the naughty cancan.

Adah Menken could not have picked a more propitious moment to arrive on the scene. The rebuilding of Paris from a medieval to a splendid, modern city, entrusted by the emperor to Baron Haussmann, was nearly completed. The elegant look that we accord to Paris today, such as the vista down the Champs-Élysées to the Arc de Triomphe, is the signal achievement of the Second Empire. The court, Europe's most gaudy, welcomed every sort of display, and the city was decorated with a multitude of ornaments, which attracted the eyes of the whole world. The Exposition would not open until April, but by early in the year pleasure seekers had focused on Paris. Tourists, adventurers, hucksters, and the merely curious flocked to admire the broad, tree-lined avenues and the cafés facing on them, to attend Offenbach operas and pack into dance halls to gawk at the cancan girls. To make sure no gent went unattended, an estimated 120,000 prostitutes plied their trade.

The premiere of Menken in *Les Pirates* was a gala event. Every seat in the house was reserved, and hours before curtain time carriages began to unload the fashionable and the rich in front of the Gaîté. They had to struggle through a crowd of celebrity hounds, standing in the cold to catch a glimpse of the mysterious star. Inside the lobby, under the blaze of gaslight chandeliers, paraded a show of court ladies in Worth gowns, diamond jewelry, and elaborate coiffures. The women of Paris attended the theater in numbers and made their views felt. Officers of high rank strutted about, and titled gentlemen were a dime a dozen. Louis's sons, the princes Jérôme and Lucien, proceeded with their suites to the imperial boxes. Mixed in with the glitterati were France's cleverest journalists, men whose opinions, printed the next day in their newspapers, could mean elation or despair to Adah.

Tension ran like a current through the house as the orchestra tuned up, men cleared their throats, and women settled into seats too narrow for their gowns. The audience did not care that *Les Pirates* was a warmed-over version of *Mazeppa*. To make the drama current, it was set in Mexico, which French soldiers had occupied. Adah played Leo (a poor youth whose tongue was cut out by Indians), a mimed role she used to great advantage. First silence, then applause greeted the curtain's rising on a wild, majestic countryside. All eyes were on the character Leo. Adah fell back on gesture and on a charisma that soared over the footlights. In the final act she scaled a higher stage mountain, strapped to a faster horse and wearing less than before. When the curtain rang down an explosion burst forth, everyone on their feet shouting, "*Vive Leo!*" Nor would the audience cease its clamor until Adah had bowed her way through nine curtain calls, throwing emotional kisses.

"Hip, hip, hurrah for Menken!" cried the *Gazette des Étrangers* next day, which summed up the universal acclaim she received. She had achieved "a triumph that was positively staggering." True, *L'Europe Artiste* carped that the well-worn play "left something to be desired."

But even this reviewer was struck by Adah's "horrifying and graceful realism," her "audacity and courage." Théophile Gautier in *Le Moniteur Universal* described Adah as "a very beautiful woman, svelte and admirably proportioned, who mimes with rare intelligence." He was captivated by the terror, mingled with a sexual thrill, of her bareback ride up the mountain of doom.

The Paris press celebrated Menken's best features. Nestor Roque-plan, a senior critic, wrote: "She has an energetic nature, with the physical harmony and balanced strength that are the signs of a perfect body." *L'Univers Illustre* raved about "the eloquence of her pantomime," adding, "her large black eyes speak fluently." Dumas *père*, in his *Mousquetaire*, preferred to catalog the presents tossed onto the stage by admirers, including jewelry worth over a hundred thousand dollars in today's money. *Les Pirates* would handsomely reward its backers with a run of 150 sold-out performances, not closing until May, when the Exposition was at its height.

The effect on Adah of being the lioness of the day was not apparent in her behavior. Night after night she played to packed houses sprinkled with counts and dukes, financiers, and "ladies belonging to the world of beauty and fashion," as Susette informed Ed James. Then, with equal gusto, Adah performed at matinees where university students howled with delight. For a time she remained at the Hotel Suez, the better to consort with her young, Bohemian friends. An English gossip saw her enter the dining room of the Hotel Byron, a hangout for poor theatrical types, dine simply with a companion, and afterward juggle knives and plates to entertain the crowd.

By the people of Paris, Menken was favorably compared to Hortense Schneider, Offenbach's leading soprano, or the diva Adelina Patti. The latter preferred to sing privately at the mansion of the Roth-schilds, where she received a fabulous sum for a few songs. Schneider would deign to be seen only at exclusive restaurants. She held a salon at her immaculate home, which she encouraged those of rank and fashion to attend. Adah, to revive her more informal salon, moved to an upscale hotel on the Rue de la Paix, where she continued to welcome firebrand journalists, needy poets, and up-and-coming actors along with the rich and famous.

Finally, however, Adah's acclaim rested on the narrow footing of her ride up that stage mountain. The paper *L'Illustration* on January 5, 1867, related an anecdote about her magnificent black thoroughbred, which Adah had thought to leave behind in London. As soon as his mistress departed for France, Gypsy began to act up and frightened people. A woman familiar with the horse, possibly Adah's maid, brought him across the English Channel, staying by his stall during the voyage. When Gypsy caught sight of Adah outside the Gaîté, he neighed with delight and licked her hands and face like a dog. A crowd of sightseers loudly cheered.

At the performance of January 19, Menken's luck ran out. Her black steed missed his footing and plunged from the ramp. The horrified audience watched the rider slip from her straps as she tumbled with the animal's large frame to the stage. Landing beside him, with an equal thud, she just missed being crushed. Adah was knocked unconscious and had to be carried backstage. The audience, some in tears, others cursing beneath their breath, were ushered out. At the hotel, the examining doctor, M. Nelaton, the emperor's personal physician, found that two fingers on Adah's left hand were broken, her head bruised, and an ear badly torn. She lay as though dead all night while he attended her, but in the morning she awoke, and in two days' time she demanded to go back onstage. Dr. Nelaton forbade it, but *La Menken* went ahead anyway. Riding a backup mount, she gave a good, if stiff, performance. Nelaton could not understand how she did it, remarking that she had great courage.

Adah could bear the pain, but she mourned the loss of Gypsy, who had to be put to rest. The episode made her still more popular, and tickets to the sold-out Gaîté changed hands at exorbitant prices. Menken, an American, thirty-one years old, had become the arbiter of fashion in the cultural capital of the world. Women drank coffee or tea from chinaware bearing the emblem of the Naked Lady, and the daring ones donned pantaloons and cut their hair *a la Mazeppa*. Men wore Menken hats and coats and Mazeppa-style cravats, collars, and handkerchiefs. Menkeniana, from scarf pins to shaving mugs decorated with her picture, was sold everywhere. Says Allen Lesser, "She was the darling of Paris, the love goddess at whose feet the pleasure-maddened capital kneeled in lavish adoration."

Although trees were bare along the boulevards, when the sun shone it felt mild enough to sit out at the busy cafés. Native *boulevardiers* had to share tables with visitors from all of Europe and places as distant as Texas. Although newly a mother, Menken's love life was the subject of their endless speculation. She was seen often in the Bois de Boulogne, wearing a dark blue, silver-embroidered riding habit, a plumed hat atop her head, cantering alongside King Charles of Württemberg. Louis Napoleon and Eugénie, both keen on horses, had purchased the land as a horse playground for Paris. Equestrianism came to be used for show, business, and flirting. Menken's expert horsemanship made a blasé crowd sit up and take notice.

Crowned and titled visitors flooded into Paris in 1867, partly to see the wonders of the Exposition, but also to court and cavort. Adah was the most desired woman in the capital, the object of attention from counts and dukes and, it was rumored, the emperor himself. She did choose a king, but an embattled one. Württemberg, with Stuttgart its capital, was a center of liberalism in nineteenth century Germany. However, King Charles I, whose reign began in 1864, sided with Austria in the Seven Weeks' War of 1866, and was forced to pay an indemnity by the victorious Prussians. Charles, with his court, had come to Paris to raise the money. But the king found time to see and be seen with the brightest star of the season.

Did he and Menken have an affair? For a change, Adah was without a husband in residence. Charles was trim, handsome, of middle years, interested in the arts and sciences, and ruler of a beautiful kingdom. He was a better catch than Lola Montez's aging King Ludwig of Bavaria. The rumor mill insisted that the pair were lovers, and Wolf Mankowitz succinctly puts the case: "One does not lightly reject the advances of a monarch in reasonable repair." Adah, no longer an innocent, felt free to make love with a man she found attractive, especially if it would make real her imagined title, "the Royal Menken."

We have anecdotal evidence about the king and the actress. Former Confederate colonel Tom Ochiltree came to Paris as correspondent and lobbyist for Texas interests. He was seated in the outdoor café of the Grand Hotel with James Bennett Jr., son of the founder of the New York *Herald*, its new editor. King Charles drove up with Adah in a carriage, his retinue following. Sly Tom offered to bet Bennett that if he spoke to Adah, she would kiss him. The latter scoffed and took the bet. Tom approached and introduced himself—they had not seen each other since youthful days—and Adah threw her arms around him and planted a kiss. Tom, a gambling man, knew it was a sure thing.

Next day over tea, Adah affirmed to Tom that she had become the morganatic bride of Charles. This implies an actual marriage, kept secret, between Adah and the king, though one that did not legally ennoble her or her infant boy. Talk of this sort became current along the boulevards, a part of the Menken myth that Arthur Conan Doyle used as the basis for his superb Sherlock Holmes tale, "A Scandal in Bohemia." Tom Ochiltree would become the confidant of American presidents and financial advisor to European royalty, and he was already a sophisticated man. Yet even he believed Adah's story. However, German sources insist that Charles was gay, and Wikipedia echoes these scholars: "Karl became the object of scandal several times for his closeness with various men." At this stage, the king's homosexuality was being hushed up, and what better way than his being seen and whispered about with *La Menken*, the great sex symbol! Adah, keenly aware of the publicity value, happily went along with this myth-making.

In any case, *La Menken* ruled the fantasy life of Paris, male and female. Imitators sprang up, but although they bared more than she, they were no match for the not-so-Naked Lady. A more serious attempt at competition was mounted by the followers of Offenbach, who cast the English courtesan Cora Pearl in the composer's classical *Orphée aux Enfers*. But on stage the vulgar Cora, though shapely, sounded like the name with which she was born: Emma Crouch. Nestor Roqueplan wrote that "she had a clown's head on a body worthy of [the goddess] Diana."

Cora was the mistress of Jérome, Prince Napoleon, Louis's cousin. He not only attended her opening but brought the entire Jockey Club to occupy strategic boxes. The pit was packed by *boulevardiers*, who had come to view the shape they could not afford: Cora was dressed mostly in diamonds and feathers. Once she began to sing, students in the gallery hooted and whistled, drowning her out. Cora quit, stuck out her tongue, and had to retreat before a fusillade of rotten fruit. This was one of numerous attempts to dethrone Adah as queen of the Parisian night, but all failed.

Gaston Jap, a critic, asked himself why the American Menken had won the hearts of his supposedly cynical countrymen. He answered:

> *Menken is one of the few happy personalities common to all nations who possess the marvelous quality of charm. To see her is to be seduced. . . . She has the gift of fascination to a supreme degree . . . her eyes give forth a curious radiance. What a pity that at the theatre her lips open but to respond to the shower of compliments poured upon her!*

Others thought it was her roguish, mischievous smile, and still others her shapely legs. Actually, Adah had an advantage over her competitors, and that was the association with her horse. The sex symbol of the Second Empire was the *amazone*, an equestrienne dressed in a skin-tight riding habit, carrying a whip, and mounted on a spirited horse. Such women could be seen cantering in the Bois de Boulogne—harlot or court lady, each for sale but under different terms. Catherine Walters (known as Skittles), who was born into poverty near the docks at Liverpool, became an accomplished horsewoman and the most expensive courtesan in 1860s Paris. It took Napoleon III's sixty-three-year-old minister of finance to keep her. The *amazone* presented an image of dominance (over her horse), freedom, and sexual vitality. In a sense, the Naked Lady was the chief *amazone*.

Adah's ride up the mountain was dangerous, and the body being admired by the audience might at any moment be broken to pieces. This was a special body that could play a man's role while looking blatantly female. Adah controlled the horse, yet at the climax of *Les Pirates,* she appeared helpless, legs spread, in bondage. Dualism generated sexual tension. That Adah was an exotic made her the more desirable to men on the town. She was an *amazone* to the highest degree: a transgressor of morals and gender. *Tout* Paris found her delicious and demanded the latest gossip about her love life.

The racists, gathering strength in the later nineteenth century, were one exception. The illustrated newspaper *La Lune* decried the attention paid to Menken, even denying that she was a real woman because she was not white. The cover of the issue depicted Adah dancing arm in arm with her black horse, he in white tie, her head enlarged to caricature Semitic features. In other words she is depicted as being no better than an animal. The sexual kick comes from the caption, MISS DADA MENKEN, which plays on the nickname given her by the people of Paris. "Dada" sounds like "Adah," and the word is a nursery name for a rocking horse. But in French street slang, "dada" is also a rude joke word for sexual congress in the astride, or so-called "Greek position." The implication is that Adah the mongrel was making it with her horse. Menken understood the innuendo. She grasped that her position at the top of the heap was as slippery as the ride up the mountain that put her there. Her reaction was similar to that of the irreverent, twentieth century Dada movement. The artists and rebels who liked to incite used the term "Dada" in its ultimate slang sense: "Up yours!" *La Menken's* next move would shock even jaded Paris.

CHAPTER TWENTY-ONE:

UNCLE TOM WITH MISS ADA

Alexandre Dumas *père* remains one of the best-known French authors, and today his novels are more popular than ever. *The Three Musketeers* has been the basis for some sixty movies, including on television, and *The Count of Monte Cristo* is not far behind. If Dumas's works, translated into one hundred languages, are as much seen as read, that is appropriate to a writer who collaborated with others but made sure his name alone appeared under the title, who favored sequels and spin-offs, and who earned large sums but spent the money like there was no tomorrow. Hollywood loves Dumas. He was a great storyteller, and his involvement with Adah Menken makes for one of his most fascinating stories.

Unfortunately, we tend to picture Dumas *père* as an old-fashioned, woolly-haired, pie-faced, obese gentleman, a fancy stick in hand. A contemporary called him, "a good-natured hippopotamus in his stiff white pique vest and high collar." However, the ambitious youth of twenty-one who arrived in Paris in 1823, hoping to find work as a clerk, was as handsome, lithe, and athletic as his well-known character, d'Artagnan. Good-natured but with a temper, his cane, if he carried one, would have sheathed a sword.

Our favorite portrayal of d'Artagnan, the fourth musketeer, is by Michael York in the 1973 film version of Dumas's classic, the first to touch on the complex erotics of the story. D'Artagnan is in love with Constance, a married woman. He is sleeping with Milady de Winter, a *femme fatale* who is married to another musketeer, and he flirts with Milady's maid. This is Alexandre writing about himself, an inveterate philanderer who boasted of his prowess: "It's sheer humanity that makes me have mistresses. If I had only one, she would be dead in a week. I have got more than five hundred children."

Alexandre made no secret of his racial heritage. His grandfather was a French nobleman who cohabited with a black slave woman in Haiti. He had a boy child, Thomas, who he brought back to France. This was Alexandre's father, a man of color who became a distinguished general under Napoleon Bonaparte. He died when his son was young, and Alexandre was raised by his mother in genteel poverty in the country. When he left for the capital, he carried letters of introduction to his father's friends, and he was determined to become a great man.

Adah Menken, who had read Dumas's novels as a young woman, idolized him. She shared with him friends such as Gautier, Sand, and Fechter, and shortly after her arrival in Paris, she sent him an autographed photo and an invitation to attend the opening of *Les Pirates*. Why did "Old Dumas," as the press tagged him, wait over a month before turning up at the Théâtre de la Gaîté? Why did he linger backstage? The famed novelist, poor and shabby, had become more highly thought of in America than in his homeland. His melodramas, once the talk of Paris, were no longer produced, and his fluency in fiction had deserted him. Yet he praised Menken in his one-man weekly, *The Musketeer*, and, like an old lion, waited for the moment to pounce. As he wrote of d'Artagnan, "He whose game is the eagle takes no heed of the sparrow."

Adah, alerted that Dumas was in the wings, ran to him once the first act was done, threw her arms around his neck, and kissed him. This was a warmer greeting than Dumas had expected. She led him to her dressing room, and while she changed costumes, she flattered him by heaping praise on his novels. The mature gentleman, dependent for support on his cranky son, the playwright Alexandre Dumas *fils*, and a joke to the fashionable, felt he had been transported back to his youth on the wings of this eagle. He set his sights on her.

In discussing the affair that engrossed Adah and Alexandre, which led to an explosive scandal that fascinated *tout* Paris—indeed, much of the world—we need to understand the motives of the participants. André Maurois, Dumas' biographer and apologist, takes the line that he succumbed to Adah's flattery and became her dupe. He presents his subject as amiable and impulsive. Dumas's son, the successful author of *Camille*, once introduced him as: "my father, a great big child whom I had when I was a little boy." Dumas *père* was a Romantic, a man who admitted to throwing away ten fortunes, who fought alongside Garibaldi in Italy, and who was an authority on dueling and cooking.

In the realm of seduction, Dumas was no fool. Experience with twenty-eight past mistresses had seasoned him enough to please even a superstar. His formula was simple: "I love those who love me." While winter dragged on, Adah and Alexandre became intimates. She visited him at his small apartment on the Boulevard Malesherbes, where his daughter Marie kept house, and the sole valuable possession was a painting given to him by his friend Delacroix. They talked of the things they had in common: books, poetry, art, the theater. Alexandre recounted incidents in his life: the Revolution of 1848, or his journey through the far reaches of Russia, and he spoke pathetically about the magnificent Château de Monte-Cristo, which he had built and lost to creditors. "[O]ne of the most delicious follies ever built," Balzac called it, "fit for a king." Adah began at once to help support the dethroned king of romance.

Writes a Dumas biographer, "At the first hint of spring the pair could be seen walking arm in arm through those quaint parts of Paris spared by Haussmann's demolition workers, with Dumas eloquently holding forth on the history and legend of the various buildings." Adah, in a sable-trimmed cape and hooped skirt, hands in a muff, Dumas dressed in a top hat, frock coat, and striped trousers, were a sight that caused the *citoyens* to buzz. The author was pleased by the attention, Adah less so. Once the trees began to bloom, the pair would get away by carriage to the sylvan suburb of Bougival.

Here the inns and taverns peered over the Seine, and their proprietors were friends of Dumas, while the boatmen on the river, as ready to sing as Italian gondoliers, were used to his amorous escapades. As the couple strolled on the riverbank, they may have run into the large figure of Gustave Courbet. He painted canvases so lifelike that they helped to dethrone the rule of an artificial classicism. The pair dined simply but well at one of the rustic inns, where Alexandre himself might cook an omelet or soufflé. The proprietor could be depended on to keep to himself the identity of the lady who spent the night.

With the opening of the Exposition of 1867, the reign of Louis Napoleon and Eugénie reached its height. In an enormous glass building on the Left Bank of the Seine, where the Eiffel Tower now stands, France showed off the accomplishments of its science and industry, arts and fashion, entertainment and cuisine. Countries from the world over exhibited their wares, and tourists from everywhere flocked to Paris. The Exposition was the ultimate showcase for the Second Empire and its last triumph. An incredible amount of money and labor had gone into the construction of "a fairyland of kiosks and domes and minarets . . . of pavilions and gardens and grottos," which over seven months' time would attract six million visitors.

On a sunny April afternoon, Alexandre, his daughter Marie, and Adah went to see the Exposition. They browsed through the galleries of labor and art, nibbled foreign foods, and pretended not to notice the many stares they received. At the studio of Pierre Petit they stopped to pose for photographs, mementos of this fleeting moment. The most important one shows the couple standing, one arm around each other. Adah, wearing a sheath garment, leans on Alexandre's paternal shoulder. He looks pleased. She, a beautiful, determined woman, looks more interested in the camera than in her escort.

In those days, when photography was still a marvel, Adah enjoyed posing before the camera with the great men in her life. However, her use for this photo was supposedly private. She sent copies, signed by both Dumas and herself, to select friends back in America. One copy went to Ed James in New York and another to Charles Warren Stoddard in California. She sent a copy to journalist Charles Henry Webb in New York, with the note: "You stick to me, and I will stick to you." Adah liked to show off her conquests, but she saw nothing improper in the photo. Father and daughter Dumas had posed for a similar shot.

One week later Adah and Alexandre again posed, this time at the studio of M. Liebert. Although two extant images seem merely suggestive, the set of photos and their bastard offspring rocked Paris and titillated the rest of the world. For one thing, Alexandre is in his shirtsleeves as Adah rests her head on his ample middle, arms about his neck. To Victorians, a man in shirtsleeves was practically undressed. Add to that, both parties look sated, as if they had just come from a bout of lovemaking.

Adah may have supposed she was affirming her identity as a woman of color, but she had been set up. Dumas owed Liebert money. To cancel the debt, he brought Adah to the studio, and afterward he looked the other way while Liebert sold to boulevard stationery shops multiple copies of the intimate photos. The shops advertised these for sale in their windows. Society, which had whispered about the affair between Dumas and Menken, now spoke of nothing else. The "mosquito press" buzzed around, making the usual assumptions about the relationship between two celebrities. One columnist offered the following rationalization: "Americans demand the right to be bizarre in their love affairs. Decayed though he may be, Dumas can be amusing, cheerful and often droll."

The porn photographers seized this opportunity. They had previously created fake nude photos of eminent persons, including Louis Napoleon and Eugénie. Soon shots of a nude young woman intertwined with a rotund older man, Adah's and Alexandre's heads pasted on the torsos, appeared at news kiosks and were hawked by boys on the street. The *boulevardiers* at the fashionable cafés, such as the twenty-four-hour Anglais, collected the lewd photos for their albums. Amusement at Dumas's latest triumph soon turned to ridicule of both parties. The poet Paul Verlaine, a café lounger notorious for his affair with Arthur Rimbaud, penned an irreverent jingle that set the crowd to roaring:

Uncle Tom with Miss Ada,
It's a show to die for.
What crazy photographer joined
Uncle Tom with Miss Ada?
Ada can ride her hobby-horse
But Tom, how long can he mount?
Uncle Tom with Miss Ada,
It's a show to die for.

The racial slur is evident, as well as the fear of racial mixing. The scandal would grow more bizarre as dozens of shop windows displayed a variety of concocted photos. De Villemessant at *Le Figaro* wrote, tongue in cheek:

> *One sees at this moment in the windows of most news agents a series of very curious photographs, accompanied by the inscription, "Portraits of Miss Menken, of her mother, and of Alexandre Dumas."*
>
> *Miss Adah Isaacs Menken is represented in tights in all sorts of poses. Some of the prints depict a majestic female in black velvet wildly clasping to her heart the young horsewoman who is in flesh-ings. Without doubt it is her mother. As for the others they show Miss Menken and Alexandre Dumas in a series of poses plastiques. Can it be her father?*

De Villemessant, meaning to be snide, had solved the mystery of Adah's attraction to Alexandre: She had found not Dada (kinky sex), but Daddy. When we recall that Menken, like Dumas, was part black, that she had never known her biological father, and that he may have been a man of color, we realize her susceptibility to the so-called "eminent mulatto." In several of her relationships she had searched for a father figure, and Dumas seemed to fit the bill. She trusted him, and she believed his assurance that he was writing a play with the dramatic role she longed for. As for Dumas's motivations in courting her, they are obvious: to restore his reputation as a lady-killer and a literary lion. He succeeded in his aims far better than she.

Enter Alexandre Dumas *fils*. Formerly a rake following in his father's footsteps, he had married his mistress, a Russian princess, and become a self-appointed guardian of public morality. He was used to his father embarrassing him, but never on the scale of the affair with Menken. To tone down the uproar, Dumas *fils* insisted that his father go to court to demand Liebert stop selling the photos and destroy the negatives. He led the charge in blaming Menken for their release.

Dumas *fils* cultivated the influential, complaining by letter to George Sand. "How distressed you must have been by those photographs," she responded. "[But] age brings consequences to bohemian life. What a pity it all is!" Dumas *père* was pressured to write to Menken, who would no longer see him, accusing her of complicity with Liebert. Her present manager, M. Karel, replied that the star had suffered from the scandal both morally and financially. She had an exclusive arrangement with Reutlinger, the leading Paris photographer, and she would have to pay him compensation. "You know Miss Menken well enough to be sure that such puffs are most objectionable to her," he reminded the toothless musketeer.

The lawsuit, which dragged on, numbed the *boulevardiers* and killed the fun in the scandal. Dumas claimed that the photos were never meant for the public and Liebert had tricked him. The photographer's lawyers countered that, for a consideration, Dumas had authorized Liebert to sell the photos of Menken and himself. It pleased his vanity to be known as the lover of *La Menken*. But when the press began to ridicule him, Dumas changed his mind. The only thing improper in the affair, concluded Liebert's lawyers, "is the philandering of M. Dumas with the pretty lady."

Adah, disappointed in her admirer, refused to testify on his behalf. Months later, Dumas won a court order banning the display of the photos and turning the negatives over to him. Adah had left for Vienna. Finally, she would realize that Dumas's faults were outsized, as were his virtues, and forgive him. But in the spring of 1867 she had cause to worry that the affair would bring down her soaring career. In fact, the result was that a sex scandal boosted her popularity. For the Naked Lady, privacy was out of the question—she was public property.

On the last Sunday in April, the one-hundredth night of *Les Pirates*, the *crème de la crème* attended Menken's performance. New scenery was built and painted, exotic costumes devised. A new musical number, "Leo's Gallop," was composed and played while Adah and her horse danced up the stage mountain. The gala event was packed with the titled and rich: Epaulets adorned the men, as they bowed to women whose smiles flashed like the diamonds in their hair. Emperor Napoleon III attended, host to the King of Greece, Prince Oscar of Sweden, and the Duke of Edinburgh. Abetted by the absence of Eugénie, whispers went around that Napoleon had succeeded in his campaign to bed Menken. In fact, he was no more the victor here than two years later at Sedan, where he lost the battle to the Prussians, along with his throne. The theatrical event, a veritable banquet of the senses, was a fitting tribute to the woman who had fascinated Europe, and to an empire that was all for show.

By the end of May Adah had played 150 performances at the Gaîté. Offers for her to appear in *Mazeppa* poured in from half the world. She considered sailing to California to do an encore tour, and then to Australia, but she could neither take her baby boy with her nor leave him for so long. Exhausted, but tempted by a large guarantee, she decided on a month's engagement at the Théâtre Impérial in Vienna. Next to Paris, it was the most important and sophisticated city on the Continent, and she could repeat Leo in *Les Pirates*, which was a less tiring role than Mazeppa. In early June, after arranging nursing care for her child, she would leave for the capital of the Austro-Hungarian Empire.

First, Adah gave a sumptuous dinner party that featured the cream of the literary world. According to the editor of the *Franco-American*, who attended, the guests included Charles Dickens; Algernon Swinburne;

drama critic John Thomson; General John Breckinridge, former vice president of the United States; opera star Hortense Schneider, *La Menken*'s rival for the role of the toast of Paris; and the guest of honor— Alexandre Dumas *père*. At the dinner, he presented his hostess with a photograph of himself, inscribed in quaint English: "To the Last Love of my Heart, to Miss Adah Menken, her faithful Alex Dumas." In this the old philanderer spoke true.

Adah had brought together a brilliant group, and we wish some record of their conversation had been kept. We may surmise, along with Allen Lesser, that "never did [she] appear more radiant nor her wit more sparkling." The famous authors represented the means to harness Adah's literary ambition, which had taken center stage in her mind. She hoped to be remembered as a serious actress and a poet. But alas, her lover Dumas disappointed and wrote no drama for her. Her friend Dickens made only a half-hearted bow to her poetry. Ironically, it was Swinburne, a drunken pariah in polite circles, who would act as midwife to the birth of *Infelicia*, her book of verse.

The gala and the dinner in the spring of 1867 represent the peak of Adah Menken's theatrical career. In Vienna on June 18, she opened to a packed house and distinguished audience, but as the evening dragged on, everything went wrong. The actors lost their lines, the props did not work, and no cheers reached Leo's ear. The curtain rang down only once to tepid applause. Next day the newspaper critics confirmed that Vienna, far from being effervescent, was too reserved a place for the antics of French melodrama. The polyglot lands over which the emperor ruled were restive, and the Prussians had made mincemeat of the imperial army. The somber tones of Brahms, Schnitzler, and ultimately Freud, rather than the cavorting of a half-naked mute waif, would mark the waning days of Austria-Hungary.

Les Pirates played on to half-empty houses. Adah was not able to connect with the audience, and without their emotional feedback, she was not herself. The productions went from bad to worse. One evening, an American reporter went backstage to find the famous star "huddled in a corner of her dressing room, like a bundle of rags, crying with rage and despair at her treatment by the Viennese." He did not know, nor would she tell him, that she had received a telegram from Paris: Her baby boy, Louis Dudevant Victor Emmanuel Barkley, had died. Once again motherhood was denied her.

At the Archduke Charles Hotel, Menken went into seclusion, brooding over her fate. She felt she was "Infelix," the unlucky one, as she had titled one of her best poems. Then, on June 24, a letter arrived from Charles Stoddard in California, who worshipped her. She replied at once:

> *My poet—I am so glad to know you. Your letter came just today when kind and beautiful things were so much needed in my heart. . . . I have today fallen down into the bitterness of a sad, reflective and desolate mood. You know I am alone, and that I work, and without sympathy, and the unshrined ghosts of wasted hours and of lost loves always tugging at my heart.*

This is the fate of a superstar, set on a pedestal but likely to be abandoned by her idolaters once she shows human frailty. It is also the complaint of a woman who feels she has neglected her true self. Adah, a Jew in a city rife with anti-Semitism, reached across the world to a gay poet similarly isolated in gold rush California: "I want us to be friends—real friends."

Adah and Charles shared a burning desire for "the true, which is always beautiful." That they hoped to satisfy this longing by collecting mementos from great literary figures, or by sharing their beds, is pathetic yet common enough. So Adah in her reply descends into gossip, relating to her faraway friend the doings of Victor Hugo (in exile in Jersey), George Sand ("a quiet little creature"), but especially Alexandre Dumas. She sends Charles his autographed portrait, adding, "Value it for his sake as well as for the poor girl he honors with his love and friendship. . . . [T]o send you this is sending a bit of my heart over the seas to you. . . . You could understand his great soul so well: the King of romance, and the child of gentleness and love."

Adah, fleeing Vienna, returned to Paris, this time with a literary intent. Writing emotionally to Stoddard on September 21, she regretted they could not meet in person. But she assured Charles:

I already know your soul. It has met mine somewhere on the starry highway of thought. . . . I am always sad and lonely. Nothing but hard work saves me from myself. And you know I am a vagabond of fancy. No home—no plans—no ideas. I was born a dweller in tents—a reveller in "the tented habitation of war." . . . Consequently, [my] views of life and things are rather disreputable in the eyes of the "just." I am always in bad odor with people who do not know me, and startle all who do. Alas!

The reference to tents seems a throwback to Adah's early, nomadic days with the circus. Actually, sensing the Grim Reaper in the wings, she did have a plan. She wanted to claim her rightful place as a poet. For that, it was necessary to collect in a book the better of her poems. Ed James had done much of the work, but she still needed to gather a few from the newspapers in which they had been published. She assigned Charles the task of finding and sending her two poems from the *Golden Era*. She repeated, perhaps to herself, that in the matter of the book, "Dickens is my friend and adviser." Thus, bound for London, she contemplated calling the collected poems simply *Writings*.

At the turn of the century, a mature Charles Stoddard recalled his youthful correspondence with Menken. He could not be sure "whether [on her part] it was the spontaneous outpouring of an impulsive and ingenuous heart, or merely the pose of an artful woman who courted admiration." Writing of himself in the third person, he knew "that her delicate flattery did not hurt him in the least, though she was at that time one of the most famous women of the world, the bright, particular star dazzling two continents, and he merely an aspiring poet. On the contrary, it inspired him to nobler efforts and filled him with a longing to achieve something worthy of her praise."

The young men fell easily for Menken. As for the older man who had been her lover, she informed Charles: "*Cher* Dumas is in the country, working hard he writes me." Indeed, the prodigious author, finished with love except in memory, had one last book in him: *La Terreur Prussienne.* The novel, which he wrote on commission, dramatized the likelihood of war with Prussia, a rising power determined to overthrow French dominance in Europe. Dumas proved all too prophetic.

At the Paris Exposition, amid the gaiety, gormandizing, and flirting, the Prussians had on exhibit a huge, thousand-pound cannon. The French thought it was a clumsy joke. Their military exhibit stressed a light new rifle, flashy cavalry, and splendid uniforms. Their forces looked unbeatable on a parade ground. But at Sedan on September 1, 1870, the Prussian cannon blew the gorgeous hussars to pieces. The French were routed, and Louis Napoleon, superbly mounted, uniform immaculate, wrinkles covered by makeup, surrendered to the German infantry. Romanticism, whether on the battlefield or stage, was passé.

Chapter Twenty-two:

THE AFFAIR SWINBURNE

The final conversion of Sam Clemens from West Coast hell-raiser to Mark Twain, author, lecturer, and husband, occured when he moved to New York and met his wealthy wife-to-be, Olivia Langdon. This change of persona necessitated a shift in his attitude toward the notorious, disturbingly front-page Adah Menken. Twain's item on her sent from Manhattan to the *Alta California* on May 15, 1867, signals not only his personal conversion to decorum but also the advent of an age of realism in the arts. This was at the time when the comet Menken lit up the night sky over two continents. Yet Twain's star was ascending, while Adah's, at a Romantic apogee, was headed down.

After describing the infamous Menken/Dumas photos and the scandal they ignited, Twain cuttingly wrote of Adah:

> *She has a passion for connecting herself with distinguished people, and then discarding them as soon as the world has grown reconciled to the novelty of it and stopped talking about it. Heenan suited her caprice well enough for a while, and then he had to vacate; the same was Orpheus C. Kerr's experience; and the same was the Davenport Brothers' [Spiritualist mediums]; and the same was the experience of some less notorious favorites of hers. And now comes the great Mulatto in the Iron Mask, and he is high chief for the present. But can he hold his position against all comers? Would he stand any chance against a real live gorilla from the wilds of Africa? I don't know. Menken is mighty shaky. Menken can't resist a splendid new astonisher. Menken is a good hearted, free-handed, charitable soul—a woman who does white deeds enough, kindly*

Christian deeds enough, every day of her life to blot out a swarming multitude of sins; but, Heaven help us, what desperate chances she takes on her reputation!

Twain exhibited the racial and gender prejudices of most Victorian men. His thumbnail sketch of Menken's troubled love life was unfair. And his mock concern for her reputation reflected uneasiness about his own past carousing. But Twain correctly realized that Adah, like a modern-day media celebrity, had to continually astonish to stay in the news. He signed off with the warning: "These photographs are to be reproduced here," meaning from New York to California. The image of Adah Menken as temptress was about to span the Western world.

In contrast, Adah's state of mind was grave. By the time she arrived in London in early September, accompanied by Susette Ellington, she was chronically ill. Latent tuberculosis had weakened her formerly robust frame, and numerous accidents onstage caused her to be often in pain. Adah's figure was losing its hourglass shape, and she was heavier in an unhealthy way. Photos taken at this time hint at a loss of physical and moral firmness. She understood time was against her, but masked the problems.

In a luxurious suite at the private Cataldi's Hotel on Dover Street, the Royal Menken renewed her open house. Among the literary notables who dropped by, or were invited to her legendary dinners, were Charles Reade and mystery novelist Wilkie Collins. Algernon Swinburne came on the rare occasions when he was sober. The actors Daniel Bandemann, a German brought over by E. T. Smith to play Hamlet, and Charles Fechter were regulars, as was Edmund Yates, a rising journalist who knew Ed James. Henry B. Farnie, who had written scathingly about Menken, was by now all compliments and attentiveness. Clement Scott, the critic who profoundly understood her poetry, remarked: "Adah Menken was an extraordinary woman, a woman with a soul. . . . She captivated in turn famous poets, and novelists of the first class, dramatists by the score and, of course, journalists."

However, Charles Dickens, secretly involved with Ellen Ternan, was overly busy preparing for a lecture tour of America. Adah still hoped he would write a foreword to her book of poetry. In compensation, she informed Brother Ed, "Alfred Tennyson called on me yesterday to read some of my poems."

Eager for publication, Adah turned to John Thomson, who worshipped the ground she walked on. He made a connection for her with Phillips and Cone, booksellers. The combination of retail bookselling and publishing was common, but this was too small a firm to do justice to The Menken. She did not realize that *Mazeppa*, scheduled for late October at Astley's, would once again attract packed houses. Despite bursts of energy, she was becoming more run-down. Weary of worldly things, Adah immersed herself more in Spiritualism, and she cultivated Daniel Dunglas Home, the great medium.

Home was born near Edinburgh in 1833, the son of a laborer who was the natural offspring of the tenth Earl of Home. When Daniel was nine his adopted family moved to Connecticut, where he received a grade-school education. At seventeen he left to seek his place in the world of Spiritualism, where he was especially gifted in communicating with departed souls through table-tipping and other phenomena in dimly lit parlors. Popular interest was growing to epidemic proportions.

From the start, the sensitive, who refused payment for holding a séance, was pampered by wealthy and powerful people. From the hospitality of the rich in America he gravitated toward the aristocracy of Europe. The Empress Eugénie consulted him, and with the approbation of the czar, he married a Russian lady of noble birth. Home was never caught in any trickery, and Adah believed in him entirely. She asked him to contribute to her album, begun in Paris, which contained the autographs and comments of those she most esteemed. "God keep and His good angels guard you," wrote Home.

But there were times when Adah did not wish to be good. Her nature was sensuous, and when aroused her nostrils would flare with an animal intensity. In the fall of 1867 she chose a young man for a lover, the librettist Robert "Racy" Reece. She wrote him a remarkably seductive letter, at once cynical and poetic. Although meant to be kept private, it later became public, to Reece's intense embarrassment. The note is Adah's invitation to a married man to come to bed:

> *Today, Roberto, I should like to see you if you are good tempered, and think you could be bored with me and my ghosts. They will be harmless to you, these ghosts of mine; they are sad, soft-footed things that wear my brain and live on my heart, that is, the fragment I have left to be called heart.*
>
> *I hear you are married—I am really glad of that. I believe all good men should be married. Yet I don't believe in women being married. Somehow they all sink into nonentities after this epoch in their existence. That is the fault of female education. They are taught from their cradles to look upon marriage as the one event of their lives. That accomplished, nothing remains. Byron might have been right after all: "Man's love is of his life a thing apart—it is a woman's whole existence." If this is true we do not wonder to find so many stupid wives. . . . Good women are rarely clever, and clever women are rarely good.*
>
> *Come when you get time, and tell me of our friends, the gentle souls of air; mine fly from me, only to fill my being with the painful remembrance of their lost love for me—even me! Once the blest and chosen! Now a royal tigress waits in her lonely jungle for the coming of the king of forests. Brown gaiters not excluded.*
>
> *Yours, through all stages of local degradation,*
> *INFELIX MENKEN.*

The woman had drunk deeply from the beaker of life, and she had her regrets, but she was not ready to depart. She had written to Charles Stoddard that the material world bored her. But the drama had time to run. Charles was gay and in far-off California. Roberto was to hand. For the time being, flesh would rule over spirit.

No new play was forthcoming from Dumas or Daly or any of the others who had promised to write one for Menken. She was not a disciplined dramatic actress in the sense of the nineteenth century theater. This didn't prevent Sarah Bernhardt, an ingenue with the Comédie-Française when Menken ruled Paris, from borrowing her expressive body language. Rather, Adah was a genuine superstar, and these rarities transcend time and place to define their own meaning.

On October 19 she opened again at Astley's in *Mazeppa*. E. T. Smith had resigned and the management was caught unprepared by an overflow house and the insistent demand for seats. At her entrance as Cassimir the page, Adah received a standing ovation, which was repeated after Mazeppa's perilous ride up the mountain. When the final curtain rang down she was greeted by thunderous applause and a shower of bouquets. The Menken was still the toast of London.

However, a book of her collected poems remained Adah's main concern. John Thomson, with Swinburne's blessing, now took the project to the latter's publisher, John Camden Hotten. In 1866 Algernon Swinburne was the *enfant terrible* of British literature. An aristocrat by birth whose father was an admiral, he was a hell-raiser by disposition. According to Matthew Arnold, Swinburne was "the favorite poet of the young men at Oxford and Cambridge." Inevitably he made enemies in the literary world. He was an aesthete, unable to play the game: "London and business or (worse) society are awful clogs on poetry," he blithely informed a correspondent.

Swinburne befriended a talented sort of lawbreaker: the half-Portuguese Charles Augustus Howell, who Dante Gabriel Rossetti had called on to open the grave of Lizzie Siddal, his wife, to retrieve his poetry buried with her; or the artist Simeon Solomon, who was arrested for sexual soliciting. Swinburne claimed to be a disciple of the Marquis de Sade, but physically puny, he was timid about acting out his fantasies. Oscar Wilde remarked that he was "a braggart in matters of vice, who had done everything he could to convince his fellow citizens of his homosexuality and bestiality, without being in the slightest degree a homosexual or a bestializer." Algernon's foppish appearance, with a huge mop of auburn hair, was simply not intimidating. Henry Adams described him as "a tropical bird, high-crested, long-beaked, quick moving, with rapid utterance and screams of humor. . . . One could call him a crimson macaw among owls."

When the publisher Moxon brought out Swinburne's *Poems and Ballads,* the duller birds got their chance to take revenge. The publisher heard from *The Times* that the newspaper had set in type a review not only denouncing *Poems* as obscene but demanding that the author and publisher be prosecuted. The result was, as Swinburne wrote, "My hound of a publisher has actually withdrawn from circulation my volume of poems." The shrewd Hotten stepped in and brought out the book. He had lived in America and had published authors close to Menken, such as Artemus Ward and Orpheus C. Kerr. He also published and sold, without an imprint, books on flagellation. Hotten understood, in an American way, that there could be no bad publicity, and he regarded the moral fury that greeted *Poems* as money in the bank. He was delighted to get hold of first Swinburne and now Menken.

John Thomson, described by Mankowitz as "part pimp, part secretary, part male prostitute," acted as go-between not only in literary but more personal affairs. Swinburne had found the precocious lad of sixteen in the kitchen of a friend's lodging house, run by his mother, reciting *Paradise Lost* from memory to cockroaches. John had begun to make his way in the world by procuring gentleman customers for the dominatrices in St. John's Wood. These imposing ladies practiced what the French termed "the English vice," sadomasochism. Beginning at public school, lads of a good class were accustomed to being whipped (with a so-called rod) on the bare buttocks as punishment for various misdemeanors. A lore developed around these public flagellations, and, to a degree, the sex life of an entire class was affected by the experience. John led Swinburne to a particular brothel, the Verbena Lodge, where two golden-haired "governesses" with hard eyes and rouged cheeks, sometimes in male drag, birched expectant bottoms. Swinburne's sex ideal was a *maitresse* with a whip.

Early in Menken's British career, Thomson had become a devoted fan, and he likely brought Swinburne to see her at Astley's. The androgynous image E. T. Smith had created for her fit the poet's kinky bill. Watching her perform in *Mazeppa*, lashed to the powerful black stallion, the danger she underwent, her revenge on the nobles who tortured her, and her swashbuckling poses all thrilled Algernon and many another former schoolboy in the audience. During this period, though he was often drunk and behaved boorishly, Swinburne wrote superb poetry. He also worked on the novel *Lesbia Brandon*, which was so far ahead of its time it would be suppressed until 1952.

In a letter to his friend, Sir Richard Burton, the explorer of exotic lands and their sexual mores, Swinburne boasted that *Lesbia Brandon* would be more offensive and objectionable to Britons than anything he had yet done. Considering that Swinburne's *Poems* had been universally denounced, rather like Whitman's *Leaves of Grass* in America, this was quite a boast. Yet his fiction is more accessible than his poetry, and perhaps more engagingly perverse, with the exception of the long poem "Dolores: Our Lady of Pain," which may have been inspired by Adah Menken. That question has been debated among biographers almost as heatedly as how Adah and Algernon went to bed and what they did there.

The accepted story goes that the Italian patriot Giuseppe Mazzini, living in exile in London, was concerned about Swinburne's drinking and frequenting the whipping houses. "All Mazzini wants is that I should dedicate and consecrate my writing power to do good and serve others exclusively, which I can't," the poet confessed to his mother. "If I tried I should lose my faculty of verse." Yet for a time Mazzini persuaded Swinburne to forget art for art's sake and write poetry, published as *Songs Before Sunrise*, dedicated to the cause of Italian democracy. That the poems are no longer read shows that, in the realm of art, Swinburne knew better than the man he called Chief and worshipped almost as a god.

Mazzini was more clever in realizing that the poet needed a woman to organize his life—someone who could "assert a moral superiority on him." The women he suggested were bluestocking types, of no interest to a disciple of the Marquis de Sade. Supposedly, Mazzini confided his concern to Dante Rossetti, who in turn told Richard Burton. Swinburne was especially intimate with Burton, and they shared a keen interest in sadistic forms of sex. According to the legend, Rossetti and Burton, at a gathering one evening in November, bet Menken ten pounds she could not get Swinburne into bed. She laughed, took the note, and at once caught a cab to his lodging at Dorset Street, Portman Square.

The part of the tale that involves Burton is nonsense. At the time, due to the machinations of his wife Isabel, he had taken a diplomatic post in Brazil. He could not get away until June 1869. But Burton's influence on Swinburne was felt through letters, along the lines of "making a man of him." The opportunity presented itself when Adah, on a bet or a tear, showed up unexpectedly at Algernon's door. Julian Field confirmed this to Edmund Gosse, the poet's original biographer:

> *I knew Swinburne intimately. He came down to Oxford many times when I was at Merton (1869–73), and how drunk he used to get! He told me all about Menken calling on him, and telling him bluntly she had come to sleep with him!! and how in the morning, when she used to speak of poetry, he said to her, "My darling, a woman with such beautiful legs should not bother about poetry!"*

Field was an Oxford graduate who became a professional swindler and served time in prison. His description of Adah's greeting to Algernon is not out of character: "I've read your poems and just love them, and I've come over here from Paris on purpose just to love the poet!" Swinburne himself told Gosse that Menken spent many nights in his bed, and that he was only bothered by her waking up early and reading her poetry to him. She would swing her bare legs off the bed in the chill air, but, to Swinburne's surprise, the passion of her poetical rhapsody kept her warm.

The twice-told tale about the bet, a biographer's chestnut, concludes with Menken returning the ten-pound note to Rossetti, remarking, "She did not know how it was, but she hadn't been able to get him [Swinburne] up to the scratch, and couldn't make him understand that biting is no use." Then why did Adah, according to John Thomson, become "a frequent nocturnal visitor" to Swinburne's lodging? Along with the gossips of Victorian London, we are left to wonder what the pair did through the long winter nights—other than sleep.

It is easier to discern what each wanted from the other. Adah was obsessed with publishing her book of poems, and by its sponsorship. When she had reminded Charles Dickens about the dedication, he wrote back:

Dear Miss Menken,

I shall have great pleasure in accepting your dedication, and I thank you for your portrait as a highly remarkable specimen of photography. I also thank you for the verses enclosed in your note. Many such enclosures come to me, but few so pathetically [movingly] written, and fewer still so modestly sent.

However, Dickens, about to leave on an exhausting tour of the United States, could not take time to write a foreword. Indeed, he did not live much longer, dying in the same year as Dumas, 1870. Adah, knowing the British prejudice against American writers, turned for backing to Swinburne. About this time the artist Whistler defended his friend's rowdy conduct before the Committee of the Arts Club, which was bent on throwing him out: "You ought to be proud that there is in London a club where the greatest poet of our time can get drunk, if he wants to, otherwise he might lie in the gutter." Adah overlooked his drinking in order to see the great man.

For Swinburne, the most desired woman in Europe had turned up as his lover—a miracle! In his way, he was a cocky and brave little fellow, and though often the butt of jokes, he could now boast of his sexual prowess. He was quick to let his friends know about the liaison, trusting they would tell the world.

The first material evidence of the affair is a letter of December 4, 1867, from journalist Thomas Purnell to Swinburne:

> *Today I have had such a letter from Dolores—such a letter! She fears you are ill; she is unable to think of anything but you; she wishes me to telegraph to her if you are in danger, and she will fly on the wings of the wind to nurse you. . . . She concludes: "Tell him all—say out my despairing nature to him—take care of his precious life. Write at once; believe in me and my holy love for him. Let him write one word in your letter. He will, for he is so good."*

We have seen that Adah, when in the mood, called herself Dolores Adios Los Fuertes. She had adopted the Spanish name to indicate her tragic unhappiness, and it may be translated as "Pain: Good-bye to Strength," perhaps referring to her chronic illness. Another friend of Swinburne's, Arthur Symons, admitted that "Adah Isaacs Menken was to a certain extent the origin of 'Dolores,'" the poet's scandalous anthem to sadomasochistic love. By 1865, while Swinburne was writing the poem, making changes up to its publication in August 1866, he had certainly seen Menken in *Mazeppa* and followed her adventures in the press. Swinburne, before he met Adah/Dolores, imagined her as his glamorized ideal: imperious, heartless, whip in hand: "Our Lady of Pain."

The next we hear of their affair, Swinburne replied to Purnell: "If you see Dolores before I do, tell her with my love that I would not shew myself sick and disfigured in her eyes. I was spilt last week out of a hansom [cab], and my nose and forehead cut to rags." The poet, once recovered, resumed his lovemaking with Dolores, or so he claimed on December 21, boasting to his influential literary sponsor (and notable collector of pornography) Lord Houghton that he was enjoying "the bonds of a somewhat riotous concubinage. I don't know many *husbands* who could exact or expect from a *wife* such indulgences as are hourly laid at my feet!"

Swinburne was playing the unaccustomed role of lover to the hilt, but others claimed to know better. Journalist Shirley Brooks, an enemy, wrote to William Hardman (a great source of Victorian gossip): "I am my own no longer, *nor my wife's neither* . . . I am Ada's . . . Swinburne is the only rival I dread—he knew her first. But I shall sit upon his corpse. He boasts—but he lies!" Swinburne's friends were equally skeptical, and Ned Burne-Jones drew a series of cartoon spoofs, titled "Ye Treu and Pitifulle Historie of ye Poet and ye Ancient Dame," which was distinctly unflattering to the libido of either party.

We believe that Swinburne and Adah did have intercourse, and its nature can be determined by Swinburne's preoccupation with acts of sodomy, which, when he got drunk in public, he described in a loud and high-pitched voice. Along with his fellow schoolboys who remained fascinated by flagellation, the buttocks were for Swinburne *the* erotic area of the body. Richard Burton, with whom Swinburne had a sado-masochistic relationship, held that anal intercourse was more natural than coitus. He liked to quote an ancient quatrain:

> *The penis smooth and round was made*
> *with anus best to match it.*
> *Had it been made for cunnus' sake,*
> *It had been formed like a hatchet!*

There were variations on lovemaking that Adah knew, since she had slept with other men whose sexual power was weak. A close reading of "Dolores" shows that it does reflect Adah's mannerisms and the acts committed between her and her latest lover:

> *O lips full of lust and of laughter,*
> *Curled snakes that are fed from my breast,*

Bite hard, lest remembrance come after
And press with new lips where you pressed.
For my heart springs up at the pressure,
Mine eyelids too moisten and burn;
Ah, feed me and fill me with pleasure,
Ere pain come in turn.

A contorted romance, to be sure, but Swinburne and Menken remained intimate for six months, during which time he continued to insist she was his mistress in the accepted sense. On January 26, 1868, he wrote to his Welsh friend George Powell: "I have been so worried of late with influenza, love-making, rather unwholesome things such as business, money, that I have 'left undone all that I should have done.'" Note that Swinburne grudgingly sandwiches in "love-making" between "influenza" and "business." If any woman could succeed in getting a rise out of him, it was the Naked Lady with her aura of androgyny and kinky sex. Such were the "indulgences" that the star laid at the poet's feet.

In the same letter to Powell, Swinburne casually writes: "I must send you in a day or two a photograph of my present possessor— known to Britannia as Miss Menken, to me as Dolores (her real Christian name)—and myself taken together. We both come out very well. Of course it's *private*." The photo in question shows a standing, smirking Swinburne, gazing down at a seated, overweight Menken. Thirty, he looks seedy, while she, though fabulously dressed, looks closer to forty. She has one hand on him in a proprietary way. Although the pair hold hands, they exhibit not a spark of passion. This might be the portrait of a surrogate mother concerned about her errant son. Although the photo lacks the warmth and innuendo of the candid Menken/Dumas shots, once circulated, it triggered a sex scandal on the order of the Parisian hullabaloo.

Copies of the photo, and another, more revealing shot, were soon visible in the windows of stationers and spread to newsboys. Unlike Paris, they were not tampered with in a pornographic way. A recent

Swinburne biographer compares the effect, in modern terms, to a shot of "Madonna photographed on the lap of a dissolute Booker Prize novelist." Actually the impact was more inflammatory, because to his young admirers, Swinburne "was not merely a poet, but a flag . . . the Red Flag incarnate." Menken, to her buttoned-up but libidinous audience, was sex appeal in the flesh. Yet, as she sought recognition as a poet, she hoped to play down this image.

Swinburne pretended to grow irate, writing to Powell in April:

There has been a damned row about [the photos]. Paper after paper has flung pellets of dirt at me, assuming or asserting the falsehood that its publication and sale all over London were things authorized or permitted or even foreseen by the sitters; whereas of course it was a private affair, to be known (or shewn) to friends only. The circulation has of course been stopped as far as possible, but not without much irritating worry. The one signed I think good—the other not, except for the pose of her shoulder and bosom.

Considering how freely Swinburne distributed the photos to friends, and the criminal tendencies of some of them, his protestations of innocence ring false. Certainly the press showed him no mercy. "There is no accounting for tastes," began one satirical piece. "The latest novelty in photographic *cartes* is a group of Miss Adah Menken and Swinburne the poet, which may be described as 'after Dumas.'" News of the scandal reached Swinburne's father, the admiral, and his mother, Lady Jane, who were upset that their son had been ensnared by a woman of the theater. All in all, Swinburne was pleased to gain a reputation as a *debauché*, one to rival his idol Baudelaire. Menken, though conflicted, could not have been surprised by the publicity. The sex scandal was becoming her most popular metier.

Mazeppa had gone out of fashion as suddenly as last year's bonnet. After the New Year a revival failed at Astley's. Managers of other theaters would have none of it, especially at Menken's price. Selling her jewelry, she collected a company of actors and musicians, and on May 11 she mounted a production of the horse opera at Sadler's Wells. Briefly, it did a brisk business. However, racked by a cough, a gnawing ache in her side, Adah was unable to stand the strain of performing nightly. An understudy took over and business fell off. *Mazeppa* minus Menken was a rusty old melodrama that its famous star, considerably poorer, had to shut down. Now that her money was nearly gone, Adah dictated a will to Susette.

She could not ignore an offer from Louis Dumaine in Paris, which was conveyed to her by George Parker, the editor of the *London Orchestra,* who acted as her manager. Dumaine had leased the Théâtre du Châtelet and offered her a serious role in a drama by respected playwright Henri Rochefort. She hoped to stay in London long enough to see her book, now titled *Infelicia,* through the press. Hotten had promised the book would be ready by spring, and he tried to placate her when it was delayed. "I am so anxious to get the book out," Menken wrote him. "I fear you put others before me. In that case we shall certainly quarrel . . . Do hurry those printers, and I shall like you better than I do now." But the star failed to speed up publication.

A pathetic note is struck in another letter. After inquiring how Hotten intended to advertise the book, Adah brought up what really bothered her:

> *I am satisfied with all you have done except the portrait. I do not find it to be in character with the volume. It looks affected. Perhaps I am a little vain—all women are—but the picture is certainly not beautiful. I have portraits that I think beautiful. I dare say they are not like me, but I posed for them. . . . Can we not possibly have another made?*

In late spring Arthur Beckett, a comedian, came to see Menken at the Westminster Palace, where she had taken a suite. He found her alone except for Susette, "having her breakfast, which consisted among other luxuries of a red herring, in a venerable morning robe.

She looked rather sallow by daylight, but was most kind and courteous, still extremely taciturn." Menken the tiger, forgetting her catty remarks about George Sand, had neglected her appearance and let her age show. The star no longer shone so bright.

To add salt to her wounds, she and Swinburne had quarreled. The gossips of London wagged their tongues over how they were drifting apart. Eight lines that Swinburne took from *Lesbia Brandon*, which he inscribed in Menken's album, tell the tale:

> *"How long wilt thou stay*
> *Faithful to me, O, fair one, say?"*
> *"For one night, and a day*
> *Lover mine, I may."*
>
> *Love flatters us with sighs*
> *And kisses on mouth and eyes*
> *For a day and a night*
> *Before his flight.*

Come June it was Adah who fled. Leaving the proofreading of *Infelicia* to John Thomson, she sailed across the Channel to what she hoped would be a royal welcome.

Chapter Twenty-three:

KNOW PARIS AND DIE

Cecil Lang, the Swinburne scholar, observed that Adah Menken had "provided Dumas *père* (aged sixty-four) with an Indian summer and Swinburne (aged twenty-nine) with a Pierian spring." For the classically challenged, "Pierian" means that she acted as his poetic muse. How greatly Menken influenced the poetry of the Victorian era's bad boy remains a matter of conjecture. In the case of Alexandre Dumas, there can be no question that the scandal triggered by their affair gave the old musketeer a last, unexpected measure of popularity. Romanticism may have been passé, but five of Dumas's plays were revived onstage during the 1867–68 season, and once again, if briefly, the King of Romance was in vogue.

Menken did not proceed directly from London to Paris. With Susette, she vacationed at Le Havre to recuperate from her frantic pace. The busy port of today was then a fashionable seaside resort, which played host in summer to many distinguished Europeans. There Adah found Dumas, lapsing into that reverie in which he lived out his remaining time. Yet she did not lack for activities or company. The newspapers reported that she swam in the sea, rode horses, and looked well. Adah was pleased that her figure had regained its svelte lines. If she felt social, she had a fine selection of notables to choose from.

A cartoon published that summer in a satirical journal called *The Mask* pictured the fashionable scene at Le Havre. "Companions of the Bath" was set at the beach and showed caricatures, in Victorian bathing attire, of political figures such as Gladstone and Disraeli, opera divas, popular clergymen, and authors such as Charles Reade, Tennyson, and Longfellow. Although they did not all frolic together as shown, they were known to frequent Le Havre. Swinburne, Dumas, and Menken were set aside as a threesome, the two men described as "a sand shrimp and a whale." While wading they were "talking together in a most affectionate way." Dumas, it was said, considered himself "the greatest swell on shore." Adah, swimming nearby, was described as wearing "a costume for the seaside instead of the usual basic fabric which leaves her reckless behind the scenes."

By the time Menken saw the print in Paris stationers' windows, she was settled into rooms in a modest hotel in the Rue Caumartin, not far from the Théâtre du Châtelet on the Right Bank of the Seine. It was a lively neighborhood, inhabited by artists, actors, and visiting foreigners of limited means. Adah enjoyed the Bohemian milieu, and the street sounds that filtered up to the third floor reminded her of happier days. Living quietly, she communed with a few English and French friends and her countrymen. Journalist H. B. Farnie, once her harshest critic, was a total convert, visiting often. Like others, he wanted to write a play for her. The expatriate poet Thomas Buchanan Read also came by. He had fought in the Civil War and was renowned for his epic, "Sheridan's Ride." From these loyal friends we learn the story of Adah's last days.

Journalist Adrien Marx brought Henri Rochefort to see Menken. They discussed her role in his *Theodorus, Roi d'Abyssinie,* which had been inspired by the British expedition of 1867 to Abyssinia (Ethiopia). It was the sort of heroic drama she had played in at the start of her career, when she hoped to become a great tragedienne. Ironically, she was born a Theodore and began onstage under that name. At last, she was coming home to her dual Jewish and African heritage. The part seemed fated for her. The author explained he was still working on the play, but a production could be mounted, and he would finish while they rehearsed.

Soon Adah met with Dumaine and his partner La Roche. Nervously, Dumaine insisted Rochefort's play was not ready to be staged. Since rent on the theater must be paid, he and his partner wondered if *La Menken* would condescend to appear, until the autumn, in . . . *Les Pirates de la Savane?* After all, Paris had adored her mimic tour de force and would pack the theater to see her. The partners promised a production on the grandest scale ever attempted.

The managers expected a thunderclap of temper, but Adah was no longer surprised that they would deceive her. She agreed to begin rehearsals immediately. The gentlemen, though relieved, brought up the matter of money. They had promised her half the nightly receipts, but there was the expense of fitting the theater for an action drama on such a lofty scale. Would the great Menken deign to accept less than half? Dumaine and La Roche were elated when their star agreed on terms, again without emotion. She had a dull pain near her heart, and she only wished to be rid of the conniving managers.

Adah was not herself, nor fit to play the heroic Leo. Once rehearsals began in the hot, stuffy theater, the actors noticed that the star was listless and dispirited. She was not the Royal Menken they knew, whose verve communicated itself to the entire cast. On the second day she collapsed onstage and lay motionless. Two doctors were summoned—a leading specialist in rheumatism, of which Adah had complained, and the other equally eminent. They revived the patient and saw that she was escorted home, but they had no idea what caused the incident.

Further examination revealed "an abscess under the left side of three or four years' duration." The doctors recommended bed rest, but offered little hope of recovery. On this they were correct, but their diagnosis is from an earlier time. It is possible that Adah had developed cancer stemming from the blows she received the previous year, when she had fallen down the mountain, along with her horse. The disease could have spread quickly due to an immune system weakened by tuberculosis. Ed James writes of her "inflammation of the lungs and a complication of disorders." Adah's early exposure to tuberculosis, combined with a daredevil lifestyle, sentenced her to an early grave. She sensed it all along, writing poetry studded with morbid or garish images. The question she asked of John Heenan in "Answer Me"—"When I am lying in my silent shroud, will you love me?"—was ultimately meant for her adoring, fickle public.

Now that Death, like an impatient bill collector, waited in the ante-room, Adah accepted its presence more easily than her intimates. She joked with Susette, Farnie, Thomas Read, and other visitors to keep solemnity at bay. She sent for Adrien Marx, who found her propped up in bed, hugging a lapdog.

"My poor boy," she said, with a sad smile. "I am lost to art and life. Yet, when all is said and done, have I not at my age tasted more of life than most women who live to be a hundred? It is fair, then, that I should go where old people go." Yet Adah was not resigned to quitting worldly cares and ambition. She reminded Marx, "Never have you written my life story, as you solemnly promised. Hurry, my dear boy, lest I die without reading your article." The superstar would have loved to read her own obituaries—at least, those on the front page.

To change the subject, the young journalist remonstrated with Adah about the dog, claiming that breathing its hair would do her harm. She replied that dogs could smell death. "So long as my little dog remains by my side, I know that I am not yet to die. If ever it should seek to fly from me, then I will understand my end is near and will duly prepare my soul for God."

Marx insisted she would get better, that *Les Pirates* was sold out, and the managers of the Châtelet were counting on her recovery. "They will find someone else to play Leo," she said. "Poor Leo!" Only then did tears well up in her eyes and overflow into sobs.

~

Adah's friends did what they could to cheer her. On July 22 Reade brought the white-bearded Henry Wadsworth Longfellow to sit by Adah's bedside and talk of poetry. Longfellow was revered in America and greatly respected in Europe. On his way to Italy, this was the one day he spent in Paris. Longfellow's sympathy for the patient is not surprising when we recall that his beloved wife had died prematurely, burned in a terrible accident.

Adah was thrilled by Longfellow's visit, and more so when he composed a poem for her, which he wrote in her album. The pastoral verse is not memorable, except that it refers to mountains, brooks, breezes, and birds, all of which Adah might never again experience. In the same album Reade wrote the following:

> *To the Menken in her illness.*
> *We nightly die ourselves to sleep,*
> *Then wherefore fear we death?*
> *'Tis but a slumber still more deep,*
> *And undisturbed by breath.*

Adah had to struggle for each breath, and the lines were to the point, but grim. According to Farnie, she suffered greatly, resigned and patient. She ate little and drank only ice water. Her face gaunt, her figure shrank down to the bone day by day. Adah left her bed only once, in early August, to try a change of air at Bougival. Accompanied by Susette, Farnie, and Reade, she drove out in a carriage to the village on the Seine where, a year before, she and Alexandre Dumas had strolled and talked of romance. Although Dumas lived on, Adah, half his age, was approaching the end.

The plan was for her to get away from the noise and heat of the city center, to inhale fresh air and hear rustic sounds. However, Farnie recalled, "The effort [of the journey] was too much for her enfeebled frame, and immediately on arrival she went to bed very ill, and there continued till her return to Paris, two days afterwards." Adrien Marx came out to visit the patient, but she was in a fever and failed to recognize him. He left to write an article in praise of the beautiful and brave Menken. She would not live to read the words she would have cherished.

On being returned to her rooms in Paris, Adah rallied briefly. She had Susette write to John Thomson about *Infelicia*. Hoping to hold the book of poems in her hands before she went, she struggled for a few days more. The book could not give her life, as she had done for it, but it might bestow immortality. Cruelly, she could wait no longer. She was becoming insensible to the life around her, inhabiting a world of pain and delirium. On the morning of August 10, 1868, Susette saw that Adah was gasping for breath. As instructed, she summoned a rabbi.

According to Farnie, "Menken died in possession of the Jewish faith, and was attended by ministers of religion. . . . [H]owever stormy her life may have been the end was peaceful and serene." On her deathbed, barely conscious, Adah was able to follow the rabbi in Hebrew prayers, and this ending strongly suggests that she was born, and remained throughout her life, a Jew. Her belief in life after death she owed to Spiritualism, to which she adhered almost as firmly. The Naked Lady was a deeply religious woman.

During the afternoon, Adah lay in a stupor. Toward four o'clock she awakened. In a whisper, she gave a few last instructions to Susette. Then she died in her arms, her little dog nearby, wagging its tail.

Once beautiful, fascinating, and desired by so many, Adah Menken was now a memory. But to Dumaine and La Roche she remained a necessity. They had postponed the opening of *Les Pirates* for a month, continuing to advertise it while hoping Adah would recover. When they called at her rooms, Susette put them off at the door by assurances that she was improving and would attend the dress rehearsal. This was scheduled for August 10 at the Châtelet, and when their star failed to show, the managers appeared with a writ and two *gendarmes*, ready to take Adah by force if needed.

Susette admitted them, pointing to the bedroom: "There she lies— it is too late now!" The men, already within, froze in horror. They could hardly believe that Adah Menken had died. The managers retreated while the *gendarmes* sealed the room.

Ever resourceful, Dumaine and La Roche substituted a French actress, Sarah Dowe, who apparently knew the role. *Les Pirates* opened next evening to a packed house. But once the audience realized *La Menken* would not appear, they grew unruly. Mlle. Dowe, lacking Menken's

face, figure, and miming ability, was hooted off the stage. Only a promise to refund the audience's money staved off a riot. The fairy tale of *Les
Pirates* died with its star.

Susette was charged with burying the corpse. Adah, since her days
on the Gold Coast, had earned more than any other actress of her
time, but she freely spent or gave away everything, except for a few
pieces of jewelry meant for Susette, and her Hebrew Bible, bequeathed
to Ed James. She died penniless. So on August 13, a modest collection of fourteen people escorted the funeral hearse, proceeding north
to Père Lachaise Cemetery. Dumaine was present, and so was Adah's
agent, George Parker, come over from London. Her unmounted horse,
Gypsy, brought up the rear of the small, solemn procession. This gave
rise to the following lines in a satirical journal:

> *Ungrateful animals, mankind!*
> *Walking his rider's hearse behind,*
> *Mourner-in-chief her horse appears,*
> *But where are all her cavaliers?*

Adah's five husbands were still living, though far off in America.
Former lovers, such as Dumas and Swinburne, were closer to hand.
Since a funeral is not a dinner party, they did not attend the event.
Although Farnie personally informed Dumas of Menken's passing, the
old musketeer remained at Le Havre. He is supposed to have remarked,
"Poor girl, why was she not her own friend!" A better question was the
one asked in *Le Petit Figaro:* "Where were you, all you good friends of
Miss Adah? And you directors, authors, and journalists, who have so
often sung the beauty and the talent of the American horsewoman?" It
was August in Paris, and the fashionable were on vacation.

Adah was put to rest in the paupers' enclave of the Jewish section of
Père Lachaise. Members of the Jewish Burial Society said *Kaddish* (the
prayer for the dead) over her, and a rough piece of black wood marked
her grave. The burial certificate, issued by the Bureau of Municipal

Affairs, claimed that under the ground lay the remains of "Menken[,] Adèle Isaac Barclay." The authorities, let alone future biographers, could not decide which husband had the best claim to his former wife's remains.

Swinburne had no qualms about claiming her memory. On August 26, he wrote from the Arts Club to his Welsh friend Powell:

> *I am sure you were sorry on my account to hear of the death of my poor, dear Menken. It was a great shock to me and a real grief. I was ill for some days. She was most lovable, as a friend, as well as a mistress.*

The shoddiness of the funeral rankled Ed James. Because he was going blind, he had been unable to visit Adah in her last days. Some months later, Ed decided to consult the renowned eye surgeons of Britain and the Continent, hoping he could save his sight. He was also determined to erect a suitable monument over his "sister's" grave. Low on funds, he appealed to "the theatrical and literary fraternity of London and Paris" to raise two thousand francs. He found that "neither Dumas nor Swinburne, nor any of the thousands of leeches who drank her champagne in life," would contribute to properly bury Menken. To his surprise, Captain Paul Barkley of California gave him the entire sum. The gambler did not long outlive the woman he loved. He was shot to death in an argument over cards.

In Paris, Ed teamed with an admirer of Menken's, Rita Percy, an actress who had worked with her at Sadler's Wells. They proceeded secretly because Jewish custom forbids the exhumation of a dead body. First, they purchased in perpetuity a site in the Jewish section of the cemetery at Montparnasse. Next, they engaged a sculptor to fashion a stone monument, severe in the Egyptian style and surmounted by an urn. To gain permission from the authorities to move the body, Ed posed as Adah's brother, which she had dubbed him. Palms were greased and the date of the transfer set for April 21, 1869.

It rained in the morning, but by noon a bright sun shone in a clear sky. Ed, Rita, the sculptor, and an interpreter went first to Père Lachaise to have the coffin raised. Just as they were about to depart, a party of American tourists came by to pay their respects. They were admirers of Adah's poetry, and they wished to place a bouquet of violets on her grave. Ed took the flowers for the new grave. The party went at once to Montparnasse, avoiding even a hint of display.

The tomb wherein Adah Isaacs Menken lies buried is near the cemetery gate. It consists of the stone, a little taller than a person, and a small fenced-in area. For years American visitors to Paris would leave wreaths or flowers there, some out of respect for the woman, others the actress, and others still, the poet. Menken's death woke up her publisher, and Hotten issued *Infelicia* one week afterward. He sent it to reviewers in mourning bands. The book has since gone through a dozen editions and is newly available online and in print.

Adah Menken's tomb gives the date of her death but not birth. This is one example of the mystery that still surrounds her life. Americans on the Grand Tour of Europe liked to stop by her grave and ponder the brief inscription on the monument, chosen by her:

THOU KNOWEST

Adah's dust lies beneath the ground, but the truth about her lives on.

CODA: THE SEXY SPIRIT

Adah's reappearances began almost immediately after her death. Daniel Home, who had known her well, was the first medium to contact her ghost. Fittingly, he would employ her spirit during the most sensational episode in the history of Spiritualism. Beginning a few days after Adah's mortal remains were buried, there occurred around Home a sequence of events with strong sexual overtones. These were recounted by Viscount Adare (later, the Fourth Earl of Dunraven) in his privately printed book, *Experiences in Spiritualism* (1872), which was promptly suppressed. At the time, there was considerable interest in Home's psychic powers, and his use of Menken's ghost to supposedly verify them.

Late in 1867 Adare, described by Home's biographer Jean Burton as "a thin, wiry, monocled, cheerfully extroverted young Guardsman in his early twenties," fell under the spell of the older Home. They began to travel and live together at Adare's expense, and to engage in late-night attempts to contact the spirit world. Adare's health suffered, which put him even more in the medium's power.

Adare, while at Dunraven (in Ireland) in August 1868, read of Menken's death. Next day he got a letter from Home, saying her spirit had visited him and was anxious to appear to the two men together. Adare returned to London to one of the family mansions, and Home moved in with him. Shortly after they had gone to bed, in the same room, they heard Adah speaking in a musical way, pronouncing her name. Both saw "a luminous cloud-like body floating in the air." Then they "distinctly heard the rustling of a silk dress moving about the room." They were reminded of a dress Adah had worn when they visited her at a hotel the year before.

Adah's spirit proceeded to take possession of Home and spoke through him. The medium, acting as Menken, went to Adare, knelt by his bed, and took his companion's hands in his own. According to Adare's account:

> *I shall never forget the awfully thrilling way in which she spoke, the desolation of the picture she drew of her feelings. . . . She spoke a great deal about Home, of his character, and a good deal about herself. . . . It appears as if our having called together upon her had some curious effect, as she could not say what she wanted till we were together again. . . . How much she wished to be sometimes near me and near Home to watch over us.*

Adah (actually Home) kissed Adare's hand and departed for the time being. As the two men traveled together on the Continent, a similar scene was played out a number of times, in which Adah acted as a psychic bridge between the athletic Adare and the sickly, feminine Home. These nights usually left Adare "in a queer state, my fingers and feet tingled as if I had pins and needles." He became a nervous wreck, and toward the end of the year he made plans to marry a Miss Kerr and travel in America. Home conveyed a stream of messages from the spirit world, advising Adare not to take either step. These were ignored, and in December the medium decided to perform a feat that would be spectacularly convincing.

One evening at Ashley House, London, before Adare and his friends Lord Lindsay and Captain Charles Wynne, Home appeared to float a few feet in the air out of one upper-story window and back in through a window of an adjoining room. The three well-educated young men each composed a written account of the levitation, the most complete one being Adare's. This manifestation of spirit in the material world has been regarded by investigators of psychic phenomena as final proof of Home's extraordinary powers. Wrote Arthur Conan Doyle in his *History of Spiritualism:* "Either the facts must be admitted to be such as are reported, or the possibility of certifying facts by human testimony must be given up."

The details of this Spiritualist incident have been rehashed and argued over, most completely in Trevor Hall's *The Enigma of Daniel D. Home* (1984). What matters to us is that Home, before attempting to levitate himself three stories in the air over the street, called on the ghost of Adah Menken to intercede with the young men he meant to impress—*seduce* might be a better word.

"Oh, good heavens! I know what he is going to do; it is too fearful," Lindsay suddenly called out. He had been informed by Adah's spirit of what Home intended but found it too terrible to repeat. However, as he told Adare, "Adah says that I must tell you: he is going out of the window in the other room and coming in at this window." Home then appeared to elongate himself in midair, slither out of a half-open window, and, after sailing along for ten feet, reappear through the second window.

Once landed, Home took the affair lightly. He remarked that if a policeman had been walking his beat and looked up, he would have been astonished. But Hall remarks, "Home was able to stimulate in these young men an emotion of fear . . . foreign to their character and training." This gave him the upper hand. Then, by associating himself with Menken, the embodiment of glamour and sexuality, he was able to dominate another side of their nature. Whether Home seduced any of them in a physical sense we don't know. Adare soon married and left for the American West, where he became a large landowner. He eventually wrote a spirited account of his doings: *Past Times and Pastimes*. It has become a classic of Western adventure.

Home was merely the first to use the life and spirit of Adah Menken as a posthumous come-on. After he retired in 1871, he was followed by another medium, Charles Foster. The Spiritualist congregation had grown bored with table rappings and ectoplasmic arms, and they favored mediums who could produce fully formed materializations of the deceased subject. Foster, an American, became famous and admired throughout the English-speaking world. Although a man of meager education, he liked to evoke the spirits of great authors, such as Virgil and Cervantes, and he would discuss with them passages from their works, which he supposedly had not read.

A remarkable illustration shows a materialization of Adah, in which her ghostly arms are wrapped around Foster from behind. It is composed of a drawing of her, perhaps taken from a photo, with a photo of the medium superimposed on it, and it represents an episode from one of his séances. Adah's attitude toward Foster appears loving and protective, which enhanced his prestige among Spiritualists. The illustration is a forerunner of attempts by Kirlian photography to image the immaterial, such as auras. It is a curious example of the manipulation that followed Adah beyond the grave.

The mediums who exploited the spirit of Menken at least understood that she had passed to the other side. Some theater managers simply overlooked her death and used her name to headline their own versions of *Mazeppa*. On stages from Broadway to the farthest reaches of North America, the Cossack prince continued to be stripped and bound, and to ride "naked" up the mountain, played by a correctly or incorrectly spelled facsimile of Adah Isaacs Menken. Late into the century, audiences continued to pay to see the so-called Menken in her signature role.

Eventually *Mazeppa* would vanish from the stage, only to reappear, beginning in 1910, on the screen. But Menken had a powerful and lasting influence on theatrical entertainment. In an obituary that dwelt on the sensational aspects of her life, *The New York Times* concluded that she was an actress "with little if any merit, yet [she] always drew full houses." The *Times* was echoing a typically Victorian sentiment: Vice must be denounced, yet it would be patronized, often by the moralists. Adah Menken conjured up nudity, flesh, action. Her thrust was soon followed in spades.

First came *The Black Crook* on Broadway in 1866. This musical melodrama featured lots of shapely girls in skimpy costumes over body stockings. By the second act they were dancing just in the stockings. The show was a huge success, and, well before Hollywood flogged sequels, it was succeeded by the *White Crook, Red Crook,* and *Black Crook Jr.* "This gimmick of dressing women in tights to play male roles, one Menken made famous in England as well as America, served for decades as a thinly veiled guise for exposing women's bodies during the prudish Victorian period," notes one theater historian.

The *Crook* series was followed by Lydia Thompson's *British Blondes* in 1868. The blondes were pretty in a hefty way, and they sang, danced, and did parody—thus the term "burlesque." Over time the satire faded, and burlesque would come to mean a girlie or leg show. The chorus girl was now firmly established onstage, showing her legs, derriere, and as much flesh as the producer could get away with. As early as 1878 the self-appointed censor Anthony Comstock railed against the so-called naked drama: "Why is it that every public play must have a naked woman? It is disgusting and pernicious to the young. It seems as though we were living in an age of lust."

Lust, or its media manifestations, would have to wait until more modern times. Meanwhile, burlesque grew more sleazy and was banned in New York in the 1930s by Mayor LaGuardia. It had already given birth to the tantalizing art of striptease, which consisted less of nudity than the promise of it. In the hands of classic artists such as Gypsy Rose Lee, the form was provocative but pleasing. The corollary art of the photo pinup also flourished.

This is another invention of the Menken/Sarony team. The pinup, an image of a scantily clad star, must be produced quickly, cheaply, and in multitudes. It required photos reproduced on treated paper rather than one-of-a-kind daguerreotypes. Not until the 1860s did paper become the dominant medium for positive photos. The cost of making an image plummeted, and the popularity of the photo album soared. At first the albums were made to hold the small *carte de visite* size, which, in spite of its limitations, became a rage during the Civil War.

Families of the boys going off to war wanted images of their heroes, and typically the boys wanted pictures of pretty actresses. Thus, a photo of Menken (often by C. D. Fredricks of New York) was lodged next to the heart of many a Union or Confederate soldier. When, by war's end, Napoleon Sarony began to photograph Menken, he employed sexier poses, clothed and unclothed, and he embellished them by adding color and tint. He also made larger, cabinet-sized reproductions, which could be framed on a wall or pinned up in a cabinet. Thus, the pinup—and, ultimately, the glossy magazine centerfold—were born. Adah, though she never posed entirely naked, began the trend toward nudity on page, stage, and screen. Her work with Sarony prefigured our age of taking it all off.

~~~

"I awoke the imagination of my century so that it created myth and legend around me," Oscar Wilde wrote from prison, where he had been sentenced for breaking Victorian-era laws against homosexuality. Wilde, in his daring, seems almost a postmodern figure. He is often credited as the first true celebrity, who stirred art, fashion, and fame into the heady brew we know as popular culture. Although Wilde was a forerunner, a generation earlier Adah Menken had pioneered the allure of notoriety. At the height of her popularity in America and Europe, she drew packed houses and crowds in the street that Wilde might have envied. The Menken was first to blend her life on- and offstage to create a seamless image both erotic and fatal. She blazoned her name in the marquee lights of a transatlantic sex scandal.

"Like P. T. Barnum, she knew the value of manufactured controversy," writes Robert Allen in *Horrible Prettiness*. For Menken it was more lifestyle than a calculated ploy. As Allen admits, she "took the Bohemian tack of declaring herself exempt from most of the strictures usually applied to women because . . . she was an artist." Marrying and divorcing freely, taking famous lovers while giving interviews, Adah fed the hunger of press and public for sexuality. Gossip about her, stamped "News" by the two-penny papers, was carried by rail and steamship to the far corners of the Earth. Consumers could take home photos of Adah and paste them into family albums. An intimacy between reader and celebrity developed during Victoria's reign, and it is going strong in the age of Victoria's Secret.

Oscar Wilde was aware of Menken. The climactic soliloquy of his *Salome* is reminiscent of her biblically inspired "Judith," and it has been suggested that he borrowed from her passionate lines. Certainly, they shared the same image maker. Wilde, landing in New York in 1882, hurried to Napoleon Sarony's Union Square studio to be photographed in his signature velvet suit, and again in a plush fur coat. These widely circulated photos set the tone for his American tour and his fame to follow.

Lillie Langtry, actress, wit, and famous mistress of the Prince of Wales, was another of Napoleon Sarony's favorite subjects. Like Adah, Lillie blended life and art. Born on the Isle of Jersey, she was raised among six brothers as a tomboy. She too had a passion for horses, and her popularity crossed the Atlantic, this time from England to the United States. How often the love goddess has a mannish side! Lillie was gorgeous but could hold her own in conversation with men of action or intellect.

Musical comedy star Lillian Russell was another (late) Victorian figure who looked swell posing as a sailor boy. At least until she started dining with Diamond Jim Brady, and the pair became synonymous with the excess of the Gay Nineties. Russell's star quality won over audiences for thirty years. As prima donna of operettas, damsel in distress of three-hanky melodramas, or performing snappy vaudeville routines, Russell became America's plump sweetheart. Her private life included four marriages and several scandals that, like Menken's, became public property. When Russell retired from the stage on the eve of World War I, she stayed in the public eye by selling war bonds and recruiting for the Marine Corps. These original superstars were super women!

Adah Menken was not content with one identity. She was such a changeling that biographers have read into her life what they please. The Western poet Joaquin Miller described a desperado, bounding on her steed one moment and the next vamping in a sheath dress made of yellow silk. Charles Stoddard, who returned to San Francisco from world travels, depicted an 1860s flower child. Mark Twain, still wet behind the ears, reported on Menken as a freak of nature, like a phenomenal jumping frog.

In the twentieth century, Fulton Oursler, author of *The Greatest Story Every Told*, pictured Adah as Venus. Dedicated Allen Lesser insisted that, at heart, she was a nice Jewish girl. Cockney Wolf Mankowitz, brought up to the porcelain trade, wrote about Adah as con artist. Recently, academic Renée Sentilles has presented a woman who was feminist, transgressive, androgynous, and continually performing. Each portrait is valid, thankfully, in a measure.

To Menken, life mattered more than her career. Yet her career demanded her life. She was first in a line that ends in mortal sacrifice. In *Harlow*, the movie based on the life of Jean Harlow, the star (played by Carol Baker) has just died. Her friend and agent (played by Red Buttons) says bitterly: "She didn't die of pneumonia. She died of life. She gave it away to everybody else. She had none left for herself." The luminescent superstar offers us her radiant self, as free of constraint as a pagan goddess. For a time, Jean, Marilyn, and Princess Diana lit up the routine of our lives. We rewarded them with bouquets of flowers on an early grave, and the showing of biopics on the anniversary of their demise.

In some form the love goddess is immortal. Menken supposed that her poetry would be her claim to lasting renown. Indeed, *Infelicia* has gone through numerous editions, including current electronic and print editions. But we need to look at the poetry differently from critics who have failed to understand it—that is, except for the Pre-Raphaelites. In 1871 Dante Gabriel Rossetti wrote to his brother William, who was preparing the first important anthology of American verse, urging him to include Menken's work: "I have her book which is really remarkable."

William did include four of her poems, noting the influence of Edgar Allan Poe on her writing. Menken's imagery is somber, sometimes macabre, like Poe's. William continued: "In the unformed rhapsodies are touches of genius which place them in a very different

category from many so-called poems of more regular construction. . . .
They express a life deeply sensible of loss, self-baffled, and mixing the
wail of humiliation with that of indignation." Here is reason of a the-
matic nature to think of Adah Menken both as a Jewish champion at a
time of mounting anti-Semitism and, in accord with New York Public's
Schomburg Collection, an African-American woman writer. Here is
the communal pain the poet has transmuted into art.

It is true that all of her life, Menken was proud of her Jewish heritage. It is equally true that she sometimes forgot about being Jewish,
claimed her natural father was Irish, and even baptized her son. Most
likely, Adah was born to a woman of color in New Orleans, into the
marginal milieu of the Creole mistresses of white men who kept them.
Lacking wealth or status, Adah still gained an education, and set out
on the road to fame and fortune by doing what was called for. She was
not a nice girl or a bad girl, since she transcends all categories—except
that of the superstar.

It seems a pity that Marilyn Monroe refused to play Adah Menken
in *The Girl in Pink Tights*. Marilyn's self-description applies equally to
Adah: "I knew I belonged to the public and to the world, not because
I was talented or even beautiful, but because I never had belonged to
anything or anyone else." Now the legend of The Menken belongs to
us all. She was as American as ambition, as human as sex, as transcendent as love.

ACKNOWLEDGMENTS

The authors hope we have written an account of Adah Isaacs Menken's public and private lives both accurate and equal to the excitement she generated. She led a brief, shooting-star life in dangerous times. To sort out reality from the tall tales and misinformation circulated first by her, and then by others, has been a sometimes frustrating adventure. Previous biographies, including reference sources, have either damned or exalted Adah. One smart aleck made her up out of whole cloth. Recent treatments concentrate on the personality she showed the world rather than the talent and force that propelled her to stardom, and the love and friendship she enjoyed with the greats of her time. We searched for the living, breathing woman beneath the scandal and her grandiose stunts. We wanted to know why The Menken was at once a superlative Victorian and a woman who still matters. We owe Allen Lesser's *Enchanting Rebel* a great debt, for he spent his life researching Adah and supplied the groundwork for others to build on. Without the cooperation and support of the persons listed below, and access to the collections cited, our biography could have added nothing new to the story of the woman who demanded top billing.

First and foremost, we thank our diligent agent, Janet Rosen, and her colleague, Sherry Bykofsky. Janet's faith in our biography never wavered, and she devoted herself to placing it with the right editor at an appropriate, high-quality publishing house. Indeed, she found the perfect editors in Keith Wallman and Ellen Urban at Lyons Press, now under the sage stewardship of Janice Goldklang. Keith's devotion to our subject and the meticulous attention he paid to our text are much appreciated.

Our thanks to the helpful, hardworking staff of the Hunter College Library, especially to Norman Clarius, the interlibrary-loan librarian, and Harry Johnson, head of Circulation. The New York Public Library has been an invaluable resource, both at the local branches—Hudson Park Library and Jefferson Market—and their Library of the Performing Arts (Billy Rose Theatre Collection, Lincoln Center). Thanks to Frederic Woodbridge Wilson, curator, Harvard Theatre Collection, Houghton Library, and his colleague, Pamela Madsen, and the staff who facilitated our research in their rich trove of Menken material, which includes original photos, print material, and Menken's letters.

We thank the staff at the Jacob Rader Marcus Center of the American Jewish Archives, Allen Lesser Collection, at Hebrew Union College (Cincinnati). The staff of American Jewish Historical Society, New York, also provided material. Dartmouth Library, our summer resource for more than a decade—with their generous librarians willing to offer guidance to their special collections—added a good deal to our fund of knowledge about Menken. The Library of Congress provided us with relevant information from books, theatrical posters, and photographs.

We also thank the staffs of the Museum of the City of New York; New York Historical Society; The Players Club, New York; Boston Public Library; Cabildo Museum, New Orleans; Rosenberg Library, Galveston, Texas; Tulane University, New Orleans; Bancroft Library, University of California, Berkeley; California State Library, Sacramento; Museum of the City of San Francisco; Wells Fargo Museum-Archive, San Francisco; Huntington Library, San Marino, California; San Francisco Public Library; and the Dallas Public Library.

In Paris we consulted the Auguste Rondel Theatre Collection, the Bibliothèque Nationale de France, and the Library of the Opera. In London we traced Menken's triumphs and affairs via the holdings of the British Museum Library; London Theatre Museum; Raymond Mander and Joe Mitchenson Theatre Collection; and the Theatre Museum at the Victoria and Albert (Entoven Collection).

We also wish to thank Lawrence Bush of *Jewish Currents* magazine, Bill Anderson of the *California Territorial Quarterly*, and Sarah Zupko, editor of the innovative website *PopMatters*, who verified Menken's importance by publishing our essays, which set forth her noteworthy accomplishments.

Finally, the splendid cover story on Adah Menken in *Nineteenth Century*, the magazine of the Victorian Society in America, reminds us of how well Menken represents this gorgeous period in history, and how relevant she remains today.

NOTES

INTRODUCTION

xi   "the man . . . unobserved": Mark Twain, Alta California, June 16, 1867, Letter 17.

xi   "head and . . . times": Ibid.

xi   "the poor . . . clothes": Ibid.

xii   "In one . . . situations": Ibid.

xii   "I went . . . age . . . bare": Ibid.

xiii   "Before Marilyn . . . reputation": Marianne Szegedy-Maszak, "In Love with a Famous Stranger," *U.S. News and World Report,* July 9, 2001.

xiv   "Nekkid, Nekkid, Nekkid": Lee Butts. *Texas Bad Girls: Hussies, Harlots, and Horse Thieves* (San Antonio: Republic of Texas Press, 2000).

xiv   "She married . . . well": Gay Gate, Internet site.

xiv   "a dimity . . . waist": Postcard, London Theatre Museum (Authors' Collection).

xvi   "Nothing is . . . lies": Joaquin Miller. *Adah Isaacs Menken* (Ysleta, TX: Edwin B. Hill, 1934) 1.

xvi   "Menken went . . . royalty": Postcard (Authors' Collection).

xviii   "'Tis love . . . strain": Allen Lesser. *Enchanting Rebel: The Secret Life of Adah Isaacs Menken* (New York: The Beechhurst Press, 1947) 237.

xviii   "To Holmes . . . she . . . sex": Arthur Conan Doyle. *A Scandal in Bohemia* (New York: G. Munro, 1896) 1.

xviii   "lollapalooza . . . who . . . sweepstakes": Billy Rose, "Pitching Horseshoes," *New York Post* Syndicated Weekly Column, 1948.

xix   "Menken's voluptuous . . . sexuality": Maria-Elena Buszek, "Representing Awarishness: Burlesque Feminist Transgression and the 19th-Century Pinup," *The Drama Review* 43 (Winter 1999): 151.

xix   "the flirtatious . . . Menken": Emanuel Levy. *George Cukor: Master of Elegance* (New York: Morrow, 1994).

CHAPTER ONE: NAKED

3   "The Accomplished . . . Tragedienne": Lisa Pegnato, "Produced in Magnificent Style," *Civil War Times Illustrated,* February, 1986: 37.

4   "an adventuress . . . disgrace": Lesser 46.

4   "most dangerous . . . world": Lesser 58.

4   "a portico . . . brothel": Robert Allen. *Horrible Prettiness: Burlesque and American Culture* (Chapel Hill: University of North Carolina Press, 1991) 75.

5   "the bright . . . men": Gary Schmidgall. *Walt Whitman: A Gay Life* (New York: Dutton, 1997) 108.

6   "the numberless . . . steamboats": "Crossing Brooklyn Ferry," *Leaves of Grass* (Philadelphia: David McKay, 1900) 86.

6   "drank out . . . due . . . love . . . world": Lesser 60.

7   "But for . . . grave": Ed James. *Biography of Adah Isaacs Menken* (New York: Ed James, 1869) 4.

8   "a woman . . . unknown": Wolf Mankowitz. *Mazeppa: The Lives, Loves and Legends of Adah Isaacs Menken* (New York: Stein and Day, 1982) 245.

8   "hit a . . . personality": Ibid.

CHAPTER TWO: TALES OF ADAH

9   "the eldest . . . standing": George Barclay. *The Life and Remarkable Career of Adah Isaacs Menken, the Celebrated Actress* (Philadelphia: Barclay & Co., 1868) 18.

11   "Obviously she . . . quadroon": Anna Bontemps and Jack Conroy. *They Seek a City* (Garden City, NY: Doubleday Doran, 1945) 99.

11   "a colored . . . Orleans": James Ivy, Letter to Dr. Stanley Chyet (American Jewish Archives), December 4, 1961: 1 (Allen Lesser Collection).

12   "All you . . . out": Ibid.

12   "deliberately . . . anonymity:" Renée Sentilles. *Performing Menken: Adah Isaacs Menken and the Birth of American Celebrity* (Cambridge: Cambridge University Press, 2003) 56.

13   "Adah Isaacs . . . reveals . . . tradition": Allen Lesser, "Adah Isaacs Menken: A Daughter of Israel," American Jewish Historical Society, 34 (1937): 147.

13   "light and . . . I . . . name": *New York Illustrated News*, March 17, 1860.

14   "Adah was . . . place": James Ivy, ibid.

15   "beautiful refined . . . spirit": Lesser, *Enchanting* 254.

15   "cottage . . . vines . . . encouragement": "Midnight in New Orleans," *The Israelite*, May 21, 1858, 45.

15   "a splendid . . . handsome": "Notes of My Life" (Material for an Autobiography), *New York Times*, September 6, 1868.

15   "a wonderful . . . love": Lesser, *Enchanting* 255.

15   "is a . . . drowned . . . Killarney . . . Life": Lesser, *Enchanting* 254.

16   "Her mother . . . Campbell": Robert Roden, "The Royal Menken," Passages from unpublished letters, Peter Gilsey Collection (Harvard Theatre Collection).

17   "In white . . . the discovery . . . banishment": Jane Gaines, "The Scar of Shame," *Cinema Journal* 26:4 (Summer 1987): 3.

17   "I cannot . . . Confederacy": Barclay 10.
18   "a true . . . things": Lesser, *Enchanting* 259.
19   "the good . . . betting": Ibid.
19   "Fickle . . . wild . . . restless . . . home": Lesser, *Enchanting* 260.

CHAPTER THREE: A DAUGHTER OF TEXAS

20   "Her dark . . . arena": Fulton Oursler, *The World's Delight* (New York: Harper & Brothers, 1929) 3.
21   "the ringmaster . . . haute-école": Richard Northcott. *Adah Isaacs Menken: An Illustrated Biography* (London: The Press Printers, 1921), 6.
21   "As a . . . gracefully": Robert C. Toll. *On With the Show* (New York: Oxford University Press, 1976) 52.
21   "in the . . . show!": Kate Wilson Davis. *Adah Isaacs Menken: Her Life and Poetry in America*, M.A. Thesis, Southern Methodist University, February 1944, 18.
21   "This was . . . Josephine . . . towns": Ibid.
22   "The Montplaisir . . . Plaza": "Notes," Appendix 1, Lesser 262.
23   "Without a . . . prostitute:" Paul Lewis (Noel Gerson pseud.). *Queen of the Plaza* (New York: Funk & Wagnalls, 1964), 46.
23   "Sexual relations . . . mores": Miguel Fernandez, *History Today* (October 1998): 3.
24   "The loveliest . . . fireflies": "Notes," Lesser 262.
25   "The culture . . . desire": Fernandez 3.
25   "Almost everyone . . . themes": Ibid.
25   "tender words . . .jewels. . . Zenea": "Notes," Lesser 264.
26   "I don't . . . friend . . . so": Davis 23
26   "In a . . . America": Enrique Piñeyro. *La Vida y Escritos de Juan Clemente, Zenea* (Paris: Garnier Hermanos, 1901) 20.
27   "I know . . . feet": Davis 64.
27   "We . . . find Mexico": Northcott 6.
28   "I always. . . go": Claude Hall, "The Fabulous Tom Ochiltree," *Southwestern Historical Quarterly* 71:3 (1967): 371.
28   "lived with . . . cabin": Francis E. Abernethy. *Legendary Ladies of Texas* (Dallas: E-Heart Press, 1981) 86.
29   "now I . . . me!": Ibid.
30   "the white . . . winter": Barclay 22.
30   "Although I . . . you": Barclay 23.
31   "If we . . . home!": Barclay 27.
31   "Adah learned . . . Texas": Mankowitz 147.
32   "As my . . . sweeter.": "A Memory," *Sunday Mercury,* June 24, 1860.

32   "Too late . . . met": Mankowitz 147.

32   "I have . . . blast": Sentilles 153.

CHAPTER FOUR: YOUNG AND FREE

33   "Shakespearian Readings . . . Reading": *Liberty Gazette,* Austin, Texas, October 8, 1855.

33   "I'm young . . . him": "New Advertisement," *Liberty Gazette,* November 23, 1855.

34   "Grayest of . . . blue": Algernon Charles Swinburne's "Dolores," *Poems and Ballads* (London: Moxon, 1866).

36   "During her . . . sadness": Abernethy 89.

36   "I never . . . once": Davis 37.

36   "Believe me . . . mother": "Women of the World," *Sunday Mercury,* October 17, 1860.

37   "She was . . . love": Davis 37.

37   "She seemed . . . Futurity": Davis 38.

37   "a lovely . . . she . . . again": Ibid.

CHAPTER FIVE: THE JEW MENKEN

41   "of some . . . adventure": Lesser, *Enchanting* 21.

42   "the debutante . . . force": Mankowitz 50.

43   "the accomplished . . . termination": Mankowitz 51.

43   "talent, joined . . . stage": Ibid.

44   "Circumstances are . . . out": Lesser, *Enchanting* 26.

44   "there can . . . days": "Shylock," *New Orleans Sunday Delta,* 4:13, September 4, 1857. Reprinted in *The Israelite,* October 2, 1857: 101–02.

44   "a combination . . . man": "Shylock" 101.

44   "Shylock is . . . Jew": "Shylock" 102.

45   "Will He . . . pine": "Oppression of the Jews under the Turkish Empire," *The Israelite,* November 6, 1857.

45   "Where the . . . grace!": Ibid.

45   "All through . . . soul": Allen Lesser. *Weave a Wreath of Laurel* (New York: Coven Press, 1983) 28.

46   "How glad . . . alike": AIM to Rosina, March 8, 1858, Brown University Library (Harris Rare Book Collection).

46   "an actress . . . acting": *The Israelite,* 4:13, May 30, 1858: 101.

46   "Adah was . . . scenes": John S. Kendall. *The Golden Age of New Orleans Theater* (Baton Rouge: Louisiana State University Press, 1952) 373.

47   "our favorite . . . meet": Lesser 32.

47   "a first-class . . . southwest": Mankowitz 54.

47   "There had . . . it": Davis 39.

48   "Never shall . . . noble": H. P. Phelps. *Players of a Century: A Record of the Albany Stage* (Albany, NY: Durang, 1880) 318.

48   "respectable four . . . air": Fredrika Bremer. *The Homes of the New World* (New York: Harper & Brothers, 1853) 100.

49   "We have. . . inspired . . . people": Lesser 37.

50   "the barbarous . . . struggle . . . die": *The Israelite,* January 28, 1859.

51   "Flattered, praised . . . lady. . . race": Lesser 32.

53   "My burning . . . light:" "Karazah to Karl," *The Israelite,* September 3, 1858.

53   "all ungentleness . . . humble . . . observant": "A Wife's Prayer," *The Israelite,* December 17, 1858.

53   "By the . . . too!": Lesser 37.

54   "vigor of . . . action . . . Pale . . . intellectual": Richard Butsch, "Bowery B'hoys and Matinee Ladies," *American Quarterly,* September 1994: 391.

CHAPTER SIX: ENTR'ACTE

56   "manager and . . . her": Lesser 39.

58   "Captain Adah . . . Guards": Lesser 15.

58   "Miss Menken . . . actress . . . like . . . down": George Odell. *Annals of the New York Stage,* Volume VII (New York: Columbia University Press, 1931) 145.

59   "When people . . . city": Odell Ibid.

59   "Purdy did . . . entirely": Odell 146.

60   "a burning . . . alone": "In Vain," *Infelicia* (Philadelphia: Lippincott, 1869).

60   "You have . . . Mazeppa": Lesser 75.

61   "But I . . . it": James Murdoch. *The Stage* (Philadelphia: J. M. Stoddart, 1880) 286.

61   "an apostrophe . . . purpose": Ibid.

61   "For the . . . receiving. . . child": Murdoch 287.

61   "Why don't . . . line": Ibid.

62   "as far . . . Jewess.": *The Israelite,* December 30, 1864: 212.

62   "requested . . . convert. . . Jewess.": Leo Wise, *The Israelite,* 1924: 31–32.

62   "Nature was . . . birthright . . . herself.": Celia Logan, "Reminiscence of Adah Isaacs Menken, *New Orleans Times Democrat* (HTC).

CHAPTER SEVEN: BELOW THE BELT

64   "As a . . . arena": Nat Fleischer. *Reckless Lady: The Life Story of Adah Isaacs Menken* (New York: C. J. O'Brien, 1941) 2.

64   "Boxing in . . . big-shots": Sam Andre and Nat Fleisher. *A Pictorial History of Boxing* (Secaucus, NJ: Citadel Press, 1959) 46.

65 "good on . . . muscle": Ed James. *Life and Battles of John C. Heenan* (New York: Ed James, 1879) 2.

66 "the most . . . city": Elliot Gorn. *The Manly Art: Bare-Knuckle Prize Fighting in America* (Ithaca: Cornell University Press, 1986) 118.

68 "carried insensible . . . battered": Richard Fox, "John C. Heenan," *Police Gazette,* 1881: 3.

68 "You took . . . thine": "One Year Ago," *Sunday Mercury,* July 22, 1860.

69 "awkward and . . . *camaraderie*": Oursler 248.

69 "festival of . . . groggeries": Gorn 79.

70 "the real . . . everywhere . . . worthiness": Barbara Rees. *The Victorian Lady* (London: Gordon & Cremonesi, 1977) 11.

70 "A modest . . . mistress": Ibid.

71 "induced . . . the ceremony. . . 1859": James, *Menken* 4.

72 "It was . . . years": Sarah Levitt. *Victorians Unbuttoned* (London: Allen and Unwin, 1986) 36.

72 "Heenan, showing . . . round": Mankowitz 64.

73 "A knowledge . . . fair-play": Gorn 10.

74 "She therefore . . . secret": Lesser 44.

CHAPTER EIGHT: THE YEAR OF METEORS

76 "Miss Adah . . . Heenan": Lesser 44.

76 "Miss Menken . . . pals": Joseph Francis Daly. *Life of Augustin Daly* (New York: Macmillan, 1917) 43.

77 "In your . . . trouble": Lesser 44–45.

78 "very pretty . . . Boy": Lesser 45.

78 "My dear . . . matter": Lesser 46.

78 "I have . . . misconstrued. . . .disgrace": Ibid.

79 "by Adah . . . in!": Lesser 47.

79 "The association . . . calling": Lesser 48.

80 "I cannot . . . experience": Lesser 52.

80 "The controversy . . . current . . . Menken . . . grace": Lesser 49.

82 "there was . . . dealing": "Heenan," *Police Gazette:* 19.

82 "No matter . . . insatiable": Gorn 150.

83 "something new . . . fight": Gorn 152.

83 "All classes . . . wait": Ibid.

83 "The first . . . Heenan": James, *Menken* 5.

83 "Commonplace people . . . occurred": Lesser 241.

84 "one of . . . does . . . she is . . . New York": Lesser 54.

84 "With her . . . celebrated": Lesser 53.

84   "a bouncing . . . eyes": Lesser 54.
85   "the battle . . . hell . . . utterance": Lesser 55.
85   "These happy . . . mothers . . . Why should . . . corpse": "Spiritual Affinity,"
      Sunday Mercury, May 13, 1860.
86   "The muster . . . Dickens": Fleischer and Andre, *Pictorial* 46.
87   "There never . . . men": James, *Heenan* 6.
87   "Every muscle . . . thoroughbred . . . expected": "Heenan," *Police Gazette:* 22.
87   "very elegant . . . dancing-master": Gorn 7.
87   "fearfully swollen . . . cushion": James 8.
87   "hit him . . . away": James, *Heenan* 12
88   "the Benicia . . . weak": "Heenan," *Police Gazette* 31.
90   "We will . . . subject": Lesser 56.

CHAPTER NINE: A SCANDAL IN BOHEMIA

91   "the vast . . . humanity": Walt Whitman. *New York Dissected* (New York: Rufus
      Rockwell, 1936) 119.
91   "tawdry, hateful . . . harlots": Whitman, *Dissected* 122.
92   "Bohemianism is . . . standards": Allen Churchill. *The Improper Bohemians* (New
      York: Dutton, 1959) 26.
93   "A foul . . . libidinousness": Ed Folsom and Kenneth Price, eds. "Walt
      Whitman," *The Walt Whitman Archive.*
93   "had been . . . Boston": Gay Wilson Allen. *The Solitary Singer* (New York: New
      York University Press, 1967) 262.
94   "He is . . . creator . . . shysters!": Albert Parry. *Garrets and Pretenders* (New York:
      Covici, Friede, 1933) 44–45.
94   "the last . . . America": David Reynolds. *Walt Whitman.* (New York: Oxford
      University Press, 2004) 37.
94   "look at . . . humanity!": Menken, "Swimming against the Current," *Sunday
      Mercury,* June 10, 1860.
94   "the girls . . . defenders": Allen 263.
94   "He swims . . . fool. . . remains": Menken, "Swimming."
95   "thousands of . . . stream": *Sunday Mercury,* May 10, 1860.
95   "that coarse . . . creature": Lesser 64.
96   "We may . . . it": Lesser 62.
96   "he was . . . gentleman": *Brooklyn Eagle,* July 13, 1901: 4.
97   "slender and . . . Bohemia": Whitman, *Dissected* 101.
98   "gay, easy . . . loose": Whitman, *Dissected* 233.
98   "To think . . . toy!": "My Heritage," *Sunday Mercury,* June 3, 1860.
98   "Soul subduing . . . spirit . . . even . . . greeting!": "Heritage."

99   "O Angels . . . door": "Drifts that Bar My Door," July 29, 1860.

99   "See how . . . moaning": "Drifts."

100 "wild soul . . . mystery": Lesser 256.

100 "The soul . . . God": Ibid.

100 "remarkably dramatic . . . confessional": Joan Sherman. *Collected Black Women's Poetry* (New York: Oxford, 1988) 121.

101 "I am . . . outcast": Roden 451.

101 "the sum . . . 1860": *New York Herald*, October 17, 1860: 5.

101 "I was . . . now": Ibid.

102 "I will . . . purpose": Ibid.

102 "the most . . . world": Lesser 58.

102 "I am . . . excitement": Ibid.

103 "As girls . . . style?": "Women of the World," *Sunday Mercury*, October 7, 1860: 2.

103 "petty jealousy . . . admiration . . . it": Ibid.

103 "What is . . . ever": Lesser 59.

105 "Pretty waiter . . . waitresses": Sentilles 153.

105 "phallus worship . . . brothel": Allen, *Horrible* 75.

105 "the greatest . . . day": Lesser 256.

106 "Ere the . . . Holofernes": "Judith," published as "The End," *Sunday Mercury*, September 2, 1860.

107 "died with . . . mother . . . handiworks": Suicide note, Jersey City, December 29, 1860 (HTC).

107 "Did some . . . heroine?": Lesser 71.

107 "one solitary . . . pleasure": James, *Menken* 4.

108 "being very . . . through": ibid..

108 "a pleasant . . . tears": "One Year Ago," *Sunday Mercury*, July 22, 1860.

CHAPTER TEN: BELLE BEAUTY

111 "I had . . . long": H. P. Phelps. *Players of the Century: A Record of the Albany Stage* (Albany, NY: Joseph McDonough, 1860) 314.

112 "her upstart . . . letter": Ibid.

113 "sank down . . . ocean": "The Ship That Went Down" (The Ship at Sea) *Sunday Mercury*, January 13, 1861.

113 "Beer pulled . . . empty": Phelps 314.

113 "youth, beauty . . . manner": Opinions of the Press (HTC).

113 "the balmy . . . storm": Ibid.

114 "Menken knew . . . steed": Phelps 315.

115 "trembling with . . . timbers": Phelps 316.

115 "Miss Menken's . . . Every. . . rehearsal": Ibid.

115 "She is . . . horseflesh": Phelps 317.

116 "Like so . . . *manqué*": Hubert Babinski. *The Mazeppa Legend in European Romanticism* (New York: Columbia University, 1974) 19.

116 "A Tartar . . . limbs": Ibid.

117 "Physically she . . . curiosity": Northcott 18.

117 "A Tartar . . . beast": Babinski 11.

118 "Aim at . . . scorching . . . thirst": Babinski 18.

119 "Ha! . . . love!": Babinski 36.

119 "A violent . . . clashing": Lesser 77.

119 "After six . . . Europe": Phelps 317.

120 "Let revenge . . . battle!": Babinski 38.

CHAPTER ELEVEN: PRO PATRIA

121 "In *cartes* . . . years": Buszek 151.

122 "Beware! . . eyes": "Pro Patria," *Sunday Mercury*, March 17, 1861.

122 "This distinguished . . . thoughts": Opinions (HTC).

123 "lovingly and . . . loneliness . . . Do you . . . love": facsimile letter, Davis, Appendix C.

124 "They are . . . comment": Ibid.

124 "the very . . . character": Opinions (HTC).

125 "a shrimp . . . Company": Lesser 86.

125 "Your heart . . . Love": Davis, Appendix C.

125 "Silence and . . . beloved": Ibid.

126 "contradict all . . . Browne . . . but": AIM papers (HTC).

126 "moral lecture . . . improved": John J. Pullen. *Comic Relief: The Life and Laughter of Artemus Ward* (New York: Archon Books, 1983) 39.

127 "stream of . . . coherence": Ibid.

127 "he loved . . . marriage . . . critter": Pullen 58–59.

128 "Gentlemen, with . . . do": Pullen 1–3.

129 "The Management . . . Union": Lisa Pegnato, "Produced in Magnificent Style," *Civil War Times Illustrated*, February, 1985: 39.

129 "sublimely terrific . . . equestrianism": Playbill, June 24, 1862 (Authors' Collection).

129 "She identifies . . . her": Opinions (HTC).

130 "It was . . . performance": Mankowitz 84.

130 "I am . . . alone": "Adah Isaacs Menken," *American Jewish Historical Society*, September 9, 1967.

131 "The fall . . . girl": Lesser 90.

132 "very smart . . . American": Allan Nevins, ed. *The Diary of George Templeton Strong*, Volume III, *The Civil War, 1860–65* (New York: Octagon Books, 1974) 300.

132 "Adah was . . . immediately": Gary Borders, "The Naked Lady of Nacogdoches," Cox News Service, August 11, 2002: 2.

133 "And ever . . . Master": Robert Newell. "The Perfect Husband," *The Palace Beautiful* (New York: Carleton, 1864) 85.

133 "He believed . . . so": *Brooklyn Eagle,* July 13, 1901.

133 "Love never . . . marriage": *Orpheus Kerr Papers*, Second Series 183.

133 "In the . . . divine": "Lenore," Newell, *Palace*, 1864: 101–02.

CHAPTER TWELVE: CIVIL WAR

135 "With all . . . gratitude": Davis 41.

136 "were removed . . . Baltimore. . . It. . . Baltimore": Mankowitz 90.

138 "My health . . . comes": Lesser 97.

138 "those states . . . Union": Pegnato, *Civil War Times*: 39.

139 "On Monday . . . fits": Mankowitz 91.

141 "It. . . kite . . . ever": Lesser 100–01.

141 "the biggest . . . branch . . . milk puntch": Pullen 82.

142 "What will . . . water": Pullen 69.

144 "the military . . . dispersed": Report of Colonel James B. Fry, Provost Marshal-General, U.S. Army, July 14, 1863, www.civilwarhome.com.

145 "The town . . . wharves": Ernest McKay. *The Civil War and New York City* (Syracuse, NY: Syracuse University Press, 1990) 203.

CHAPTER THIRTEEN: THE GREAT MENKEN

146 "Napoleon of . . . stage": Lois Rodecape, "Tom Maguire: Napoleon of the Stage," *The California Historical Society Quarterly* 21 (1942): 39.

147 "The interior . . . Louis XV": *Virginia City Herald*, April 20, 1859.

148 "head of . . . Belvedere . . . eyes": Charles Warren Stoddard, "La Belle Menken," *National Magazine*, February 1905: 47.

149 "Garments . . . pure": Stoddard 479.

150 "I am . . . born": Roger Austen. *Genteel Pagan: The Double Life of Charles Warren Stoddard* (Amherst, MA: University of Massachusetts, 1991) xxvi.

150 "Men lined . . . curls! . . . waist": Rodecape 59.

152 "I had . . . footlights": Joaquin Miller 3.

153 "all her . . . silk": Joaquin Miller 4.

153 "The road . . . Our . . . Africa": Joaquin Miller 3.

153 "with her . . . lion color . . . color": Ibid.

154 "fell with . . . broken . . . die": Joaquin Miller 4.

154 "my dog . . . death . . . grandfather": Ibid.

156 "She showed . . . motion": *Daily Alta*, September 25, 1863: 2.

156 "Menken's superlative . . . skill": Sentilles 218.

156 "The Menken . . . it": Henry Nash Smith, ed. *Mark Twain of the Enterprise: Newspaper Articles and Other Documents, 1862–1864* (Berkeley: University of California Press, 1957) 7.

157 "He could . . . joke": Thomas Shirer. *Mark Twain and the Theatre* (Nuremberg: Verlag Hans Carl, 1964) 14.

158 "Though most . . . marriages": Andrew Hoffman. *Inventing Mark Twain* (New York: Morrow, 1997) 77.

158 "the bare . . . thigh": Paul Fatout. *Mark Twain in Virginia City* (Bloomington: University of Indiana Press, 1969) 159.

158 "*Mazeppa* proved . . . played": Nash Smith 9.

158 "Livery stable . . . clothes": Edmund Gagey. *The San Francisco Stage* (New York: Columbia University Press, 1950) 91–92.

159 "About this . . . families": Edgar Branch and Robert Hirst, eds. *Early Tales and Sketches, 1864–1865: The Works of Mark Twain*, Volume II (Berkeley: University of California Press, 1981) 120.

159 "a wonder . . . island": Stoddard 481.

160 "fixes its . . . clouds . . . illusory . . . Eternity": "Aspiration," *Golden Era*, September 20, 1863.

161 "Died this . . . prayer": "Resurgam," *Golden Era*, September 29, 1863.

161 "I stand . . . here": "Infelix," *Golden Era*, January 3, 1864.

161 "Prudery is . . . pays": "Tom Maguire," *Sacramento California Historical Society:* 60.

162 "A thing . . . forever": Franklin Dickerson Walker. *San Francisco's Literary Frontier* (New York: Knopf, 1939) 169.

162 "the most . . . seen": Walker 146.

162 "European intellectualism . . . oysters": Walker 120.

163 "It has . . . nights": Lesser 113.

163 "from the . . . Passion": "Aspasia," Newell, *Palace* 31.

CHAPTER FOURTEEN: GOLD EAGLE GUY

164 "Pearls are . . . beaming": Newell, *Palace* 29–33.

165 "This is . . . her": Ibid.

165 "Hers was . . . studies": *Brooklyn Daily Eagle*, July 13, 1901.

166 "He represented . . . so": Ibid.

166 "What is. . . lightly?": Newell, *Palace* 29-33

166 "he was . . . deliver": Mankowitz 112.

166 "You know . . . are": AIM to Ed James, January 29, 1864 (HTC).

167 "her winnings . . . denomination": Davis 51.

167 "bright and . . . activity": Pullen 83.

168 "one sweet . . . forever" Ida Egli, ed. *No Rooms of Their Own* (Berkeley: Heyday, 1992) 305.

168 "beautiful, accomplished . . . brilliant": *Golden Era,* February 7, 1864.

168 "They seem . . . place": Egli 304.

169 "There is . . . stupid": Ada Clare, "The Man's Sphere and Influence," *Golden Era,* April 3, 1864: 4.

169 "to her . . . woman": "Aspasia," Newell, *Palace* 29–33.

169 "handsome enough . . . enter": Tess Ardenne, *Golden Era,* April 24, 1864: 5.

169 "You never . . . affection": Ibid.

169 "the most . . . produced": Constance Rourke. *Troupers of the Gold Coast, or the Rise of Lotta Crabtree* (New York: Harcourt Brace, 1928) 185.

170 "an odd . . . yellow": Rourke 184.

170 "a wonderful . . . rapidity": *Alta California,* January 20, 1864.

171 "Miss Menken . . . success": Walter Lehman. *Memories of an Old Actor* (San Francisco: A. Roman, 1886) 301–02.

CHAPTER FIFTEEN: SUN MOUNTAIN

172 "haunted by . . . dust": George Lyman. *Saga of the Comstock Lode* (New York: Scribner's, 1934) 3.

173 "dressed in . . . war": *Gold Hill Daily News,* February 27, 1864.

173 "There were . . . times . . . it": Mark Twain. *Roughing It* (Berkeley: University of California, 1972) 289.

173 "Wildcats dubious . . . spending": "What We Owe Nevada," *San Francisco Chronicle,* January 31, 1892: 4.

174 "receptacle for . . . hopes": Rodecape 57.

174 "In Washoe . . . syllogism": Bernard DeVoto. *Mark Twain's America* (Boston: Little, Brown, 1932) 128.

175 "They civilized . . . Comstock": DeVoto 124.

175 "To the . . . gentility": Robert Wallace, "The Frontier's Fabulous Women," *Life,* May 11, 1959.

177 "open-eyed . . . voice . . . melody": Lyman 273.

177 "consummated the . . . melodrama": DeVoto 126.

177 "in attack . . . dangerous": Dan DeQuille, *San Francisco Examiner,* March 9, 1893: 13.

177 "Her body . . . desire. . . orgasmic": DeVoto 126.

178 "a goddess . . . virgin": Lyman 276.

178 "exalted Menken . . . contempt": *San Francisco Theater Research Monographs,* Volume V, Series 1, Number 15: 81.

178 "Like all . . . Menken": Albert Bigelow Paine. *Mark Twain's Autobiography* (New York: Harper & Brothers, 1912) 248.

179 "She delighted . . . step": Lyman 280.

179 "There was . . . bullion": Lyman 282.

180 "Think of . . . others!": "Aspasia," Newell, Palace 33.

180 "great actress . . . passions": Reprinted *Golden Era*, March 11, 1864.

180 "the local . . . performance": Fatout 163.

180 "The editors . . . go": Ibid.

180 "Miss Menken . . . cap . . . familiar": Edgar Branch, ed. *The Works of Mark Twain: Collected Letters I, Uncorrected Galleys* 224.

180 "She has . . . manuscript . . . now": Ibid.

181 "The dinner . . . removed . . . half ": *San Francisco Examiner*, March 19, 1893: 13–14.

182 "the object . . . song": Ibid.

183 "I began . . . prince": Lesser 127.

183 "Her left . . . conjure": Lyman 290.

183 "In the . . . decoration": Ibid.

184 "the circus . . . dollars": Mankowitz 106.

185 "priestess among . . . pagans": Walker 202.

185 "decidedly of . . . style": *Stockton Independent*, May 31, 1864 (Bancroft Library).

185 "a brazen. . . were. . . California": *Nevada Gazette*, May 31, 1864 (Bancroft Library).

185 "The star . . . forever:" *Golden Era*, April 7, 1864.

186 "a study . . . days . . . notoriety": Gary Scharnhorst, ed., *Selected Letters of Bret Harte* (Norman: University of Oklahoma, 1977) 346.

186 "yellow hair . . . eyes": Tony DiMarco, ed. *The Days I Knew* (Brooklyn: AMS Press, 1925) 3.

188 "Don't *live* . . . outrageously": Hoffman 87.

188 "corrupting America's . . . fame": Shirer 31.

188 "Adah was . . . horse": Wallace, Life, May 11, 1959.

CHAPTER SIXTEEN: THE TALK OF LONDON

191 "You know . . . photographs": Lesser 132.

192 "Bret Harte's . . . coat-tail": Mankowitz 151.

193 "*coup de foudre* . . . passion": Ibid.

193 "She felt . . . knew. . . *years*": Lesser 143.

194 "is to . . . style . . . preposterous": Lesser 132.

195 "Thanks. Menken . . . America": Horace Wyndham. *Victorian Sensations* (London: Jarrolds, 1933) 168.

196 "Miss Adah . . . fashionables": Wyndham 170.

197 "There is . . . protest. . . corruptions. . . community": Bernard Falk. *The Naked Lady: A Biography of Adah Isaacs Menken* (London: Hutchinson, 1952) 86.

197 "To begin . . . taste": Northcott 21.

198 "Grand Stud . . . Ballet": Wyndham 172.

199 "real swells . . . West-End": May 15, 1912, AIM Clippings (HTC).

199 "this served . . . phlegmatic": James, *Menken* 9.

199 "as if . . . photographers": Wilson Disher. *The Greatest Show on Earth* (London: Bell, 1957) 234.

200 "For heaven's . . . fussing": Falk 89.

200 "goes through . . . predecessors . . . course": Northcott 22.

200 "the country . . . somewhat. . . apparel": Northcott 24.

200 "vividly. . . the female . . . masculine": Ibid.

201 "beauty of . . . *Mazeppa*": Northcott 28.

201 "emulated the . . . man": Mankowitz 135.

201 "a bare-backed . . . steed . . . Jewess": Mankowitz 136.

201 "The attraction . . . impurity": Wyndham 176.

201 "Menken is . . . manager": Ibid.

202 "breakfasts, dinners . . .Ed. . . die": James, *Menken* 6.

202 "At the . . . note": James, *Menken* 7.

202 "Her generosity . . . herself . . . creature": Anonymous Introduction to *Infelicia* (Philadelphia: Lippincott, 1888) xiii.

203 "applauding shouts . . . actress": Falk 93.

204 "None left . . . Mrs. Heenan!": Falk 101–02.

CHAPTER SEVENTEEN: FOUR ACES

205 "She lands . . . up": Wyndham 189.

206 "I am . . . part": Mankowitz 153.

206 "Have you . . . all": Ibid.

206 "I shall . . . once": Ibid.

206 "she had . . . crest": James, *Menken* 7.

207 "the same . . . good": Falk 96.

208 "I will . . . me": Roden.

208 "Pray keep . . . sake": Falk 106–07.

209 "There is . . . suffering . . . I do . . . Alas!": Mankowitz 156–57.

210 "a notorious . . . arms": Falk 104.

211 "My good . . . Press": Falk 102.

211 "I have . . . me . . . again": Ibid.

212 "was as . . . could": Falk 132.

212 "the satisfactions . . . home": Michael Slater. *Dickens and Women* (Palo Alto, CA: Stanford University Press, 1983) 135.

213 "a pretty . . . figure": Slater 202.

213 "came like . . . him": Slater 203.

214 "a great . . . *Laurel* . . . used-up . . . it": Falk 108–09.

215 "Spiritualism, Mormonism . . . worthlessness": Falk 118.

215 "the excitement . . . immense": Lesser 154–55.

216 "I'll tell . . . victim . . . life": Roden, December 12, 1864.

216 "You know . . . of ": Ibid.

217 "the most . . . Mazeppa . . . guy:" James, *Menken* 7.

217 "I presume . . . too!": Lesser 140.

218 "While she . . . her": Disher 233.

219 "run to . . . New York": Lesser 158.

219 "a swathed . . . one . . . harp": Rose Eytinge. *The Memories of Rose Eytinge* (New York: Stokes, 1905) 310.

CHAPTER EIGHTEEN: THE ROYAL BENGAL TIGER

222 "The Menken . . . had": Falk 130.

223 "At the . . . *do*": Ibid.

223 "A clever . . . spectral": Falk 132.

224 "Miss Menken . . . advantage . . . order": Lesser 161.

224 "They have . . . title": Roden 450.

224 "My carriages . . . Menken": Ibid.

224 "I cannot . . . crucifixion": Falk 134.

225 "The manager . . . remained": Falk 140.

226 "She ignored . . . box . . . spot": Falk 111.

227 "a dream . . . dreams . . . evil": Michael Booth. *English Melodrama* (London: Herbert Jenkins, 1965) 14.

227 "Why doesn't . . . talents?": Falk 138.

227 "I am . . . annoyed": Falk 144.

CHAPTER NINETEEN: ONE LAST MARRIAGE

231 "charming flights . . . vagabondism": Falk 4.

233 "dirty and . . . democratic": James, *Menken* 9.

233 "Not a . . . ago": Ernest McKay 295.

234 "It's worth . . . birds. . . cakes": Busch, "Bowery B'hoys": 391.

234 "longed for . . . Paris": James, *Menken* 9.

234 "for the . . . leaves": Ada Clare. *Only a Woman's Heart* (New York: M. Doolady, 1866) 29.

234 "a life . . . sweets": Clare, Only 327.

235 "I have . . . life": Whitman, *Dissected* 233.

236 "All attempts . . . failures": *The Photo American,* September 18, 1894: 324.

236 "When the . . . did": Ibid.

237 "the confluence . . . photographer . . . a magic . . . while": Marianne Fulton, "Publish or Perish," *The Digital Journalist,* March 2000: 151.

238 "all life . . . action": Ben Bassham. *The Theatrical Photographs of Napoleon Sarony* (Kent, OH: Kent State University Press, 1978) 4.

239 "The photograph's . . . sexuality": Buszek 151.

239 "Adah Isaacs . . . years. . . clothes": Ibid.

240 "The sale . . . tumbler": Buszek 156.

240 "Marilyn is . . . heiress": Arthur Miller, "Fabled Enchantresses," *Life,* December 1958: 11.

241 "She gave . . . it": Marilyn pages, ellenspace.net/images

242 "Adah Isaacs . . . petticoats": Bassham 36.

242 "The female . . . come": Falk 155.

243 "the person . . . see": Lesser 175.

243 "a woman . . . nudity . . . the coarsest . . . vulgarity": *Theaters,* "Mazeppa at the Broadway Theatre," May 1, 1866: 3.

244 "the eloquence . . . hall . . . spite": AIM to Gus Daly, May 3, 1866 (ALC collection).

244 "inner force . . . successes": Lesser 179.

245 "She wore . . . dissipation": Lesser 180.

245 "By universal . . . glow": Falk 158.

246 "She was . . . nobody": James, *Menken* 10.

CHAPTER TWENTY: CITY OF LIGHT

249 "a beautiful . . . interest": Lesser 169.

249 "I am . . . you": Falk 142.

249 "the marvelous . . . body . . . war": Lesser 170.

250 "It is . . . narrow-mindedness": René Doumic. *George Sand: Some Aspects of Her Life and Writings* (New York: Putnam's, 1910) 6.

251 "it would . . . nymphomaniac": *Britannica Online.*

251 "Geo. Sand . . . telegrams": Mankowitz 191.

252 "to go . . . muse": Francis Gribble. *George Sand and Her Lovers* (New York: Dutton, 1907) 322.

252 "the age . . . egotism. . . noble": Doumic 10.

253 "at the . . . Barkley!": Lesser 197–98.

254 "Israelites . . . Faith": Falk 166.

254 "She was . . . theater": Lesser 186.

255 "I shall . . . useless": Mankowitz 168.

255 "a great . . . kind": S. C. Burchell. *Upstart Empire* (New York: Atheneum, 197) 223.

256 "vagabonds, disbanded . . . brothel-keepers": Burchell 32.

256 "a gauche . . . eyes": Burchell 37.

256 "a ringmaster . . . drunk": Ibid.

257 "From a . . . all": Burchell 21.

258 "Hip, hip . . . staggering": Falk 168.

258 "left something . . . courage": *Opinions des journeaux de Paris sur Miss Adah Isaacs Menken, artiste Americaine,* Paris, 1866–67 (HTC).

259 "a very . . . intelligence": Ibid.

259 "She has . . . body": Ibid.

259 "the eloquence . . . fluently": Ibid.

259 "ladies belonging . . . fashion": Lesser 192.

261 "She was . . . adoration": Lesser 193

262 "One does . . . repair": Mankowitz 171

263 "she had . . . Diana": Falk 177.

263 "Menken is . . . her!": *Opinions des journeaux de Paris* (HTC).

CHAPTER TWENTY-ONE: UNCLE TOM WITH MISS ADA

265 "a good . . . collar": Herbert Gorman. *The Incredible Marquis* (New York: Farrar & Rhinehart, 1924) 436.

265 "It's sheer . . . children": André Maurois. *The Titans: A Three Generation Biography of the Dumas* (New York: Harper & Brothers, 1957) 351.

266 "He whose . . . sparrow": Petri Liukkonen. *Books and Writers* 3 online

267 "my father . . . boy": Peter Quennell, "The Three Musketeers Named Dumas," *The New York Times Book Review,* February 9, 1958.

267 "One of . . . king": F. W. J. Hemmings. *Alexandre Dumas: The King of Romance* (New York: Scribner's, 1979) 147.

267 "At the . . . buildings": Hemmings 208.

268 "a fairyland . . . grottos": Burchell 125

269 "You stick . . . you": Lesser 200.

269 "Americans demand . . . droll": Falk 186.

270 "Uncle Tom . . . for": Lesser 194.

270 "One sees . . . father?": Falk 198.

271 "How distressed . . . is!": Maurois 358.

271 "You know . . . her": Falk 200.

271 "is the . . . lady": Falk 203.

273 "To the . . . Dumas": Mankowitz 178.

273 "never did . . . sparkling": Lesser 203.

273 "huddled in . . . Viennese": Mankowitz 190.

274 "My poet . . . heart . . . friends": Mankowitz 191.

274 "a quiet . . . Value . . . love": Ibid.

275 "I already . . . Alas!": AIM to Stoddard, September 21, 1867, *National Magazine:* 487.

275 "Dickens is . . . adviser": Mankowitz 193.

275 "whether on . . . admiration . . . praise": Stoddard, *National Magazine:* 487

276 *"Cher* Dumas . . . me": Mankowitz 193.

CHAPTER TWENTY-TWO: THE AFFAIR SWINBURNE

277 "She has . . . reputation!": *Alta California,* May 17, 1867.

278 "These photographs . . . here": Ibid.

278 "Adah Menken . . . journalists": Falk 223.

279 "Alfred Tennyson . . . poems": Roden 453.

279 "God keep . . . you": Lesser 221.

280 "Today, Roberto, . . . MENKEN": Northcott 32.

281 "the favorite . . . Cambridge": Donald Thomas: *Swinburne: The Poet and His World* (London: Weidenfeld and Nicholson, 1979) 11.

281 "London and . . . poetry": Philip Henderson: *Swinburne: Portrait of a Poet* (New York: Macmillan, 1974) 138.

281 "a braggart . . . bestializer": Henderson 140.

282 "a tropical . . . owls": Edmund Wilson. *The Bit between My Teeth: A Literary Chronicle of 1950–1965* (New York: Farrar, Straus, and Giroux, 1965) 236.

282 "My hound . . . poems": Georges Lafourcade. *Swinburne: A Literary Biography* (New York: Morrow, 1932) 134.

282 "part pimp . . . prostitute": Mankowitz 215.

283 "All Mazzini . . . verse": Lafourcade 155.

284 "assert a . . . him": Lafourcade 156.

284 "I knew . . . poetry!": Algernon Charles Swinburne. *Adah Isaacs Menken: A Fragment of Autobiography,* April 24, 1913 (London: Privately Printed, 1917).

284 "I've read . . . poet!": Thomas 147.

285 "She did . . . use . . . visitor": Mankowitz 216.

285 "Dear Miss . . . sent": Wyndham 196.

285 "You ought . . . gutter": Henderson 152.

286 "Today I . . . good": Ricky Rooksby. *A. C. Swinburne* (London: Scholar Press, 1997) 158.

286 "Adah Isaacs . . . 'Dolores'": Thomas 146.

286 "Our lady . . . Pain": *Swinburne's Collected Poetical Works* (New York: Harper & Brothers, 1927) 176.

286 "If you . . . rags": Rooksby 156.

287 "the bonds . . . feet!": Rooksby 158.

287 "I am . . . lies!": S. M. Ellis. *The Hardman Papers* (London: Constable, 1930) 320.

287 "Ye Treu . . . Dame": Lesser 230.

287 "The penis . . . hatchet!": Thomas 180.

287 "O lips . . . turn": Ibid.

288 "I have . . . done . . . I must . . . *private*": Swinburne, *Fragment of Autobiography*, xi.

289 "Madonna photographed . . . novelist": Rooksby 159.

289 "was not . . . incarnate": Thomas 111.

289 "There has . . . bosom": Rooksby 159.

289 "There is . . . Dumas": Falk 239.

290 "I am . . . now": Mankowitz 197.

290 "I am. . . made?" Ibid.

290 "having her . . . taciturn": Disher 243.

291 "How long . . . flight": Falk 236.

CHAPTER TWENTY-THREE: KNOW PARIS AND DIE

292 "provided Dumas . . . spring": Cecil Lang, ed. *The Swinburne Letters*, Volume I (New Haven: Yale University, 1958) 276.

293 "a sand . . .talking. . . shore . . . scenes": Falk 250–51.

294 "an abscess . . . duration": Falk 253.

294 "inflammation of . . . disorders": James, *Menken* 11.

294 "When I . . . me?": "Answer Me," *Sunday Mercury,* January 5, 1861.

295 "My poor . . . go . . . article": Falk 253.

295 "So long . . . God . . . Leo!": Ibid.

296 "To the . . . breath": Lesser 237.

296 "The effort . . . afterwards": Northcott 36.

297 "Menken died . . . serene": Ibid.

297 "There she . . . now!": James, *Menken* 11.

298 "Ungrateful animals . . . cavaliers?": Falk 260.

298 "Where were . . . horsewoman?": Falk 260.

299 "I am . . . mistress": Swinburne, AIM fragment.

299 "the theatrical . . . neither . . . life": James, *Menken* 12.

CODA: THE SEXY SPIRIT

301 "a thin . . . twenties": Jean Burton. *Heyday of a Wizard* (New York: Knopf, 1944) 191.

301 "a luminous . . . room": Burton 224.

302 "I shall . . . us": Viscount Adare. *Experiences in Spiritualism* (London: Privately Printed, 1869) 36.

302 "in a . . . needles": Adare 37.

302 "Either the . . . up": Sir Arthur Conan Doyle. *The History of Spiritualism* (New York: George Doran Company, 1926) 198.

303 "Oh, good . . . fearful . . .Adah . . . window": Trevor Hall. *The Enigma of Daniel D. Home* (Buffalo: Prometheus Books, 1984) 110.

303 "Home was . . . training": Hall 129.

304 "with little . . . houses": *The New York Times*, August 12, 1868: 4.

305 "This gimmick . . . period": Robert Toll. *On With the Show* (New York: Oxford, 1975) 216.

305 "Why is . . . lust": Lesser 296.

306 "I awoke . . . me": Oscar Wilde, *De Profundis (Excerpts from his Prison Writings)* BunnyBlu.wordpress.com.

306 "Like P. T . Barnum . . . artist": Allen, *Horrible* 100.

308 "I have . . . remarkable": Falk 19.

308 "In the . . . indignation": William Rossetti. *American Poems* (London: E. Moxon, 1925) 444–45.

309 "I knew . . . else": "Personal Quotes," Biography for Marilyn Monroe, www.IMDB.com.

BIBLIOGRAPHY

SPECIAL COLLECTIONS AND ARCHIVES, UNITED STATES

Adah Isaacs Menken Collection
Allen Lesser Collection (ALC)
American Jewish Archives, Hebrew Union College, Cincinnati, Ohio
American Jewish Historical Society, New York
Bancroft Library, University of California, Berkeley
The Billy Rose Collection, New York Public Library
Boston Public Library
Cabildo Museum, New Orleans
California State Library, Sacramento
Dallas Public Library
Harvard Theatre Collection (HTC), Harvard University
Huntington Library, San Marino, California
Library of Congress
Museum of the City of New York
Museum of the City of San Francisco
New York Historical Society
Players Club, New York
Rosenberg Library, Galveston, Texas
San Francisco Public Library
Tulane University, New Orleans
Wells Fargo Museum-Archive, San Francisco

SPECIAL COLLECTIONS, LONDON AND PARIS

Auguste Rondel Theatre Collection, Paris
Bibliothèque Nationale de France
British Museum Library
Library of the Opera, Paris
London Theatre Museum
Raymond Mander and Joe Mitchenson Theatre Collection, London
Theatre Museum at the Victoria and Albert Museum (Entoven
    Collection)

BOOKS

Abernethy, Francis. *Legendary Ladies of Texas*. Dallas: E-Heart Press,
    1981.
Adare, Viscount. *Experiences in Spiritualism*. London: Privately Printed,
    1869.
Allen, Gay Wilson. *The Solitary Singer*. New York: New York
    University Press, 1967.
Allen, Robert. *Horrible Prettiness: Burlesque and American Culture*. Chapel
    Hill: University of North Carolina Press, 1991.
Austen, Roger. *Genteel Pagan: The Double Life of Charles Warren Stoddard*.
    Amherst: University of Massachusetts, 1991.
Babinski, Hubert. *The Mazeppa Legend in European Romanticism*. New
    York: Columbia University, 1974.
Barclay, George. *The Life and Remarkable Career of Adah Isaacs Menken,
    the Celebrated Actress*. Philadelphia: Barclay & Co., 1868.
Bassham, Ben. *The Theatrical Photographs of Napoleon Sarony*. Kent,
    OH: Kent State University Press, 1978.
Burchell, S. C. *Upstart Empire*. New York: Atheneum, 1971.
Burton, Jean. *Heyday of a Wizard*. New York: Knopf, 1944.
Butts, Lee. *Texas Bad Girls: Hussies, Harlots, and Horse Thieves*. San
    Antonio: Republic of Texas Press, 2000.
Clare, Ada. *Only a Woman's Heart*. New York: M. Doolady, 1866.

Bibliography

Daly, Joseph Francis. *The Life of Augustin Daly.* New York: Macmillan, 1917.

DeVoto, Bernard. *Mark Twain's America.* Boston: Little, Brown, 1932.

Disher, Wilson. *The Greatest Show on Earth.* London: Bell, 1957.

Doumic, René. *George Sand: Some Aspects of Her Life and Writings.* New York: G. P. Putnam's Sons, 1910.

Egli, Ida, ed. *No Rooms of Their Own.* Berkeley: Heyday, 1992.

Ellis, S. M. *The Hardman Papers.* London: Constable, 1930.

Falk, Bernard. *The Naked Lady: a Biography of Adah Isaacs Menken.* London: Hutchinson, 1952.

Fatout, Paul. *Mark Twain in Virginia City.* Bloomington: University of Indiana Press, 1969.

Fleischer, Nat. *Reckless Lady: The Life Story of Adah Isaacs Menken.* New York: C. J. O'Brien, 1941.

Gorn, Elliot. *The Manly Art.* Ithaca: Cornell University Press, 1986.

Henderson, Philip. *Swinburne: Portrait of a Poet.* New York: Macmillan, 1974.

James, Ed. *Biography of Adah Isaacs Menken.* New York: Ed James, 1869.

Kendall, John S. *The Golden Age of New Orleans Theater.* Baton Rouge: Louisiana State University Press, 1952.

Lehman, Walter. *Memories of an Old Actor.* San Francisco: A. Roman, 1886.

Lesser, Allen. *Enchanting Rebel: The Secret Life of Adah Isaacs Menken.* New York: The Beechhurst Press, 1947.

Lyman, George. *Saga of the Comstock Lode.* New York: Charles Scribner's Sons, 1934.

McKay, Ernest. *The Civil War and New York City.* Syracuse, NY: Syracuse University Press, 1990.

Mankowitz, Wolf. *Mazeppa: The Lives, Loves and Legends of Adah Isaacs Menken.* New York: Stein and Day, 1982.

Maurois, André. *The Titans: A Three Generation Biography of the Dumas.* New York: Harper & Brothers, 1957.

Menken, Adah Isaacs. *Infelicia*. Philadelphia: Lippincott, 1869.

Miller, Joaquin. *Adah Isaacs Menken*. Ysleta, TX: Edwin B. Hill, 1934.

Nevins, Allan, ed. *The Diary of George Templeton Strong*. Volume III, *The Civil War, 1860–65*. New York: Octagon Books, 1974.

Newell, Robert. *The Palace Beautiful*. New York: Carleton, 1864.

Northcott, Richard. *Adah Isaacs Menken: An Illustrated Biography*. London: The Press Printers, 1921.

Odell, George. *Annals of the New York Stage*. Volume VII. New York: Columbia University Press, 1931.

Parry, Albert. *Garrets and Pretenders*. New York: Covici, Friede, 1933.

Phelps, H. P. *Players of a Century: A Record of the Albany Stage*. Albany, NY: Durang, 1880.

Pullen, John J. *Comic Relief: The Life and Laughter of Artemus Ward*. New York: Archon Books, 1983.

Reynolds, David. *Walt Whitman*. New York: Oxford University Press, 2004.

Roden, Robert. "The Royal Menken," Passages from Unpublished Letters. Peter Gilsey Collection. Harvard Theatre Collection.

Rooksby, Ricky. *A. C. Swinburne*. London: Scholar Press, 1997.

Rourke, Constance. *Troupers of the Gold Coast, or the Rise of Lotta Crabtree*. New York: Harcourt Brace, 1928.

Schmidgall, Gary. *Walt Whitman: A Gay Life*. New York: Dutton, 1997.

Sentilles, Renée. *Performing Menken: Adah Isaacs Menken and the Birth of American Celebrity*. Cambridge: Cambridge University Press, 2003.

Shirer, Thomas S. *Mark Twain and the Theatre*. Nuremberg: Verlag Hans Carl, 1964.

Slater, Michael. *Dickens and Women*. Palo Alto, CA: Stanford University Press, 1983.

Smith, Henry Nash, ed. *Mark Twain of the Enterprise: Newspaper Articles and Other Documents, 1862–1864*. Berkeley: University of California Press, 1957.

Swinburne, Algernon Charles. *Adah Isaacs Menken: A Fragment of Autobiography.* April 24, 1913, London: Privately Printed, 1917.

Thomas, Donald. *Swinburne: The Poet and His World.* London: Weidenfeld and Nicholson, 1979.

Walker, Franklin Dickerson. *San Francisco's Literary Frontier.* New York: Knopf, 1939.

Wyndham, Horace. *Victorian Sensations.* London: Jarrolds, 1933.

PERIODICALS

Borders, Gary. "The Naked Lady of Nacogdoches." Cox News Service (August 11, 2002).

Busch, Richard. "Bowry B'hoys and Matinee Ladies." *American Quarterly,* 46 (September 1994).

Clare, Ada. "The Man's Sphere and Influence." *Golden Era* (April 3, 1864).

Fulton, Marianne. "Publish or Perish." *The Digital Journalist* (March 2000).

Lesser, Allen. "Adah Isaacs Menken: A Daughter of Israel." *American Jewish Historical Society,* 34 (1937).

Miller, Arthur. "Fabled Enchantresses." *Life* (December 1958).

Pegnato, Lisa. "Produced in Magnificent Style." *Civil War Times Illustrated* (February 1986).

Rodecape, Lois. "Tom Maguire: Napoleon of the Stage." *The California Historical Society Quarterly,* 21 (1942).

Stoddard, Charles Warren. "La Belle Menken." *National Magazine* (February 1905).

Szegedy-Maszak, Marianne. "In Love with a Famous Stranger." *U.S. News and World Report* (July 9, 2001).

Wallace, Robert. "The Frontier's Fabulous Women." *Life* (May 11, 1959).

AUTHORS' PRINT AND INTERNET ARTICLES ON MENKEN

FOSTER, BARBARA AND MICHAEL:
"Adah Isaacs Menken: An American Original." *North Dakota Quarterly* (Fall 1993).

Adah Isaacs Menken: An American Jewish Original." *The Jewish Quarterly* (Winter 1993–94).

"Adah Isaacs Menken Wins the West." *Journal of the West*, 33:4 (October 1994).

"Adah Isaacs Menken: Broadway's First Star." *Culturefront* (Summer 2000).

"Adah Isaacs Menken: 19th-Century Superstar." *Nineteenth Century: Magazine of the Victorian Society in America*, 22:1 (Spring 2002).

"From Adah Isaacs Menken to Marilyn Monroe." *Moondance Magazine* (October 2003).

Women in Judaism. Online Encyclopedia (2004).

"Lights, Camera, Adoration: From Adah Isaacs Menken to Marilyn Monroe." *Salome Magazine* (2005).

"Adah Isaacs Menken: The Naked Lady." *Jewish Currents* (January–February 2006).

"The Great Bare: Adah Menken, the Naked Lady, Dazzles the Gold Rush and the Young Mark Twain." *California Territorial Quarterly*, 69 (Spring 2007).

"The Invention of Celebrity." *Miranda Literary Magazine* (2007).

"Adah Isaacs Menken: The First Broadway Star." *PopMatters* (2008).

FICTION

Conan Doyle, Arthur. *A Scandal in Bohemia.* New York: G. Munro, 1896.

Harte, Bret. *The Crusade of the Excelsior.* New York: Houghton Mifflin, 1896.

Oursler, Fulton, Sr. *The World's Delight.* New York: Harper & Brothers, 1929.

Rossen, Steven. *Naked Angel.* New York: 1979.

FILM

Mother Wore Tights, 1946 (inspired by Adah Isaacs Menken [AIM],
starring Betty Grable).

Heller in Pink Tights, 1959 (Sophia Loren as Adah; directed by George
Cukor).

Sherlock Holmes in New York, 1976 (Charlotte Rampling as AIM).

TV series: *Bonanza* (aka, *Ponderosa,* AIM played by Ruth Roman).

Sherlock Holmes, 2009 (Irene Adler based on Arthur Conan Doyle
on AIM).

PHOTOGRAPHY

Adah Isaacs Menken, until her death in 1868, was the prime subject of
the first celebrity photographer, Napoleon Sarony. She was the first to
extensively use her photographs for publicity. Copies may be found in
a number of the archives listed above, as well as websites listed below.
Originals are avidly collected by private individuals, including the
authors of *A Dangerous Woman.*

INTERNET SITES

The authors' ongoing website, www.TheGreatBare.com, is dedicated
to Adah and her friends and lovers, as well as those who have followed
in the path blazed by the Naked Lady. It includes information on Adah,
numerous photos, the authors' scheduled appearances (in person and
in the media), and the Nude News.

The authors have installed a slide show of Adah's photos at myspace
.com/adahmenken.

Internet reference sites tend to repeat errors of fact about Adah's life
and character, and are mostly useless. For example, en.wikipedia.org/
wiki/Adah_Isaacs_Menken is patronizing and mistaken; www.sfmu-
seum.org/bio/adah repeats an old radio script by Samuel Dickson, and
is at least amusing. At *Performing Menken: Adah Isaacs Menken and the Birth
of Celebrity,* there is a perceptive review by scholar Gregory Eiselein of
Renée Sentilles's doctoral thesis. "This scholastic rigor has not, however,
culminated in an authoritative biography." The search continues.

INDEX

Page numbers in *italics* refer to pages in the photo insert.

Adare, Viscount, 301–3
Adler, Stella, xviii, 164
Albany, 111–13, 114–20
"A L'outrance" (Menken), 59
Ardenne, Tess, 169
Arnold, George, 92, 106
"Aspasia" (Newell), 97, 164–65, 166, 169, 180
"Aspiration" (Menken), 160
Astley's, 194–204, 210–12, 214, 221–27, 281, 289
Avedon, Richard, 240, 241
Avon, Albert, 254–55

Baltimore, 135–37, 138–41 217–218
Barbarian, The, 43
Barclay, George, 9
Barkley, James Paul (husband)
    Adah's burial place, 299
    affair with Adah, 192, 193–94, 205–6
    brownstone built for Adah, 232
    career, 192–93, 208
    illness, 229, 230
    marriage to Adah, 245–46
Barkley, Louis Dudevant Victor Emmanuel (son), *12,* 253, 272, 274
"Battle of the Stars" (Menken), 98–99
Belasco, David, 152
Belle Beauty (horse), 113, 115
Billings, Josh, 141–42
Black Crook, The, 304

Black-Eyed Susan, 136, 159, 169, 217
Bohemian life, 92–98, 106–7
Bontemps, Arna, 11
Booth, Edwin, 53–54, 58
Booth, John Wilkes, 120, 139
Booth, Junius Brutus (June), 151, 152, 167, 186
Bourgeois, Anicet, 229, 254
Bowery Theater, 83–85
Boyd, Belle, xvii, *11,* 140
British Blondes, 305
Broadway Theater, 235–36, 242–44
Brougham, John, 214, 216
Brown, Thomas Allston, 112, 123, 138, 142
Bulette, Julia, 175–76, 179
burlesque, 305
Burton, Richard, xvii, 284
Byron, Lord, xv, 25, 27, 60, 116

California, voyage to, 143–46, 147–48
Campbell, J. C. (stepfather), 10, 16, 18
Canterbury Concert Hall, 104–5
Cataldi's Hotel, 278–79
Chapman, Henry, 60
Charles, James S., 42, 46
Charles I (king of Württemberg), 261–62
Child of the Sun, The, 10, 214, 216, 221, 222–24, 225–27
Choate, Rufus, 96
Cincinnati, 47–51, 61–62, 245
Civil War, 127–28, 137, 143
Clapp, Henry, 92, 93–94, 97, 106

Clare, Ada
  as Bohemian elite, 5, 92, 97–98
  death, 235
  Only a Woman's Heart, 234–35
  pregnancy, 106
  San Francisco, 168–69, 183–85
  sexual relationship with Adah,
    probable, 125
  Stoddard, Charles, and, 187
  Virginia City, Nevada, 169, 173,
    180, 181–82
  Whitman, Walt, and, 94
Clemens, Samuel. *See* Twain, Mark
Coburn, Joe, 66, 205–6, 227
"Come to Me" (Menken), 79
"Companions of the Bath"
  (cartoon), 292–93
Conroy, Jack, 11
Crabtree, Lotta, 125, 169–70, 186
Crampton, Charlotte, 60, 117
Crusade of the Excelsior (Harte), 186
Cukor, George, xix
Cusick, Jim, 65, 66, 71, 74, 82, 84

Dada caricature, *12*, 264
Daly, Augustin (Gus), 15–16,
  79–80, 231
Davis, Camilla G., 21, 23, 36, 37
Davis, Jefferson, xi, 95, 138
Day in Paris, A, 46, 56, 58–59
Dayton, 51–52, 53
Deborah (Biblical prophet), 50
De Quille, Dan, 176–78, 181–82, 183
Dickens, Catherine, 211, 212, 213
Dickens, Charles, xvii, 3, 9–10, 203–4,
  210–13, 285
Dietrich, Marlene, 121, 169, 239–40
"Dolores: Our Lady of Pain" (Swin-
  burne), xvii, 34, 283, 286, 287–88
Dowling, Frank, 86, 88
Doyle, Arthur Conan, xviii, xix,
  262, 302
draft riots, 143–45
"Drifts that Bar My Door"
  (Menken), 99

Dugué, Ferdinand, 229, 254
Dumaine, Louis, 249, 250, 254, 290,
  293–94, 297
Dumas, Alexandre (elder)
  affair with Adah, xvii, 266–72,
    273, 274, 292
  life and career, 265–66, 276, 292
  photographs with Adah, xii, xiii,
    13, 268–71
Dumas, Alexandre (younger), 266,
  267, 271
Dumas, Marie, 267, 268, 269

Eagle Eye, 30–31
Ellington, Susette, 232, 233–34,
  244–46, 296–97, 298
Emancipation Proclamation, 128
Enchanting Rebel (Lesser), 13
Etyinge, Rose, 219–20
Eugénie, Empress, 256
"Evening with Poets," 100–101
Exposition (Paris, 1867), 256, 268, 276

Farnie, H. B., 197–98, 200, 293, 296
Fazio, or The Italian Wife's Revenge,
  42–43
Fechter, Charles, 210–11, 221–22
Fernandez, James, 226
Field, Julian, 284
Fish, Provost Marshal, 138–39, 140
Foster, Charles, *16*, 303–4
"Fragment of a Heart" (Menken), 96
Franconi, Victor, 20–21, 27
French Opera House, 10, 13, 18
French Spy, The, 130, 159, 239
Front Street Theater, 136–37, 138, 139
"Full and Reliable Account of the
  Extraordinary Meteoric Shower
  of Last Saturday Night, A"
  (Twain), 159

Garbo, Greta, 241
Gautier, Théophile, 214, 229, 259
Gayety Theater, 73, 77, 101, 104, 112,
  113, 120

Gerson, Noel, 22–23, 251–52
Girl in Pink Tights, The, xix, 309
Glasgow, 215
Gold Eagle Guy, 164
Golden Era, 148, 160–61, 162, 168
Goodman, Joe, 167, 173–74,
    176–78, 180–82
Gottschalk, Louis, 168, 184, 234–35
Great Expectations, 124–25
Greeley, Horace, 59, 69, 83, 93–94,
    122, 136
Green Street Theater, 111, 112, 117
Gypsy (horse), 260, 298

Hamilton, Allen, 183
Hardinge, Emma, 184–85
Harlow, Jean, 308
Harney, General, 31
Harte, Bret, 162–63, 186
Havana, *3*, 22–27
Heenan, John Carmel (husband)
    affair with Adah, 59–60, 68–70
    betrayal of Adah, 3, 4, 101–2,
        107, 123
    bout with Morrissey, 66–68
    bout with Sayers, 71, 73–75,
        81–83, 86–89
    Canterbury Concert Hall, 105
    courts Adah again, 204,
        207–8, 209
    death, 229–30
    divorce from Adah, 123, 131
    early life, 64–65
    initial meeting with Adah, 55–56
    marriage to Adah, 63, 71–72,
        73–74, 84
    marriage to Adah, press
        controversy about,
        76–79, 80–81, 90
    painting of, 183
    photograph, *5*
    as prizefighter, 64, 65, 69
    as world heavyweight champion,
        3, 4, 89–90
Heller in Pink Tights, xix

Herald, 101, 102, 103
Hoffman, Andrew, 188
Hogarth, Georgina, 212
Home, Daniel Dunglas, 279, 301–3
Hope Chapel, 100–101
Hotel de Suez, 250, 259
Hotten, John Camden, 281, 290, 300
Howard Atheneum, 125–26

Illustrated News, The, 83
Imperial Hippodrome, 20–21, 27
Infelicia (Menken)
    Adah's anxiety about delay in
        publication, 290, 296–97
    Dickens, Charles, and, 211, 212,
        285
    editions, 308
    James, Ed, and, 211–12
    Newell, Robert, and, 96
    publication of, xviii, 300
"Infelicia" (Zenea), 27
"Infelix" (Menken), 161
Israelite, The, 44–46, 47, 49–50, 51, 53,
    62
Ivanhoe, 54
Ivy, James, 11–12

James, Ed
    Adah's funeral and burial place,
        299–300
    Adah's suicide attempt,
        107–8, 112
    Bowery Theater engagement, 83
    life and career, 7, 9–10
    photograph, *5*
    relationship with Adah, 135, 191,
        206, 224–25, 231–32
Judaism, 10, 13, 45–46, 48–51,
    96, 297
"Judith" (Menken), 105–6, 307

"Karazah to Karl" (Menken), 53, 79
Kendall, John S., 1, 12–13
Kneass, Nelson (husband), 13, 34,
    35–36, 37

Lady of Lyons, The, 42
Langtry, Lillie, 307
La Roche (manager), 293–94, 297
Laulerack, 30–32
"Laulerack" (Menken), 31–32
Lawrence, Joe, 162, 186
Le Havre, France, 292–93
"Leonore" (Newell), 133–34
Lesbia Brandon (Swinburne), 283, 291
Lesson for Husbands, A, 43
Liberty, Texas, 33–37
Liebert, M., 269, 271
Life and Remarkable Career of Adah Isaacs Menken (Barclay), 9
Light Guards (Dayton), 51–52, 53
Lincoln, Abraham, 120, 121–22,
  127–28, 135–36
Lindsay, Lord, 302–3
Liverpool, 213
Logan, Celia, 47–48, 62
Lola Montez, 113–14
London, 191, 194–214, 217–18,
  221–29, 249–50, 278–91
Long Branch, New Jersey, 141–42
Longfellow, Henry Wadsworth, xviii,
  15, 295–96
Louisville, 53–54, 245

Macbeth, 60–61
Maguire, Thomas
  Adah's quick-change pieces, 163
  Crabtree, Lotta, and, 170
  meets Adah at dock, 146, 148
  negotiations for Adah's perfor-
    mances, 138, 142
  personality, 153
  publicity for Adah in Virginia
    City, 172–73
  as theater producer, 146–47,
    171, 186
Manceau, Alexandre, 215
"Man's Sphere of Influence, The"
  (Clare), 169
Marx, Adrien, 249–50, 255,
  295, 296

Masset, Stephen, 102–3, 107–8,
  112, 185
Masters, Edgar Lee, 205
Mazeppa
  accidents, 115, 131
  Albany, 117–20
  Baltimore, 136–37, 138
  costume, xii, xiv, *1*
  horse riding in, xv–xvi, 60, 113,
    115, 118, 131
  imitations of, 141, 217, 304
  London, 197–204, 210–12, 214,
    217, 227, 281, 289–90
  New York, 128–30, 235–36,
    242–44
  opening night, 117, 119–20
  plot, 117–19
  postcard featuring scene from,
    xv, *1, 6*
  reception of, 119–20
  rehearsals, 114–15, 198–99
  reviews, 129, 155–59, 200–201,
    242–44, 245
  San Francisco, 148, 151–53,
    154–60, 163, 185
  Smith, John B., and, 111–12, 113
  tour in British Isles, 214–15
  tour in U.S., 244–45
  Virginia City, Nevada, 176–78
Mazeppa (Byron), 116
Mazeppa, Ivan, xv, 116
Mazeppa, or the Wild Horse of Tartary
  (Milner), 117
Mazzini, Giuseppe, 283–84
McCord, James (stepfather), 9, 10, 14,
  18–19, 21, 22
McDonald, Jack, 82, 86, 89
McKenna, John, 213
Menken, Adah Isaacs
  accidents, 115, 131, 225–26, 260
  adolescence, 20–32
  advertising for beau ideal, *3,*
    33–34, 36–37
  arrest as secessionist, 138–39,
    140–41

as ballet dancer, 27–28
bigamy accusations, 78, 80–81
birth name, 12–13
bisexuality, 31–32, 123, 124, 125
burial places, xviii, 298–300
as captive of Indians, 30–31
childhood, 14–19
as circus performer, 20–22
clothing, xi–xii, xiii–xiv, *2*, 130,
  152, 169, 251
conflicting information on,
  xiv, xvi
death and funeral, 297, 298–99
divorce, from Heenan, 123, 131
divorce, rabbinical, from Alex,
  61–62
education, 18, 29–30
ethnic heritage, xiv, 9, 10, 11–15,
  16–18, 62
fame, xiii–xiv, 163, 209–10
in fiction, xviii
gambling, 167
as horse rider, xv–xvi, 60, 113,
  115, 118, 131
illness, 130, 138, 141–42, 160,
  244, 278, 294–97
literary salon, xvii, 202–3, 205,
  278–79
marriage, attitudes toward, 36–37
marriage to Barkley, 245–46
marriage to Heenan, 63, 71–72,
  73–74, 84
marriage to Heenan, press
  controversy about, 76–79,
  80–81, 90
marriage to Kneass, 13, 34,
  35–36, 37
marriage to Menken, 41–42, 78
marriage to Newell, 131, 132–35,
  142, 145, 164–67, 185
media portrayals of, xviii–xix
as minstrel performer, 34–36
money, generosity with, 202, 205
parents, 9, 10, 13, 14–18
patriotism, attacks on, 129

photographs, *1–4, 6–7, 9, 10,*
  11–15
photographs, seminude, *7,* 104
photographs, spirit, *16,* 304
photographs, with Dumas, xii,
  xiii, *13,* 268–71
photographs, with Swinburne,
  14, 288–89
physical appearance, 34
postcards featuring, xiv–xv, xvi, *1*
pregnancy, *11,* 72–73, 85,
  245–46
prostitute, accused of being,
  79, 102
singing voice, 30
smoking, 218
son, first, 4, 99, 100
son, second, *12,* 253, 272, 274
suicide attempts, 3, 5–7,
  107–8, 246
theatrical entertainment,
  influence on, 304–9
Menken, Alexander Isaac (husband)
  Adah's poems about, 53
  bigamy accusations, 78, 80–81
  Dayton Light Guards, 52
  divorce, rabbinical, from Adah,
    61–62
  family, 41, 46, 47–48
  marriage to Adah, 41–42, 78
  relationship with Adah, 56
Mexico, 27–28
Miller, Arthur, 240
Miller, Joaquin, xvi, *10,* 151–54,
  162, 186–87
Miller, Minnie, 152, 154, 186
Milner, Henry, xv, 117
mining, 175
Monroe, Marilyn, xix, 240–42, 309
Montez, Lola, 113–14, 148, 170,
  183, 195–96
Montplaisir troupe, 22
Morrissey, John (Old Smoke), 64–65,
  66–68, 77, 82, 88
Mortara, Edgar, 50, 51

Murdoch, James, 60–61
"My Heritage" (Menken), 98

Nacogdoches, Texas, 28–30
Napoleon, Louis, 256, 257, 272
Nashville, 60–61, 245
National Theater, 56, 57, 58–59
Nelaton, Dr., 260
New Advertisement!!! (Menken), 33–34
New Bowery Theater, 128–29
Newell, Robert Henry (husband).
    See also Sunday Mercury
    Adah's fame, 163
    Adah's suicide attempt, 107
    "Aspasia," 164–65, 166, 169, 180
    California, voyage to,
        143–46, 148
    Canterbury Concert Hall, 105
    cast off by Adah, 204, 208
    character, 96–97
    courtship of Adah, 131
    death, 208
    early life, 95
    marriage to Adah, 131, 132–35,
        142, 145, 164–67, 185
    photograph, *8*
    publishes Adah's writings, 95, 96,
        100, 103, 112
    San Francisco, 152
    theater as crass environment, 161
    Virginia City, Nevada, 173,
        181, 182
    Ward, Artemus, and, 167
    writings, 97, 131–34
New Orleans, 11–12, 14–19, 42–47
New York City, 56–64, 91–108,
    143–45, 192, 218–20, 231–46
"Notes of My Life" (Menken), 15–16,
    17, 22, 24–25

O'Brien, Fitz-James, 92, 106
Ochiltee, Thomas P., 28–29, 262
"One Year Ago" (Menken), 68–69
Only a Woman's Heart (Clare),
    234–35

Opera House (San Francisco), 142,
    146–47, 151–53, 154–60,
    163, 185
Opera House (Virginia City, Nevada),
    176–78, 186
Oursler, Fulton, Sr., 20, 26, 69
Overall, John W., 43, 46
Oxenford, John, 198, 200, 217,
    222–23, 224

Palmer, Pamela Lynn, 36
Papers of Orpheus C. Kerr, The
    (Newell), 97, 131–32
Paris, 214, 250–73, 275–76, 293–300
Pearl, Cora, 263
Peasley, Tom, 178–79, 182–83, 186
Percy, Rita, 299–300
"Perfect Husband, The" (Newell),
    132–33
Pfaff, Charlie, 5, 92
photo pinups, 305–6
Pinkerton, Allan, 135–36
Pirates de la Savane, Les, 253–54, 258–60,
    264, 272, 273–74, 293–94,
    297–98
Pittsburgh Theater, 56
Poems and Ballads (Swinburne),
    282, 283
"Pro Patria" (Menken), 121–22, 129
prostitutes, 79, 91–92, 102, 175–76
Pullen, John, 127
Purdy, A. N., 56, 57, 58, 59
Purnell, Thomas, 286

Queen, Frank, 59, 73, 79, 107, 123
Queen of the Plaza (Gerson), 22–23

railroads, 56–57
Reade, Charles, 203, 212, 223, 296
Reece, Robert "Racy," 279–80
"Resurgam" (Menken), 160–61
Rochefort, Henri, 290, 293
Rookwood, 163
Rossetti, Dante Gabriel, xvii, 100,
    228–29, 284, 285, 308

Rossetti, William, 247, 308–9
Rothschild, Lionel de, 39, 49–50
Russell, Lillian, 307
Russ House, 148, 183–84

Sand, George, xvii, *14*, 250–53
San Francisco, *9*, 146–64, 165–71,
    183–86
Sarony, Napoleon, xviii, 236–40,
    241, 242
Sayers, Tom, 71, 73–75, 82, 86–89
"Scandal in Bohemia, A"
    (Doyle), xviii
Second Empire (France), xvii,
    256–57, 263, 268
Shakespeare, William, 44–45
"Ship that Went Down, The"
    (Menken), 112–13
"Shylock" (Menken), 44–45
"Silva" (Zenea), 26–27
Sixteen-String Jack, 51–52
Smith, E. T.
    carriage for Adah, 206–7
    Child of the Sun, The, 221,
        226–27
    Mazeppa, 194–96, 197–98,
        200, 201, 203
Smith, John B., 111–12, 113,
    114–16, 117–18
Soldier's Daughter, The, 43, 46, 51, 58
Spirit of the Times, 76–77, 78,
    80–81, 84
"Spiritual Affinity" (Menken), 85–86
Spiritualism, *16,* 184–85, 218,
    279, 301–4
Stirling, Edward, 194–95
Stoddard, Charles Warren, 148–50,
    159, 185, 187, 274–75
Sunday Mercury, 77, 85–86, 94–95,
    96, 98, 101
"Swimming against the Current"
    (Menken), 94–95
Swinburne, Algernon, xvii, *14,* 34,
    281–89, 291

Tacón theater, 22, 24–25
Tale of Two Cities, A (Dickens), 9–10
Ternan, Ellen, 213, 279
Territorial Enterprise, 156–57,
    176–78, 180
Texas, 20–22, 28–37
Théâtre de la Gaîté, 229, 249, 250,
    253–54, 258–60, 266, 272
Theodore, Josephine (Annie) (sister)
    cares for dying mother, 80
    as chaperone, 36
    death, 100, 130
    as performer, 10, 18, 21, 76–77
Théodore, Marie (mother), 14–18, 21,
    22, 80, 90, 100
Theodorus, Roi d'Abyssinie
    (Rochefort), 293
They Seek a City (Bontemps and
    Conroy), 11
Thomson, John, 281, 282–83
Three Fast Women, 170–71
"To the Sons of Israel" (Menken),
    50–51
Twain, Mark
    on Adah, xi–xiii, 277–78
    Billings, Josh, and, 141
    life and character, 157–58,
        187–88
    Mazeppa, 155, 156–57, 158,
        159, 176–78
    photograph, *10*
    Virginia City, Nevada, 173,
        176–78, 180–82
    Ward, Artemus, and, 127, 167
Tweed, Boss, 232–33
Tyng, Hattie, 32, 123, 124, 125

Under the Gaslight (Daly), 79–80
Utica, New York, 113–14

Vienna, 273–75
Virginia City, Nevada, 171–83

Ward, Artemus, 92–93, 125, 126–28,
    141, 167, 219

Webb, Charles Henry, xii, 162
Westchester House, 101–2
Westminster Palace Hotel, xvii, 191, 196, 202–3, 205
Whitman, Walt
    as Bohemian elite, 94–95
    Civil War, 137
    Clare, Ada, and, 97, 98
    homoerotic poetry, 149
    on New York City, 63, 91
    photograph, 8
    slave culture, inability to adapt to, 47
    "Year of Meteors," 85
"Wife's Prayer, A" (Menken), 53
Wilde, Oscar, 306, 307

Wilkes, George, 60, 76–78, 80–81, 84
Wilkins, Ned, 92, 97, 106
Winter, William, 58–59, 101, 129, 243–44
Wise, Isaac Mayer, 44, 47, 48–49, 51, 62
Wise, Leo, 49, 51, 62
"Women of the World" (Menken), 103
Wood, George, 235–36
"World's Delight, The" (Kendall), 12–13
World's Delight, The (Oursler), 20, 26

"Year of Meteors" (Whitman), 85

Zenea, Juan Clemente, 22, 25–27, 37

ABOUT THE AUTHORS

Michael Foster, novelist, biographer, and historian, graduated from Cornell with honors in philosophy. He received an MFA from the Writer's Workshop, Iowa, and did extensive graduate study and taught at NYU. His first novel, *Freedom's Thunder,* was praised by Nobel laureate Isaac B. Singer.

Joint publications of the Fosters also include *Forbidden Journey: The Life of Alexandra David-Neel,* a classic of adventure travel; and *Three in Love: Menages a Trois from Ancient to Modern Times,* the history of the romantic triangle. Praised by *Entertainment Weekly,* the *Washington Post,* and *Bookwoman, Three in Love* has been published in German, Polish, Spanish, Portuguese, Korean, and Turkish.

The authors' most recent book is the highly acclaimed and widely translated *The Secret Lives of Alexandra David-Neel: A Biography of the Explorer of Tibet.* The Fosters have written articles for magazines as diverse as *Travel and Leisure, Topic, The Evergreen Review,* the Anglo/French *Chimera,* and the Internet's *PopMatters.* They are the authors of a dozen print and Net articles on Adah Menken, including a cover story for *Nineteenth Century.* The Fosters host an interactive website devoted to Adah Menken and her heritage: *TheGreatBare.com.*

Barbara Foster, former professor at CUNY, specializing in women's studies, has co-authored three trade books. She has published many articles on education and travel and some 200 poems in journals in various countries. She lectures often in the United States and abroad and has packed auditoriums from Washington's Smithsonian to Cal Tech, Sidney, Buenos Aires, and Prague. Barbara appears on television, radio, and in print and online interviews.

They live in New York City.